Conference series organized by the
»Association Luxembourg-Harvard«
with Harvard University

THE WESTERN COMMUNITY AND THE GORBACHEV CHALLENGE

edited by Armand Clesse and Thomas C. Schelling

 Nomos Verlagsgesellschaft
Baden-Baden

Coverphotos: APN

CIP-Titelaufnahme der Deutschen Bibliothek

The **Western Community and the Gorbachev Challenge:** [conference series] / [organized by the »Assoc. Luxembourg-Harvard« with Harvard Univ.]. Ed. by Armand Clesse and Thomas C. Schelling. – 1. Aufl. – Baden-Baden: Nomos Verl.-Ges., 1989
    ISBN 3-7890-1789-2
NE: Clesse, Armand [Hrsg.]; Association Luxembourg-Harvard with Harvard University

1. Auflage 1989
© Nomos Verlagsgesellschaft, Baden-Baden 1989. Printed in Germany. Alle Rechte, auch die des Nachdrucks von Auszügen, der photomechanischen Wiedergabe und der Übersetzung, vorbehalten.

Contents

5

Part Two: The Economic Policy Challenge

Part Three: The Foreign and Strategic Policy Challenge

7

Foreword

The conference on »The Western Community and the Gorbachev Challenge« has been the second academic colloquium organized with Harvard University. It is part of a relationship between Luxembourg and this prestigious American university, a relationship which involves students as well as scholars. A few months after the December 1988 conference, a group of Luxembourg students paid a second visit to Harvard, and two weeks later the second Harvard Model Congress Europe took place in my country with some 300 high school and college students from all over Europe. All of these activities are very important for Luxembourg, for its intellectual endeavours and for the education of its youth. The relationship with Harvard owes much to the dedication of people on both sides of the Atlantic, people such as Dean Epps and Dean Shinagel of Harvard University or the members of the Association Luxembourg-Harvard around Dr. Clesse.

I believe that the conference on the Gorbachev challenge has been a strong success due above all to the overwhelming quality of the participants. Looking at the names it is hard to cite anybody. Should I mention such personalities as Professor Galbraith or Professor Schelling on the Western side, Professor Zagladin or Professor Abalkin on the Soviet side? Of course, I should not forget the some one hundred students from many European universities as well as from Harvard who participated actively in the conference.

The topic of the conference was well chosen. No other issue raises more attention among the public, not only in Europe or in the East-West dimension but worldwide, than the action and the fate of General Secretary Gorbachev.

His ambition to reform his country seems unyielding, but so seem the problems facing him. We must not and cannot be indifferent to the outcome of his endeavours. It can mean continuation of the often frustrating politics we have experienced for decades or it can entail a new quality in the relationship between East and West, between Eastern Europe and Western Europe, the beginning of a new and creative interaction.

9

The experts who accepted our invitation to attend the conference in December 1988 were, by their knowledge and their insights, eminently qualified to examine what really is at stake for the Soviet Union and beyond. Major parts of their work during the days of the colloquium are taken up in this book. I hope that the latter will be viewed as a modest but valuable contribution to an exciting and even vital global debate.

Jacques Santer
Prime Minister of Luxembourg

Harvard and the Gorbachev Challenge

The Luxembourg-Harvard Colloquium on the Western Community and the Gorbachev Challenge was a collaboration made possible by Prime Minister Jacques Santer and Dr. Armand Clesse, President of the Luxembourg-Harvard Association. I am grateful for their friendship and support and congratulate them on the success of the conference.

Joining members of the Harvard faculty who contributed papers to this volume were twenty-five Harvard undergraduates with expertise in Soviet, European and Western Community affairs. We felt it was important that our students take part in the spirited debate going on within the western community over the short- and long-term significance of the Gorbachev reforms. We wanted the students to hear directly from Soviet scholars knowledgeable about these reforms and listen to western scholars respond to them. By participating in the conference, the students saw how government works and learned about the role of ideas in shaping foreign and domestic policies.

Harvard has always encouraged its students to enter public service. Many have done so and served with distinction. It is only when the most talented and thoughtful students in every nation assume public responsibilities that it is possible to foster and preserve traditions of excellence in the life of the world. The difficult choices facing political leaders East and West call for vision, hard thinking and the spirit of cooperation.

The manner in which politicians and scholars who understand politics interact is of no small concern to the university. Conferences such as this help to bring open-mindedness and reflection to complex international and domestic public-policy questions that call for unusual discernment. We at Harvard are proud to have participated. We hope that these papers will give you a better understanding of the new world we are entering.

Archie C. Epps
Dean of Students
Harvard College

Introductory Remarks

This volume is not only about the new relationship between the Soviet Union and the Western democracies: it is a demonstration of it. It is a book that could not have been produced three years ago, just as the conference reported here is not one that could have been held three years ago. Soviet scholars and Soviet officials are saying things today, saying them in public, saying them in this book, that were impermissible three years ago. And the Western scholars and officials enjoyed at this conference what for most of them was a new experience – listening to the thoughtful remarks of their Soviet colleagues and crediting them with the same sincerity and candor that they expect from each other.

The changes taking place in both the intellectual and the political climate of the Soviet Union, and in the intellectual and political relations between East and West, have been so breathtaking these last few years that we have to expect, for a while at least, continuing rapid evolution of both the Gorbachev challenge and the Western nations' response.

This book offers a wide-ranging spectrum of opinions on what is going on in the Soviet Union of Mikhail Gorbachev, on the scope and the depth of the reform process and on the chances for success. Is Mikhail Gorbachev just trying to improve the system or does he intend to foster essential changes? What are the effects of his action upon the West? How should the West react: Should it limit itself to benign observation or opt for active concern and involvement? What are the potentialities for East-West relations in different realms, such as arms control, trade, cultural exchanges?

The intention of the book is not to give a message, except perhaps that there are no clear-cut conclusions to draw for the time being, that everything is on the move. It does not come up with ready-made concepts or definitive answers. The diversity of the opinions expressed reflects the uncertainty of the reform process.

The discussions during the conference were uninhibited, even candid, taking place, without any political reservation, in an exciting intellectual atmosphere that was warmly received by all participants.

13

Since the colloquium, many things have happened in the Soviet Union. Gorbachev has suffered partial setbacks. The nationality problems are far from being solved, the economic situation has not improved. The democratization, however, has continued. The General Secretary, with will-power and skill has strengthened his power basis, weakened the position of his actual or potential opponents above all in the Central Committee and consolidated the whole process. Supporters of perestroika have been publicly endorsed through the elections for the Congress of People's Deputies.

Generally speaking, this book reflects the work of the December conference even if this means that there are some redundancies and also some contradictions. Most of the papers have been submitted to the editors at the time of the conference, a few before the start of the conference, some a few weeks or even a few months later. The latter, of course, were able to take into account developments that have occurred since mid-December whereas the others represent the state of knowledge of the time of the colloquium, i.e., December 1988. Some of the papers submitted during the conference may be more vivid but also less systematic, some of those presented later may be more elaborate but also less lively.

But this book is more than a piece of academic art. It also is a reminder of a rewarding experience, of privileged moments of intellectual and human encounters. The meeting in December once more made clear how important it is to meet, to discuss, to exchange ideas and thus contribute to a better understanding between people from different parts of the world. In this sense, the conference and the book constitute a sound basis for future endeavours and future meetings, to explore further the vital issues facing mankind, to discover that beyond ideologies, political concepts, economic choices and strategic preferences there exist fundamental common aspirations, a longing for a better condition for man wherever he may live.

Armand Clesse   Thomas C. Schelling

14

Acknowledgments

The book »The Western Community and the Gorbachev Challenge« is the direct offspring of the conference which was held under the same title from 19th to 22nd December 1988 in Luxembourg. We have to thank all those people who through their unselfish commitment made this conference and this book possible.

There are those who provided their material help to set up an ambitious and of course expensive event. Here we have to cite first and above all the Government of Luxembourg and especially Prime Minister Jacques Santer for their unwavering support.

Many banks and firms from Luxembourg made a financial contribution: Banco di Napoli International, Banque Générale du Luxembourg, Banque Indosuez Luxembourg, Banque Internationale à Luxembourg, Banque de Luxembourg, Banque Nationale de Paris, Berliner Bank International, BP Luxembourg, Caisse d'Epargne de l'Etat, Cactus, Crédit Lyonnais, European Investment Bank, Mr. Harold Gans, IBM Bruxelles, International Bankers Incorporated, Kredietbank, Mr. Henry J. Leir, Philips Luxembourg Professional Systems, Shell Luxembourgeoise, Société Européenne de Banque, Société Générale Alsacienne de Banque and Paul Wurth S.A.

Harvard University also made a substantial financial contribution for this conference. The US Embassy in Luxembourg gave a reception for the conference participants.

We have then to thank those who lended us their expertise and their energy for the preparation and the implementation of the conference. From the Harvard Administration we have to cite Dean Archie Epps, Dean Michael Shinagel, Mrs. Ellen Towne, Mrs. Nancy Sinsabaugh, Mr. Alexander Shustorovich, Mr. Steven Solnik and Mrs. Debora Spar. From Luxembourg the members of the Association Luxembourg-Harvard: Jules Christophory, Gaston Gengler, Jean-Marc Hoscheit, Aloys Jacoby, who manages with considerable skill the financial assets of the common venture, Jean-Jacques Kasel, Ernest Michels and Gilbert Trausch. There is Mr. Alexandre Avdeev, Ambassador of the USSR in Luxembourg, who endeavoured to convince all the outstanding experts from his country to come to Luxembourg, Mr. Vadim Loukov, First Secretary at the same embassy, who helped prepare the conference, who did simultaneous translation during the conference and worked on a number of manuscripts. There is Miss Denise Schauls, who besides her normal working time devoted hundreds of hours during the months preceding the conference and again innumerable hours during the preparation of the book and without whom the whole project would not have come true.

Finally, we would like to thank those who gave their professional advice during the preparation of the conference and who therefore have a strong merit in its outcome, even if some of them were not able to participate themselves: Abram Bergson, Robert Blackwill, John Kenneth Galbraith, Marshall Goldman, Charles Maier and Adam Ulam of Harvard, Jonathan Dean of the Union of Concerned Scientists, Renata Fritsch-Bournazel of the Institut d'Etudes Politiques in Paris, Raymond Garthoff, Ed Hewett and Michael MccGwire of the Brookings Institution, Jerry Hough of Duke University, Robert Legvold and Marshall Shulman of the Averell Harriman Institute in New York, Alex Pravda of the Chatham House in London, Eberhard Schulz of the Gesellschaft für Auswärtige Politik in Bonn, Gerhard Simon and Heinrich Vogel of the Bundesinstitut für ostwissenschaftliche und internationale Studien in Köln and Philip Windsor of the London School of Economics.

We thank all of them and we hope that they are not too disappointed about the result of our joint efforts.

A.C.

Keynote address:
by John Kenneth Galbraith

Capitalism and Socialism in Our Time: The Dynamics of Change

John Kenneth Galbraith

I must begin with a word of thanks and appreciation for my hosts here in Luxembourg and for all who planned this conference. You have, indeed, paid me a compliment in inviting me to give the opening address. But I am even more pleased by the opportunity, to which I greatly look forward, to participate in and benefit from the discussion of these next days. I am, to repeat, much in your debt.

There has not for many years been an address such as this that hasn't opened with a reference to change. You have all heard it: »I speak to you in a time of great political, economic and social change.« I am firmly in this tradition. I am led to speak of great changes that are now occurring on the world scene. But I wish also to speak of the very great forces that, in modern political life and thought, are in resistance to change, in resistance to any acceptance of a greatly changed reality. The change I cite is in the powerful circumstances affecting economic, political and military life and the relationship between the great powers. The resistance to change lies in what I shall call our commitment to institutional belief – institutional belief as opposed to the reality of the times.

The change or changes of which I wish to speak are in the internal character and external manifestations of the two great economic, social and political systems, capitalism and socialism, more often called Communism, which for seventy years have been dominant on the world scene. The institutional belief with which I deal is strikingly revealed in the organizational or bureaucratic resistance to acceptance of those changes.

The changes in the socialist *cum* communist world dominated by the Soviet Union and in the capitalist world epitomized and led since World War II by the United States are not in doubt. They are visibly obtrusive. In the case of some, there is an element of *déjà vu* in mentioning them.

All, nonetheless, are in conflict with, and in striking degree denied by, institutional belief.

For many years after the noted American writer Lincoln Steffens returned from Russia in 1919 to tell his friend, the great financier Bernard Baruch, »I have been over into the future and it works« – one of the more spectacularly premature economic observations of all time – there was an uneasy, deeply subjective feeling in the United States that, in our relations with the Soviet Union, we were contending with a dangerously compelling economic order. It was, however much we wished to deny the thought, on the wave of the future. This fear was evident in the impassioned oratory that condemned the Soviet system; beneath the rhetoric was a strong current of concern. And in the years between the wars the Soviets built a powerful industrial base, avoided the unemployment and general economic disaster of the Great Depression and then sustained the vast armies that defeated Hitler. This contributed notably to a common social phenomenon, which is the compelling belief of fortunate people, rejoicing greatly in their good fortune, that somewhere there lurks an infinitely powerful, deeply insidious design for its expropriation. American conservatives, in particular, were always more committed to the Marxist inevitability of socialism than Marxists themselves.

American and Western paranoia, in turn, had its Russian counterpart. The 1918 military intervention of the Allies, the onslaught of Hitler bent on destroying communism and the years of exuberant capitalist success following World War II were all seen as a threat to the socialist system. Capitalism was not thought disposed to tolerate a rival system; it was awaiting the opportunity to obliterate it.

There was similarly a source of fear for both Soviets and Americans in what appeared to be a common commitment to aggressive, and for a time successfully exercised, international influence – Soviet expansionism as it was called by the West, American or capitalist imperialism as it was denoted in Moscow. And here too there was substance. In 1961, I went to India as American Ambassador – a point man, as it were, for American imperialism. Soviet power at the time seemingly stretched undiminished from the Brandenburg Gate in Berlin to the port of Haiphong. The commonplace reference, lodged in all professional conversation, was to the Sino-Soviet bloc.

The Eastern European satellites, the most visible evidence of Soviet expansionism, also seemed solid, successful and secure. There were socialist/communist outposts of marked importance in North Africa, Indonesia and in the Western Communist parties. The Korean conflict had, in the general view, made evident this commitment to expansion, as did the overt Soviet promise of support to wars of national liberation. There was at the time a formidable concern in Washington as to how we could prevent India from falling under Communist control, a misfortune I then thought no really perceptive Communist would wish to contemplate.

Similarly evident was the American and Western influence – SEATO, CENTO, NATO. Also the web of John Foster Dulles's bilateral treaties. Also a strong moral position on the part of the United States in Central and South America and much of Africa. The Soviets saw all this – as we saw the Sino-Soviet bloc and its ancillary outposts – as evidence of imperialist intention. Or, at a minimum, as a determined policy of encirclement.

Next there was the military experience. In World War II there was the Western vision of the enormous power of the Soviet armies as they drove the Wehrmacht back to Berlin and beyond and the combination of gratitude and fear that this engendered. And again there was the counterpart concern of the Soviets – the evident American advantage in naval and aerial strength and, above all, the pioneer breakthrough in nuclear weaponry. Here, along with economic achievement and imperial ambition, was the third source of reciprocal fear and tension.

Finally, there was the compelling question of human rights, the evident incompatibility of one system that avowed them and another that did not. The American commitment was admittedly imperfect as regards minorities, especially blacks. It was also, as it is still, unduly identified with the private ownership of productive property. Dictators who accepted this could be forgiven much else. Nonetheless the difference here between the two systems was great, inescapable and an evident cause of friction. To be too friendly with the Soviet Union was to be acquiescent on this great issue of human rights.

It is a mistake, I believe, to make light of these differences and these fears in their time. They, especially the fears, were very real. And it was inevitable that they would become the foundation of foreign and military policy in both the great powers. In doing so, they became, I suggest, the sources of the institutional belief that controls and guides policy to this day. And the singular and inescapable fact is that the sources of this fear have, as regards substance, greatly diminished.

Reciprocal and threatening economic success as a source of fear has totally disappeared. The Soviet Union, China and the Eastern European countries, their considerable past achievements notwithstanding, are now openly struggling with grave, perhaps even intractable, economic problems. The confidence of an earlier time has greatly diminished. The present socialist preoccupation is with bureaucratic sclerosis and the strategies of release and reform. Or, a somewhat neglected point, with the difficulty that a planned economy has in meeting the demand for the highly diverse products, designs and services of the modern high-consumption society. What served well in the time of Lenin or Stalin for satisfying primitive wants or building basic industry does not satisfy modern consumer wants. Marx did not see cosmetics, fashionable women's clothing or automobiles as objects of mass proletarian consumption. A primary concern now in all the socialist world is how concessions can be made to the market without surrendering the basic fabric of socialism.

Similarly in the capitalist world and especially in the United States. In the United States we have been sustaining our living standard only by massive internal and external debt creation. In our traditional areas of industrial achievement, we are no longer competitive with Japan, Korea, Taiwan and the other new countries of the Pacific Basin. For each speech in the American Congress on the socialist threat of the Soviet Union, there are now at least ten on the economic threat of Japan. The dollar, once above challenge as the reference currency of the world, is now viewed with caution and, on recent occasion, with disdain.

Thus the first conclusion. Neither American capitalism nor Soviet socialism any longer project the image of success which once induced fear in the other country. In the United States we have still, to be sure, the normal manifestation of conservative paranoia as regards socialism. Increasingly, however, we recognize it as such.

Change has been even more spectacular as regards the once-avowed dangers of Soviet expansionism and capitalist imperialism. Here the retreat has been massive and inescapable. The Soviets have experienced the traumatic break with China; a visibly weakened position in Eastern Europe; the loss of effective influence in Egypt, Algeria,

22

Ghana, Indonesia; the shrinkage or near disappearance of the Western European Communist parties; the disaster in Afghanistan and now even the dissent of ethnic communities within the U.S.S.R. itself.

Our experience viewed over the last twenty-five years has not been different. Central and South America are no longer ours on call. Only Grenada and perhaps Honduras are now available for the asking. Those who seek expansion of American power are confined to the unfortunate republic of Nicaragua. SEATO and CENTO have gone with the wind of which they largely consisted. So also nearly all of the Dulles bilateral treaties. NATO survives, but it no longer accords the United States the automatic support we once enjoyed. Travel by American leaders to NATO meetings is pleasant and much enjoyed; no one for some years has suggested that the meetings themselves are intellectually demanding. And, as the Soviets have had Afghanistan, we have had the traumatic experience and lesson of Vietnam.

We and the Soviets have, in fact, run into the same two problems. The first has been the intense, unrelenting desire of all countries and their governments to be free from external authority; this in the post-colonial era is one of the most powerful influences in our time. It has overcome the tendency and error since Rome to see one's own imperial authority as a reward and blessing to others.

The second problem we have both encountered is the manifest inapplicability in the Third World of the model of either mature socialism or developed capitalism. The socialist disaster, evident in Afghanistan, Ethiopia and Mozambique, has been particularly great. And this should not have been to any good socialist's surprise. On nothing did Marx insist more adamantly than that socialism could come only after the preliminary socializing influence of capitalism. But we too have suffered from the supposition that what is sound economic policy in the United States must somehow be appropriate for India, Africa or Latin America. Against nothing in my years as ambassador did I struggle so hard as the belief in economic and social matters that what was right for the United States was automatically right for India.

Next there has been the massive change in the military relationship. Here one risks a rapid descent into the obvious. Any modern military conflict brings the risk of nuclear exchange. This neither capitalism nor communism, both highly sophisticated designs for ordering economic process, would survive. Accordingly, capitalism and communism now

23

sit on the same side of the table facing the common threat of nuclear war.

Some months ago I read of a draft proposal emanating from some imaginative precinct in Washington that called for the construction of special underground shelters for safeguarding real estate deeds, stock certificates, other evidence of property ownership and perhaps their principal custodians, so that in the aftermath of a nuclear war, survivors would have a valid claim on their assets. Were there, indeed, such survivors, their claim would be small as compared with what they could have from the newly available public domain.

There is a further change in the larger military nexus. That concerns the question of whether the modern industrial state can be an object of successful military action and occupation. From the earliest times agricultural regions were a useful fruit of conquest. Farmers or peasants, whatever their ethnic, religious or other objection, would perform more or less equally well whoever were their ultimate masters. They would provide revenue and manpower to one master about as well as to another. No one can suppose this to be so of the modern, complex, intricately demanding industrial economy.

Can the Russians imagine that they could take over and operate the Japanese economy, a thought that, as they contemplate military expenditure, has almost certainly occurred to the Japanese? Or the Italian economy, as we hear alarming references to the undefended »southern flank« of NATO? Or do Americans wish to have responsibility for the Polish economy? Or that of Russia? I mention these matters not as final judgment but as things we should be discussing. Do we need armed troops along every frontier? Is what lies behind any longer that enticing? Last winter one read of the alarm over the required withdrawal of the F16 aircraft from the environs of Madrid. I wondered at the time, as surely did others, if the worry was not over a new Ottoman onslaught against the Knights of Malta.

Finally there has been change as regards human rights. The Soviet Union has taken long steps toward open intellectual and political expression; it is now engaged in a debate of startling vigor on economic and social policy and the means to a greater democratic participation in the affairs of the state. Even if much remains to be done, one cannot doubt the extent of its recent change. And in the West we need also to remind ourselves that our own position on these matters is far from

24

perfect. We still support repugnant dictators whose justification is only that they do not interfere with the rights of private property. I am disturbed by the number of my fellow citizens for whom poverty, homelessness and deprivation are fully as effective forces in the denial of freedom and liberty. Nothing more constrains liberty and action as abject, all-embracing poverty.

More broadly, we should recognize that human rights are for all advanced industrial countries, capitalist or socialist, less a virtue than a necessity. In all Western industrial countries there is a greater or lesser measure of freedom of expression. And also of participation in the processes of government. That is because while the people of the poor peasant economies who are subject to the daily grind of existence can be kept in subordinate silence, in the advanced industrial country this is not possible. Businessmen, trade union leaders, scientists, professors, journalists, poets and students all demand to be heard and to participate in the tasks of government. So it is in the Western industrial countries; so it is coming to be in the U.S.S.R. There are more articulate Americans than can be kept quiet; there are coming to be more articulate Russians than, as a practical matter, it is possible to subdue. We are right to avow the moral case for human rights. But we should not deny their inevitability in the modern highly developed, highly diverse economy of educated people.

Let me now turn from these matters – from the great and largely undisputed changes I have cited – to the role of institutional belief.

A certain stability in public thought and policy is not to be deplored. This is especially so in the United States, where, every four or eight years, the White House and the departments of government, especially the former, are invaded by men (and some women) with an unduly imaginative vision of what is theirs to change. We now risk a recurring coup d'etat. We must also recognize, however, that all great organization, all great bureaucracy, has a deeply intrinsic resistance to change. And both public and private life today are dominated by great organizations. So in the United States; so in the other Western countries; so even more in the Soviet Union.

The organizational or bureaucratic factors resisting change are five. In all great organization there is, first, the need for a unifying system of thought, commonly called a policy or in military organization a military doctrine. To this all participants in some measure must then adhere.

The alternative – everyone proceeding on his or her independent, undisciplined course – would, indeed, be chaos.

There is, second, both a release from mental effort and a measure of pride in accepting a ruling idea or doctrine. Tolstoy tells in *War and Peace* of the relief, even pleasure, men have in surrendering all decision to the rule of the regiment. Institutional belief is likewise an alternative to the painful processes of thought that we all seek in some measure to avoid.

Third, there is personal safety in such surrender to the organizational or bureaucratic view. It is a hard but inescapable fact that in all organized effort, it is often safer for the individual to be wrong with the majority than to be right alone.

Fourth, there is the strong tendency of all organization to exclude the inconvenient voice. Here I venture to cite personal experience. In the earlier stages of our involvement with Vietnam I was more than marginally concerned with our policy there. I felt, from some personal knowledge of the larger region, that, as in India, while capitalism and communism were concepts irrelevant to most of the population, foreign intervention (in Vietnam, the Chinese, French, Japanese and now ours) was not. Also, from my days as an agricultural economist, that herding people into strategic hamlets, so-called, was a particularly efficient design for the alienation of those so saved. Also that the government we supported in Saigon was oppressive, corrupt and incompetent. And also, a later view, that our sophisticated military establishment was badly designed for the elementary warfare there required, where only the most discerning ideologist could tell a capitalist jungle from a communist jungle.

But I learned in those years that urging these matters was far from being a formula for popularity. Or even participation in policy action. »We know where Galbraith stands; he is not useful.« And there was always a more disagreeable thought. Perhaps the individual motivated to dissent had fallen under some adverse external influence: »Maybe they have got to him.« Such was one experience; such is the frequent fate in organization of the individual who challenges institutional belief.

Fifth and finally, there develops a vested personal and pecuniary interest in established belief. Not many of us wish to deny our past or admit to past error. I have many countrymen who have committed their lives to the concept of inevitable conflict with the Soviets. It is a hard, cruel

26

thing to have that commitment destroyed. My sympathies as a professor should be especially great; who in academic life wishes to see those old lecture notes made obsolete?

There are, however, even greater pecuniary rewards in established policy – in holding to the accepted institutional belief. Here I verge on the trite. No one doubts the great financial interest in present military policy and the concept of continuing strain and tension that sustains it. The danger here was implanted in American thought and language by Dwight D. Eisenhower and his enduring reference to the military-industrial complex. That a counterpart vested interest exists in the military operations of the Soviet Union we must surely assume.

All of the foregoing bears as institutional belief on American/Soviet relations. Especially it bears on the military nexus. On the one hand, change; on the other hand, the strong resistance to change – the power of institutional belief and the vested intellectual and economic interest that it expressed. The consequence is the present and highly visible anomaly in foreign and military action and policy. In the United States we have a dual policy or, at best, a wonderfully bifurcated policy. Through the force of the changes I earlier cited in the relation between the two great systems and their two principal exponents, we have the compelling pressure for association and compromise. Here the reality asserts itself. This has been made evident in the four summit meetings of Ronald Reagan and General Secretary Gorbachev, in the closer working relationships between American Secretary of State and Soviet Foreign Minister, the INF Treaty and an unprecedented increase in scientific, artistic and other association. These, to repeat, are in response to the underlying changes – changes that no leader and certainly none in our politically responsive democracy can resist.

At the same time, and notably on military matters where institutional belief rules most strongly, where vested economic interest is great and perhaps decisive, we still have the full force of that institutional belief. The two great systems, ours and that of the Soviet Union, are held to remain in bitter conflict. Expansionism is still assumed. Military parity, if not preeminence, is still sought. All frontiers are deeply vulnerable. Both presidential candidates in the recent American election, urged on by their professional advisers, affirmed their commitment to »a strong defense.«

We accept that change has altered the basic relationship between the

27

two superpowers, as by courtesy they are still called. But institutional belief, as reflected especially in military doctrine or policy, effectively denies that there has been any change. We have one policy in response to reality; we have another policy in response to institutional belief.

It will be evident that I regard the case for reality as being stronger than that for institutional belief. I urge that we understand the wonderfully conflicting forces which, in a world of great organization and great change, come to control attitudes, speech and action. And I ask you, a most distinguished and influential audience, to join in accepting and urging not the institutional belief but the new reality.

Part One:
The Domestic Policy Challenge

Gorbachev's Agenda for Domestic Policy Reform

Michel Tatu

There is no question now in the West about the depth of changes in the U.S.S.R. under Gorbachev. Since 1987 and especially since the beginning of this year, there has been a new and increasing momentum of change. Everybody agrees on the will of Gorbachev to change the system he has inherited: he is a genuine reformer. But there is disagreement over the feasibility of these changes, the nature and strength of resistance to them, as well as Gorbachev's ultimate goal, if and when he can overcome the present difficulties.

What is the path and the substance of »gorbachevism«? His first aim was, as for all other new leaders in Moscow since Stalin, to revigorate the economy, i.e., to reduce the technological and economic gap with the West. Nothing original so far. But two elements are new in this old equation, especially if we compare the present stage with the last period of reform in the early 1960s.

In the first place, the consequences of the same old evils were much worse in the 1980s, after 20 years of Brezhnev's »stagnation,« than in the 1960s. In all areas other than the military, the Soviet Union had regressed to the status of a »third-rank provincial power« predicted long ago by Andrei Sakharov – and even lower: for example, in the area of infant mortality, the Soviet Union occupies place 50 in world rankings, »behind Barbados and Mauritius,« as Evgueni Chazov, the Minister of Health, confessed in June at the Party Conference in Moscow. While alcohol consumption doubled, a broad-range disintegration of elementary discipline among the cadres led to wide corruption practices, as can now be witnessed by the trial in Moscow of Churbanov, Brezhnev's son-in-law, and the so-called »Uzbek mafia.«

In addition, the remedies are different from those found with past reforms. Gorbachev came to realize that the traditional approach, which was advocated during the brief tenure of Andropov, was no longer sufficient: more discipline and less corruption, less alcohol and harder work are easy enough to announce but more difficult to achieve. He

31

decided that economic reform alone is inadequate and is doomed to failure if it is not accompanied by political reform. In the initial period of the perestroika wave, from January 1987 through the beginning of 1988, this was illustrated by glasnost. At the end of the spring of 1988, glasnost was supplemented by an open appeal for political reform, with the overall change being called a revolution. This was the aim of the National Party Conference at the end of June and of the changes in the Constitution and the electoral law adopted by the Supreme Soviet in November.

I leave to following speakers the question of economic reforms. Let me talk here about the two main aspects of the political reform: glasnost and political changes.

What is glasnost? The Russian word means a situation where everything is made public. It could be translated by »transparency,« but it would in fact be more correct to see it as a process instead of a situation; the English word »openness« is more suitable, and that is the way glasnost is translated by Soviet officials.

As for substance, we can see in glasnost a late conversion to very old Western concepts of normalcy in the areas of information and culture: more objectivity in the relation of facts, and more common sense in their interpretation and analysis. In particular, glasnost means: the publishing of many books and works not published before and no more, or much fewer, taboos on both negative facts and topics open to debate; a discovery of the existence of public opinion for purposes other than propaganda – see, for example, the proliferation of opinion polls; Western-style media coverage of natural phenomena and catastrophes – see the progress made between the Chernobyl accident in 1986 and the Armenian earthquake of 1988; and, finally, the liquidation of »black spots« in most periods of the past, including the whole of the Stalin era (and not only for the 1936-1939 period, as was done under Khrushchev). In fact, one can see that the Party has abandoned a large part of its monopoly on the interpretation of history, leaving historians and writers free to work in this field without having to wait for Party guidelines.

To be sure, this liberalization profits mainly the intelligentsia, writers and journalists. But we should not underestimate its impact on the readers, the Soviet public at large, which has for at least 60 years not read such exciting press. Even should the reform soon come to an end, something will remain of this period of fresh wind and fresh ideas, in the same way as something remained – and is now being positively recalled – of the much more limited reforms implemented by Khrushchev in the 1950s.

At the same time, we have to see the limitations on glasnost. Some of them are, for foreign-policy considerations, self-imposed. For example, nearly everything can be said about Brezhnev's actions and practices, except with regard to what the late Soviet leader did to Czechoslovakia in 1968. Many aspects of Soviet-Polish relations remain a dark spot in the history of Stalinism. But there are also inconsistencies between the »state of law« announced by the General Secretary and some of the dogmas that, simply because they belong to Lenin's heritage, he is unable, or unwilling, to throw away. It was Lenin, not Stalin, who disbanded the only freely elected assembly in Russian history, banned all political parties except the CP and closed all newspapers except Communist ones. But while some Soviet historians hint timidly at some »errors« by Lenin, the »liberalization of history« has not been extended to that chapter.

Another limitation is that while glasnost has given us a mass of valuable information about history and the present state of Soviet society, very little is said about the current political debate in the Party, particularly that going on at the top. The proceedings in the Politburo and the Secretariat, even among the 300 or so members of the Central Committee, are off limits to the foreign student (and the Soviet one, too); they remain as secret as under Stalin and Brezhnev.

In fact, these limitations derive from those we find in the second aspect of the political reform, the institutional changes. Even if we accept the view that the one-party system cannot be abandoned at the present, the democratization desired by the leadership would make it necessary to abandon another dogma of Lenin's heritage: so-called »democratic centralism,« according to which once a decision has been made, debate over its merits or those of alternatives has to cease. The leadership is supposed to be »monolithic« in its implementation.

This is probably the single biggest obstacle to the general democratization desired by the General Secretary. First of all, it is difficult to determine at what point a critical discussion becomes political opposition. One significant example is the refusal at the June Party Conference to rehabilitate Boris Elstin, a party leader who in October

1987 had voiced many ideas less radical than those published in the press a few months later. Indeed, the condemnation of his October speech as »politically erroneous« was erroneous from the outset and an illustration of the weight of the Stalinist past.

Second, and more important, in order to escape the »stubbornness in the error,« which has characterized nearly every period in the history of the regime, criticism has to be applied after, and not just before, a decision is made. Up to now, this »after« has come many years too late, when the ruler was long gone. Would the Soviet Union stand where it is now if »stagnation« had been denounced 15 years earlier, as it was by most foreign observers in the 1970s and even before?

Unfortunately, Gorbachev cannot abolish »democratic centralism,« since it was created by Lenin in 1921. To compensate, he has introduced the idea of »socialist pluralism,« while admitting that a coexistence of past and new practices, authoritarian and democratic, is unavoidable at this point. A good example is the way he has consolidated his authority: inside the Party, he reversed the stand he had taken at the Party Conference and imposed at the end of September deep personnel changes by purely administrative methods; at the state level, he accelerated a concentration of power into his own hands in a way that provoked criticism even within the ranks of his most dedicated perestroikist allies.

To be sure, a presidential system is not incompatible with democracy, as we see, for example, in the United States and France. We also have to take into account a strong Russian tradition of consistently imposing reforms from above by an »enlightened« czar. Nevertheless, given the fact that modernization today clearly means democratization across the board, the exercise is more difficult and less credible, even more so in a one-party system where the Party apparatus has not been freed from the bias of past practices.

The new electoral law adopted in November is clearly disappointing in that respect: First of all, while several candidates can be admitted to the competition, the choice of these candidates will remain in the hands of a »preliminary electoral assembly« to be dominated by the Party. Second, voting will in fact be indirect, since the real Supreme Soviet will be designated by a »congress of people's deputies« and not directly by the voters. Finally, one-third of the deputies will be elected by »social organizations,« one of them being of course the Communist

Party, whose members will have the privilege of voting twice. And it is not entirely sure that the other associations entitled to this second vote will include the non-Communist popular fronts created in the various regions.

All in all, the political reform is certainly an important attempt to democratize the institutions and to restore a role for the republics at the expense of the Party and its apparatus. The »state of law,« together with the law on the press and the reform of the criminal code, will undoubtedly introduce better guarantees for individual freedoms. But what we are witnessing is only a first step in that direction; further reforms are planned for 1989 in the areas of interethnic relations and organization of power at the local level. The first stage seems, however, to have been rather hastily conceived in certain respects, with a strong inherited »Soviet« bias. It is clear that some aspects will have to be reexamined at a later stage. This might be the case with the rule obliging local Party leaders to chair their regional soviets, a point that is still strongly criticized by many officials at all levels.

This brings me to a second type of limitations on the reform, namely, the strong opposition encountered today by Gorbachev's program in Soviet society and in the Soviet apparatus. This opposition can be divided into three groups:

(1) »Inertial« opposition. By this I mean resistance by the Soviet population at large, for which perestroika has not yet born any fruit in terms of better living conditions and which has seen only the bad points – more hard work, quality controls in the factories (which can lead to production refusals and the suppression of bonuses), less alcohol, and less leeway in benefiting from the parallel channels of distribution and/or corruption. Furthermore, economic reform brings with it price hikes and new social inequalities, which Soviets citizens, in general, are less inclined to accept than the Chinese, for example. One should be reminded that the last big price increase for food products in June 1962 provoked grave riots in Novocherkassk in southern Russia.

(2) Structural opposition. Some 18 million persons are employed in administrative functions, including several million in the 79 federal ministries (the Soviet government is the largest in the world, with more than 60 purely economic or technical ministries) and the nearly 600 republic ministries. This apparatus was reduced – but

not abolished – in the summer of 1987, but it is unable or unwilling to adapt to modern, market-type methods of management. The same can be said for many factory directors and, even more, for Party functionaries, who have practiced »command-like« methods their life long.

(3) Ideologic opposition. Not only do all cadres know only the Stalin-Brezhnev system, but many more or less genuinely believe that »socialism« is precisely this system and nothing else. While admitting that perestroika is a necessity for overcoming the illnesses of Brezhnev's stagnation and supporting some kind of economic reform, they are reluctant to accept political reform and adamantly oppose glasnost, the new style in the media and the reappraisal of history, as could be witnessed in many speeches at the Party Conference last June. These people have found new fuel for their grievances in the nationalist turmoil of the past few months – something that can easily be attributed to the destabilization engendered by Gorbachev's policy – all the more so since they find strong support from the Russian-nationalist group in the intelligentsia.

We find these various categories of resistance – in particular, the last two – at two main levels of political institutions:

(1) In the Central Committee. The »parliament of the Party,« which has not been renewed since the last regular congress in March 1986, has clearly not adapted to the drastic changes that have taken place since then. Its composition in 1986 reflected Gorbachev's still unconsolidated power, with 56% of the members occupying the same seat since Brezhnev's time and more than half with an age of at least 60 (see table). This situation has become aggravated: nearly 60% of the full members are at least 60 years old, and the number of septuagenarians (51 members or 16.7%) is nearly as great as at the highly »gerontocratic« congress of 1981 under Brezhnev.

Furthermore, although more than 60 members have been demoted or retired in the past two years, these »dead souls« still occupy their seats at the expense of many »new souls.« The latter have taken key positions in the Party and government and are invited to the CC plenums, but they have no right to vote. 56% of the Party's regional first secretaries have seats in neither the CC nor the auditing committee, as compared to 28% in 1986. The same is true for the five new first secretaries in the republics, including the most troubled republics of Armenia, Azerbaidzhan and Estonia. Gorbachev clearly intended to use the National Party Conference to organize new elections to the CC, but this attempt failed in the face resistance by the apparatus. Although the Conference reiterated a 1939 regulation providing for up to 20% rejuvenation of the composition of the CC at a given conference, this was to apply at the next conference and not at the present one. We can nevertheless expect a campaign for an extraordinary Party congress prior to the regular meeting in 1991. If unresolved, the present deadlock could lead to a withering of the importance of the CC in favor of such bodies as the Supreme Soviet (where partial elections are regularly held), an evolution not exactly favored by Gorbachev.

It should also be mentioned that new rules have been enacted, whereby mandates to all elected bodies are limited to two terms. A reform of this sort was undertaken by Khrushchev in 1961 but then quickly forgotten by Brezhnev. This regulation will as well first become applicable with the next Party congress, such that Gorbachev is entitled to remain in power until 2001, when he reaches the age of 70.

(2) At the top level. The Politburo remains the dominant force in all areas – a sort of government and parliament at once. As has often been the case in the recent past, there has been less reshuffling in the Politburo than in the Secretariat, which was divided a few weeks ago into six specialized commissions; the reform was also accompanied by important changes in the departments of the Central Committee. Despite the usual statements about »full unity« of leadership, tough discussions are permitted, and a clear distinction has evolved between radical reformers and the conservative (or, at least, cautious) wing under the leadership of Egor Ligachev, who has long occupied the second-highest position in the Party.

With the September reshuffle, Ligachev suffered a setback, but he and other like-minded leaders remain in the Politburo. It will be impossible to exclude a showdown at a later stage of the political reform, especially if interethnic disorders continue. In this respect, it is to be mentioned that the present leadership is not particularly well-suited to handling this problem; non-Slavic nationals have never been so poorly represented at the upper levels in Moscow, with only Georgian Shevardnadze, the Foreign Minister, numbering among the top thirty officials.

In summary, one can see a strong discrepancy today between, on the one hand, the brilliant image achieved by Gorbachev abroad and in the area of foreign policy and, on the other, the protracted struggle and often aggravated difficulties confronting him domestically. While the triumphs abroad have helped him in the domestic arena, his success is not guaranteed, and the reforms cannot yet be considered irreversible. To be sure, a return to Brezhnev's practices and stagnation has now been ruled out, and in any case, something will remain of the Gorbachev era (just as with the lasting effects of the Khrushchev era). However, a return to a more orthodox approach to problems – either with or without the present General Secretary – cannot be ruled out.

Gorbachev is basically betting on the optimist's vision of socialism – on the idea that the system is fundamentally sound and in need only of a dose of democracy to improve it. But he must nevertheless deal with a good many pessimists, who believe that the system will be unable to withstand the pressure of free expression. Gorbachev's greatest strength lies in the fact that all are in agreement that the past system was a failure. Whether the future belongs to the optimists is, however, open to question.

THE EVOLUTION OF THE CENTRAL COMMITTEE OF THE CP BETWEEN MARCH 1986 AND DECEMBER 1988 *

	March 1986	%	15 December 1988	%
Full members, total	307		304	
Seniority				
Already full members in:				
1981	172	56.0	165	54.2
1976	112	36.4	106	34.8
1971	61	19.8	59	19.4
1966	29	9.4	27	8.8
Age				
More than 70 years	33	10.7	50	16.4
More than 60	126	41.0	169	55.5
50 to 60	145	47.2	166	38.1
Less than 50	36	11.7	19	6.2
The »new souls«				
Regional Party secretaries who are (1)				
– CC members	77	49.0	41	27.7
– CC candidates	28	17.8	20	13.5
– Members of Audit.C.	7	4.4	4	2.7
– without any seat	45	28.6	83	56.0
Ministers of the USSR:				
– CC members	50	59.5	38	48.1
– CC candidates	24	28.5	16	20.2
– Members of the Audit.C.	6	7.1	4	5.0
– without any seat	4	4.7	23	29.1
The »dead souls«				
– Full members of the CC who no longer have any function:			41	
– Full members who have been pensioned and have only secondary functions:			21	
Total			62	20.3

* These tables have been computed using the »SOVT« data base system created in »Le Monde«.

Will Gorbachev Be Able to Reform Soviet Society?

Philip Windsor

Nobody knows what *perestroika* means. In the Soviet press, or on Soviet television, when the subject is discussed, it is variously described by the clichés arising from the prevailing political debate. Sometimes, it is called »better work.« Sometimes, *perestroika* is identified with *glasnost*. But, even though others at this Conference have a far more detailed understanding of Soviet society and of the Gorbachev era than I have, I would venture to suggest that *perestroika* has undergone significant changes of meaning since Gorbachev came to power.

In the first instance, it was largely identified with »acceleration.« It turned out, however, that acceleration itself implied a vastly increased exploitation of natural resources, which would have sped the Soviet Union even more rapidly towards the abyss than the policies of the Brezhnev era. Subsequently, it came to mean a set of loosely related economic experiments and reforms. There was not, and has not yet been, any systematic attempt to overhaul the economy in the sense which the word »restructuring« should imply – simply because every experiment represented a political compromise between radical and conservative elements in the Party. In its third phase, *perestroika* represented an attempt to introduce not only greater freedom of discussion (in itself an extension of *glasnost*) and a determined attack on corruption but also a broadening of rights and freedoms within the framework of what might be called a new form of socialist legality. This has been no better coordinated than the programme of economic reform, not only because of the necessity of political compromise but also because powerful elements in both the Party and the KGB have been actively opposed to it. And that consideration leads directly to the fourth and current meaning of *perestroika*, which is quite straightforwardly a struggle for political power. The question of who actually exercises power, and with the consent of whom, is a question which dates from 1988. It was raised as such even in 1987. It was above all the Nineteenth Party Conference which brought it into the open, and in which Gorbachev disclosed the full extent of his ambition: »The Soviet people deserve nothing less than a full-blooded and unconditional democracy.«

Obviously, it is somewhat schematic to divide the process of *perestroika* into particular phases as I have just done. There are continuing elements of all the first three which can be identified virtually from the beginning and which are actively at work today. But the fourth phase, that of the definition of power and consent, is the new and determining element of the current situation. It also indicates why it is necessary to begin this discussion with some attempt at defining *perestroika* – since the issue of whether it can succeed now depends more clearly than before not on structural questions concerning the nature of Soviet economics or Soviet society but on the outcome of a power struggle.

That power struggle is characterized by a paradox. Since the Nineteenth Party Conference in particular, Gorbachev has concentrated very great power in his own hands – so much so that Andrei Sakharev was impelled to warn against the possible consequences during his recent visit to the United States. In the past, when a Soviet leader held such offices and exercised such power, his political utterances were faithfully repeated at all levels of Soviet society, including those of the Party, the State ministries, such intellectual organisations as the Writers' Union and the media. This is not the case with Gorbachev. The price of *glasnost* is that his political opponents feel free to speak out and challenge him. Indeed, the notorious Andreyeva letter was widely and rightly regarded as a kind of political manifesto of the conservative opposition. The paradox therefore is that Gorbachev has had to concentrate so much power because he has so little of it. At the top of the Party structure, he has been able to concentrate a considerable number of articulate and determined supporters – though it would still be a wild exaggeration to say that he has been able to surround himself entirely with such people. But lower down in the Party hierarchy, at the senior *oblast* level and within the ranks of the Central Committee, there is every evidence of a highly conscious political opposition to the Gorbachev programme. Such eminent Soviet analysts as Professor Zaslavskaya aver that this opposition is not only conscious but well organised. Many is the apparently autonomous economic enterprise, brought into being by *perestroika*, whose work has been stopped or effectively nullified by a telephone call from the local party headquarters.

But the paradox goes further. If Gorbachev has needed to take on the power structure within the Party, including those »far from Moscow,« he has had of necessity to rely on other forms of power. These of course include popular support (of which more will be said later) but they have also included the KGB. Everyone is aware that the Gorbachev rise to power can in part be attributed to the support of Andropov and the KGB itself. (Some resolutely sceptical figures in the West argue that »therefore« he is little more than a master propagandist, whose fundamental aims are the same as those of his predecessors, except that he would like to be more efficient. By the same logic, King Juan Carlos of Spain is clearly a Franquist in democratic disguise!) Such interruptions apart, it seems to me that not only has Gorbachev had to move slowly with respect to the KGB but also that at times he has needed its support for his onslaught on Party nepotism, corruption and the perpetuation of power structures. Others at this Conference will know more, but I would hazard a guess that the reign of Chebrikov was testimony to such considerations. Now, a word of caution is necessary here. Generally speaking, most people in the West think of the KGB as a kind of Soviet Gestapo. In some respects they are right. But its functions are more variegated than such an image would convey. To give an analogy: when the operations of firms and banks in the City of London were opened up to new forms of scrutiny by new legislation a few years ago, it was rapidly found that a number of them were operating in an unethical and illegal manner. In these circumstances, the Fraud Squad of the Metropolitan Police was detailed to investigate. In Moscow, such a task would be the work of the KGB – and indeed it was KGB investigation which uncovered such monumental frauds as that of the cotton scandal in Uzbekistan (with the help, that is, of satellite photography) and which led to the trial, among others, of Brezhnev's son-in-law. In other words, the KGB was at times a useful instrument for Gorbachev in the earlier phases of *perestroika*. But it also clearly represented a danger, particularly as *perestroika* enters the phase of increasing emphasis on legality. Perhaps the turning point came with the »Begun riot,« in which it appears that not only Jewish demonstrators but also carefully selected Western correspondents were beaten up in the Arbat as part of a KGB plot. Since that time Gorbachev appears to have distanced himself from the KGB, at least as far as it concerns the power centre in Moscow. The implication is that he is now conducting a campaign on several fronts. He is taking on the Party bureaucracy, the state bureaucracy and the KGB bureaucracy. In such a context he has had to make new concessions even while claiming more power. The law on demonstrations which followed so soon after the brave words spoken at the Nineteenth Party Conference is a case in point.

In waging these campaigns on different fronts, Gorbachev enjoys the support of most intellectuals, whose work as advisors and in research institutes has become more influential, of a numerous echelon of senior Party officials – many of whom of course owe their seniority to Gorbachev himself – and, in an inarticulate manner and to a varying and unpredictable extent, the man in the street. But this last contention must be more clearly differentiated if it is to carry any meaning, particularly when it must be weighed against the opposition which is important at the middle and regional levels of the Party hierarchy.

Party opponents know what they don't like: the devolution of power, the threat to entrenched privilege, the prospect of accountability for their actions. Their rearguard action can be quite skilled, particularly while they are still responsible for implementing many of the policies of *perestroika*. It is still common for example, in drawing up new economic measures, for the local Party organisation to instruct the local Soviet to carry them out. If they succeed, the Party officials get the credit. If they fail, the Soviet gets the blame. So much, so far anyway, for accountability. But whereas such people can identify what they oppose, it is much harder for the populace at large to identify what it supports. If *perestroika* means better living standards, the only conclusion that most people seem to have drawn so far is that living standards have actually declined – and that is certainly the case in those areas of production where workers are being made financially responsible for quality control without having the means to exercise such control in the first place. If it means greater freedom of expression, there is a limit to their rejoicing when any amount of freely voiced complaint seems to do nothing to bring about actual change. If it means that, in contrast to the almost paranoid seclusion with which the *khozain* (»the bosses«) kept themselves apart from the people, Gorbachev and a few others now actually make some effort to meet them and see for themselves what their living conditions are like, then it also means that such meetings end with exhortations for greater efforts and more patience and with very few concrete promises. If, finally, it means the freedom to assemble, organise and demonstrate, then the new Popular

43

Fronts which have sprung up are highly ambiguous in character. In the Baltic Republics, they are religious or nationalist in nature. In Moscow, much Popular Front activity has been dominated by an extreme Russian nationalist group partly characterized by a virulent anti-Semitism – so much so that a kind of counter-Popular Front has now been formed to withstand its activities. In the Caucasus, Popular Front movements have been swamped by explosions of populist nationalism, which have led not only to great numbers of deaths and atrocities but also to the danger of a violent confrontation between Christian and Moslem. In other words, *perestroika* is capable, at the popular level, of an enormous variety of interpretations, and also of an almost kaleidoscopic pattern of frustration.

In such circumstances, it is going to be of the greatest importance that Gorbachev is able to channel popular support towards definable political objectives, and in a manner which will go at least some way towards raising living standards within a very short period of time. Lenin's Revolution was defined by its maker as »the Soviets plus electrification.« Gorbachev's second socialist revolution, as he likes to call it, might be defined as tolerable living conditions plus human rights. One of the questions that this implies is whether an adequate Western response has been determined. The countries of the Continent of Europe seem at least to appreciate the importance of *a* response. Mrs Thatcher's reaction, which unfortunately seems to be shared by most members of the outgoing and incoming administrations in the United States, might be summarised in the proposition »when you've solved all your problems, we'll be ready to help you.« I shall return to these considerations, but in the meantime it is worth noting that the internal and the international dimensions of the prospects for the Gorbachev reforms are very closely related.

In one sense, that is a very familiar point, as the debate among West Europeans and Americans over whether there should be a human rights conference in Moscow amply testifies. Whether they oppose or support such a prospect – or simply keep changing the minds – the message is clear. The reception accorded by the West to the Gorbachev reform programme will depend very much on its internal dimensions. The implication is that even if the Soviet government were to undertake significant and verifiable negotiations with the West on a large number of issues, including arms control and economic exchange, the Western

44

powers would still insist that these be tied to tangible evidence of progress on the questions of democratisation and human rights inside the USSR. Western politicians seem to be quite clear in their minds about that kind of linkage. At the same time, few seem to appreciate that the Gorbachev programme also has its own form of linkage: »new thinking in international relations« is as much a part of what he is trying to achieve as *glasnost* and *perestroika*. Indeed, the success of the latter two might well depend on what happens in terms of the first. Some Europeans do seem to appreciate this. Yet, apprehension was almost universally voiced, and profound relief later expressed, when the question arose as to whether the USSR would seek to link arms control negotiations in Vienna with a human rights conference in Moscow. It would appear that the West is allowed to play linkage games but the USSR is not. (In any event, in the end, the Soviet Union did not try: arms control negotiations will go ahead in Vienna whatever the outcome of the debate over the conference in Moscow.) But something more fundamental is at stake here.

It might be defined as the difference between a static analysis of the Soviet Union and a feed-back analysis. The first one would effectively argue that: »they are like that«. The system militates against change; Gorbachev is a brilliant propagandist whose radical ambitions are limited and who is very possibly not likely to last for very long in any case. If that is so, why should we make concessions now which might prove economically expensive and possibly perilous in terms of Western security, when we might well find ourselves up against a determined and hostile leader in the not-too-distant future? The feed-back analysis would say: »that's precisely the point.« It is to our advantage not to argue about what the Soviet Union, or Mr. Gorbachev *are* like, but to decide on how we can best influence their evolution through Western reactions and a Western input in the changing nature of the Soviet internal debate. The criterion should not be what the Soviet Union *is* like but what it can *become* like, given a properly measured Western set of responses. That raises questions of criteria, which I shall touch on later; but for the moment, I would wish to make it emphatically clear that I am in favour of the feed-back analysis rather than the static analysis.

In that context, the earlier analysis of *perestroika*, and of the stage that it has now reached, becomes particularly relevant. The earlier passages suggested that Gorbachev was coming increasingly to depend on popular support, as he was fighting on several fronts against the bureaucracies of the Party, the State and the KGB – but equally that this popular support was ill-defined and liable to turn into manifestations of popular discontent. In such circumstances, Gorbachev needs to harness popular energies for a sweeping transformation of Soviet society: what he has called »the second Russian Revolution.«

There is more than an element of paradox in such terminology. First, revolutions are not supposed to be directed from above. Even Lenin, who did direct what was in effect the second Russian Revolution from above, did so not from any position of legitimacy or entrenched authority, but as a direct challenge to those in such positions, whether they were inherited from the Ancien Régime in Russia or those thrown up by the first Revolution of February 1917. Gorbachev, on the other hand, is trying to direct this »second Russian Revolution« (perhaps more properly called the third) by his own established political authority. Insofar, that is, as it is established. It is for that reason that the question of the power struggle in the current state of *perestroika* has become particularly acute. The paradox at this level is that, were his power secure, he might not need to appear so revolutionary in terms of what he is trying to achieve; but since his power does not appear to be secure by any means, he has both to insist on the revolutionary nature of his objectives and at the same time to try to contain and direct the historical process by which these can be achieved – from a position which reflects political weakness at least as much as it reflects political power. At another level, the paradoxical nature of his programme becomes even more evident.

Revolutions seldom occur within a properly constituted civil society. But in any event, when they do occur, they sweep away the existing structures of any particular society. Gorbachev's ambition, on the other hand, appears to be to create something like a civil society in the Soviet Union – for the first time in fact in Russian history. The growing emphasis on legality, the promises to re-examine certain clauses of the Soviet constitution, the attempts to curb Party power and in particular the power of Party officials, the commitment to an elected Parliament with a plurality of candidates – all of these could come to represent the institutions of civil society. Obviously, he continues to emphasize that all his reforms must operate within the framework of socialism;

46

and a plurality of candidates will still fall short of what is meant by pluralism in the West. Yet, as he put it in his speech to the Supreme Soviet just before it voted itself out of existence: »We are all students in the school of democracy.« It is precisely on this point, of course, that his opponents voice their hostility.

There appears to be an extensive and fairly vociferous political debate at present about what actually constitutes socialism. Gorbachev insists that he is attempting to put socialism into practice after the years of terror and the years of stagnation. Others argue that his economic reforms are re-introducing capitalism and that his political reforms are incompatible with a Leninist party. Gorbachev's emphasis on collective decision also fits ill with the degree of personal power that he himself has accumulated, which worries not only his opponents who mutter about a new cult of personality, but also his supporters such as Andrei Sakharev. Yet even in this respect, it is interesting that he has effectively re-opened discussion about the nature of socialism itself, and that is a change which appears to be irreversible.

Given the degree of opposition, however, Gorbachev, as suggested earlier, needs public support more than ever. It was also suggested that he is not getting much of it. But it is important to draw a distinction here. Popular support, in terms of positive acclaim for the Gorbachev programme, still seems to be lacking; but popular revolt against the *khozain* is certainly growing. Seven First Secretaries have been removed from power at the regional level by popular demand, including in a famous case, that of Sverdlovsk. Clearly, popular discontent with the system is not necessarily a reliable ally for Gorbachev. The ethnic and religious confrontation in the Caucasus and the explosion of nationalist feeling in the Baltic Republics might prove very threatening. Gorbachev is trying to co-opt nationalist feeling and a sense of cultural rediscovery among the different nationalities into the process of *perestroika*. If he succeeds, he will then genuinely have a powerful ally – but so far it seems that nationalism is ambiguous in terms of the positive/negative distinction I have outlined.

Given time, the reform programme might find another powerful ally: the educated youth. It is now being taught at least a part of the true history of the Revolution and its consequences. One of the most significant measures of this year was the cancellation of the history examinations in schools and the withdrawal of previous text books while new and more truthful ones are being prepared. Soviet schoolchildren and students have already been told that they have not been taught the truth, and for them there can presumably be no return to the old system, which had lied to them so extensively and for so long. In the context of Gorbachev's promises to create a form of civil society in the USSR, extended and amplified by his emphasis on the need for legal guarantees of free speech and free assembly as he spoke to the world forum of the UN General Assembly, Soviet youth is bound to contrast the prospects of the future with the lies of the past. Given the choice, there is very little doubt as to where it would cast its weight.

But, as I have just suggested, being given the choice means being given time. It would seem to me that it is vital, both for the preservation of hope in the East and for the future of security in the West, that the Western powers use their utmost endeavours to buy as much time as possible for the success of the Gorbachev reform programme. I suggested earlier that *perestroika* has now reached a critical stage, at which it is essential for Western analysts to abandon a static mode of approach in favour of a feedback analysis, depending not so much on what »we« think the Soviet Union is like now but on what we can do to assist in its development towards becoming a recognisable, normal, peaceful member of the international community. This is exactly the prospect that Gorbachev held out in his UN speech – and, incidentally, it was interesting to note that he did so within the perspectives of a Marxist interpretation of history. In other words neither Marxism *per se* nor the Russian Revolution condemn humanity to continuing confrontation. So what is the West waiting for?

One answer might be that it is in fact very difficult to translate the fine aspiration of »helping« and »buying time« into practical action – even assuming that such Western governments as those of the United States and Britain abandon the attitudes which I have tried to characterize in an earlier paragraph: namely, when you have solved all your problems, we'll be ready to help. But, even assuming that the West *wants* to help, what can it actually do?

Some grandiose suggestions have been made in the recent past. One such, by Signor de Mita, the Italian Prime Minister, was that there should be a new kind of Marshall Plan for the Soviet Union and Eastern Europe. That now appears to have been dropped – and rightly so. At the first of the Luxembourg-Harvard conferences a year ago, which in fact commemorated the 40th anniversary of the original recovery programme, it was noted that »you can't clone the Marshall Plan.« The success of that endeavor depended, apart from American generosity and political will, on the fact that in spite of the destruction of the Western European industrial superstructure brought about by the Second World War, the infrastructure had survived in a readily reparable state; and recovery was therefore astonishingly fast. If the main problem in the Soviet Union and Eastern Europe is the nature of the infrastructure itself (in terms not only of transport and distribution facilities, but also in those of distribution procedures, price formation and economic as well as political accountability), a new Marshall Plan would amount to little more than throwing a great deal of money at a set of intractable problems in the hope that some of it would stick. Grandiose proposals of this nature seem in fact to have little practical content.

Other alternatives appear on the face of it to be less grandiose. The Soviet Union, for example, has been trying for some years to join the GATT. GATT is in theory a global organisation, but in practice it is dominated by Western economic power, Western belief in the liberal values associated with the free market, and by rules of entry which are virtuously dictated by the West. In these circumstances, it is perhaps hardly surprising that the American reaction to the Soviet application verged on the contemptuous, declaring that the Soviet economy was organised in a manner philosophically and practically antithetical to the principles of the GATT. But if one applies the feedback criteria to dealings with the USSR – in this case how to help it change both the philosophy and the practice of the Soviet economy, which is Gorbachev's avowed aim – is there not a case to be made after all for Soviet membership? One should not forget that Roumania has been a member for quite some time, and it is hard to imagine any country whose philosophy and praxis could be more antithetical to the GATT principles. But it was allowed to join because of its hostility to the Soviet Union; and the fact that it has not observed any of the »surrogate rules« which were a condition of its membership has not made the slightest difference to its status. In these circumstances it is hard to gainsay the Soviet content that there is a political bias on the part of the Western powers which precludes it from membership. But that does not indicate the real difficulties of the case.

Even with political goodwill, the GATT would still find it hard to absorb the Soviet Union (especially since negotiations about the renewal of Chinese membership are now going on) without distorting the entire nature and the functioning of the organisation. Once these two enormous economies joined GATT, its rules would be virtually meaningless, and its value as an international forum for the promotion of free trade would effectively break down. It is no doubt for that reason, quite apart from political calculations, that the United States is at present placing so many obstacles in the path of the Bulgarian application to join. A small economy like Bulgaria's would really make no difference; but it would set a *political* precedent for the huge Soviet economy to disrupt the workings of the GATT. Quite apart from the question of political will, therefore, there are real technical difficulties here. Even if the Western powers as a whole were determined to encourage *perestroika* and the transformation of the Soviet economy, they might, in GATT terms, find themselves doing so at the expense of what has been hitherto a reasonably effective operational system in many parts of the globe. In other words, goodwill only serves to heighten dilemmas. But governments, if they are worthy of the name, should be at home with dilemmas. That is what they are for. And in the case of this particular dilemma, it seems that a model is available for at least a partial resolution. Neither the Chinese nor the Roumanian model, but the Jugoslav. That is to say, a gradual extension of the GATT provisions, negotiated on a case-by-case basis, of the Most-Favoured-Nation principles in return for observable measures of »transparency« on the part of the supplicant country. (Recent Jugoslav experience does not provide a happy guide to the application of these principles but does not invalidate them in themselves.) In the case of the Soviet Union, however, such a process of extension would appear to be exactly what the present government has in mind – as evidenced by recent Soviet declarations at the Uruguay Round. The politics and economics of the »Jugoslav model« could in fact provide a way forward for the Western powers to engage in an increasingly interacting set of methods of dealing with the East, of creating a framework for feedback policy-making, without venturing into the grandiose nullities of a »new Marshall Plan,« on the one hand, or the structural distortions implied in immediate Soviet membership of GATT, on the other. Lateral thinking might be the key to the unlocking of confrontational issues.

The USSR has by all accounts also proposed its own form of lateral thinking. In meeting after meeting with European leaders, Gorbachev has emphasized the need for a relaxation of the COCOM rules. If one regards these proposals in the light of a static-confrontation analysis, they obviously represent an attempt to gain strategic advantages at virtually no cost. If one looks at them again within the framework of an attempt to move from an offensive-defensive strategy to a defensive-defensive strategy, which can be based on broader criteria of what constitutes security than the simple measurements of a military balance in Europe, they might make a lot of sense – within the context of *Western* security aspirations. In other words, a redefinition of what constitutes security is now involved. At the risk of sounding rather too much like Hans-Dietrich Genscher, I would strongly suggest that it is high time for the West to reconsider what Western security actually entails. That is not a defineable or easy process. Apart from anything else, it involves questions of time-scales as well as criteria. One might suggest at first that a »Jugoslav« approach to the question of GATT membership and a discriminate relaxation in the COCOM rules would help. Beyond that, one would also have to judge by new, evolving criteria: namely, whether a feedback policy were doing its job. If not, »we« might have to think again – and much there would obviously depend on the evolving social and political relations in the USSR itself. In such historical circumstances, *festina lente* is bound to be the name of the game. But while the policy might have to be slow, the criteria are those of how to hasten the pace of change.

Now behind all this lies a fundamental consideration: no government in the West knows how to deal with the phenomenon represented by Mikhail Sergei Gorbachev. Questions as to what constitutes »propaganda« as opposed to »new departures,« as to what he means by »a new era of peace« as opposed to particularistic advantages for the USSR in its dealings with the other superpower, as to whether his internal reform programme is likely to succeed or is even sincere, abound in all Western countries. Such questions have almost become a Western luxury – and have also produced the response which suggests that if the Soviet Union can solve its problems, the West will be willing to help ... Why?

It has just been suggested that a pragmatic approach to the problems of how to deal with a new Soviet Union is indeed possible: whether in terms of a »Jugoslav« solution to the problems of its accession to GATT, or in terms of a relaxation of the COCOM restriction designed to encourage the Soviet Union to economic and technological collaboration, or indeed in terms of arms control criteria, which have scarcely been mentioned so far but which *might* become very important in 1989 if the CST talks get seriously under way. A range of pragmatic possibilities is indeed available. Yet the Western powers find that these are causes for dispute among themselves. Genscher and de Mita at one extreme; Shultz and Thatcher at the other. That in itself is an interesting phenomenon.

NATO, to the best of my knowledge, is the only alliance in history whose Treaty contains a preamble stressing that it is founded on common values. Gorbachev is now threatening the NATO countries with the prospect that the Soviet Union (while no doubt remaining a competitive power) will join those values. In such circumstances, can Europeans and Americans, left and right, hold together against what is no longer perceived as a unifying threat? Can they even agree on a course of pragmatic action?

The words of the great Alexandrinian poet Cavafis might come in handy here. In his poem, *Waiting for the Barbarians*, he describes the confusion in Alexandria as it became apparent that the barbarians were not going to attack after all. The last lines of the poem go like this:

>»But what shall we do without the barbarians?
>They were a kind of solution.«

That is the problem with which Gorbachev has confronted the members of the Atlantic Alliance. How can we change ourselves to respond?

The Foreign Policy Implications of Soviet Economic Reform

Jerry F. Hough

Mikhail Gorbachev ended his interview with *Time Magazine* in August 1985 with a deliberate concluding statement:

>»In conclusion I would like to emphasize a point that has been the main one in our conversation. It has been rightly said that foreign policy is a continuation of domestic policy. If this is so, I ask you to ponder: if we have a grandiose program in the domestic sphere, than what are the external conditions in which we have an interest? I leave the answer to you.«

This teasing question led to a major debate in the United States that still continues. On one level, the answer was simple. It was necessary, as Soviet Foreign Minister Eduard Shevardnadze put it in 1987 »to ›economize‹ our foreign policy, if such an expression is permissible, since, until it is linked with the economy, it will be unable to help in restructuring our domestic economy and society.«[1] Thus it was necessary to play down the promotion of revolution and concentrate more on the promotion of trade. It was necessary to follow a détente policy and to seek arms control in order to divert money from the military to the civilian sector.

But beneath these general propositions were a series of very specific questions on which there has been the most profound disagreement. The underlying assumptions of each side in the debate have not always been made explicit, but the debate rests on a most profound disagreement about the nature of the Russian people and about the domestic policy that Gorbachev is following and must follow.

I.

Everyone who has given any serious thought to Soviet economic reform knows the problems that must be faced and solved. Monopolistic

[1] Vestnik ministerstva inostrannykh del SSSR, no 3, 1987.

ministries must be broken up, and competition between enterprises or firms introduced into the economy; a planning system that inevitably creates a sellers' market with demand in excess of supply must be replaced by an economic system in which producers have an incentive to economize on labor and supplies and meet consumers' demand. Such a system depends on prices that are more or less in line with supply and demand, and this means an increase in the price of a number of sensitive goods, such as meat.

And, finally, although most Western economists for some reason do not emphasize it, the Soviet Union must attack the massive protectionism that is imbedded in the system itself. Because the very planning system ensures that demand – especially for capital goods – is in excess of supply, Soviet manufacturers do not lose any business when foreign goods are imported, and hence they are not compelled to raise the quality of their goods to meet the competition. Because manufacturers have a guaranteed market at home (or in Eastern Europe with similar conditions), they are not compelled to export manufactured goods and meet competition in the foreign market as the Pacific country manufacturers have to. The protectionism of the communist societies has made Japan look like an open economy, and the consequences. of the protectionism in terms of quality, innovation, efficiency, and so forth have been just what a Western economic textbook would predict. As experience showed, the Brezhnev policy of importing technology without forcing domestic manufacturers to compete with it was a failure. The rate of economic growth continued to decline, and the Soviet Union slipped further behind in the technological race. The Soviet Union must accept major foreign investment, it must develop its own multi-national corporations with plants abroad, it must engage in cooperative productive relationships with Western firms, and it must adopt a very vigorous export strategy. Many Westerners say that the Soviet Union cannot possibly export goods because of the low quality of those goods, but the experience of the Pacific countries indicates otherwise. If low-quality goods are priced low enough (that is, if the exchange rate is set at the right level), they will sell. The Pacific countries began to export when the quality of their goods was low precisely in order to force their manufacturers to compete on the world market and improve the quality of their production.

II.

The essential debate in the United States is whether the Russian people
– and I literally mean the Great Russians, not the Soviet people as
a whole – will accept the kind of steps which are necessary. Many
analysts argue that they will not, and instead would revolt at any
change in the status quo. Although ten-twenty years ago, we saw
the Soviet Union as a repressive dictatorship, we now talk as if the
Brezhnev regime were virtually a democracy for the masses. Income
distribution is recognized as having been egaliarian, and bureaucrats
and managers had little power to discipline workers. Russians are
described as people who crave order and security and who, above all,
want to be protected from corrupting Western influences and unsettling
Western market forces. We use the term »social contract« to refer to
the agreement between the wishes of the public and the policy of the
Politburo in the Brezhnev period.

If the Soviet people were basically happy with Brezhnev's policy, then
Stephen Cohen was right in 1979 when he wrote, »the real obstacle to
reform in the Soviet Union is ... the profound conservation that seems to
dominate ... all ... Arguably the Soviet Union has become, both upstairs
and downstairs, one of the most conservative countries in the world.«[2]
Or perhaps analysts such as George Feiffer and Andrei Amalrik were
right that the conservatism is so ugly that it might easily support a more
fascist regime. In Feifer's words in 1981,

> »My friends are convinced that 60 years of Soviet rule which has taught
> schoolchildren to lie, and destroyed civic virtue, have turned the Russian
> people into a rabble ripe for envy, violence, demagogery, but not for
> responsible citizenship. Where is the social material fore a more progressive,
> tolerant government, they ask. The country had quite enough handicaps dur-
> ing the 50 years before the revolution, when it made unsteady unpredictable
> progress toward constitutional monarchy and democracy. Almost all the
> people who achieved that progress were subsequently shot or otherwise
> silenced if they had not already fled. Almost all the needed habits are gone.
> If the hated regime were to collapse overnight, fierce nationalists would
> be more likely than enlightened liberals to replace it, if only because few
> enlightened liberals manage to develop in that sort of environment, and
> few understand or want them. Even if something more humane were to be

---

2 Stephen Cohen, Rethinking the Soviet Experience (Oxford University Press, 1985),
  p. 146.

somehow pieced together, it would quickly be torn apart by the dumb anger Soviet rule has inculcated.«[3]

Feifer expressed a virtually identical view in *Harper's* in October 1988.[4]

Obviously if this view of the Russian people is correct, then Gorbachev has a Herculean task in conducting a reform that would undercut the »social contract« that they cherish. He would be particularly unlikely to take serious steps in the foreign economic realm that would begin subjecting the Russians to foreign competiton. But since he is presiding over a declining economy, be desperately needs photo opportunities with Western leaders, recognition of Soviet super-power equality abroad, control of military spending through arms control, and importation of foreign technology to try to stave off economic collapse. To get these – so the argument goes – the Soviet leadership must make concessions to the United States. It must retreat in the regional conflicts, permit freer emigration, and make the major concessions in arms control negotiations.

This view, in one form or another, to one degree or another, permeates Washington thinking, and, in my opinion, underlies the hard-line policy of the Reagan Administration. It was articulated with unusual sharpness and frankness by a former Reagan administration official, Stephen Sestanovich, in the *Washington Post*:

> »Gorbachev's is a foreign policy of concessions. To maintain the momentum of change and innovation, he's prepared to meet the demands of his adversary ... But other governments are bound to ask the obvious question: Why reciprocate, rather than simply wait for another concession? Why not add new demands? There's a dawning sense that Gorbachev may be a man who can be had: on arms control, Afghanistan and other issues ... Only the most serious internal preoccupations can explain such an experimental diplomacy with such an uncertain payoff ... Western policy continuity is important ... because he ... will keep backpedaling if we let him.«[5]

There is, of course, another possible policy conclusion that can be drawn from the analysis that societal pressures make reform virtually impossible. One can argue that we should help Gorbachev, and some liberals make it. However, the argument is unconvincing. If the Stalin

3 George Feifer, »Russian Disorders,« *Harper's*, February 1981, p. 53.
4 George Feifer, »The New God will fail,« *Harper's*, October 1988
5 Stephen Sestanovich, »Gorbachev: Giving Away the Store?«, *Washington Post*, December 11, 1988, Outlook, p. Cl.

empire can be toppled, if (as Harvard historian Richard Pipes says) Russian foreign policy has been most nonexpansionist during times of trouble, the logical conclusion is that the United States should welcome the Soviet disorders that weaken Gorbachev, and it should seek to promote the disorders through any means it can – including dragging its feet on arms control that would save Gorbachev money, restraints on economic activity, propaganda that increases a sense of unhappiness in the Soviet Union, convert funneling of money to democratic movements in the Soviet Union, and so forth. Indeed, I think that that has been the policy of the United States.

III.

In my opinion, however, the analysis of the Russian people and the chances of success for reform on which the American policy rests is an incorrect one. Those who are currently saying that the Russian people will not permit reform were the same ones who previously were saying that the »partocracy« or the military or the »nomenklatura« or whoever would not permit the selection of an innovative leader. As George Feifer and his friends expressed it in 1981:

> »The party-KGB-military oligarchy is seen to be developing into a hereditary ruling class that passes position and luxury to its offspring ... ›Every one of these party bosses is a drab, empty functionary‹... ›These second-rate hacks have the fewest qualities for anything resembling genuine leadership‹.«[6]

So much for Mikhail Gorbachev who spent his whole life in the party apparatus. Michael Voslenskii and Konstantin Simis were only two among a number of immigrants presenting a similar view.[7]

It seems to me, however, that we should see the Russian people – including those working in the party and state apparatus in light of modernization theory. We understand that when a country does not have an educated middle class – as, for example, in Haiti and Panama today – it finds it almost impossible to develop a real democracy. But when a country does develop such an educated middle class, its

6 Feifer, »Russian Disorders,« p. 54. The statements in small quotes are from Feifer's friends.
7 Michael S. Voslenskii, *Nomenklatura: The Soviet Ruling Class* (Garden City, N.Y.: Doubleday, 1984), and Konstantin Simis, »The Gorbachev Generation,« *Foreign Policy*, no. 59 (Summer 1985), pp. 3–21.

population generally becomes increasingly intolerant of dictatorship. This has certainly been true of countries such as Argentina, Brazil, South Korea, and Spain.

In my opinion, Russia society has been becoming increasingly middle class in character.[8] In 1959, 14 percent of the population had a high school diploma or better, but this figure had risen to 41 percent by 1980. We do not say that the black middle class in American suburbs in 1988 have the same political culture and attitudes as the illiterate black sharecropper in the south in 1918, and there seems little reason to believe that the Russian middle class of 1988 is the same as the illiterate peasant muzhik of 1918. In my opinion, education, urbanization, and the like are having the same impact on attitudes that they had in countries such as Spain, Argentina, and Brazil – and earlier in Western Europe. Already in the 1950s the educated youth were showing themselves different from the xenophobic Brezhnev generation by their attraction to Western music, Western films, Western clothes, and so forth. As early as 1959, Edward Crankshaw, one of the most perceptive observers of the time, argued that this generational change was found among party and governmental officials as well:

> »Nothing in this world is more depressing to contemplate than the average Soviet official of high or low degree at present between the ages of forty and sixty [that is, born between 1900 and 1920] ... The Soviet Union's great hope lies in the young – those under thirty-five [that is, born after 1924] ... In a dozen professions in which Party control is particularly rigid – in the Foreign Service, in the Law, in journalism, in economics, in the higher civil service with its many branches, in the armed forces, in the University faculties, you will meet well-turned-out young men in their thirties, usually Party members, relaxed and easy in manner, often with a pleasantly ironical approach to life, and very much in touch with realities of every kind ... I have been talking of the cream of the younger men beginning to rise in what are called the liberal professions and the State and Party service. Until the last decade young men of comparable ability would not have dreamt of this sort of career.«[9]

The crucial fact about the 1970s was that this group was moving towards middle age (a man born in 1924 was 56 in 1980) and was replacing the Brezhnev generation among the country's middle-level

8 For a comprehensive presentation of this case, see Jerry F. Hough, *Soviet Leadership in Transition* (Washington, D.C.: The Brookings Institution, 1980).
9 Edward Crankshaw, *Khrushchev's Russia* (Baltimore: Penguin Books, 1959), pp. 90–91 and 130.

officials. The younger age groups who were coming along were progressively better educated, and in 1983 S. Frederick Starr could write correctly that »the present young adult generation is the first in Soviet history to share fully in European and American popular culture.«[10] Those Russians who some dismissed as bureaucrats were really the educated middle class, and with the number of people with a high school diploma or better increasing from 20 million in 1954 to 100 million at the time of Brezhnev's death, the latter came to be not the representative of the dominant Russian social forces, but a powerful dam holding back their demands for change.

In this view Brezhnev might hold on for a few years, but a new general secretary with a time horizon that extended into the 1990s would have to reform the system if he wanted to maintain political stability. That is, with the growing middle class, it would have been the maintenance of Brezhnevism that would have caused revolt, not a movement away from the so-called social contract. Gorbachev understood this. A Western visitor to his office in the Central Committee in 1981 – while Brezhnev was still alive – found it furnished with modern Scandinavian furniture, a powerful symbol to the officials visiting him that his campaign promise was Westernization. Gorbachev's last major speech in the Chernenko period called, in the words of Serge Schmemann at the time, »for a transformation of the nation as radical as the one wrought by Stalin in the brutal industrialization drive of the 1930s.«[11] Gorbachev judged correctly that the Brezhnev Central Committee would support this appeal, and, of course, the 40 percent turnover in the Central Committee at the 27th Party Congress in 1986 strengthened his hold on that body even more.

As a consequence, we have in the Soviet Union a bureaucracy, a middle class, that wanted blue jeans and jazz when they were young, a general secretary who rests his policy on an appeal to their values, and both a general secretary and a middle class who have an unanswerable argument to use against the conservatives. They can say that the old social contract and the isolation from the West was a disaster for Russian power because of the protectionism it created. They could

10 S. Frederick Starr, *Red and Hot: The Fate of Jazz in the Soviet Union, 1917–1980* (New York: Oxford University Press, 1983), p. 321.
11 »The emergence of Gorbachev,« *The New York Times Magazine*, March 3, 1985, p. 44

seize the banner of nationalism and patriotism that had been such a powerful support for the conservatives in the past and use it to support a diametrically opposed policy.

IV.

If Gorbachev not only can, but must have radical economic reform to maintain stability, then what are the foreign policy consequences? First, Gorbachev must change his ideology to accommodate the new foreign economic necessities. He must speak, as he did at the United Nations, of the world economy as »a single organism,« not as two separate capitalist and socialist economies. He must say, as Shevardnadze said in 1987 that »we should become a more organic part of the world economic system, and we can and are obliged to become so if we accept and assimilate the forms extant in it.«[12] He must talk about Europe as »a common home,« not as an appeal for the breakup of NATO, but to say that Russia is part of Western civilization and that a free flow of information about the outside world is necessary if the Soviet Union is to have a successful export strategy.

Second, while Brezhnev had an interest in maintaining a threatening army that made it difficult for reformers to say stagnation was weakening Soviet defense, as well as an interest in nuclear arms control negotiations that created the impression that American technology was under control, Gorbachev had an opposite set of interests. He had no domestic need to create any illusions about Soviet power, but rather found it useful to emphasize the Strategic Defense Initiative as a symbol of the totally devastating result that technological backwardness might have. He needed to reduce conventional forces both to save money and to reduce the Western sense of threat and, thereby, to smooth the way for foreign investment.

Third, the internationalized and multilateral character of modern economic relations means that integration into the world economy inevitably undercuts the image of a two-bloc world that lay at the heart of a bipolar foreign policy. To some extent, foreign policy would

12 Vestnik ministerstva inostrannykh del SSSR, *no. 3, 1987,* op. cit.

inevitably become more multi-polar. Moreover, in practice, the United States was inclined to a very hard-line policy on questions such as technology transfer and most-favored-nation treatment, and it tended to draw the conclusion from Gorbachev's concessions that Sestanovich did: if Gorbachev's domestic situation was so desperate to require such concessions, a continuation of the economic restrictions might produce a collapse or near-collapse of the Soviet empire. If the United States is going to try to maintain a technological and economic semi-blockade, then Gorbachev has to try to break it by reaching out to Western Europe, Japan, and the large, industrializing Third World countries.

In actuality, Gorbachev wanted and sought American legitimization of his improvement of relations with America's allies, and he insisted on periodic summits to achieve it. Indeed, he even invited himself to the United Nations to obtain the latter. The link was often clear: When Shevardnadze visited Washington in September 1987 to agree to the Washington summit, Chancellor Kohl was able to receive Erich Honecker in West Germany as an equal several weeks earlier, and then Shevardnadze flew to Brazil and Argentina directly from Washington. Just before Gorbachev flew to the United Nations, the West German government felt it possible to announce the end of division-size maneuvers of West German troops in West Germany.

While Sestanovich was right in saying that the Soviet Union was making the concessions in the Soviet-American relationship (although, as Fedor Burlatsky said, President Reagan was making ideological concessions), it is striking how little the United States was gaining from these concessions. The only arms control treaty, the INF Treaty, removed a significant American missile – the Pershing 2 – that was aimed at the Soviet comand-and-control system without removing a single missile aimed at the United States. The removal of SS-20s aimed at Western Europe simply removed part of the glue in the U.S. alliance system. The U.S. did not take advantage of Gorbachev's 1986 proposal for conventional arms control to reduce its military spending in Europe, and it did not facilitate economic relations with the Soviet Union in a way that would have benefitted American businessmen. It concentrated its attention on getting the Soviet Union out of Afghanistan – something that would complicate American relations with Pakistan – and getting Cuban troops out of Angola – something that would benefit Castro – instead of making compromises with the Soviet Union in other parts

61

of the world to solve problems in its own sphere of influence in the Caribbean and Central America.

There was another reason for early ambivalence in Gorbachev's policy. Soviet geostrategic and economic interests have been in conflict under Gorbachev. The essence of the postwar period, intended or otherwise, was American geostrategic hegemony over Western Europe and Japan and Soviet hegemony over Eastern Europe. This has created a very stable situation in the industrial world for forty years – a sharp contrast with the situation that had prevailed in the previous forty years. West Germany basically accepted the division of Germany, and the domestic politics of neither West Germany nor Japan featured any pressure for the acquisition of nuclear weapons. NATO provided the excuse for the maintenance of the Warsaw Pact. No intelligent Soviet leader would want to challenge this stability lightly.

For this reason there was no need for the Soviet Union to take the risks of destabilizing the Western alliances prematurely. Certainly there was much to be said for trying to alleviate fears in Western Europe, Japan, and elsewhere so that their people and governments would be responsive to later moves, but the latter could be postponed. There was no reason to take real risks for the sake of economic reform until economic reform reached the stage where the risks needed to be taken. Economic reforms in the Soviet Union, it must be remembered, are an extremely complicated process, quite aside from any opposition to it. Extraordinarily radical innovations, such as privately owned cooperatives and joint ventures with foreign capitalists had to be introduced on a very small scale the first year or two so that experience could be gained and the detailed rules adjusted before a large-scale program was launched. In addition, the various parts of the reform had to be carried out in the proper sequence. A law giving the enterprise more independence could not have meaning until the supply system was loosened, and the planning of supply always occurred the previous year. Any real loosening of supply required a toleration of inflation, and this had to wait until cost-of-living clauses were introduced into the pension legislation. The joint venture law could never have much meaning until the enterprise gained some independence from the ministries. And so forth.

As a result, there never was any reason for the Soviet Union to encourage large-scale foreign investment in the Soviet Union or to challenge the American economic-technological blockade for the first three to four years of the Gorbachev period, even if there were no opposition to radical reform and if Gorbachev were determined to plunge ahead. And if there was no realistic possibility of an accelerated foreign economic policy during this period, there was consequently no reason to sacrifice Soviet geostrategic interests prematurely.

By the summer of 1988, however, the preparatory period for economic reform seemed to be drawing to a close. The cooperatives law passed by the Supreme Soviet in May was a radical improvement over the first experimental law; Gorbachev began talking much more urgently about fundamental agricultural reform, and all signs suggested major change in the winter of 1988–1989. The Council of Ministers decreed that some 20 percent of the supply system should not be centrally planned in 1989, and the minister of finances announced that shares of state enterprises would be sold, with a stock market introduced. Joint ventures would no longer have to be owned 51 percent by the Soviet side.

If the analysis presented in this article is correct, then the fall of 1988 should have been a time for a change in foreign policy. And, precisely at this time, leading Americanists in the foreign policy establishment (Gromyko, Dobrynin, and Vorontsov) were retired or demoted, while two leading proponents of an Europe- and Japan-centered policy, Yakovlev and Falin, became head of the foreign policy committee of the Politburo and head of the international department of the Central Committee respectively. When the membership of the foreign policy commission was announced, it included the first deputy minister for Europe (Kovalev), but neither Vorontsov (officially still a first deputy minister) nor Bessmertnykh, the new first deputy minister for the United States. At the same time, relations with China improved to such an extent that a summit meeting was possible, and a steady stream of European leaders visited Moscow. Soviet-West German relations improved markedly.

It remains to be seen how thoroughly an economic reform or a change in foreign policy will take place. It also remains to be seen how a new American administration will react. If it repudiates the very hard-line policy of the Reagan Administration on conventional disarmament and economic relations with the Soviet Union, then the Soviet Union need not change its own policy drastically. The change in personnel in

September and October 1988 had, however, much of the appearance of the replacement of the pro-Western Maxim Litvinov with the hard-line Viacheslav Molotov in May 1939. If the warning is ignored as it was in 1939, the consequences may be quite severe. Soviet domestic imperatives for an opening to the world economy are absolute, and Gorbachev will do what he has to do to meet these imperatives.

Perestroika and the Nationality Question: An Assessment

Gerhard Simon

I. Mass Mobilization of Small Nations

1988 will become memorable as the year of unprecedented mass mobilization of small nations in the Soviet Union. The main actors were the Baltic nations, the Armenians and the Azerbaidzhanis. There are about 1 million Estonians; 3 million Armenians living in Armenia; and the Azeris are a nation of about 6.5 million. One has to have in mind these figures in order to evaluate properly the mass demonstrations during 1988. 300,000 Estonians assembled on September 11 in Tallinn on the occasion of the festival »Estonia's Song 1988.« 500,000 Lithuanians met on August 2 in Kaunas for the largest demonstration in the Baltic republics after World War II. The topic in Kaunas was the growing ecological crisis in Lithuania. Mass meetings had started in Armenia in February, when up to one million people took to the streets in Erivan, parallel to walkouts in Stepanakert and other cities. Finally, mass mobilization reached Azerbaidzhan in November, when also hundreds of thousands gathered for anti-Armenian demonstrations in all major cities.

Such political mass mobilization has few parallels in European history and is surely unprecedented in Soviet history. The demonstrations by virtually the entire population of metropolitan areas occurred either in sharp contradiction to the clear political will of the party leadership in Moscow or – as in some instances in the Baltic republics – with its grudging toleration. In neither case were the mass movements part of Gorbachev's *perestroika* from above. Just the opposite; they were a demand for *perestroika* in the area of national relations.

Two conclusions stand out:

1. The amazingly quick and complete self-organization of small nations is a signal of a serious crisis of the Soviet political system.

65

2. National and democratic forces are on the rise and they are demanding changes leading to a transformation of the political system.

The national movements were successful because they were able to incorporate a wide range of grievances and demands exceeding the limits of the national sphere proper. To put it in the words of a member of the Armenian Karabakh-Committee, Ambartsum Galstjan: National requests joined forces with the overall dissatisfaction. »Discontent about social injustice, a corrupt leadership, a disastrous ecological situation, discontent about the moral and cultural decline.« This reminds us of the well-established fact that there is no nationalism as such. Nationalism forms all sorts of coalitions with intellectual currents, social movements and political parties. Nationalism can combine forces with liberal and democratic endeavors or with reactionary movements. Its adaptability guarantees its universality.

II. Grievances and Demands of the Nations

Let me summarize the demands of the small nations before reflecting on some main features and consequences of their self-organization:

1. The central issue for the Armenians is the unification of Mountain-Karabakh with Soviet Armenia. Why did this irredentist demand become the central issue of Armenian national consciousness? Irredentism characterizes Armenian nationalism in the 20th century in general; it is the essence of the »Armenian question.« Contemporary Soviet Armenian territory constitutes a mere north-eastern border province of the medieval Armenian state. Today, Armenian claims to Turkish territory are illusionary, all the more so since the Armenian population in Anatolia has been killed or expelled. The percentage of the Armenian population is also approaching zero in the Autonomous Republic of Nakhichevan, an Azeri enclave on Armenian soil. The only region outside the Armenian republic with a solid Armenian majority is Mountain-Karabakh, which by a decision of the Soviets could be united with Soviet Armenia.

A redemption of Mountain-Karabakh is not only feasible, it would clearly be an act of self-determination for the Armenians living there and in Armenia. Claims for unification date back to the 19th century and since the 1960s an ever-mounting popular oppositional movement fought for it. In this sense, a unification of Mountain-Karabakh with Armenia would constitute a step towards democracy in Soviet society.

2. The Azerbaidzhanis fiercely oppose the Armenian claims, arguing that Mountain-Karabakh never belonged to Armenia in modern times, but constituted an Islamic *khanat* in the 18th century and was later incorporated into the *gubernija* of Elizavetpol (earlier Ganja, today Kirovabad), also an overwhelmingly Islamic province of the Russian Empire. In 1988 crowds of hundreds of thousands in Baku and other Azerbaidzhanian cities demanded the dissolution of the united autonomy of Mountain-Karabakh and its degradation to a normal district of the Azerbaidzhanian SSR.

But in Azerbaidzhan, as in Armenia, the basic national conflict is reinforced by other factors. The declining economy in general and the decline of the oil industry in particular have sharpened social tensions. The Armenian minority in Azerbaidzhanian cities is better educated, holds better jobs and has a higher standard of living compared to the Azeri majority. The Armenian minority fulfills a scapegoat function similar to the one Jews used to fulfill in many European states. The Azerbaidzhanis also envy the Armenians for preserving their cultural heritage, intellectual superiority and language more strongly than the Azeris. The Azerbaidzhanis now openly demand from Moscow more cultural autonomy and the return of the Arabic script as the symbol of their distinct cultural identity, arguing that the contemporary generation is not even able to read the tombstones on the graves of their forefathers.

3. The Baltic nations have articulated their demands for economic, cultural, and political decentralization much more clearly and boldly than the Transcaucasian nations. They argue for the realization of Soviet federalism, which on paper guarantees sovereignty to the Union republics, but in practice does not even allow them to set the price for a bottle of beer or to change the recipe of a cake without permission from Moscow.

Particularly the Estonians – the smallest nation with an own Union republic – developed a model for economic autonomy of the republics which boils down to the establishment of special economic zones in the USSR. The Baltic nations are also demanding an improved status for the titular language and culture within one's own republic, guaranteed and enforced by law. All three republics in 1988 amended their constitutions with articles stating that the mother tongue of the titular nation is the state language in the given republic.

No other issue has aroused so much national resentment as the Russification drive during the late Brezhnev era, and in no other field have *all* Soviet nations now turned from submission to counter-attack. In 1978 the Brezhnev leadership tried hard – although in vain – to erase the state language articles from the constitutions of the Transcaucasian republics. Today, liquidation of state-language articles is out of the question. On the contrary, more and more republics are coming up with demands to protect their languages by law.

4. From the point of view of the nationalities *perestroika* has to mean decentralization. It cannot be otherwise. Apart from the general demands applying to all nations the Balts have aired their own specific grievances. They want a halt to the massive immigration of Russians into Estonia and Latvia that is endangering national culture and identity. More than half of Tallinn's population is »Russian-speaking« (russkoja-zyčnye), and according to unofficial estimates, Latvians today constitute less than half of the population of their republic. Immigration of Slavs and rapid industrialization are directly interrelated. Therefore, the Balts are opposed to new huge industrialization projects, which could also turn the current ecological crisis into ecological disaster.

The memory of the independent sovereign states between the two World Wars and their liquidation by the Stalinist Soviet Union in 1939/40 motivates the self-organization of the three Baltic nations. National flags and anthems have now been officially readmitted. To hoist the national flag could have led to imprisonment a few years ago.

III.   Self-Organization of Nations

Let me now turn to the instruments and consequences of the self-organization of the small nations. A preliminary remark on non-violence and violence is in order. To my mind, one of the most remarkable features of the self-organization of the nations is that it was carried out by and large without violence. Hundreds of thousands took to the streets, and in

Armenia demonstrations several times took the form of general strikes. Emotions were running high, but there were no incidents, no brawls, no knifings. The most obvious exceptions from general non-violence came with the terrible pogroms in Azerbaidzhan at the end of February and again at the end of November in Sumgait, Baku, Kirovabad and in other places. Their victim was the Armenian minority in Azerbaidzhan. Although the pogroms were partly organized, partly tolerated by local Azerbaidzhani officials, we have to keep in mind that the hundreds of thousands in the streets of Baku and other cities are not *pogromščiki*.

1. The most notable feature of the self-organization of the nations is the establishment of political organizations, which enjoy tremendous authority and, to a considerable extent, de facto rule society. The Karabakh-Committee, which directed the Karabakh-campaign, the demonstrations and strikes, emerged in Erevan in February. It was not only able to bring virtually the entire population to the streets, but – more important – also to call demonstrations off and send people back to work. Gorbachev de facto recognized the Karabakh-Committee when he first received its representatives on February 26 before talking to the now-dismissed Armenian First Party Secretary Demirchjan 10 days later. The Karabakh-Committee possesses a fairly dense network of committees in factories, organizations, schools and institutions of higher learning. It is headed by leading figures from the cultural and intellectual community. The official ban on the Karabakh-Committee in summer 1988 seems not to have diminished its authority and power. In this sense Polish conditions are developing in Armenia. The real authority rests with the opposition which has been forced underground. This opposition is able to mobilize the intelligentsia and the workers alike.

In the Baltic republics the institutionalization reached a provisional culminating point with the establishment of popular fronts in October. The »popular fronts for support of perestroika« have been crystallizing since late spring. In October formal founding congresses were held; elected delegates adopted programs and statutes. The popular fronts serve as umbrella organizations for numerous so-called informal groups, ranging from pop-music groups and folklore associations to clubs for local history and political discussion circles. The popular fronts stopped short of incorporating two demands into their programs, namely introduction of a multiparty system and separation from the Soviet Union. But there are strong currents within the popular fronts advancing just these points.

The strong authority of the popular fronts may be gleaned from the following facts: They pushed hard and succeeded with the installation of new, more liberal and progressive men on top of party or state apparatuses in all three republics. The mass media in the titular languages, including local TV, have to a certain extent become mouthpieces of the popular fronts. The popular fronts openly opposed the amendments to the Soviet constitution which became effective on December 1. The same holds true for the Karabakh-Committee and informal oppositional groups in Georgia. Opposition against the amendments of the Soviet constitution had only limited success.

Relations with the party are ambivalent. On the one hand, party members are invited to cooperate with the popular fronts, on the other hand, functionaries of party and state apparatuses are explicitly not eligible for its leading organs.

2. Soviet organs, and to a lesser degree, party organs have been co-opted into the national movement. Neither in Armenia nor in the Baltic republics did the leadership try to stem the self-organization of the nation. On the contrary, the official authorities either stood passively aside or joined the movement. To jump on the bandwagon seemed the only way for the party leadership to save at least some of the steadily dwindling credibility of the party. The self-organization of the nation did not develop against the party but bypassed the party.

The most conspicuous cases of co-optation of the Soviets by the national movement occurred in Armenia and Estonia. On February 20 the Regional Soviet in Stepanakert called upon the Supreme Soviets in Erevan and Baku to decree the unification of Mountain-Karabakh with Soviet Armenia. On June 15, the Supreme Soviet in Erevan agreed to the incorporation of Mountain-Karabakh into the Armenian Soviet Republic. Finally, on July 12, the Regional Soviet in Stepanakert declared the formal unification of Mountain-Karabakh with Armenia.

In the Baltic republics the situation got critical in connection with the proposed amendments to the Soviet constitution. On November 16, the Supreme Soviet in Tallinn disagreed with crucial points of the amendments and resolved that henceforth laws were to be valid in Estonia only after approval by the Estonian Supreme Soviet. Although the Presidium of the Supreme Soviet in Moscow and Gorbachev personally declared this resolution null and void, the Supreme Soviet in Tallinn stuck to its decision and reaffirmed it in a resolution on December 7.

All these events were obviously not intended and not foreseen when the Gorbachev leadership newly advanced Lenin's slogan »All power to the Soviets!«

IV. Why now?

Why have nationality problems become so acute since 1986, approaching a preliminary climax in 1988? I have dealt here only with the most publicly visible nationality conflicts. But there are also the Crimean Tatars who in 1987 forcefully resumed their struggle for return to the Crimea. There are Germans and Jews who are leaving the Soviet Union in record numbers. Ukrainian writers and journalists have, in an unprecedented way, criticized the Russification drive in the Ukraine and are demanding the Ukrainization of public life. There have been local incidents of *djihad* in southern Tadzhikistan, near the Afghan border.

There are two sets of reasons which can help to explain why conflicts are simultaneously coming to a crisis in faraway regions of the empire with nations differing very much in size, history and culture.

1. *Glasnost* has opened mouths. In the more relaxed atmosphere of the present thaw, people are inclined to articulate their grievances. *Glasnost* is the invitation to call black black and injustice injustice. Since Gorbachev terms his policy »revolution,« he first has to state clearly that the present situation is so bleak that it needs a revolution. Many nations are meanwhile demanding a revolutionary *perestroika* of relations between center and periphery.

2. National consciousness has been on the rise in the Soviet Union for decades. This was officially recognized after the death of Brezhnev. General Secretary Andropov stated in his speech on the occasion of the 60th anniversary of the USSR in December 1982 that the growth of national consciousness is »a lawful, objective process« in a socialist society. As in many other parts of the world, the social basis and the social bearer of the new nationalism is the national intelligentsia educated after World War II.

71

National tensions are aggravated by two additional factors: the declining economy and the growing spiritual vacuum. In a situation of economic stagnation and decline, economic shortcomings and social frustration are easily transformed into national tensions. Marxism-Leninism has long ceased to be a mobilizing value conveying spiritual force in society. A large spiritual vacuum has opened up, which is partly filled by national consciousness.

All these reasons for rising national tensions have been at work for quite a while. They are well-known also from outside the Soviet Union. Many of them can be termed classic causes for nationalism. Two new driving forces for national consciousness in the Soviet Union appeared recently: ecology and anti-Stalinism. Siberian writers such as Valentin Rasputin and Viktor Astafev first sounded the alarm because of the ecological crisis of Lake Bajkal and the taiga. To them, the decay of the Siberian nature is tantamount to the destruction of »rodina Rossija,« its moral essence and tradition. During the last five years or so, the ecological movement has united forces with the national cause in many other republics. Silva Kaputikjan became famous as a campaigner against the contamination of the environment in Armenia before she emerged as one of the leading figures of the Karabakh-Committee. Ukrainian writers and scientists are fighting against the building of more atomic power plants in the Ukraine and against plans for the construction of a Dnepr-Danube canal. The same persons speak out in favour of more Ukrainian-language schools and new laws to protect the Ukrainian language in the public sphere. In Lithuania the campaign against more atomic power stations has partly been successful; the construction in Ignalina has been temporarily halted. Also plans for extraction of phosphate in Estonia will not materialize as envisaged earlier by the central planning authorities in Moscow. These plans would have turned a whole region in north-east Estonia into an industrial desert.

Anti-Stalinism became a forceful ally of the national cause. The Balts are demolishing the historical myth about their allegedly voluntary incorporation into Stalin's Soviet Union in 1940. In Byelorussia the terrible exhumations of the victims of Stalin's terror in Kuropaty have spurred efforts to found a Byelorussian popular front. Byelorussian writers, such as Vasil Bykov and Ales Adamovič, are at the same time fighting for full and detailed »pravda« about the extermination of the people in Byelorussia, for the reintroduction of Byelorussian as language of instruction in secondary schools, and the revival of the Byelorussian historical heritage.

V. Conclusion

National conflicts in the Soviet Union are on the rise. They will increase further because of objective conditions. A *perestroika* of national relations could ease tensions. There is no *perestroika* as yet. *Perestroika* in nationality relations would encompass decentralization in the fields of economy, culture and domestic affairs.

Mass mobilization of the small nations in 1988 does not only show the strength of national consciousness but also the weakness of the party. People have lost confidence in the party. They are rallying around the national cause, which is considered as a political alternative.

Self-organization of the small nations has been remarkably disciplined, democratic, and non-violent – the pogroms against the Armenian minority in Azerbaidzhan being the sad exception.

The national movements are fighting for basic human rights such as self-determination, democracy, and freedom. Marxism once boasted it had overcome nationalism, now it may turn out that democratic nationalism fighting for emancipation will help to overcome a centralized, still dictatorial one-party system.

The Ideological Dimension: Obstacle, Realpolitik or Productive Power?

Dietmar Schössler

1. *Preliminary Remarks*

With the thaw following Stalin's death, there began a debate in the West, which has continued ever since, over whether Soviet ideology represents nothing more than an obstacle, erected by conservative groups, to the dynamics of technological and social change. Such change had begun rapidly to threaten the postwar establishment and seemed to push forward the entire Soviet system toward a more convergent pattern, as compared to the Western manner of industrialization and modernization. In those days, the philosophy of convergence formed an influential trend in Western public opinion, as can be witnessed with Toynbee, Sorokin, Rostow and Tinbergen, to name just a few. The policy of détente is a direct outcome of this approach. The foremost issue was whether the socialist camp was, in the long run, converging with similar trends in Western post-industrial societies, resulting in an evolutionary resolution of the East-West conflict.

As a result of the frustrations and irritations stemming from the process of détente – during which period the Soviet Union became an uncontested world power – Western attitudes began gradually to change. It now seemed clear that Soviet political conduct was dominated by neither ideology nor convergence but rather by Realpolitik – power politics. When Gorbachev came to power in the mid-1980s, Western observers once again reappraised. Ideology, convergence and Realpolitik faded, and a »new thinking« became the concept of the day, in other words, a completely innovative approach transcending all former perceptions of political and social reality.

However, in opposition to this prevailing Western view, I question whether it is not indeed ideology that guides Soviet conceptions and actions. This perspective – ideology as a productive power – is shared not only by a small group of unshakeable Western analysts but also by the Soviet political class itself. I contend that the latter – to some degree, in accordance with modernity in general – employs ideology as a powerful tool in permanently constructing or fabricating reality. From the aspect of general modernity theory, developed by classical German philosophy and by Marx and Engels, modernity is an historical pinnacle, where mankind itself is for the first time able to construct reality unassisted by transcendent forces. According to Karl Marx, modernity is the period or key historical point at which the world becomes philosophical and philosophy, worldly.

In discussing briefly this central proposition, I will proceed along three analytical lines:

– the general pattern or character of modernity, in particular, the revolutionary relationship between theory and practice;
– the manner in which Lenin attempted to transfer this Western heritage to a completely foreign context, which he defined as »semi-asiatic«; and
– the special qualities of the Gorbachev approach.

2. The Ideological Pattern of Modernity

One may observe that in sharp contrast to the Middle Ages, there has been a tendency toward a new relationship between, on the one hand, theory and philosophy and, on the other, practice. It is characterized by a scientific, technological orientation toward nature and – as a logical consequence – man and society. Theory ceased to be passive and contemplative and became active and instrumental: theoretical knowledge strives ultimately to power, i.e., mastery over nature. With his famous Novum Organum, Francis Bacon formulated the novel understanding that human knowledge and power coincide; to be commanded, nature must be obeyed. He felt that man needed to begin anew from his very foundations in order to prevent him from eternally revolving in a circle with mean and contemptible progress.

In sum, the general pattern of modernity must necessarily be described in terms of this drastic change in the theory-practice relationship. Theory now has to be scientific, i.e., instrumental and technological. This is the new idea of philosophical knowledge: instead of aiming at patterns as lofty as they are useless, it ought to bear fruits in works. Science should be practical, that is, applicable to technological progress and to an industry serving mankind.

75

3. Lenin's Approach

Lenin's main difficulty was the translation of the Baconian-Hegelian-Marxist understanding into the semi-asiatic context of late Czarist Russia. Being a contemporary of Sorel and Pareto, Lenin combined the former approach with an elitist understanding of revolutionary politics. In keeping with this late 19th-century thinking, he defined ideology as an active weapon of the professional revolutionary elite. His party took on a novel form, designed to instrumentalize permanently the official philosophy of dialectical and historical materialism. As a theory of scientific socialism, ideology is now defined in the sense of a true consciousness of total reality. It is important to note that under Lenin's elitist approach, three main aspects of ideology are inseparably united: theory (i.e., philosophy), organization (of the new party) and strategy (tactics of the communist movement). Contrary to the common Western understanding of Marxist-Leninist ideology, there is no distinction between ideology and science. Followers of Marx and Lenin view ideology as the sum of the essential results of the philosophical, historical and economic sciences.

With regard to Lenin's approach to ideology, the problem of the relationship between theory and practice thus exhibits the following elements:

– Social revolution is no longer to be understood as a process of objective historical development; rather, it is the result of the strategy and tactics of a professional revolutionary elite, which constructs reality by political decision and action.

– In contrast to traditional Marxist doctrine, it is now the superstructure that dominates social existence; the material substructure is a product of the planning and programming system created and implemented by the new party.

– Philosophy, political/societal institutions, and strategy/tactics are to be perceived as a living totality.

4. Gorbachev's Approach

In my view, Gorbachev is to be viewed as a true disciple of Lenin. As is clearly reflected in published speeches and documents, his assessment of the situation turns on the above-mentioned relationship between superstructure and substructure. Faced with national stagnation and international expansion, Gorbachev has noted an emerging contradiction

76

between socialist productive forces and socialist economic and production relations. This internal conflict, developing within the material substructure, seems likely to spread, in view of the unquestionable fact that the superstructure as well is becoming contradictory. Thus, Gorbachev has had to take into account a growing antithesis between the socialist material substructure and the corresponding socialist superstructure. This relationship poses a serious threat both to internal political stability and to the capacity for the global projection of power; both aspects are undisputed prerequisites for superpower status.

Marxist-Leninists are, however, able to solve this problem by defining socialist contradictions as non-antagonistic. The strategy is first to stabilize the non-antagonistic character of the contradiction and then progressively to supersede the whole problem. This has been advanced in three directions: rebuilding the political superstructure in order to underscore the Party's claim as the leading political force in the Soviet state; reconstructing the material substructure to achieve greater flexibility, especially with regard to socialist property relations; and accelerating socialist productive forces, in particular, with respect to the subjective factor.

In this context, the Soviet political leadership's new thinking is guided by potentiality as opposed to reality. Potentiality is defined as the philosophical concept characterizing the developmental tendencies inherent in the appearances and processes of objective reality, and it is determined by the laws of development underlying such appearances and processes. Provided that the necessary conditions are present, potentiality at some point passes into reality. In addition, a real potentiality is found when these conditions already exist, such that in realizing the entire spectrum of conditions, all potentiality passes over into reality. Under Marxist-Leninist doctrine, the relationship between potentiality and reality describes precisely what is needed to solve the problem of superseding all contradictions in a non-antagonistic manner.

It is readily evident to me that the Soviet political class has chosen this path for proceeding toward modernity. But history will show whether this social technology will fit to the real interests of the people and the individuals.

The Cultural Dimension of Political Reform

Luigi Vittorio Ferraris

The Gorbachev challenge confronts us in the West with the need to give to our approach and to our reactions a cultural dimension. Such a cultural dimension presents two interrelated aspects: the free flow of information and ideas and consequently of culture in the widest sense; and the problems of the recognition or discovery of a cultural identity in Europe, both East and West, not only through words but also through deeds.

It is clear to all that the perspective of more intimate and open relations between East and West that do not impinge on the different political structures cannot be implemented if cultural barriers prevent a free flow of ideas and information and free movement for those persons who are to interpret and voice culture, ideas and information. More is required than simply implementing fully the provisions of the Helsinki Final Act and of the recommendations of the follow-up conference in Madrid and other meetings, since all these provisions reflect compromise, which is perhaps now outdated.

The West has always considered the Helsinki process an instrument to influence dynamically the East, putting pressure on it in all areas related to the implementation of Western concepts of freedom, concepts that did not correspond to the Eastern view of democracy. It is difficult to deny that the greatest success of the CSCE is to be found in the acknowledgement of the possibility, even the right, to interfere in the internal affairs of the East in order to foster democracy, freedom and mobility and to bring about a peaceful evolution of Eastern societies. The aim became legitimate, because the society envisioned by the Final Act closely resembles the Western model and is far removed from the so-called communist model.

Nowadays, the »new thinking« follows different paths. The barriers have not fallen, but they are much less difficult to overcome than was formerly the case. The recognition of »universal human interests« and the newly formulated relationship between »communist morality« and

»universal human morality« open the way to a common appraisal of the shared values of human rights, with a wide spectrum for the expression of these rights. The approach to the problem would be false if we were to jump to the conclusion that between East and West the views on political and social freedom are now equal, although the wording of some recent Soviet documents could justify such an impression. Assimilation or convergence is prevented not merely by differences in the ideas on the ways and means through which public opinion is to have the right of expression; there is also a lack of identity with regard to the final aims that society should aspire to for the benefit of individuals. In addition, a set of concepts should as well be submitted to new analysis: détente, coexistence, balance of power, sufficiency, cooperation and so on.

The concept of a common cultural identity in Europe only partially reflects the reality of Europe of recent centuries. Europe's geographical boundaries could be debated at length, and if Europe hopes to become a viable political entity, it is difficult to ignore the United States. It is still open to question whether the Soviet Union is integral to a common European identity, especially insofar as the Soviet Union also has an Asiatic dimension (one should not forget that in Moscow efforts are underway to build an Asian house!). It is not enough simply to recall the influence that those writers and artists who are the glory of Russia have had on Europe, above all, in the last 150 years. The idea of a common European house, regardless of how attractive this may sound, is a political statement rather than an objective recognition of cultural reality. Soviet leaders have clearly stated that the building of such a »European house« in no way implies a retreat from the so-called »Yalta partition,« which, on the contrary, is to be recognized as still valid.

But even if we need to live with this reality for the time being, the realization of the importance of »interdependence« and a certain degree of »pan-European« integration is a step in the right direction. Nevertheless, this alone is not enough, as it is far too ambiguous. Pan-European integration, as conceived of within the CSCE process, presupposes an undifferentiated Europe composed of states to be treated as equal regardless of the differences in their political systems or alliances. Western European integration, on the other hand, views states as having equal political and economic consistency. We should look for a way out of this contradiction in the cultural field, not in the political field.

The challenge confronting us is to enhance cultural relations within the whole of Europe and to reinclude within the framework of Europe as a living body those parts of the Continent that have been artificially separated by political events. The walls dividing Europe – not only physically but also spiritually – close out those countries and peoples that have never ceased to consider themselves a part of the more general European context.

What makes Europe distinct is the European consciousness, which holds itself to be different; it is the origin of a set of great ideas that have permeated the whole of the world, without which modern societies would not be able to exist. On the other hand, this reality should not lead to a new form of »Eurocentralism,« one no longer founded on military strength but merely on the conviction that it is the sole producer of ideas. European ideas are being confronted by new sets of beliefs, which seek to give voice to a new *Weltanschauung*. European identity should not be a superficial assimilation of different cultures but rather should recognize pluralism, which is the very foundation of Europe as a whole. This identity lies in the diversity of national cultures connected not only with different languages and traditions but also with different political traditions, which suggest various solutions to problems theoretically common to all.

An important element of this variety is the European Community, which in its efforts to create a political unit, could create new diversity or even a new partition within Europe. The two halves of Europe would follow different paths: in the West, toward political integration and supranationality to overcome national temptations; in the East, toward the resumption of sovereignty and national independence as a reaction to ideological solidarity or suffocation.

This involves various aspects of an evolution that began in the Soviet Union and then pervaded Eastern Europe, but it concerns all of Europe in a very direct way. We must not ignore the difficulties facing the task of implementing change in the Soviet Union or reinterpret communist theories. At the same time, we must not give in to the temptation to take any change, real or potential, at its face value.

We in the West are both morally and politically compelled to evaluate in a different light the profile of a changing Soviet society. This is first and foremost a cultural evolution, which is leading toward uncharted waters. One could be led to believe that the East is on the verge of abandoning its ideological and cultural tenets, with so-called capitalist tenets – the logical result of a long Western philosophical tradition – gaining the upper hand. Although such a trend could in itself provoke a new ideological struggle with the socialist or communist *Weltanschauung* in the East, we should nevertheless seek to interpret this evolution in a different, more sophisticated fashion, to be qualified by future events. Many important political steps have already been taken in this direction, but it is open to question whether these steps, though courageous, have also brought about a cultural change and how deep such change will run.

The West must be open to all novel approaches, since it was always our fundamental belief that the status quo, as supported in the East in the 1970s, cannot offer real and effective solutions for strengthening peace in Europe. We have always maintained that a given society cannot avoid peaceful change, as indicated, for instance, by the Helsinki Final Act. In the West, we enjoy the advantages of a political and cultural structure that permits change without jeopardy to internal peace and international stability. This political and cultural belief is the basis for Western policy towards 'the East.

Before working on a common house or a common cultural identity, both East and West must act slowly, but with great spiritual force, to promote the opening of our societies. As we emerge from the postwar era, which began in Helsinki, the pace and magnitude of the processes at work are impressive.

For the West, the challenge lies in not forfeiting fundamental elements of freedom in the search for peace, since without freedom, peace would be very weak. Openness should not destroy the diversity of our cultural heritage or the expression of different European cultures. However, we are witnessing the decay of ideologies based on a philosophy that interprets history as being dictated by utopian or deterministic objectives.

It is a very complex challenge. Culture is not simply determined by the thoughts or actions of ruling groups; it is what percolates through public opinion as a whole. It cannot be decided by governments; it is the result of the evolution of peoples, which increasingly see national or ideological boundaries as very fragile indeed. The peoples of Western

Europe have taken important steps to reconcile Europe and its citizens with their history. Is it possible to hope that a similar reconciliation will take place in Eastern Europe? This is the challenge of any political reform in the East. It is a challenge for all of us, in East and West alike – in the whole of Europe.

Constitutional Reform in 1988:
The First Phase of Political Perestroika

M. A. Krutogolov

With the implementation of political reforms in December 1988, which included the introduction of major changes to the Constitution of 1977 and the adoption of new laws on the election of people's deputies, our country entered a new phase of political *perestroika*. These measures are aimed at establishing sovereignty of the soviets (the legislative bodies elected by universal suffrage at all levels, from municipal to national) and creating a state subject to socialist legality.

The decision to democratize Soviet society and to reform the Soviet political system was made in early June 1988 at the 19th Party Conference. Thus, the implementation of a wide spectrum of radical changes in the organization of the highest organs of state power took place in a mere five months. This is a feat in itself. By way of contrast, the decision to draft the 1977 Constitution was made at the 21st Party Congress in 1959, such that some 18 years were required to implement it. The current reforms are thus perhaps an example of a modern catchword born of *perestroika* – *uskoreniie*, or acceleration.

If the first years of *perestroika* went to interpreting the situation at hand in the mid-1980s – the time when the concept of *perestroika* was formed – then the current period represents the stage where ideas increasingly obtain the character of political directives and legal statutes. Today, *perestroika* sets priorities for all activities in the USSR, and we consider it necessary to increase the force of this process, such that no circumstance will be able to slow it down, to say nothing of threatening or reversing its progress; the task at hand is to make *perestroika* irreversible.

The continued development of our country is increasingly met with the imperfection of political institutions. We will be unable to make our way quickly out of the conditions of stagnation unless life in the USSR is democratized and the soviets are revived as the representative organs of power and self-government by the people. Furthermore, only with a combination of economic reform, political change, democratization and *glasnost* will we be able to solve the problems of today and tomorrow. This is precisely why past attempts to repair the state of affairs in the economy were unsuccessful: no changes were made in politics, and broad democratic transformations were not carried out. The ossified political system acted as a brake on the development of society. Even today, when *perestroika* of the economy and the social sphere has made obvious the interdependence of economic and social development, we are faced with such difficult problems as the necessity of expanding *glasnost*, democratizing economic management and completely reforming the political system.

The first phase of the reform targeted the renewal of the structure of the soviets, the reorganization of the highest organs of power and their activity, and modifications in the election system. As is well known, the organs of state power in our country are the soviets of people's deputies. In practice, however, the soviets have long exercised the mere role of formally approving or ratifying decisions already made. One of the most important ideas generated by the 19th Party Conference – the revival of sovereign soviets and self-government by the people –has now fundamentally changed the attitude toward soviet activity. This was demonstrated by the nationwide discussion surrounding the draft reform of the Constitution in 1988, which was published in *Pravda* on Oct. 22, 1988. The ensuing free exchange of opinions and heated debate promptly exceeded the proposed framework for the discussion, revealing the complexity and variety of the processes of democratization of public life and, at the same time, the objective necessity of these processes.

The Presidium of the Supreme Soviet alone received more than 300,000 corrections, remarks and amendments. The most pointed issues, which provoked sharp differences of opinion, were the »painful issues« of the country's economic development as a whole and in individual geographic regions, the priorities of *perestroika*, the necessity of continually supporting the process of revitalizing socialism and, finally, the improvement of interethnic relations and the demarcation between Union and Republic sovereignty.

After having gone through a general public revision, legislation on changes and additions to the Constitution has taken on a noticeably different appearance: of the laws approved by the session, nearly half of the articles were elaborated and supplemented. This very fact, unheard of until quite recently, speaks for the raised level of public consciousness, the liberation of social initiative and energy and society's readiness to break with dogmas of the past.

The substance of the 1988 political reforms has frequently been analyzed in the world press, and I would simply like to recall some of their most important aspects. To begin with, four new institutions have been introduced into the Soviet state system by the draft Constitution:the Congress of People's Deputies, the Supreme Soviet (which has retained only the name of its predecessor), the Chairman of the Supreme Soviet and the Committee on Constitutional Supervision. In addition, the role and functions of many other organs have been significantly altered (for instance, the Presidium of the Supreme Soviet or the People's Control Commission).

The highest organ of state power is the Congress of People's Deputies (arts. 108-110). It consists of 2,250 members elected for five-year terms, of whom 750 are elected from national-territorial regions and 750 from social organizations (this is an innovation). Persons serving in organs accountable to the Congress cannot simultaneously be deputies (with the exception of the Chairman of the Council of Ministers and the Procurator General). Belonging to the exclusive jurisdiction of the Congress are the most significant questions of national life. These include the adoption of the Constitution, the determination of basic directions in foreign and domestic policy, the confirmation of both economic plans and the most important economic- and social-development programs and the election or confirmation of all organs of power and administration in the USSR.

The Congress selects from among its ranks the Supreme Soviet (arts. 111-113). This legislative organ of state power, composed of 542 deputies, is divided into two houses – the Soviet of the Union and the Soviet of the Nationalities – and is presided over by the Chairman of the Supreme Soviet. Deputies are elected for five-year terms, and none may serve more than two consecutive terms. Whereas the Congress meets only once a year, the Supreme Soviet is continuously at work, with two sessions per year lasting from three to four months each. The Supreme Soviet is provided with many of the plenary powers that, in Western countries, would be entrusted to a parliament. The Presidium of the Supreme Soviet is comprised of various public servants; it ensures the proper organization of work for the Congress and the Supreme Soviet, and it fulfills the functions of both a bureau of parliament and, in Western terminology, the head of state

The post of Chairman of the Supreme Soviet (arts. 120-121) previously did not exist in the USSR. The Chairman is the highest official of the Soviet government and represents the USSR within the country and in international relations. I would like to point out that the draft Constitution does not make the Chairman the »head of state«; as mentioned above, this function is exercised by the Presidium of the Supreme Soviet.

Finally, the Committee on Constitutional Supervision (art. 125), made up of 23 members, is elected by the Congress for a term of ten years. It is responsible for ensuring that normative acts are carried out in conformity with the Constitution, suspending acts that contradict it.

The new principles for organizing the activity and structure of these institutions spell a crucial step in the development of the Soviet state system, i.e., democratization and self-government by the people. The authoritarian methods of ruling that were built up during the years of Stalinism and stagnation, the command-bureaucratic system of management and the repression of elected organs of power by the apparatus are all beginning to break up. New laws have created conditions that make it possible to surmount these negative phenomena, which for many years slowed the progress of our society. Laws regarding important constitutional issues or those that subject to review any issue affecting the state are now to be confirmed by the Congress of People's Deputies. At the same time, the fact that the Supreme Soviet is continuously in session enables it to implement such laws, to take into its own hands the complex process of preparing laws, to wield control over the budget and to ensure in-depth, skilled analysis of the work of ministries and agencies. No less than once a year, the government must report before the Supreme Soviet. The strengthening of the soviets' control functions and the creation of the Committee on Constitutional Supervision serve as guarantees against relapses of past mistakes and allow the higher organs of power to restore justice quickly and decisively when it is violated.

Thus, an entirely new structure has been created for higher organs of state power (the congresses of soviets, which were in operation until 1937, were only a prototype of the current Congress of People's

Deputies). However, not all participants in the public discussion approved of this rather complex, multilayered structure, since the functioning Supreme Soviet is not elected directly by the voters but rather by the Congress. I personally favor a parliament with a single layer and the direct election of its deputies. But in the final analysis, content – and not form – is what is important. Even if the new Supreme Soviet becomes the functional center of the nation's political life, the interests of all citizens will be represented – non-Party individuals as well as Communists, believers and non-believers, people from all classes and strata of society and of all nationalities. It is also important to note that the newly created institutions are not considered permanent and unchangeable. As more experience is gained, corrections can be made in the organization of elections, in the work of the chambers and in the system's other institutions. One step leads to others. But for the time being, we cannot afford to lull ourselves into thinking that we have found absolutely perfect, ideal solutions, as was pointed out in an extraordinary session of the Supreme Soviet.

In the voting by the Soviet of the Nationalities on the law to change the Constitution, 657 votes were cast in favor of the law and 3 votes against it, with 26 abstentions. The Soviet of the Union registered 687 votes for, 2 against and 1 abstention. The rejection of unanimous voting, which occurred for the first time in Soviet history at the preceding session in October 1988, reflects the pluralism of opinion among deputies. However, regulations of both the Congress of People's Deputies and the Supreme Soviet provide for technical voting safeguards and, when necessary, a name count, so that the electorate can know how their deputies voted (provided that voting is not secret). When a voting count is taken (not without technical irregularities, as this is such a new procedure for the Soviet Union), then a name count is not.

In the course of preparing the constitutional reform, not everything was well thought out. As is known, things were a bit rushed, some formulas were not acceptable to all, and not all of the provisions of reform were clarified as they should have been. In addition, the Soviet state for the first time met with objections from several republics to a number of its propositions. The differentiation of plenary powers between the Soviet Union as a whole and the individual republics has led to an improvement of relations between national groups in the USSR, which is becoming the focus of the second stage of political reform. Indeed, in preparing the reforms in 1988, the central authorities learned a good lesson for future efforts. As Mikhail Gorbachev declared in his final remarks at a recent session of the Supreme Soviet, »all work in this regard will be conducted in close cooperation between the central, republican Party and state organs, social organizations, scientists, specialists and the general public, and it will proceed openly and with glasnost.« Our ideal can be expressed in the following motto: »A sound Union is made up of a strong center and strong republics.« Bringing this about is, of course, no simple matter, and in any case there will be no attempts to introduce local changes through guidelines from Moscow.

During the course of public discussion on the draft Constitution, wide attention was given to the decision made at the 19th Party Conference to combine the position of chairman of the soviet with the position of secretary of the Party committee at the corresponding level. This was to be implemented at all rungs of the political ladder, with the position of Chairman of the Supreme Soviet being united with that of General Secretary of the Central Committee of the Communist Party. Such a measure raised various reactions among the Soviet people. Having put forward this idea at the Party Conference, Mikhail Gorbachev proposed that the delegates discuss it. However, instead of giving this most important step the discussion it deserved, the delegates merely took sides on the issue. Now it seems that this measure, which is new for our country, will be first tested in practice in order to answer all questions concerning it.

I personally support the uniting of these two positions at the top of the pyramid. In other countries as well, the head of the political party usually leads the country, either as head of state or of the government. Combining the positions of Chairman of the Supreme Soviet and the General Secretary of the Central Committee of the Communist Party is a very important and timely political step, for under current conditions of conflict between supporters and opponents of *perestroika*, this measure signifies a strengthening of Gorbachev's position. In any case, one can now be assured that a progressive, energetic leader will no longer be able to be removed overnight from his post – »for reasons of health« – by a »unanimous« show of 300 hands prompted by a scant dozen. Now, at the very least, a public discussion at the Congress of People's Deputies is required, with secret voting by its 2,250 members. However, a number of delegates to the 19th Party Conference expressed doubts that this principle might spread to the soviets, including local ones. Similar doubts were raised at an extraordinary session of the Supreme Soviet.

It is, of course, heartening that the soviets are being strengthened and that their new chairmen are insisting that they be reckoned with – something that did not happen too often until now. On the other hand, a weakness lies in the fact that the only guarantee against abuse of power rests with the Party Secretary, i.e., the chairman of the local soviet. However, a legal measure cannot be created for a specific individual, no matter how popular with the people he may be, for at some point his term will come to an end. With the reform of 1988, the Constitution was amended in order to limit the length of time a position may be held to two terms, i.e., ten years.

Legal and juridical issues have also received special attention in the public discussion of the constitutional reform, in particular, the issue of the independence of the judiciary. In a country where for many years Stalinist terror and utter lawlessness held sway, public interest in the future role of the courts is to be expected. Great progress was made at the 19th Party Conference in this area, principally by way of changes in the elections procedure. Under the proposals, judges were to be elected to ten-year terms by the immediately superior soviet: a judge at the *raion* level was to be elected by the *oblast'* soviet; a judge at the *oblast'* level, by the republic soviet; etc. However, the published draft of the revised Constitution in art. 152 took no note of this: people's judges at the *raion* level were to be elected by the *raion* soviet; *oblast'* judges, by the *oblast'* soviet, etc. It was unclear how the decisions made at the 19th Party Conference were able to be so fully distorted; we do not know who wrote the draft. But it seems that the democratizing of the judiciary was not without its adversaries. Opponents of *perestroika* sought to attack the independent judicial structure by humiliating judges – »putting them in their place.« Apparently these objections found their way into the draft.

The conflict was resolved in a speech given by Mikhail Gorbachev at a session of the Supreme Soviet, where he noted the »great debate on this issue.« No support was found for the disputed article in public discussion, and after taking into account public opinion, the text introduced in the Constitution conformed in all respects to the decisions of the 19th Party Conference. In addition to adopting the procedure whereby judges are elected by the immediately superior soviet, the Constitution does away with the »telephone law,« the notorious practice in which legal cases were decided by means of a telephone call from an important figure. Local officials will no longer be able to pressure the local judge, and officials at the superior level will generally not be interested in provincial matters.

With regard to the election of deputies to the soviets, somewhat less optimism is called for. Art. 100(3) of the draft Constitution reads: »As a rule, voting ballots are to include a greater number of candidates than the number of mandates available.« Many citizens voiced objections to the proviso »as a rule« and proposed that it be dropped. In an interview in *Pravda* on Nov. 18, 1988, V.G. Lomonosov, the head of the committee of deputies, stated in this connection: »Various statements give the impression that the possibilities for nominating candidates for the position of deputy of a soviet are narrowing. Article 100 makes clear that this is not the case. The number of candidates for the position of people's deputy is not limited; each participant in the pre-election meeting can propose that the candidacy of any person be discussed, including his own. In addition, our commission has proposed that the words ›as a rule‹ be removed from the draft article.«

The Supreme Soviet also took up the issue at its session on Nov. 29, 1988: »Many participants in the discussion supported the amendment that states that elections can be held only on the condition that there are no less than two candidates for every position. There were, however, a not insignificant number who did not want to limit the right of voters to decide for themselves on the number of candidates. Taking this into account, the draft of the law will include this clarification: ›the voting ballots can include any number of candidates‹.« This version became the text of Art. 100(3). Notably, »any number« can also mean only one candidate. As is well known, there has been a »tradition« in the Soviet Union, although not set down in any normative act, according to which Soviet voters »preferred« to elect their deputies from a field of one candidate. It is not likely that this practice can be rapidly changed everywhere, and it is regrettable that the constitutional reform did not unambiguously oppose this tradition by opting for a different solution. Nevertheless, we will soon see what substance will result from the practical interpretation of the words »any number« and in how many

90

cases the conservative strata of the apparatus will be able take this to mean the »right of voters« to choose from among a single candidate. The next elections for people's deputies at the Union level are scheduled for Mar. 26, 1989 and are to be conducted in accordance with the new law allowing for alternative candidates.

The democratic election of deputies, who will for the first time be taking up difficult responsibilities in the plenary soviets, is a decisive step toward the creation of *perestroika's* political mechanism. These deputies will be given the task of ensuring the further economic restructuring of the Soviet Union and the well-being of society. They will also be responsible for setting forth the first stage of political *perestroika*. Among the laws to be adopted at the first sessions of the Congress of People's Deputies in the area of political *perestroika* are those on the press, youth, freedom of conscience and judicial-legal reform.

It has already been mentioned that the second stage of *perestroika* will target the improvement of interethnic relations, to be followed by local self-management. This growing democratization will make *perestroika* irreversible, leading to the creation of a socialist legal state – to a Soviet pluralistic democracy.

Linkages between Domestic and Foreign Policy in the Soviet Union

Alex Pravda

It has become commonplace to note the strength of links between domestic and foreign policy under Gorbachev. When asked about the rationale underlying the radical shifts in policy, Soviet officials claim that we need look no further than domestic needs. Gorbachev himself has highlighted the unprecedented priority of internal factors – as he told Mrs Thatcher, »our foreign policy today stems directly from our domestic policy to a greater extent than ever before.« Theoretically, of course, Soviet leaders since Lenin have placed domestic requirements first. Yet the priority accorded them is now certainly higher than at any time since the early Khrushchev period. Arguably, domestic considerations have figured more prominently in the last four years than in any peace-time period since the years immediately following the Revolution. Indeed, Soviet observers have drawn parallels with the domestic priorities that led to the Treaty of Brest Litovsk as well as with the New Economic Policy.

If the Gorbachev years stand out in the salience of domestic factors in foreign policy, they are perhaps even more noteworthy for the congruence in the direction of change on the internal and external front. This is where the linkage between the two spheres is particularly tight by comparison with previous Soviet administrations. In most previous cases the relationship between domestic and foreign policy has been an incongruent one. Even in the late Lenin years, moves towards greater participation in the international system, particularly in the economic sphere, were congruent with economic reform measures at home yet at odds with political centralization. Inconsistency between domestic and foreign policy strategies grew in the mid- to late 1930s with an opening up of contacts abroad with the Left, and a closing down of what remained of political dialogue within the Soviet Union. Khrushchev introduced a reformist congruence with his early drive for de-Stalinization in domestic and foreign policy, followed by a return to a more militant stance on both fronts in his later years in office. Under Brezhnev a reformist foreign policy of détente went hand-in-hand with rolling back economic reform and tightening political controls at home. Indeed, the moves towards greater economic and political contact with the West were meant in part to reduce pressure for change within the Soviet Union. Foreign policy reform was thus in a sense a substitute for domestic change. Only the last years of Brezhnev's rule saw greater consistency between the two fronts, with foreign policy hardening and thus coming more into line with domestic circumstances. This alignment was the product not so much of any positive steering as of caution and fear of change – what is now dubbed *zastoi* (stagnation).

The current period stands out in the consistency of reform on both home and international fronts. Far from movement towards greater accommodation with the outside world being seen as a substitute for domestic decompression and democratization, the two approaches are complementary and even symbiotic. As the process of domestic and foreign policy change has become more radical over the last two to three years, so the linkage between the spheres has thickened. As *perestroika* has broadened from the economic to political reform and foreign policy has moved from tactical shifts to programmatic and strategic innovation, so the domestic and international dimensions of *perestroika* have become increasingly symbiotic. In fact there is some correspondence between the pace and depth of change on the internal and external fronts reflecting perhaps the political strengths of reform forces. For instance, the later months of 1986 and 1988 saw particularly rapid advances on both fronts (Reykjavik and *glasnost'* in autumn-winter 1986; leadership changes, further political reform and unilateral cuts in ground forces in late 1988). It is scarcely possible to envisage the domestic changes that have taken place in the Soviet Union recently without concomitant changes in foreign policy. Similarly, the transformation in the Soviet Union's international image is inconceivable without many of the radical internal reforms. More importantly, the dynamics of the processes of change on both fronts are interdependent: progress in one sphere draws on advances made in the other, albeit in unequal proportions with dependency being predominantly on domestic development. The following sections look briefly at three major areas in which the linkages between domestic and foreign policy are most evident: policy impetus or drive; the general framework and type of policy thinking; the policy process, where the last three to four years have seen a growing politicization of foreign policy issues.

Policy Impetus

If one looks at the rationale underlying Gorbachev's major policy departures on the domestic and especially the international front, the interaction of external and internal considerations figures prominently. Rather, while the most powerful flow of influence is from domestic to foreign policy, influence also clearly flows in the reverse direction. External factors have played an important role in shaping the domestic reform agenda in at least two major respects: by reinforcing the case for radical reform and by influencing its content and direction.

Among the considerations that prompted the Soviet leadership initially under Andropov to begin a shake-up of the system and subsequently under Gorbachev to embark on radical reform, external performance undoubtedly played a key role. The fact that the Soviet Union was seen to be falling further behind advanced Western states probably had a dual effect on decision makers faced with a variety of alternative strategies, ranging from muddling through to radical restructuring. First, the unfavourable comparison between Soviet performance and that of capitalist rivals focused critical attention on the gravity of the situation at home. It was not just a case of a widening gap between the USSR and traditional rivals, such as the US and Western European states, but of the Soviet Union lagging behind China and the NICs. Second, the depth of performance failure, the degree of slippage of the USSR in the international league table, highlighted the urgent need to take drastic steps. Many decision makers may well have shared the view later expressed by Gorbachev, admittedly in retrospect, that *zastoi* (stagnation) endangered the Soviet Union's status as a superpower. The positive side of this argument was of course that only if stagnation were reversed through *perestroika* could the Soviet Union build a solid base for its superpower status. The arguments that inaction was putting Soviet security at risk may well have been an effective counter to any objection by conservatives that radical change was too risky and might undermine national security.

International comparisons not only served as a mirror reflecting the

94

weakness of the Soviet economy and system, giving a powerful impetus to the case for change. Reforms in other countries have also provided ideas about the form and content of such change. Chinese modernization has acted both as a stimulus to change and as a source of reform ideas, especially in the sphere of agriculture and external economic relations. Soviet economists and politicians are well aware of the peculiarities of the Chinese rural situation, yet the success of effective reprivatization may have added the case for introducing more widespread family contracts and leasing arrangements. Chinese experience in »opening the door« to capitalist trade and investment has certainly had an impact on Soviet moves in the same direction. The influence on the content of Soviet policy change has been a mixed one: lessons on what to avoid are as valuable as positive pointers to reform. A similar mix of negative and positive lessons has been drawn in Hungary. Apart from influencing the areas where the Chinese example figured importantly, the Hungarian reform experience – the longest and most successfully sustained in any socialist state – has exercised particular influence in the areas of economic decentralization, self-accounting, financial and banking changes and the development of a cooperative sector as well as in more general terms moves towards a more entrepreneurial system. More recently, as *perestroika* has overcome nearly all remaining ideological taboos, Sweden has gained in stature as a source of progressive ideas on how to marry capitalist efficiency with an acceptable level of socialist welfare and distributive justice. For instance, Soviet economists are showing considerable interest in Sweden's taxation system. With the upgrading of elections and parliamentary bodies and the acceptance of the principle of checks and balances, Soviet politicians and specialists are paying increasing attention to Western constitutional arrangements. If the influence of external developments on the domestic agenda may be somewhat indirect and diffuse, the impact of internal upon external policies is more focused and powerful. Domestic needs have shaped a wide range of foreign and security policy priorities. It may be useful to distinguish between two broad sets of domestic imperatives: those demanding a respite from pressure, an easing of international constraints and those requiring interaction, fuller involvement with the international system.

Domestic reforms place a premium on two kinds of respite: environmental and resource-based. Environmental respite involves a general easing of international pressure on the Soviet system, largely by way of reducing general East-West tension. It would clearly have been very difficult to undertake a radical, indeed revolutionary, change in a state traditionally obsessed with vulnerability to a hostile capitalist world, in conditions akin to a second Cold War, as the late 1970s and early 1980s have been labelled. It was therefore politically vital for Gorbachev to change the reality and perception of the international climate in order to undermine conservative objections to reform, also voiced in the Andropov period, on the grounds that it would expose the Soviet Union and weaken national security. He and others have been quite explicit about *perestroika's* need for a quiet international environment. And indeed it is difficult to envisage the process of *glasnost'* and decompression, with its accompanying disruptions, taking place in an international setting as tense as that of the early 1980s.

Resource-based respite relates to the need to remove outside constraints on Soviet economic development. The central constraint here of course is arms competition to maintain military parity with the West in general and the United States in particular. While a major achievement of the Brezhnev era, parity is now acknowledged to have imposed a burden on the Soviet economy that seems incompatible with successful economic reform. It is not so much a case of domestic resources being wholly inadequate for the task of keeping up with the United States in military technology. Rather, it is the unacceptability of the opportunity costs involved for the civilian economy. Having taken the decision to modernize the whole economy in order to improve Soviet standards of living and quality of life, Gorbachev cannot afford, both materially and politically, to maintain traditional military priorities. *Perestroika* involves the reorientation of Soviet economic development so as to make the civilian sector rather than the military the top priority, the cutting edge of excellence. Even if ultimately economic modernization will benefit the military by building the broad technological base necessary to sustain weapons competitiveness, in the short term this requires at the very least a slowing of the growth in military spending and, ideally, a real easing in the military burden. With what is now admitted to be a hundred billion rouble budget deficit (amounting to 11–12 % of GNP), Gorbachev is under enormous pressure to cut back wherever possible; the large military budget – usually estimated at 15–17 % of GNP and possibly bulking far larger – presents an obvious target. Hence determined Soviet international action to reduce the pace of military technological development.

Efforts to constrain on SDI through the ABM Treaty and the emphasis on both arms control and disarmament in both the nuclear and the conventional sphere point to the priority of meeting domestic imperatives to shift resources from military to civilian development. While the elimination of intermediate nuclear weapons and even the projected 50 % cut in strategic arsenals is unlikely to bring net savings – given the cost of destruction and verification the final balance sheet may be in the red – they do help to strengthen the case against further expensive modernization. Cuts in conventional forces, on the other hand, do bring real savings. More generally, the calmer international climate which the process of arms control and disarmament creates, politically helps Gorbachev to take steps to reduce the status of military priorities and cut the military budget (such as those announced by Gorbachev in December 1988–January 1989). Thus easing international tensions opens the way to reducing the military burden and diverting military facilities increasingly to civilian use, both by transferring actual production and by placing light industrial plants under defence industry management.

Because the domestic need for easing constraints is highlighted by Soviet leaders and has had such spectacular effects on Soviet international conduct in general and shifts in security policy in particular, the respite imperatives are sometimes seen as the only real domestic driving force behind shifts in Soviet external strategy. However, it is important to give due weight to what we have called the interaction imperatives for greater contacts with the international system, particularly the global economy. Less spectacular so far in their effects on Soviet foreign policy, these interaction imperatives have wider ramifications and greater long-term significance. In economic terms more extensive contact with the capitalist system does not mean merely more trade. Gorbachev has made clear that the strategy of the 1970s, centred on importing technology, is not appropriate to the *perestroika* enterprise. He is anxious to avoid Brezhnev's strategy of imports as a substitute for domestic innovation. Gorbachev wishes, by contrast, to help modernize by exposing the Soviet Union to international standards, by absorbing foreign expertise, learning from the successes of the capitalist world. At the heart of this strategy lies the development of contacts of all kinds,

97

particularly direct investment, joint production and joint ventures, all of which are supposed to act as catalysts of domestic modernization. In a wider sense, interaction goes beyond the narrowly material sphere and extends to what may be called the sphere of economic culture. Since *perestroika* seeks to promote initiative and entrepreneurship, it needs to foster those qualities in the Soviet manager, workers and the population as a whole. One way to do this is by making all aware of the absurd backwardness of the Soviet Union in these respects. *Glasnost'*, information about the outside world, including its living standards and successes, forms the necessary complement to the direct comparisons that joint ventures on Soviet soil will make starkly apparent.

This bid to catalyze modernization by exposure to and interaction with the capitalist economic system lies at the heart of Gorbachev's whole *perestroika* enterprise. It underscores the westernising essence of his strategy. We sometimes tend to forget that there could have been alternative kinds of radical change in response to the Brezhnev legacy of stagnation. One alternative lay in a autarkic reform, a fortress strategy concentrating on rebuilding Soviet strength before risking exposure of the country to any interaction in the shape of allowing outside information to penetrate the Soviet system or foreigners to run and even own plants on Soviet soil.

Policy Thinking

The depth of connection between these strategies emerges fully if we turn from questions of policy impetus to ones of policy thinking. Here it is far more difficult, though, to generalize about flows of influence, since the linkage involves parallel and interacting strands of perspectives. Many of these views straddle domestic and foreign policy spheres, insofar as they represent general approaches that apply to both areas. Indeed, some influential policy specialists have advocated cognate changes in external as well as internal policy, drawing on a common pool of policy thinking. Bovin, Burlatsky, Butenko, Shmelev and Shakhnazarov all come to mind as examples of what might be called »dual« policy specialists. They highlight the large overlap between what are two parts of a common policy climate and culture. The overlap found among specialists is paralleled by the dual domestic/foreign policy orientation among top decision makers. Shevardnadze retains a strong interest in domestic policy as he spent his entire previous career in that area; Medvedev, now in charge of ideology, for a time oversaw relations with socialist states. Yakovlev has also held key internal and external affairs posts, being both one of Gorbachev's closest associates in the general area of ideology and now head of the International Affairs Commission of the Central Committee, thus effectively in charge of coordinating foreign policy.

To do justice to the connections between policy thinking in domestic and international fields would require a comprehensive analysis of recent theoretical innovations in both areas as well as their interplay. The far more modest aim of this paper is to sketch some of the major traits of »new thinking« that straddle the internal-external divide. Most of the traits amount to tendencies of analysis rather than specific recommendations, even if some do suggest fairly clear policy options. The first trait is analytical eclecticism, a strong tendency away from narrow Marxist-Leninist approaches to analysing policy problems to one employing a wide range of social science theories and methods. Gorbachev has called for innovative approaches in analysis of international development. Rather than asking social scientists in traditional style to elaborate new variations on ideological themes, he now urges them to use any kind of analysis that will produce accurate assessments. After all, in many instances, American and Western literature is of infinitely more use than the works of Marx or Lenin for dealing with critical areas of security policy such as arms control. The fact that the political leadership now applies criteria of effectiveness rather than orthodoxy has cleared the way for a plethora of new policy perspectives and concepts derived from Western specialist literature and »alternative« thinking. In the security policy area, these include the action-reaction process of the arms race, the role of enemy images, non-provocative defence, reasonable sufficiency, mutual security and interdependence.

This broader eclectic approach to policy problems has raised to prominence two traits of policy thinking that figure particularly importantly in domestic and foreign policy innovation: the strength of diverse interests and the need to compromise. There is a strong logical as well as practical link between changing views of differences of interest within Soviet society and in the international arena. Rather than trying to fit domestic and international interests into the Procrustean bed of class analysis, »new thinking« acknowledges that the situation is far more complex, that interests have deep historical, national, psychological as well as class-linked roots. Pluralism, once rejected as a bourgeois concept, has now, with the important qualification »socialist«, become part of Gorbachev's lexicon. Along with the recognition of the strength of plurality goes a far more sober view of the tractability of interests. Neither groups within Soviet society nor societies in the Third World or even Eastern Europe, it is now admitted, lend themselves easily to moulding in a socialist or progressive socialist direction. To assume an ineluctable tendency, in traditional fashion, towards the new socialist man, an overall Soviet identity for all ethnic groups, or towards a socialist community of nations and an international communist movement is viewed as an unsatisfactory basis for the conduct of domestic or foreign policy. It is seen as similarly unrealistic to set up one model to which all developments, domestic or international, should conform. Rather than striving to impose uniformity, policy should seek to manage interests by recognizing their complexity and building on commonalities.

Recognition that overlaps exist between most if not all sets of interests underpins the second policy principle, that favouring compromise. Instead of thinking in traditional zero-sum-game terms, Gorbachev stresses the importance of positive-sum relationships, of seeking to reconcile interests both within society and between states and systems. As Stalin once projected his thesis of class struggle from the domestic to the international arena, Gorbachev now sees the need to exclude confrontation from both domestic and international settings. In the domestic context this means harnessing rather than hampering individuals and small groups striving for material gain and striking a balance between their interests and those of the state. Internationally it involves highlighting the potential for reconciliation between what were previously seen as antagonistic forces, for instance in regional conflicts. It means playing down ideological zero-sum elements in East-West relations and pointing up interdependence and the need for cooperation. This line of thinking is justified on the pragmatic grounds that compromises produce effective results. Removing or at least severely downgrading the ideological element from the management of interests means adopting an almost wholly pragmatic policy stance. It is in terms of effectiveness that Gorbachev defines »socialist quality«

(»sotsialistichnost«) just as Shevardnadze makes »profitability« the key criterion of foreign policy.

These far more pragmatic policy strategies also involve a marked shift in policy means, away from coercive towards more open and legalistic methods in both domestic and international affairs. At home, vigorous criticism of Stalinism has spilled over into a questioning of more recent uses of coercion to deal with opposition and dissent. Recent steps to regularize procedures, to ease restrictions on religious practices and on emigration, to release almost all prisoners of conscience and to establish greater permissiveness towards public protest all suggest a move away from coercive methods. Though the security machine survives intact, the Gorbachev leadership seems to regard maintenance of domestic security in less strongly coercive terms than its predecessors. Similar trends are evident in the international sphere, where Soviet security is viewed increasingly in economic and political rather than military terms. A recurrent theme of »new thinking« is the declining utility of military force – its use rarely yields gains but often creates alliances among previously disunited opponents. Complementing this shift away from coercive means is the more tentative, yet equally significant, move towards legal frameworks and instruments to manage conflict both at home and abroad. Gorbachev's declared aim to create a law-based state (pravovoe gosudarstvo) parallels his stress on the importance of international law and international bodies. The new quality of commitment to law is still largely a declaratory one. Yet steps taken to codify and clarify domestic laws, to strengthen the judicial process and constitutional review all point in the direction of serious intention to create a legal culture. Steps in a similar direction on the international front include acceptance of the jurisdiction of the International Court, measures to bring human rights legislation closer into line with international covenants, and increased financial as well as political support for the United Nations.

Developments in policy means thus run along parallel domestic and international lines. Both tend in the direction of pragmatic, flexible and civil or, as Gorbachev has put it, civilized politics. However, the lines of development have different starting points, speeds and limits. Socialist pluralism denotes markedly greater strictures on variety in the domestic context than »freedom of choice« indicates for the international community. At home the leading role of the Party, albeit

101

couched in less administrative and extensive forms, remains valid; in Eastern Europe, Moscow's guidance retains *de facto* preeminence. In the Third World, however, the days of advancement of Soviet socialism through military influence seem numbered and the coming of global socialism appears to have been postponed *sine die*. With Gorbachev and Shevardnadze now seeking to exclude military and ideological confrontation from international relations and co-development the order of the day, scarcely anything seems to distinguish the foreign policy of the Soviet Union from that of a »normal« Great Power.

Politicization

Both sets of linkages we have discussed reflect and further a third: the growing politicization of foreign policy. International issues have of course always played an important part in Soviet domestic politics. Still, the changes associated with »new thinking« and *perestroika* are arguably bringing a broader public role in international affairs and introducing greater controversy into the realm of foreign policy strategy and tactics.

At the public level, *glasnost'* has brought greater awareness of international affairs in Soviet foreign policy. While the quality of information and critical analysis still limps far behind the debate on domestic issues, historical reassessment – including key foreign policy events such as the Katyn massacre, the Molotov-Ribbentrop Pact and Stalin's conduct of the War – and debates on key recent and current issues, notably SS–20 deployment, Afghanistan and nuclear weapons, all serve to highlight popular awareness. The extent to which *glasnost'* has increased the absolute salience of foreign policy issues and how far international affairs bulk larger in the public consciousness relative to domestic issues is very difficult to gauge. Public attention to political matters has increased dramatically, but given the naturally closer absorption with domestic issues at a time of turmoil, it would be surprising if the *relative* salience of foreign affairs has not declined somewhat.

Nonetheless, particular foreign policy issues, nuclear weapons and Afghanistan being the most prominent, have attracted public concern. On both these questions the Soviet people are now better informed and able to voice opinions more fully than ever before. Public opinion polls are conducted on an increasing range of foreign policy issues; published data cover attitudes to some Western states and aspects of arms control. Polls reveal some scepticism about the feasibility of official goals, notably the complete elimination of nuclear weapons. Overwhelmingly, however, the public endorses the thrust of Gorbachev's arms control policy. Given the anxieties fostered by the rather alarmist propaganda that surrounded tension in 1983–84, the vast majority of the population is relieved at the thaw in relations with the United States and the reduced danger of war. Only a small minority seems concerned about the asymmetrical nature of reductions and the general dangers of letting down the Soviet security guard against what was portrayed until very recently as an imperialist military threat. On Afghanistan, opinion of course is less equivocal, strongly welcoming the decision to withdraw Soviet troops. Even if some in the military see the decision as denting national pride, the vast majority of the population was anxious to see an end to the bloodshed as casualties had begun to affect families throughout Soviet society. Precisely what part rising public disenchantment with Afghanistan played in Gorbachev's decision to cut losses and pull out remains uncertain. Yet, considering the ground swell of complaints from the public, and particularly from veterans, plus the leadership's concern to enlist popular support for *perestroika* as a whole, mounting public dissatisfaction must have weighed heavily in estimates of the costs of continuing the war.

It would be wrong to exaggerate the strength even of indirect public influence over Soviet foreign policy. Decision makers in Moscow are selectively sensitive rather than directly responsive to public preferences, even when clearly voiced. The new parliament and its standing commissions may provide a channel for some public oversight and even influence, yet the active public »voice« in foreign affairs, for which Shevardnadze has called, lies some way in the future.

In the meantime it will remain difficult to gauge the overall impact of foreign policy on the Gorbachev leadership's popular standing. Apart from minority concerns about asymmetrical reductions reducing national security, Gorbachev's extrication from Afghanistan and success in reducing tension and boosting the Soviet Union's international reputation can only have enhanced his popular standing. Popular support flowing from foreign policy success contrasts with disappointment on the economic and domestic front. The vast majority of the population

103

probably rightly sees little connection between the small cuts in military expenditure and future improvements in their standard of living. Even if it is no substitute for material improvement, further progress in de-militarizing East-West relations should clearly redound to Gorbachev's political advantage.

As far as elite opinion goes, the balance of advantage is less clearly favourable. The fact that the Gorbachev leadership has broken with so many of the traditional ground rules of Soviet foreign policy tactics, particularly in accommodating Western demands, might lead one to anticipate considerable internal criticism and controversy. However, key conservative elites are largely preoccupied with fighting rearguard actions on major domestic fronts, especially against deep cuts in the bureaucratic machine. They concentrate on economic reform where perestroika is most vulnerable. While those critical of *perestroika* do not align exactly on domestic and international issues, the contours of political divisions are broadly similar. Conservative leaders do make a point of linking domestic reforms with those in the international arena. The notorious Andreeva letter attacked the whole notion of opening up the country to nefarious influences. Ligachev in his Gorkii speech in the summer of 1988 pointedly criticized both moves towards the market and the attempt to de-ideologize peaceful coexistence (specifically the statement that peaceful coexistence no longer constitutes a form of class struggle), identifying these moves as planks in a single political platform. So while the conservative attack is focused on domestic rather than international innovation, the tight political linkage between them makes foreign policy vulnerable to political attacks motivated by domestic purpose. (Obviously, should Gorbachev meet with a major foreign policy failure, this will be used against the whole programme of reform.)

Three sets of issues lie at the centre of conservative concern and form foci for the politicization of foreign policy changes: human and civil rights; demilitarization of security; and economic interaction with the West. Specific human rights moves tied to foreign policy probably give rise to less political controversy than the general easing of controls over society. Jewish and ethnic German emigration, while most clearly serving foreign policy ends, affects fewer interests than the climate of wider liberalization of which it forms part. Easier access to Western information, the more tolerant attitude to public protest and plans for freer foreign travel all cause concern with the conservative circles. The fact that all these moves are in part motivated by international considerations means that they redound politically upon the new departures in foreign policy.

For most conservatives a strategy of demilitarizing security and »normalizing« relations with the West stands out as the most disturbing aspect of foreign policy change. Many find it difficult to accept the new stress on the economic rather than the military nature of the Western threat, with its clear implications for Soviet security policy. While some in the armed forces may agree that traditional policy tended towards military »over insurance«, most feel uneasy about the stress now placed on »reasonable sufficiency« and »non-provocative defence«. Even key Gorbachev appointees such as Defense Minister Yazov insist on using the term »reliable« sufficiency, stressing the need to keep pace with Western capabilities and retain in any defensive postures the capacity to launch counter-offensive operations. Gorbachev's general strategy of disarmament has encountered little if any direct opposition, but its speed and asymmetry have aroused concern, particularly within military circles. The Soviet moratorium on nuclear testing, the unfavourable asymmetries of the INF treaty and the unilateral cut in conventional forces stand out as politically controversial moves. This is not to say that the military's response overall to Gorbachev's arms control policy has been predominantly negative. The younger and more forward-looking members of the military establishment appreciate the role which disarmament can play in freeing resources for technical modernization which in turn holds the key to future military competitiveness. They may see the military merits of leaner and more flexible armed forces. Still, important groups in the military elite, especially its older contingent, view with apprehension the mounting chorus of deprecation from politicians, journalists and writers alike of the utility of military force and the performance of the armed forces. It is in the context of what many generals see as a decline in the military's traditional status that they find the prospect of deep cuts in forces and budgets particularly worrying. The larger these cuts and the greater the economic transfers from military to consumer production, the more will security policy become enmeshed in domestic political controversy.

Economic issues provide a less obvious yet potentially more important avenue for the politicization of foreign policy. External economic policy has long attracted political controversy in the Soviet Union – witness the sharp discussions around the foreign policy dimension of the NEP or debates on the economic aspects of détente. Attuned to the political sensitivities surrounding any signs of higher economic dependency on the West, Gorbachev has come out against taking large new credits to purchase consumer goods. Nonetheless, political sensitivities have been raised by his thrust to open up the Soviet Union to the international economy, to increase trade and in particular direct cooperation with capitalist states. Even leaving doctrinal objections to one side, the current moves towards greater interaction involve and presage a greater politicization of foreign policy in general and external economic policy in particular. If a greater penetration of the Soviet economy and society by foreign commercial interests materializes from present policies, it will bring a large number of foreign policy related issues onto the domestic political agenda. The development of foreign trade links and joint ventures (now totalling over 160) by a large number of ministries, local authorities and enterprises will mean a dramatic extension of the range of groups with direct interest in Soviet foreign relations. This multiplication of constituencies with international policy concerns is likely to alter the environment for foreign policy makers. For the first time they will have to deal with a wide array of pressures outside the major institutions on various aspects of foreign policy within the framework of a changing political system, which may afford far greater opportunities for lobbying activity. Among the most powerful potential lobbyists are associations of foreign trade enterprises, republics and the economic regions and the special enterprise zones now under active consideration. Shevardnadze has indeed urged republics to develop their own external economic strategies. As far as future republican roles in foreign policy are concerned, Estonian developments suggest that we may see the increasing pursuit of distinctive external economic policy, which in turn will affect the republics' general foreign relations with key commercial partners.

All this, when added to the domestic social and political repercussions of joint ventures, promises to make the running of Soviet foreign policy a far more complex political process. Opening the Soviet Union to global economic influences will inevitably expand the role of what is often called »low politics« in the foreign policy process. In this sense *perestroika* is likely to change the web of connections between domestic and foreign policy into something more akin to that found in Western states. A broader, more complex, variegated and ultimately thicker web does not of course necessarily mean any particular shift in the direction of Soviet foreign policy. However, it makes likely a more open debate and foreign policy process involving a larger number of constituencies, which will bring to bear a wider range of domestic considerations and interests. Greater interdependence between East and West may therefore bring about closer links between domestic and foreign policy within the Soviet Union.

Part Two:
The Economic Policy Challenge

Economics of Perestroika

Abram Bergson

Since his elevation to Party General Secretary on March 11, 1985, Mikhail S. Gorbachev has made institutional and policy restructuring, or *perestroika*, as that process is now known everywhere, a feature of the Soviet scene. While bent on reshaping Soviet society generally, Gorbachev has been seeking with particular intentness to reform the economy. Under his sponsorship the Party and government have adopted a host of measures projecting such restructuring.

Many of the more important measures are quite new and have been at best only partially implemented; and further actions are clearly in prospect. It is possible by now, however, to discern essentials of a more or less inclusive program. It should not be too soon to try to gain an overall view of the reform process that is unfolding and to consider what Gorbachev is trying to achieve through it, and with what prospects for success.

I.

We must begin where Gorbachev did, with the economy that he inherited from his predecessors. The essential facts are broadly familiar. When Gorbachev became General Secretary, the Soviet economy still was administered by a planning system that had originated with Stalin and was organized much as it was under the Dictator. Proverbially bureaucratic and cumbersome as Soviet centralist planning is, it once performed quite well in a sphere that the Soviet leadership considered cardinal. Tempos of growth under Stalin and for a time under his successors were once quite respectable by Western standards.

Nevertheless, such tempos did not persist. Soviet national income, which was still growing by an impressive 5.1 percent annually in the sixties, has progressively slowed since that time. By 1981–85, the tempo had fallen to 1.8 percent [Table 1]. I cite unclassified estimates relating specifically to the gross national product (GNP) that were compiled by the United States CIA. Western students of the Soviet economy generally consider these data as more reliable than similar

111

measures of growth of so-called net material product (NMP) released by the Soviet government. The Soviet official data, too, show a protracted and marked decline in growth, but tempos throughout are higher than found by the CIA. Interestingly, the reliability of the Soviet official data has lately come in for much questioning even in the USSR.[1]

While growth rates were once high, as not always understood, they were generated in a rather novel way: under this process, initiated under Stalin, output expansion was achieved primarily by the sheer multiplication of labor and capital inputs, and only to a limited extent by increases in their productivity. Output per worker, it is true, grew rapidly, but that was due chiefly to economy of labor induced by a notably rapid increase in accumulated capital stock (plant, equipment, etc.), that in turn being funded by a dramatic increase in the volume of new capital investment in relation to the GNP. Output relatively to inputs of labor and capital together, or factor productivity, as it is called, grew only very moderately [Table 1]. This »extensive« growth process, thus, contrasts with the »intensive« one familiar in the West, where output expansion tends to be fueled in good part by increases in productivity. The expansion of labor and capital inputs, however, necessarily also has a significant place in the West.

The difference in growth processes is not inconsequential. Originating in advances in technology and in efficiency more generally, factor productivity growth often requires outlays for R & D, but costs of additional output tend to be not nearly as great as those incurred through

---

1 Soviet criticism of Soviet official data on growth is not new, but it has flourished lately under the impact of *glasnost'*. In the upshot the CIA measures too have come into question. Very possibly even those reduced rates, it has been held, are too high. This is a large theme that I cannot really pursue here, but a principal argument for the indicated view is the striking contention of Abel Aganbegian (1988, pp. 2–3) that the Soviet NMP during 1981–85, rather than growing at 3.2 percent annually as officially claimed, did not grow at all! Such a contention by a leading Soviet economist, and a principal advisor of Gorbachev, has to be pondered carefully, but Aganbegian provides no documentation for his contention, and one cannot ignore that the Gorbachev administration may find it difficult to be fully objective in evaluating Soviet economic performance under its predecessors.

In this essay, we shall have to consider measures of growth not only of national income but of diverse components. Here, too, there is good reason often to prefer Western data that are at hand to related official data that have been released. As with the measures of national income, however, I take note of both sorts of data. Only the official data are congruent with published plan goals.

expansion of factor inputs. In the case of capital, of course, such costs ultimately take the form of imposed consumer saving and abstinence. Such costs had hardly been a deterrent in Stalin's day, but the dictator died on March 5, 1953. His successors felt impelled to ameliorate Stalin's onerous priorities. That must have seemed imperative if only from a concern for morale and incentives for an increasingly literate and sophisticated labor force. Resultant consumer benefits, apparent even in relatively conservative CIA estimates [Table 1], have nevertheless dwindled as output growth has slowed. But, in order to achieve them, further increases in the volume of capital investment had to be progressively limited.

And that has inevitably fed back into a slowdown in output growth itself. As a cause of that slowdown, however, the declining rate of increase in investment volume has only compounded the impact of another, widely reported trend. The Soviet labor force, which expanded by about 1.4 to 1.8 percent yearly during the sixties and seventies has lately been increasing at less than half of that tempo.[2] Increases in labor supply that have been materializing recently are restricted predominantly to peripheral areas (Central Asia, Kazakhstan, Transcaucasus). The population there is apparently reluctant to migrate to major industrial centers elsewhere.

Curiously, as output growth has declined, it has remained of the costly extensive sort. While factor input growth has slowed, so too has the growth of factor productivity. Recently, such growth has been negligible, if not actually negative [Table 1]. As a source of productivity increases limited gains in efficiency have apparently been offset by diminishing returns in natural resource exploitation.

Such was the Soviet growth process as it evolved under Gorbachev's predecessors. In the upshot it permitted a once backward country to become in the course of time a military superpower. Nevertheless, in 1985, when Gorbachev became General Secretary, Soviet per capita consumption was still little more than 30 percent of that in the USA.[3]

---

2 The falling labor force growth reflects reduced increases in labor participation rates as well as demographic factors. See Murray Feshbach (1983); Stephen Rapawy and Godfrey Baldwin (1982, Part 2) and CIA (1987, p. 70).

3 The relation for 1975, 34.5 percent, given in Abram Bergson (1988, ch. 4), must be reduced by several percentage points in order to allow for 1975–85 trends, as indicated by CIA (1987, pp. 53, 66), and *Economic Report* (1988, p. 279).

Careful as I believe they are, the calculations underlying this estimate could only allow very partially for the pervasive deficiencies
in product quality that have characterized extensive growth under
centralist planning in the USSR. They do not take into account at all
the continually disorganized retail market under that process, with its
proverbial sell-outs and queues, and the resultant inconvenience to the
Soviet consumer.

Lately, it has become customary in the USSR to describe the immediate
pre-Gorbachev years there as ones of stagnation (*zastoi*). In respect of
the economy, that must be considered hyperbole to a degree,[4] but on his
elevation to General Secretary, Gorbachev had reason to be concerned
with Soviet economic performance. He was in fact deeply concerned.
So much is manifest not only in his pronouncements but in his actions,
to which we must now turn.

II.

The economic reform measures that Gorbachev has initiated are wide-
ranging as well as multitudinous. The reform of industrial planning,
however, has been a priority concern; actions initiated to that end are
patently central to Gorbachev's efforts at economic restructuring. The
nature of the transformation of industrial planning that is being sought
has evolved in the course of time and no doubt will continue to do so.
But it apparently reached a relatively advanced stage, at least in design,
with a series of decrees issued in June and July 1987.

Contrary to some commentary, the government is by no means projecting an abandonment of centralist planning. But to a greater degree
than in the past use is to be made of market processes in the direction
and coordination of enterprises, the agencies immediately in charge of
operations.[5] While decision making at all bureaucratic levels is still to

4 See, however, above, n.1.
5 On the decrees of June-July 1987: *O korennoi...* (1987). These decrees, and earlier
  ones that have been absorbed into the program now unfolding, have been subject
  to extensive comment and analysis. Particularly useful are Ed. A. Hewett, Victor
  H. Winston, *et al.* (1987); Gertrude Schroeder (1986; 1987); Hewett (1988); Joint
  Economic Committee (1987; 1988); Abel Aganbegian (1988); Padma Desai (1988).
  Also of interest is a further decree of January 1988 regulating labor employment and
  dismissals, on which: Vladimir G. Kostakov *et al.* (1988); *FBIS*, March 4, 1988, pp.
  32 ff.

be controlled by plans, the enterprise is to enjoy increased autonomy in formulating and implementing those applicable to it. The enterprise will still be obliged to accept state orders for a substantial, though purportedly diminishing, volume of output, but central rationing of materials is to give way increasingly to different forms of wholesale trade.

While gaining in authority, the enterprise is to be subject to greater financial discipline, and profits are to serve as a summary index of its performance. That is not novel, but norms determining profit shares allocated to the government budget and to incentive and other funds are to be more stable than they have been hitherto. Rewards are thus to be more dependent than previously on the enterprise's financial performance. Subsidies to enterprises operating at a loss, now widespread, are declaredly to cease to be so after a projected reform in prices, and enterprises that remain insolvent will be candidates for liquidation. Hitherto that has been a practically unheard of phenomenon in the USSR. Staff curtailment to achieve cost reduction, traditionally impeded by regulatory restrictions, is apparently to be facilitated.

Wages for workers at all levels will usually continue to be, as they have been previously, of a conventional sort, comprising a basic return plus premia or bonuses for exemplary performance. The collective of workers, however, will now have the option, subject to approval by the enterprise's bureaucratic superior, the ministry, to have incomes determined rather differently: as a residual claim to income after material and other expenses are met and required allocations to the budget and other assignments are made. Without explicit reference to the Yugoslav system of labor self-management, the Soviet reforms appear here to be emulating it. The emulation is the more marked so far as an elaborate system of workers' representation is established in each enterprise. Among other things, the director is to be elected by the enterprise collective. The outcome of the election, however, is subject to approval by the ministry. Depending on how this legislation is administered, it could represent a striking departure from past Soviet practice.

Insofar as they affect labor incentives, the foregoing shifts carry further earlier ones initiated under Gorbachev, most importantly a wholesale change in wage structure under a decree of September 1986, whose main thrust is towards greater emphasis on incentive pay differen-

115

tials.[6] The legislation of June and July 1987 also leaves intact a measure of July 1986 providing for control over industrial output quality by extra-enterprise acceptance commissions. Previously quality control had been left to the producing enterprise, a feature hardly conducive to excellence in this important sphere.

While for Gorbachev the reform of industrial planning has been pivotal to economic restructuring, it has by no means been exhaustive of that process. Indeed, one may wonder whether reform in another sphere, not so much stressed initially, has not come to be regarded as of at least comparable urgency to that of industrial planning. The principle shifts that are occurring regarding property relations have understandably attracted much attention in the West, but may not always be well understood. Since Gorbachev came to power, the government has affirmed the legality of a wide variety of private enterprise activities that previously had often been at best legally dubious. Subject to local licensing, private enterprise is now legally permitted in such diverse fields as handicraft production, construction, repair services, and medicine. Individuals who are normally employable in the social sector, however, may work on their own account only after hours, and employment of hired labor is not allowed.[7]

While opportunities for private enterprise are thus still restricted, a near counterpart of such enterprise is seemingly to be allowed much scope. In the USSR, the cooperative has long enjoyed only an attenuated existence, chiefly as a quasi-state enterprise in trade. The government has now proclaimed the cooperative to be a fundamental form, along with state enterprise, of socialist economic organization and has acted to codify its widespread use as a substantially autonomous entity in industry, trade and services.[8] Whatever the sphere, members must actively participate in its work, but employment of hired labor is permitted.

I refer to cooperatives apart from collective farms. Those too are cooperatives, but they have always enjoyed a special and not exactly

---

6 On the September 1986 decree, and recent developments in the sphere of income differentiation more generally: Janet G. Chapman (1987). For the text of the decree, *Sobranie postanovlenie ...* (1986).

7 For the main legislation: *Pravda*, November 21, 1986. See also Roger Blough *et al.* (1982, Part 2); Libor Roucek (1988); Stanislaw Pomorski (1988).

8 See *Pravda*, June 8, 1988; *Radio Liberty Research*, March 15, 198, June 10, 1988.

enviable status. In a degree that is still to be so, but here too liberalization is the order of the day. Thus, arrangements, formerly rare, are now to be promoted, by which small groups of farm members or even individual families contract to assume responsibility for entire cycles of farm operations. For purposes of such an arrangement, a segment of the farm may be leased. Such contractual arrangements, with a lease as long as 50 years, have been authoritatively recommended for government approval. The new arrangements are now in order not only for collective farms but for so-called state farms, that is, farms that have been organized as state rather than cooperative enterprises.[9] Among the rearrangements in industrial planning and property relations that I have mentioned, a number are intended to boost incentives for effective management, and for skill and productive effort generally. While addressed to one or another economic sphere, such shifts also manifest still another facet of Gorbachev's restructuring endeavor more generally. But, in seeking to harness the »human factor,« as he phrases it, Gorbachev has been concerned not only with enhancing incentives. He has also urged the need for increased discipline on the part of workers at all levels. To achieve that result, it was made clear early on in his administration that the government would persist in efforts initiated under Iurii Y. Andropov to curb absenteeism and heighten labor discipline in other ways as well.[10] A host of dismissals of officials, promptly initiated after Gorbachev's elevation, must have been motivated variously but can only have underlined what was being emphatically affirmed: »exactingness« was the order of the day at high as well as low stations.[11] As has also been left in no doubt, »exactingness« demands not only competence but freedom from corruption, a vice held not always to have been fought with sufficient vigilance by previous administrations.

Last but not least, Gorbachev's attention-getting campaign against alcoholism manifestly derives in part from extra-economic concerns. It is properly seen, however, as still another dimension of his endeavor to

9 See above, n. 5; also *FBIS*, August 29, 1988; *Radio Liberty Research*, August 29, 1988, pp. 44 ff.
10 *Pravda* August 7, 1988; *Radio Liberty Research*, October 16, 1985.
11 With Gorbachev not yet in office a full year, some two-fifths of all government ministers and state committee chairman, and nearly one-third of all Party secretaries at the provincial (*oblast'*) level had been replaced; *Pravda*, April 12, 1985, *Radio Liberty Research*, January 22, 1986.

promote »exactingness« and a beneficent »human factor« more generally. Government action to curb alcohol abuse is not new in the USSR,
but the current campaign is notable for its vigor and decisiveness. The
government has drastically curtailed legal sales of alcoholic beverages.
By 1986, such sales had fallen to about one-half the 1984 level. I refer
to sales of legally produced supplies; not surprisingly, illegal production
has spurted.[12]

III.

Gorbachev has elucidated on more than one occasion what it is that
he is seeking in restructuring the Soviet economy. His cardinal aim, he
has affirmed, is acceleration of growth (*uskorenie*), or reversal of the
economic slowdown. As he explained rather dramatically at the outset
of his administration:[13]

> The historic fate of the country, the position of socialism in the modern
> world in large part depends on how we proceed from here ... We must
> achieve a significant acceleration of social-economic progress. There is
> simply no other path.

Uskorenie, moreover, must be achieved in a particular way. As Gorbachev also made clear early on, the extensive growth process that
prevailed under his predecessors could no longer serve. In its place,
the Russians must »achieve a decisive turn in the transition of the
economy on the rails of intensive growth,«[14] growth, that is, that is
propelled primarily by advances in technology and overall efficiency.
What are the prospects for *uskorenie*? Seemingly not too bright when
we consider the usually meager payoff to previous Soviet economic
reforms. Even the highly touted Brezhnev-Kosygin reform of 1965,
as it turned out, left the system functioning much as before.[15] The
restructuring that Gorbachev has initiated has properly been called

---

12 On legal sales of alcoholic beverages, *Pravda*, January 26, 1986, January 18, 1987; on
   Gorbachev's campaign and its predecessors in the USSR, David E. Powell (1985) and
   Vladimir E. Treml, in *Radio Liberty Research*, March 18, 1987; also *Radio Liberty
   Research*, August 3, 1987.
13 Report to the Party Central Committee, April 23, 1985; quoted in Hewett (1988, p.
   31).
14 *Pravda*, March 12, 1985.
15 Hewett (1988, ch. 5).

»radical« in the USSR; it represents by far the most substantial shift of Soviet economic institutions and policies projected since Stalin. If only on that account, any easy extrapolation from past experience would be out of place. As the daily news suggests, however, the current restructuring is not exactly off and running.

Owing in good part to good weather and a good agricultural harvest, growth spurted in 1986, but fell again to a very low level in 1987.[16] Probably more important, the market for consumers' goods, never well organized, appears lately to have deteriorated, with shortages and queues even more frequent than usual. For some foodstuffs, rationing has been initiated in a number of localities. Paradoxically, supplies generally may not be much diminished. The difficulty appears rather to be that an always disproportionately large household money demand has lately become even more so.

For that, however, the government itself is much at fault. It has deferred to 1990–91, even for highly subsidized food products, the price reform that might bring about a better overall balance of supply and demand for consumers' goods. It has also refrained from resorting to an alternative instrument – higher income taxes – that might achieve such a balance. Indeed, the government itself has compounded the imbalance, among other things, through its draconian curtailment of legal sales of alcoholic beverages, and the resultant release of purchasing power previously absorbed by the high taxes and prices of such goods. An incidental effect: because of the increased demand for bootleg production, sugar has joined the list of rationed goods.

The imbalance in the consumers' goods market is but the obverse of the budgetary deficit which the government has now acknowledged but seemingly still understates. According to Western accounting practice, the shortfall of revenues from expenditures could be as large as 7 percent of the GNP.[17] In financing the deficit the government has apparently resorted to wholesale currency emissions. If too many rubles are chasing too few consumers' goods in the USSR, that must be a principal cause.

---

16 The Soviet official growth rate for national income utilized and the corresponding CIA figure for the GNP: 1988, 3.4; 3.9; 1987, 1.4; 0.8; TSSU (1988, p. 388); CIA (1988 A, p. 61).

17 On the evolving state of the government budget and the consumers' goods market: Jan Vanous, in *Plan Econ Report*, November 4, 1988; CIA (1988 B).

Even for a casual observer, the government's hesitation to bite the bullets of retail price reform and increased income taxes is politically understandable, but the resulting disorder in the consumers' goods market is not auspicious for economic restructuring. It is not only that consumers are much inconvenienced by pervasive queues and sell-outs. The disorderly market also tends to impair the incentives for initiative and effort that the government is seeking to enhance.

Reform is properly projected for prices not only of consumers' goods but also of more basic industrial products; here too the delay is costly, for the financial controls, including profitability, that are projected increasingly to shape enterprise behavior necessarily depend for their rationale on the degree to which prices reflect prevailing commodity scarcity values. More basically, the delay in reforming prices has proved to be an impediment to the enterprise's exercising the autonomy that is supposedly being conferred on it. But there have been other impediments as well. Most importantly, with all the authority that the enterprise is to gain, the superior ministry is still responsible for fulfilling its own plan. With obligatory state orders it still has at its disposal a potent instrument to bend the enterprise to its will. While the chief rearrangements in question are very new, the resulting confusion must already be exacting a toll of economic performance.[18]

If all is not well with Gorbachev's »radical« economic reforms, that is not very surprising. Initiation of such a sweeping program could be expected to be disruptive and economically costly for a time. Soviet economists themselves have been careful to caution against any high expectations of results in the short term. The immediate prospect, it has been held, is rather for a »difficult and painful« time. Only after a more or less protracted transition period can any marked progress materialize.[19]

Pending achievement of favorable results, however, even one who is sympathetically inclined must conclude that Gorbachev's ambitious restructuring program is still at risk. That might be true in any event,

---

18 See the writings of Hewett and Winston, *et al.*, and of Schroeder, cited above, n. 5; *FBIC*, May 23, 1988, pp. 81 ff; June 22, 1988, pp. 64 ff; July 25, 1988, pp. 65 ff; September 15, 1988, pp. 65 ff.

19 Soviet economists may be optimistic, though, in thinking that the transition will occupy only two or three years. See Aganbegian and Leonid I. Abalkin, in *FBIS*, Feb. 12, 1988, pp. 66 ff; May 11, 1988, pp. 81 ff; May 23, 1988, pp. 81 ff.

but it is all the more so in view of the divided public response that the program has provoked. Among elite personnel, by all accounts, many are less than enthusiastic, to say the least. That is understandable when we consider the threat that restructuring poses to traditional Soviet beliefs as well as the material status of the persons in question. Soviet commentators report variously on attitudes to economic restructuring among the public more generally.[20] For the first time under the five year plans, though, Soviet workers are threatened with wholesale staff dismissals. While the government has been reassuring as to reemployment, it would be surprising if the operative cause should be very popular.[21] Increases in income differentials under way also appear to be provoking a very mixed response, high earnings of cooperative and private enterprise being a special target for criticism.[22] And while many wives are said to have welcomed the curtailment of alcohol sales, no one has to be told that many husbands are not similarly disposed.

But it would be wrong to close on such a somber note. Concerning the future of Gorbachev's restructuring initiative, there are grounds for optimism as well as pessimism. Radical reform of the Soviet economy is an endeavor whose time has come. Such reform is difficult to accomplish, but it would also have been difficult not to undertake it. One need not ponder long on the deteriorating pre-Gorbachev economic performance to become convinced of that.

Granting the defects of Gorbachev's reform initiative, its thrust is clear: to a degree, bureaucratic are to give way to market-like processes, and state to private enterprise and to quasi-private cooperatives. Much Western economic thought and experience suggests that that is a promising course. We must be wary of mechanically extending to the USSR the experience with centralist planning reform elsewhere, but no one at all informed on that will dispute that here too there is evidence that Gorbachev's reform measures are shifting the Soviet economy in a potentially favorable direction.

Experience elsewhere also suggests what in any case might be inferred,

20 For almost diametrically opposing accounts: *Current Digest of the Soviet Press*, June 22, 1988, pp. 18 ff; *FBIS*, August 12, 1988, pp. 50 ff.
21 On prospective dismissals, and measures to cope with them, above, n. 5.
22 The deep division of public opinion on cooperative earnings in particular is doubtless the principal reason for the government's widely reported vacillation on the question of whether such earnings should be subject to a progressive income tas: *FBIS* August 1, 1988, p. 55, August 8, 1988, pp. 47–48; *Radio Liberty Research*, July 15, 1988.

that what is called for in the USSR is not a program, in any definitive sense, but a process. Reform must be followed by reform of the reform, and then by reform of that, for the task is far too complex to admit of any once-for-all disposition. Such a process, however, is already under way in the USSR. Perhaps most important is the increased emphasis, remarked earlier, on cooperative and private enterprise. Not a few careful Western observers consider that this could be all to the good, especially in agriculture and services.[23]

Finally, even modest success in the actuation of such a reform process must require exceptional leadership qualities, but they are also qualities with which the present director of Soviet affairs appears to be well-endowed. In seeking to reinvigorate the Soviet economy, Mikhail S. Gorbachev has undertaken an awesome task, but if anyone can do it, he can.

This is still not at all to say that fulfillment is assured of the latest Soviet five-year plan that was approved by the Party and government in Gorbachev's second year in office, or of the longer-term goals that were proclaimed at about the same time [Table 1]. The marked growth acceleration that these programs projected seemed ambitious when they were announced. They seem more so now.[24]

---

23 Reform of the reform has also had a more specific character, as where a »temporary law« has been enacted to regularize the issuance of state orders for the balance of the Twelfth Five Year Plan. How much remains of the additional autonomy the enterprise was to gain under previous legislation, however, is not very clear. See *FBIS*, July 25, 1988, pp. 65 ff; August 22, 1988, pp. 30 ff.

24 The acceleration projected is even more marked than it might seem, for plan targets are not afflicted with the upward statistical bias that distorts Soviet official measures of past performance. While under the five-year plan investment volume is to grow disproportionately, note that the entire 1986–90 increase in industrial output is to be achieved by increasing labor productivity and not at all through expansion of employment. That fairly clearly attests to the »intensification« that the plan is purportedly to achieve. Work on the five-year plan must have been at an advanced stage before Gorbachev came to office, but it went through several drafts after that. It presumably reflects to a degree Gorbachev's policies, and that must be still more true of the longer-term goals. See Hewett (1985, pp. 286–287); Keith Bush, in *Radio Liberty Research*, August 2, 1986; and compare the goals in *Pravda*, November 9, 1985 and June 20, 1986.

Table 1. Selected Economic Indicators, USSR, Average Annual Rate of Growth[a] (per cent)

	1961–70	1971–75	1976–80	1981–85	1986–90	1986–2000
1. Net material product (NMP), Soviet official[b]	6.4	5.1	3.9	3.1	4.1	4.7[c]
2. Gross national product (GNP), CIA estimates[d]	5.1	3.7	2.2	1.8	n.a.[e]	n.a.
3. Gross fixed capital investment, Soviet official[f]	6.9	6.8	3.5	3.5	4.9	n.a.
4. Factor productivity, Bergson[d]	1.4	...[g]	...	...	n.a.	n.a.
5. Industrial output, Soviet official	8.5	7.4	4.4	3.7	4.6	4.7[h]
6. Industrial output, CIA estimates[d]	6.6	5.9	2.6	1.8	n.a.	n.a.
7. Agricultural output, Soviet official[i]	n.a.	2.5	1.8	1.0	2.7	n.a.
8. Agricultural output, CIA estimates[d],[i]	n.a.	1.4	0.4	(-) 0.6	n.a.	n.a.
9. Real income per capita, Soviet official	6.5	4.3	3.4	2.1	2.7	3.2–4.0
10. Consumption per capita, CIA estimates[d]	3.8	2.9	2.0	1.9	n.a.	n.a.

a   Sources: Soviet official data and plan goals, TSSU (1986) and earlier volumes in the same series; *Pravda*, March 9, 1986; June 19, 1986; June 20, 1986, CIA data, John Pitzer (1982), CIA (1985, pp. 64 ff), Gertrude E. Schroeder and M. Elizabeth Denton (1982 B); CIA (1988 A, pp. 47, 60 ff). For consumption, 1981–85, and agricultural output, 1976–85, unclassified CIA data supplied to author. Factor productivity is calculated with inputs as in Bergson (1988, ch. 6) for 1960–75; as in CIA (1987, p. 70) for 1975–85, and input weights as in Bergson (1988, ch. 6).
b   »Utilized for consumption and accumulation«
c   »Almost«
d   Output valued in 1970 prices for growth rates for 1961–75, and in 1982 prices for growth rates for 1976–86.
e   n.a.: not available.
f   CIA estimates essentially accord with Soviet official data
g   Negligible
h   »Not less than«
i   Yearly growth rate of average for five year period over average for previous five year period.

Perestroika of the Economy: The Soviet Point of View

Leonid Abalkin

A radical *perestroika* of the economy occupies a central place in the transformations that are being realized today in the Soviet Union. The results of this *perestroika*, regardless of their dimensions, have exerted a direct influence on the life of literally every person, and of every Soviet family; these results affect people's mood and their social activity.

Moreover, the results that have been achieved in the economy – as opposed to other spheres of life – can be quantitatively measured and compared both with what has been done in the past as well as with announced intentions. This, however, does not exclude differences in the interpretation of the course and the results of *perestroika* of the economy.

»The Soviet point of view« for the course of economic *perestroika* is a broad idea and is very conditional. Officials of the planning organs, scholars and representatives of various social groups by no means evaluate in the same way what has happened. Various specialists assess the economic reform in substantially different ways. The same applies, it seems, to the »Western point of view.«

In addition, it is possible to single out a few particular points that are inherent to the approach of Soviet scholars and specialists in evaluating the design, course and results of the *perestroika* of the economy, and in evaluating the path and speed of further progress of the reforms.

First, at the foundation of our approach lies new political and economic thinking, which has arisen in the process of working out the theory and policy of *perestroika*, as well as a new view of socialist society and its place in world development. We look at socialist society and its economic system not only as the negation of the old, but also as a natural successor of everything good that human civilization has amassed. In many ways this determines the new approach toward the idea of the cooperative and of the marketplace, toward enterprise, competition, democratic institutions and moral norms.

Second, in Western evaluations there dominates a comparison of *per-*

estroika of the Soviet economy, with the results achieved from models or reforms that already exist and are being implemented in other countries. Soviet scholars and specialists follow different criteria, which are founded in the concepts of fulfilling the possibilities of the socialist system, of its economic and social efficiency, of its capacity to insure an economy receptive to scientific and technical innovation and to ensure flexibility toward constantly changing social and individual needs.

Third, the distinguishing characteristic of the Soviet approach is defined by the inclusion of scholars and specialists in the process of *perestroika*. They are therefore able to perceive the changes that are transpiring, the successes and failures, as a stimulus for the search for the most effective decisions, for the elaboration of earlier conclusions and recommendations. Taking into account the increased interest of society in *perestroika* of the economy, this situation, in my opinion, requires significantly more realism and a more pointed critical approach in evaluations of the course of economic reform and its results.

Design

Perestroika of the Soviet economy is not an autonomous process. It is a constituent part of a gigantic plan, connected with the renovation of socialism and giving socialism a qualitatively new appearance. It is a response to an historical challenge, the essence of which is contained in making maximum use of the potential of socialism while preserving its characteristic system of social values and ideals. Our goal is to ensure the mastery of the newest achievements of science and technology, the high efficiency of the economy, the conditions of life worthy of modern man, and of free development.

The Soviet Union has projected a period of time – a relatively short one, in historical terms – in which to renew its industrial apparatus, to review the structure of the economy, to move the economy in the direction of intensive development, to raise radically the productivity of labor, and to ensure the high quality and competitiveness of production. It will be necessary to resolve the problem of foodstuffs and housing, to reform education and health care, and to saturate the consumer market with high-quality goods and services.

It is clearly impossible to solve these tasks using the structure of

125

property relations and the forms and methods of management that have taken shape in the past. This is what determines the necessity of radical reform of the economic mechanism – reform that is genuinely revolutionary in its essence and consequences. Half-measures, only partial adjustments of the existing system of management, cannot bring about the expected results. The distinctive feature of the Soviet point of view is a clear understanding that economic reform must be realized simultaneously with the *perestroika* of the political system and with the renewal of social relations and of the spiritual-ideological sphere.

Special attention is given to the *perestroika* of all relations of socialist ownership, to the enrichment of its forms, to the surmounting of accumulated deformations. Various types of property ownership are developing-cooperative ownership, ownership by public organizations, ownership by the individual, and special forms of ownership. However, the main problem – and the main difficulty – is the renewal of the internal structure of public property ownership, which until recently has been identified with state property ownership. It will be necessary to overcome the alienation towards property ownership and management that might be felt by workers, labor collectives, and regional groups of the population. These groups must be established as having all rights and responsibilities in the workplace, in the city and in the republic.

The primary element of reform is the transfer from administrative-command to economic methods of management. A new concept of centralized management is being formed which is based on the programmed resolution of strategic tasks and on the wide use of economic regulators – prices, taxes, payments for resources, interest rates, etc.

The plan of *perestroika* presupposes the formation and development of a socialist market both for the means of production as well as for consumer goods. There is the question of a credit market, a market for investment resources and for securities. A whole program of measures will be implemented, directed for the broad development of economic competition and for the battle with extremely dangerous monopolistic phenomena and tendencies.

It is important to emphasize that the economic model taking shape in the Soviet Union will be very complicated in structure. Primitivism, one-sided thinking and opposition of some elements to others are inadmissible in the evaluation of this model. A qualitatively new model for the functioning of the Soviet economy must combine the following:

126

the highest level of efficiency of production with humanistic goals in developing it; reinforcement of wage differentials with the developed system of social guarantees; disengagement of manpower from industrial production with general and efficient employment; revival of the cooperative and the broad development of the principles of the cooperative while strengthening and renewing the public sector of the economy; and establishment of the socialist market, the strengthening of its influence upon production with improvement of the methods of centralized planned management.

One of the key questions concerning the principles and fate of *perestroika* of the Soviet economy, which has been exposed to international discussion, is the possibility – or impossibility – of combining such contradictory principles. What can be said in this regard?

First, public life – both in the past and in the future – is woven out of similar contradictions. Examples are the contradictions between personal freedom and the norms of human society and morality, as well as those between the growing interdependence of nations, born of the division of labor, and their national sovereignty.

Second, the question of the capacity to combine the above-mentioned contradictory principles is the essence of the historical challenge that has been put to socialism. We accept this challenge and by means of our *perestroika* are prepared to answer it. Time will be our judge.

I would like to emphasize still another particular feature of the plan of *perestroika*. It emanates from the denial of the ideal model – a type of philosophers' stone – the search for which occupied medieval alchemists. One must recognize a reality of modern society – that today there exists in no country a model that has proved capable of resolving all problems and that is suitable for everyone. By the way, evaluations »by analogy,« which are used by many experts, emanate from the presence of a suitable model (either ideal or existing in reality).

Human civilization, in principle, develops into different variants. Any functional economic model will be effective only if it takes into account the sum total of historical traditions, national characteristics, and the culture of the given nation. This, of course, does not deny the necessity of studying and exchanging experiences, applying forms and methods of regulation of economic life that have proven effective and become, with time, the common property of human civilization.

This feature of the plan of *perestroika* can be called the principle

127

of diversity, applicable broadly also to the formation of a model of economic management proper. On the basis of this formation are determined the conditions of regulation of the economy in its different spheres and regions (Soviet republics), the expediency of combining different types of economic activity – of large, medium and small enterprises, of a variety of forms of *khozrashchet* [economic self-accountability].

To accomplish such a grandiose plan like *perestroika* and the renovation of socialism, a sufficiently protracted period of time is required. The question concerns an entire stage of historical development, as measured in decades. Of course, within the framework of this stage stand out the immediate and ensuing phases, with their own specific problems.

Results

Real *perestroika* of the Soviet economy on any sort of significant scale began relatively recently – only about a year and a half ago. The time preceding this was consumed by a critical interpretation of the situation that had arisen toward the beginning of the 1980s – a search for ways out of the pre-crisis condition of the economy, a working out of the plan and program of *perestroika*.

Over this above-mentioned time, further economic decline leading to a crisis was checked, hope in the possibility of radical improvement was revived, and dormant forces were activated. Soviet society and its economy began to move forward. Very interesting and efficient sectors of the economy are arising (in the scientific-technical sphere, in industry and agriculture, and in the sector of the cooperatives), even though they remain for the time being removed islets and have not changed the general situation in the economy as a whole.

There is a noticeable turning point in the economy, toward a resolution of social problems. Over a relatively short period of time – from 1984 up to and including 1987 – the average life expectancy increased from 67.7 to 69.8 years. The long period of stagnation in housing construction gave place to the following rise:

128

Completed housing space (in millions of square meters)

1970	106.0
1975	109.9
1980	105.0
1985	113.0
1987	129.3

In 1987 for the first time in our country, the entire increase of the national income and output of all branches of material production was accomplished at the expense of the productivity of labor, with an overall reduction of the number of employees in those branches of the economy. However, it must be recognized that the very rates of growth of the productivity of labor remain low for the time being.

The portion of production and labor, achieved at the expense of raising the productivity of labor (in percentages):

	1976-80	1981-85	1987
Produced national income	78	87	100
Industrial output	75	86	100
Gross agricultural output	100	100	100
Construction	94	87	100

The dynamic of such general indicators as the national income and the real per capita income is significant for the evaluation of the successes of *perestroika* of the economy. In past years this dynamic was very irregular. However, after a serious fall in 1987, a certain improvement of these indicators is now expected.

The rates of growth of national income and of the real per capita income (in percentages):

	1981-85	1986	1987	1988[x]
Produced national income	3.6	4.1	2.3	4.6
Real income per capita	2.1	2.5	2.0	3.5

x – expected fulfillment

Currently, the Soviet Union has set about to calculate and publish data on the size and rates of growth of the gross national product, according to the methodology of the United Nations. This makes it possible to analyze in depth the current economic processes and to broaden international comparisons. In 1987 the gross national product of the USSR amounted to 825 billion rubles, of which 668 billion rubles (or 81%) were created by enterprises from the sphere of material production, and

129

157 billion rubles (or 19%) by enterprises, organizations and institutions from the non-industrial sphere (according to the classifications accepted by the USSR's *Goskomstat* [State Statistical Administration]).

Taking into account the strengthening of the social orientation of the Soviet economy, as well as the emphasis put on the development of the sphere of services, the gross national product is growing at higher rates than the national income.

Rates of growth of the gross national product and of the national income (in percentages):

	1980	1985	1987
Gross national product	100	122	131
Produced national income	100	119	127
Gross national product		100	108
Produced national income		100	106.5

On the whole however, there was no radical improvement in the economy over the above-indicated years. Scientific-technological progress, as earlier, is developing sluggishly, the quality of products is slowly improving, economic growth is occurring primarily on an extensive basis. As a result of an unjustified rise of monetary incomes, the condition of the consumer market worsened, and the deficit in the state budget grew.

It is important not only to establish all of these facts but also to analyze thoroughly the reasons that did not allow the achievement of fundamental improvements in the economy. Here, as in other problems, the picture must not be simplified; it is improper to blame everything on any one single cause or on one single set of circumstances. The results of *perestroika* of the economy seem to be affected by a number of things.

First, during the above-mentioned years there emerged a number of factors that, although extraneous to the reform itself, harmed it greatly. These are: the tragedy at Chernobyl, the elimination of whose after-effects cost 8 billion rubles – almost 1.5% of the nation's national income; the sharp reduction of prices on the world market, which led to a lowering of the USSR's foreign trade turnover (in current prices) in 1987 by almost 10% in comparison with 1985; and the lowering of receipts into the budget of taxes from the turnover because of the anti-alcohol campaign.

Second, the results of the reform were very negatively affected in that the reform itself was not carried out in an all-embracing manner; in particular the transition of enterprises and associations [*ob"edineniia*] to new conditions of economic management was not supported by *perestroika* in the higher echelons of management. Many measures were introduced half-heartedly.

Third, the lack of *perestroika*'s effectiveness was a result of a number of social and psychological factors: bureaucratism, which became deeply rooted in the apparatus of management; an extreme insufficiency of cadres familiar with the economic methods of management; a severe lack of people acquainted with commerce and capable of leading in an innovative way; the passivity of wide layers of the population – a passivity connected with the preservation of stereotyped views of consumption and of labor motivation.

The difficulties with which *perestroika* of the Soviet economy came into conflict are not unexpected – if, of course, we are to remain realistic and not to draw up illusions. It was clear from the very beginning that such a grandiose transformation of social-economic life could not take place smoothly, without obstacles, and that there are no revolutionary changes without a battle between the old and the new, between the forces of renewal and stagnation.

In addition, a realistic evaluation of the situation requires certain corrective measures into the original plans to bring about reform. The final goal and strategic idea remain the same, but the tactics and the sequence of measures to be taken – as well as their timing – are in need of clarification.

Perspectives

A program of urgent measures to revitalize the economy and to achieve the material-financial balance of the entire economy has now entered the number of measures that must be taken immediately. It will take, probably, two to three years to carry out this program. And only after its completion can new, large-scale steps be taken to ensure a deepening of radical reform of the management of the economy.

What is the basis for such a conclusion? Namely, this: it is impossible to carry out some measures without taking into account conditions

131

that must be present for those measures to be taken. Objective factors impose corresponding limitations upon our wishes. Not to come to terms with these factors is tantamount to losing one's footing and to embarking on the slippery path of arbitrary decision-making.

This should in no way be taken as a suspension of reform or as a deceleration of its pace. On the contrary, it will be necessary to carry out enough serious steps to clear the way for subsequent transformations. The particular issue here is the sharp reduction in the state budget deficit by limiting the scale of capital building construction, by lowering military spending, by discontinuing financing of unprofitable enterprises by the state, etc. On the other hand, it is necessary to widen the scope of available goods and services by establishing additional incentives to produce them, by maneuvering resources in necessary ways, by developing the cooperative and concept of rent, and by reexamining the politics of imports.

Together with this program of urgent measures, the preparation and gradual realization of an entire complex of projected measures are also required. It will take time to complete this work, which could possibly happen towards the mid-1990s. It is particularly important to ensure that the reforms are not just of an external, purely formal character, but rather increasingly include in their scope the deep structures of the economy and the basic relationships within it.

The initial experience of economic reform showed how dangerous it is when new approaches and concepts are used only as screens for the preservation of obsolete forms and methods of economic management. This happened, for example, in 1988 with *Goszakaz* [State Orders for Goods and Services]. The following year, its proportion in all branches of the economy is being substantively reduced.

The portion of *Goszakaz* in the production of basic industrial complexes (in percentages):

	1988	1989
Machine-building	86	25
Fuel-energy	95	59.4
Metallurgy	86	42
Chemical-forestry	87	34
Ministry of light industry	96	30

However, the issue here concerns neither the form nor the proportion of *Goszakaz*. *Goszakaz* might, even with a reduction of its role, be nothing but an administrative lever; it could become an instrument of a qualitatively new system of management and be based upon the utilization of economic methods. In many ways this relates to the development of *khozrashchet* [economic self-accountability] of enterprises, of rent and of the cooperative.

Therefore, in the near future it is likely that the primary »rent« of *perestroika* will be the struggle over filling the now-arising forms and methods with new substance – this assumes the qualitative revitalization of basic production relations.

Yet another characteristic feature of the nearest phase of economic reform will increasingly be the interweaving of reform with *perestroika* of the political system, with a renovation of the institutions of social democracy, with the changes in the social and spiritual-ideological spheres of life. In order for the current transformations to become stable, time also is needed, and no small amount of it. The skills and experience in using the democratic institutions must be combined; a whole galaxy of a new brand of political leaders and economic managers must be formed.

The formation of a socialist market and a system of price setting adequate for such a market will require a significant amount of time. It is impossible to incorporate these by decree and without creating corresponding conditions. In the face of a profound deformation of the circulation of money, of the exclusive situation of economic producers, and of the undeveloped system of economic competition, price reform not only will not achieve its goal but, on the contrary, will only provide the basis for uncontrollable growth of inflation.

As has been discussed above, the new stage of *perestroika* of the Soviet economy will continue approximately to the mid-1990s. Its success in many respects depends upon the substance and quality of the new, thirteenth five-year plan. Past years have shown how difficult it is to combine the traditional model of the five-year plan with the new methods of economic management. It is important to learn from acquired experience and to develop a five-year plan that will, in full, correspond to the new philosophy of economic management, to both the spirit and letter of economic reform. The model and substance of the thirteenth five-year plan will in the very near future become yet another payment in this fierce struggle.

The enormous energy required to solve the problems of the current stage of reform should not displace questions of strategy and perspective from their places of primary importance. By this is meant the fundamental changes in the structure of the entire economy, the carrying out of large-scale social and scientific-technical programs, and the preparation for the convertability of the ruble.

The subject of particular concern is the formation of a new generation of economic managers, capable of working in new conditions, possessing economic methods of management, well able to orient themselves in the domestic and world market. New, nontraditional solutions must be sought, and broad-based international cooperation is needed. No less important is the general raising of the economic culture – the technological culture, the culture of labor in the broadest sense of the word, the culture of commercial relationships, the culture of managerial activity. The low level of this culture is the deep-rooted weakness of our economic system, and this weakness will be more evident when measured by *perestroika*. Therefore, even today we must have a clear, well thought out program to raise our economic culture.

A realistic attitude, inherent in the Soviet point of view on the process of *perestroika* of the economy, enables us to give a balanced evaluation of the path already trod, to see the successes and deficiencies and the complicated nature of the tasks ahead. This approach does not give cause for exaggerated optimism, nor for despondency or dismay. The choice has been made and there is no going back. As far as difficulties and failures are concerned, they will only stimulate the creative energy of the true fighters for *perestroika* and will increase the necessity for scientific recommendations and practical actions.

Ends and Means in Gorbachev's Economic Agenda

Ed A. Hewett

I.

Any analysis of *perestroika* should include a sober examination of the underlying roots of current difficulties encountered by that process. In my view these difficulties lie in the lack of a coherent strategy for the transition from a centrally planned economy to some form of a socialist market economy, and in the absence of a consensus on the character of that new socialist market system.

If there were a textbook written on transitions – alas, there is no such textbook – I am sure that there would be something like three basic points about the course of the transition from a centrally planned to a market economy. First, there would have to be a decision in principle that the existing system was unable to meet the needs of the society whatever those needs might be, and that therefore the system had to be changed. Second, it would be necessary to forge a consensus on a new system which would better meet the needs of society. Third, a strategy would have to be devised for the transition from the old system to the new system.

So far the Gorbachev reforms constitute a much less orderly transition than that depicted in my hypothetical textbook. Indeed they seem to be an unusually messy transition even by the standards of the usual gap between reality and textbooks. Only in one sense is there no gap; it is virtually a unanimously held view in the Soviet Union that the existing system, the one inherited from Stalin and from Brezhnev, is unacceptable. Across the entire political spectrum – from very conservative to very radical – the one point of agreement in the USSR seems to be that the current system will not do, and therefore must be changed. That is probably the only point on which there is complete consensus now in the Soviet Union. On the other two points – the outline of the new system and how to get there – there is very little consensus.

II.

Four years into Gorbachev's reign – the equivalent of one term in the American presidency – the outline of the new system remains very general, with even important details (for example, the nature of property rights) still unresolved. It was not until the June 1987 Plenum that even the general outline emerged in the form of a document approved by the Party, and a set of accompanying decrees defining what might be called the »contours« of the system.[1]

The system Soviet leaders hope to create can be summarized in three principles. First, the center will plan much less than it has in the past, but it will plan much better. The idea is that central authorities will focus on those aspects of the system which are most important to them – the structure of investment, the level of investment, the general direction of technological change – matters which some Western societies address through industrial policies.

The second principle is that lower-level units in the system, most notably, enterprises, will have much more room for maneuver than in the past, much more authority to make decisions; but on the other hand they will assume much more responsibility for the decisions they make. So that now there are provisions amounting to a bankruptcy law in the Soviet Union: enterprises can fail. On the other hand enterprises can make substantial profits and retain much of them, which is a departure from the past. I am only talking about the principle codified in law, not about how it has been implemented so far.

The third principle follows from the first two, namely, that the price and financial systems will have to be much more flexible than in the past, assuming the guidance of resource allocation, a task previously handled by the central administration. Prices will have to be flexible, reflecting supply and demand; the financial system will have to move capital around, responding to economic criteria and not to political criteria; and so on.

There is a fourth principle that some Soviets might mention and that is worker control of enterprises, but that principle has received to my mind less attention so far than the first three. To be sure, there is a good deal of discussion of »democratization« of economic decision-making in the USSR. But that essentially is a code word for the decentralization embodied in the first three principles.

Beyond these very basic, and generally laudatory, principles, very little seems to have been resolved. It is still not at all clear to Soviet leaders, or to their advisors, what socialism will or should actually look like in the 21st century. This becomes quite clear when you ask Soviets, as I have, to characterize even in the most general terms the USSR of the 21st century which they have in mind. Will it most closely resemble today's Sweden? Or will it be closer to Hungary? Or, will it be *sui generis*, a system we cannot now picture? Is it possible to at least sketch out what the approach will be to the mix of private and state ownership of the means of production? What ownership rights will accrue to individuals in the new system? One could add a long list of additional questions. There is now a very interesting public debate on these issues in the USSR – and Leonid Abalkin is one of the most active participants – but it is still rather unfocused, and there is certainly no consensus on the answers.

III.

Attention to the third principle in my hypothetical textbook – the transition strategy – was almost non-existent during 1985–86. The approach was cavalier, and the results predictable. By 1988 Soviet leaders had begun to realize, in light of some very hard lessons, that a transition without a strategy is a very dangerous thing.

The basic approach in 1985–86 was to work on various parts of the reform, then introduce them as they were ready, with little regard for the interconnections in the economy, and even less regard for the internal consistency of the myriad measures being codified into law. Even today, with the benefit of four years of hindsight, the approach is not dramatically improved.

I can cite many illustrative examples; Soviet economists could offer many more. To take just one example, consider enterprise autonomy. Soviet leaders genuinely believe in the principle that enterprises should be given much more autonomy than they have had in the past. The enterprise law under which all enterprises operate as of January 1989

137

enshrines that principle into the law. On the other hand Mikhail Gorbachev has retained most of the forty-odd ministries that guide industrial and agricultural production in the Soviet Union. He has even created a new administrative level in the superministries and superministerial bodies – for example, the machine-building *biuro*, and *Gosagroprom* – led by deputy prime ministers. Moreover, the administrative apparatus still faces quantitative planning targets generated by Gosplan.

This fundamental contradiction in the reforms has led to some marvelous battles. Consider, for example, the showdown between Uralmash, Nikolai Ryzhkov's old factory, and its ministry, *Mintiazhmash* (Ministry of Heavy, Power and Transport Machinebuilding; formerly simply Ministry of Heavy and Transport Machinebuilding). At the end of 1987, *Mintiazhmash* sent to its factories detailed plan targets for 1988 in direct contradiction to the provisions of the enterprise law under which all of these enterprises would be operating in that year. Seventeen of the enterprises protested that the ministry's targets were illegal. *Mintiazhmash* persisted and sixteen of the enterprises backed down, sensitive to the still enormous power of »their« ministry. Uralmash stood its ground and called *Izvestiia*. (*Izvestiia*, March 23, 1988, No. 83, p. 3.) The result was a fascinating look at the consequences of this contradictory tendency in Gorbachev's reforms to talk of decentralization, while retaining, and using, a central apparatus.

Uralmash wanted to set lower targets for some products, including earth-moving equipment, because its orders did not justify the quantities *Mintiazhmash* was calling for in its (illegal) plan. *Mintiazhmash*, on the other hand, argued that it had to set those targets because Gosplan had set targets for the ministry. In the end no one was terribly happy. Uralmash ended up with a visit by a commission from the machine-building *biuro*, but a generally clean bill of health. The ministry ended up claiming, by implication, that it, not Uralmash, had been right all along. (*Izvestiia*, December 15, 1988, 2). And, at least for this observer, the conclusion was that both sides were right; it is the inconsistency in the basic design of the reform that is the source of the difficulties, not perfidious ministries or uppity enterprises.

This is merely one of thousands of stories from the Soviet Union, illustrating the contradictions inherent in this transition, in which some things are changing, and some things are not.

If there are any overall criteria that are guiding the transition, they seem to be of two sorts: political and opportunistic. The notion seems to be that work proceeds simultaneously on various parts of the reform. When one of the parts is ready, and if it appears that it is politically acceptable, then it is introduced. If, on the other hand, other parts aren't ready, or if they are politically too sensitive, then they wait, irrespective of the interconnections in the system.

This approach has not only led to rather colorful confrontations such as that between Uralmash and *Mintiazhmash*; it has led to a fatal flaw in the entire process. The enterprise law came into effect in January 1988, and as of January 1989 all enterprises in industry formally operate in the new regime. It gives enterprises formal autonomy in many of the decisions they make, telling them in essence to go out and earn money. At the same time the price system remains rigid, with prices that are ten, twenty or thirty years old. Many of the prices are totally detached from economic reality, so that enterprises perceive some products as profitable which are not, at the same time perceiving other products as unprofitable which actually are quite profitable for society. The price reform should have come at the same time as the enterprise reform. But it hasn't, because the fate of price reform was linked to the retail price reform, and the retail price reform is too sensitive to do now politically. So the politicians have said to the economists, »Yes, this is important. We should do it. But we must wait.« Under that set of criteria the transition goes ahead with the predictable problems now so obvious in the reform.

IV.

What are the reasons for the mayhem? Why is the transition going wrong? In the first place, it is understandable that Soviet society, and certainly the Soviet economics profession, was simply unprepared in 1985 to introduce or even think about a new system which they had been forbidden to discuss for the last six decades. It is too much to expect that the Soviet economists suddenly, by some miracle, would be ready to talk about a new system, when for decades they have been unable to discuss anything other than »further perfection« of an almost »perfect« system. As one Soviet economist said to me, »For years we were ignored, and suddenly now we have to go visit the Council of

139

Ministers or the Central Committee every week to give advice. They expect us to reach into our back pocket and to pull out a new system. I reach into my back pocket, and there is nothing there. It is not my fault, but that is not a very satisfactory thing to say to the leadership.« The second reason for what I would call mayhem is that politicians perceived that the economists were not ready to come up with a new system, yet it was clear that something had to be done, that they could not afford to wait five or ten or fifteen years for their economists to work something out. So they went ahead, sometimes simply issuing, with some modification, decrees worked out by the Brezhnevite bureaucracy, at the same time pressuring their economists and a restructured bureaucracy to come up with something more coherent and far-reaching. All of this took longer than expected, and the sense of urgency grew during 1986–87, leading to the pressure to introduce new measures, even if only parts of the new system were prepared. If there is one word which best captures the four years of reform under Gorbachev it is »improvisation.«

The fact that it has taken (and is taking) longer than expected reflects not only difficulties Soviet economists have in adjusting to their new task, but also to the fact that there are no satisfactory theories anywhere in the world to guide a transition of the sort now being attempted in the USSR. The experience of socialist economies which have tried it – Hungary and China being the most prominent examples – are far from encouraging. Western economic theory focuses primarily on how to regulate market systems already in existence, while offering little advice on how to create a market system, particularly in a country such as the USSR. Thus Soviet economists find themselves, like it or not, on the frontiers of applied economics. They are under pressure to produce results quickly, yet they are not wholly unconstrained in the recommendations they can put forward. On the whole it is an unenviable position.

I myself do not have a theory of transition to offer, or at least not one sufficiently prepared to see the light of day. But, short of that theory I can offer several observations on the current process, and my concerns about it, in the form of two Confucian proverbs which probably exist, although I have yet to find them. Until I do, I will have to rely on my own formulations.

The first Confucian proverb goes something like this: »If you start off on a journey without knowing where you are going, you may not like where you end up.« And what I am thinking of there is that by relying on improvisation to design a transition, the economic system can end up in some very unpleasant situations which will be difficult to reverse. For example, the commitment to decentralization in the Soviet Union is extremely strong, extremely deep, particularly among reform economists. The commitment to competition – I mean competition the way that we think of it in the West (in Russian the word would be *konkurentsia*) – is not as strong as the commitment to decentralization. Therefore it is quite possible that this reform will bring about a decentralization in a system in which monopolies are prevalent and that therefore monopolies will run rampant, raising prices and reducing quality. In other words, unless sufficient thought is given to the ultimate nature of the reformed system, the Soviets could end up with a decentralized monopolized system.

Secondly, it is certainly the case in the Soviet Union that the disenchantment with central planning runs very deep. It runs so deep now that there is a danger that Soviet economists will advocate a total rejection of central planning, even in areas where it should be used. That is, a revulsion with central control could lead to excessive decentralization. The second Confucian proverb, which I have made up, is the following: »When you do figure out where you would like to go, you might find that it is harder to get there than it would have been if you had known from the beginning where you were going.« What I am thinking of here for example is that improvisation can lead to mistakes which discredit the entire reform process. The Soviet population is naturally suspicious of the reform process because of the very real possibilities for inflation, unemployment, and major shifts in the income and wealth distributions. If the early measures, taken without serious planning, lead to high rates of inflation, to chaos, to greater shortages, then it may be very difficult to convince people to go further when Soviet leaders finally figure out where they want to go. Moreover if the first tentative and somewhat mistaken moves towards economic reform use up reserves (political and economic) that would have been very useful and important later on, then it will be that much more difficult to move decisively when the final goal of the process is much clearer.

There are, of course, advantages to the approach to *perestroika* that has emerged in the Soviet Union. In 1985 the population was not really

141

ready to accept a radical reform. The leadership might not even have been really ready to do what indeed they now seem to be ready to do. Partial measures can be very useful in breaking down resistance, in beginning to force a rethinking. Coops are in that category. Coops, despite the fact that they haven't gone as well as some would have hoped, may be useful in showing people the possibilities of a more radical reform in the supply of services. Joint ventures may also play that role.

The other advantage of improvisation is that if the population is not ready for radical reform, it is possible to use *glasnost* and the debate associated with *glasnost* to create a dynamic which may lead to changes that go much farther than would have been acceptable if everything had been mapped out from the beginning. Matters can get out of control in a good way.

V.

I conclude with a few remarks on the accomplishments of *perestroika* and the threats to *perestroika*. The greatest accomplishment of *perestroika* is *glasnost* itself and the debate that has come from it. *Glasnost* has revealed information about the workings of the system which has had the effect of discrediting the past, a very important thing for politicians to do. Gorbachev has brought tremendous enthusiasm to this task. Now in any speech he gives, he discredits the past in order to cut off any possibility of retreat. In fact I think in some ways he has gone overboard. I joke with some of my Soviet colleagues that they should publish a quarterly bulletin on Brezhnev's GNP, because it keeps falling. *Glasnost* is also important because it is bringing us new economic information, although on that front progress is not nearly as rapid as it should be.

The second accomplishment comes from *glasnost* and that is the debate itself. As you can see from listening to our Soviet colleagues here, and as any of you know who have been to the Soviet Union or who read the Soviet press, the debate now in the Soviet Union is extremely exciting. Soviet society is now thinking about itself again, thinking about socialism in a way they have not done since the 1920s. I can only say that if I were given a choice of when to be born and what to

142

do, I would want to be born when I was as the Soviet specialist that I am. It is a very exciting time to be watching the Soviet Union, to play a part, however small, in the awakening of this society.

Finally, the opening to the West is an accomplishment of *perestroika*. Although it is primarily an opening in the realm of ideas, it is also an opening in the economy itself. Much more serious attention is being given now than in the past to the need to open the Soviet economy to the world, to integrate the Soviet economy with the world economy. Indeed it is now understood that economic progress of the sort that is desired in the Soviet Union would not come without such an opening. What are the threats to *perestroika*? The obvious one is that there is very little change in the real economic situation; and to the extent that it has changed, it has come primarily as a result of central measures and not as a reform itself. For example, the improvements in housing construction come primarily as central measures, because the twelfth five-year plan is a traditional five-year plan and not because of the better workings of the economic system.

The new economic mechanism, which is indeed very new and very young, has brought nothing yet. Moreover, some of the policy changes that have been made may have led to problems and not to improvements in economic performance (for example, the financial consequences of the anti-alcohol campaign). Furthermore, Mikhail Gorbachev has been in some ways a very unlucky man. He came into office in 1985 and oil prices fell, devaluing the USSR's major export. Chernobyl was an economic blow, Armenia another. It would have been much easier to do some of the things he wanted to do if he had not had some of the unpleasant surprises he has had.

A second major threat to *perestroika* lies in the lack of theory about the transition and the new system. Therefore it is extremely important that Soviet economists spend much more time now in the theory of transition and in the theory of a new system. It is time to think through what the new system will look like, moving beyond yet more justifications for rejecting the old system, and it is clearly well past time to think about the economics of the transition, because there are serious dangers here, and of course the people who are thinking least about it are the politicians (who govern the transition).

A third point I would make is that *glasnost* has led to many interesting stories, but less interesting statistics. The liberalization and reform of

143

economic statistics is going at a snail's pace. Soviet economists need better statistics, and they need them now in order to guide them in the reform and also to guide them in the critique of the old system. There is a disturbing tendency in the Soviet Union to rely on rumors, anecdotes, or half-baked analysis of the past to guide important policy choices. For example, I think Soviet economists are too quick to talk about the economic crisis the Soviet Union is now in, based primarily on the fact that the General Secretary talks that way, or the fact that they know it is true without trying to document it. If they did want to document it, they would have to use primarily CIA data to do it, because Soviet data are so unreliable. Or, they are too quick to talk about shortages in the Soviet Union, when we know that the supplies of many goods have improved and from my point of view it is still a question of whether shortages have actually grown worse. When I ask Soviet economists, »How do you know they have grown worse?« the answer is »Because we know it.« That is not a good enough answer for an economist. Better data would support the development of stronger empirical traditions, which would improve the quality of analysis supporting policy.

I do not envy the task that Soviet economists have set for themselves. It is easier to criticize a reform than to figure out how to do it. I very much support them in their effort and I know many of my colleagues are ready to be of assistance where they can, although we know that we have very little to provide.

Pricing Policy and Financial System Adjustments as Major Factors in the Reform of the Soviet Economic Management System

Nikolai Petrakov

A major strategic factor promoting long-term dynamic development of the Soviet economy is the restructuring of the management system. The essence of radical reforming the management system seems to involve the integrated change in the planning system, new ways of allocating production inputs and the restructuring of the pricing and monetary-credit system. Major issues are concerned with the following transitions:

- from detailed planning in real terms to planning economic norms (standards);
- from rigidly determined allocation of material resources and centralized assignment of consumers and producers to the creation of a capital-goods market;
- from cost-based pricing to a balanced, planned one;
- from tax schedules established for individual firms and enterprises to a uniform system of taxes and payments to the government and local budgets; and
- from the monopoly by a single bank to a flexible banking system.

The above transformations in the economic management system are aimed at providing flexibility and dynamic properties to the socialist economy. However, a necessary condition for their successful development is to change radically two key factors in the management system of the planned economy, i.e., prices and finance. Therefore in this paper we will focus particularly on various aspects of modernization of pricing policy and the finance-credit system in the entire mechanism of managing and controlling the Soviet economy.

It would have been an exaggeration to claim that the planned price system represents a frozen, absolutely static element in the management mechanism. For example, through 1980 wholesale and purchase prices have been repeatedly revised, the methods of setting prices for new

145

engineering products have been changed, and prices for quite a few consumer goods and services have been adjusted. But perhaps due to these activities on the »pricing battlefield,« we are facing a very grave situation. The point is that these changes and numerous corrections to the rules of setting price levels for individual product groups have been carried out incoherently, without a unified methodological background and without analysing and forecasting market response or supply-demand dynamics. Consistency between wholesale prices for industrial products, purchase prices for agricultural raw materials, and food products and retail prices has been broken. An especially great gap has emerged between purchase and retail prices. At the same time, wholesale prices for industrial commodities have deviated considerably from purchase prices (which creates the necessity of setting two price levels for many goods delivered to the agricultural sector) as well as from retail prices (which necessiates government subsidies for some products and artificially high turnover tax rates for other products).

A marked distortion is observed not only between prices for industrial, agricultural and consumer goods but also within each price category. Thus, relative prices for various food products have been significantly biased (for instance, meat-fruits, bread-vegetables), as is also the case for manufactured consumer goods (especially clothing, footwear, household goods, etc.).

The overall wholesale-price pattern does not meet current trends of economic development and is inconsistent vis-à-vis the production-costs structure. The Soviet Union belongs to highly industrialised countries that are distinguished by relatively cheap (vis-à-vis raw materials) manufactured goods. Yet, the relationships between current wholesale prices still produce the opposite picture. As a result, the profit included in the prices of products manufactured by the engineering complex exceeds by almost 200 percent the investment requirements for extended reproduction. Contrary to this, accumulated capital in the fuel-power complex is 25 – 30 percent less than is needed to grow at the rate envisaged by two recent five-year plans and the socio-economic development plan of the Soviet Union for 1986-1990.

Artificially low pricing of primary goods creates economic obstacles for implementing advanced production technologies, broad diffusion of resource-saving technologies and combined methods of resource use. »Fundamental Principles of Radical Restructuring the Economic

146

Management System« stresses that »in carrying out the radical pricing reform, *all categories of prices and tariffs must be revised on a unified basis* and an inherent coordination between wholesale *purchase and retail prices and tariffs has to be ensured.*«[1] An integrated approach requires that for all categories of prices, common problems be specified and solved in the first instance. Among such key problems is the problem of implementing a fundamentally new approach to price-setting practice in primary extracting and manufacturing industries.

One of the reasons for extensive trends in resource use is that differential rent is completely neglected in price setting. To remove this deficiency, it is necessary to proceed from the principle of setting prices based on average industry costs to that based on incremental or marginal costs. The price would then indicate what additional costs will be incurred in producing an additional million tons of coal or metal or, alternatively, what extra resources will become available, should it be possible to save these costs.

At present, a heated debate is raging in the Soviet Union on the opportunities for changing price relationships between extracting and manufacturing industries without causing dramatic inflation. It is from this aspect that one should consider the accumulation-demand balance of financial resources in the industrial sector. In this instance, we may be satisfied with aggregate data, since we are interested here in the general trend and basic relationships, and moreover, the statistical agencies as yet, unfortunately, prefer to publish only aggregated indicators.

The table below demonstrates that a stylised »pillow« of more than 100 billion rubles exists between actual selling prices of industrial goods and self-financing prices. This magnitude allows in fact a minimal reserve for maneuvering when a change in relative prices is to be effected. A considerable portion of this amount may be »transferred« to the agricultural sector in the course of the purchase-price reform based on the elimination of regional differentials, the introduction of rent payments and a unique price for a use-value unit. This would create favorable economic conditions for the optimal concentration of agricultural production in the regions of effective farming and cattle breeding, for regional specialization and for reducing costs due to

1 Proceedings of the CPSU Central Committee Plenary Meeting, June 25-26, 1987, Moscow, Politizdat, 1987, pp. 86 – 97.

rational allocation of agricultural production and its intensity. Transfer of financial funds to agriculture through a price system (instead of finance-credit instruments) would radically improve the economic situation in this sector. One should bear in mind that collective – and state – farm profits (21 billion rubles in 1985) conceal the heavy credit debt of agricultural enterprises. At the beginning if 1986, this reached 143.9 billion rubles, and a considerable portion of repayments have been postponed to the twelfth five-year period.[2]

Intra-industry reallocation of accumulated funds should also be radically changed as a result of revising the pricing policy for fuel industries products. At present, the profits earned in the fuel industries' sector comprise 9.1 percent of total profits in the entire industrial sector; in terms of investments, the fuel industries' share is 28.4 percent.[3]

It is important to stress that we are speaking here of intra-industry (or, if we take into account the introduction of rent in the prices of agricultural produce, intra-economy) reallocation of funds. As a result of dramatic change in relative prices, the necessity of substantial budget injections for the fuel industries and agriculture will be removed. The budget will no longer be used as a huge »pumping system« that uselessly transfers financial assets from one sector of the economy to another.

The transition to the intensive type of socialist economic development radically changes requirements placed on the financial policy and also defines in a new way the role of the state budget. The sources of budget revenue must be closely »pegged« to the performance of individual enterprises and associations in terms of efficiency in using economic resources. By realizing the property right for means of production, the state must tax the actual income produced in proportion to the amount of economic resources granted to an enterprise (capital, land, mineral reserves, etc.). In this way the state establishes some form of leasing relations with groups of people representing socialist enterprises and imposes normative conditions for minimal efficiency in using a portion of the public production potential that has been transferred to a specific group of workers. Due to this, the major sources of budget revenue must be represented by capital and labor taxes and rent payments. Of course, this does not mean that a progressive tax on quasi-rent as a means

2 Problems of Economics (Voprosy Ekonomiki), N° 8, 1986.
3 USSR Statistical Yearbook, 1985 (Narodnoje Ckozyajstvo SSSR v 1985 godu), pp. 550, 368.

of some sort of income-equilibrating instrument should be completely eliminated, since quasi-rent is generated due to unredictable fluctuations in the economic system.

Under the intensive type of social production, changes in financial policy are predominantly expressed in a radical change between the sources for financing the process of economic growth. Budget finance continues to contribute a significant part of the total amount of investments. At the same time, the leading position of budget expenditures for the development of production starts to shift toward large-scale national programs of an inter-industry nature, toward the development of new regions, toward the transport and communications network and toward other elements of the production infrastructure. Budget support for inefficiently performing enterprises and inefficient economic decisions has to be severely cut. Concurrently, the weight of budget allocations for financing public programs and the development of the arts, culture and basic science should be considerably increased. In the light of these changes in budget expenditures, the financing of enterprises, associations and industries in terms of self-support for expanded reproduction by money funds acquires a much more important dimension. The self-financing system represents a form of implementing business policies for a considerable portion of investment activities.

Shareholding forms of investment concentration will be ever more widely used in the next few years. In terms of improving dynamic properties of the economic system, the use of shareholding types of funds accumulation and reallocation enjoy a number of advantages. First, stock companies make it possible to avoid solving economic problems at the expense of the state budget. Second, they provide an opportunity to concentrate investments at the most important sites. And third, real democratic principles begin to be employed in the area of formulating investment policies. The stockholding form of attracting funds for construction purposes is based on the principle of free will and mutual commercial involvment in the development of economic entities. When a state (public) enterprise purchases shares of another enterprise from its own development funds, this may be taken as a peculiar form of voting, as a public expression of confience for particular economic initiatives. By buying (or not buying) shares issued by socialist enterprises, firms and associations actually participate in the social process of establishing economic priorities.

149

Thus, stockholding forms for creating and developing socialist enterprises are a means of removing the investment monopoly held by the central management agencies. The latter previous by made a considerable contribution to large-scale structural changes, but in recent years, they have grown to be retarding forces for economic progress. Excessive investment centralization not based on real needs of economic development leads to non-economic motivations in the determination of investment policies.

Relationship between funds of industrial enterprises in 1985 and demand for them[1]:

	billion rubles
1. Profits	100.6
2. Other accumulated funds, including turnover tax	49.9
3. Depreciation	34.7
4. Total (1 + 2 + 3)	185.2
5. Investments	65.5[2]
6. Incentive fund (production development fund excluded)	13.3
7. Total (5 + 6)	78.8
8. Excess of accumulated funds and depreciation over total demand under self-financing conditions (4 – 7)	106.4

1 Calculated from »USSR Statistical Year book«, 1985 (Narodnoje Ckozayistvo SSSR v 1985 godu), Moscow, Finansy i Statistika, 1986, pp. 336, 550, 557 – 559.
2 In estimate prices as of January 1, 1984.

Perestroika and Foreign Economic Dependency

Georges Sokoloff

1. Dependency and Stagnation

Between 1958 and 1975, the economic development of the Soviet Union was largely based on a policy of investment, which increasingly favored the importing of foreign equipment. By the end of this period, 25 % of invested equipment was of foreign origin,[1] with Western equipment suppliers possessing a major share of imports. From 1965 to 1975, their market share in the Soviet Union rose from 19 % to 40 %. It was also during this period that the Soviet convertible-currency debt largely arose (roughly $7.5 billion in 1975).

Although this strategy had certainly been expensive, it was able to be justified by the fact that respectable economic achievements were maintained. However, in the mid-1970s, things changed dramatically. Economic growth slowed, eventually coming to a complete halt – undoubtedly due to the sudden restrictions imposed on investment.[2] Equipment imports also slowed, although probably to a lesser degree than investment. This seems to be indicated by the fact that at the beginning of the 1980s, imported equipment valued at 5 billion rubles were not being used, remaining instead in depots.[3] By 1986 more than half (51%) of the invested equipment stemmed from imports, with 15 % being of Western origin.[4]

The acquisition of unfinished goods, which are indispensable for maintaining industrial equipment from Western countries, formed a major share of purchases in strong currencies. However, currency reserves had been heavily depleted by the large imports of corn, which

---

1 G. Sokoloff »The Economy of Detente, the Soviet Union and Western Capital«, Berg Publishers, Leamington spa, Hamburg, New York, 1987.
2 For one of the first of the numerous studies of this phenomenon written by this analyst, see K. Val'tukh »Investicionnyj kompleks i intensifikacia proizvodstva«. Eko, 1982, 3.
3 A. Ivaščenko »Čto mešaet Merkuriju«. Pravda, 16/8/88.
4 B. Djakin, »Napravlenija korennoj perestroiki vnešneekonomičeskogo kompleksa«. Planovoe khozjajstvo, 1988,1.

151

had been necessary due to an extended period of poor agricultural performance. Revenues from oil exports, which had been a major source of income during the period of high prices, dried up with the sudden drop in prices in 1984, which led to a worsening of the trade balance with Western countries. The net debt in strong currencies has more than tripled since 1975, reaching some $24.5 billion in 1987.

The turn thus taken by the Soviet economy in the last 12 years has been rather uncharacteristic for this socialist country (at least for a period of peace): stagnation accompanied by increasing foreign dependence. Due to the deterioration of political relations between East and West during the 1980s, this situation gave rise to economic xenophobia. The president of the Academy of Sciences, Alexandrov, attributed in this fashion the economic misfortunes of his country to the »plague of imports.«

Since Gorbachev has arrived on the scene, the administrative system of allocation of productive goods is being questioned. At the end of 1984, a senior Soviet planning official had to admit that »the apparatus of Gosplan is no longer able to master economic activity.« The new willingness, however, to give up administered economy does not exclude the traditional willingness to get rid of excessive dependence towards foreign countries. The present Soviet authorities have adopted a principle widely applied in the West whereas Brezhnev had replaced reforms by imports. And it seems evident that they have even been tempted to adopt a particularly audacious corrolary: would it not be conceivable that, amongst other benefits, the reforms could replace imports? As a matter of fact, the decisions taken in view of a reconstruction of the mechanism of Soviet economic relations[5] are of this kind although this is not put in such harsh terms.

2. Reforms and Economic Balance

Most of the decisions taken by Soviet authorities in this area stem from three major measures: the decrees of August 19, 1986, of January 13, 1987 (concerned solely with mixed companies) and of September 17, 1987. The decree of August 1986 dealt with reforms in the administration of foreign economic relations and forecasted the

5 For a comprehensive overview, see G. Sagalov » Novyj mekhanizm vnešne-ekonomiceskikh svjazej i mězdunarodnogo sotrudnijčestva«. Voprosy ekonomiki, 1988, 5.

152

implementation of the economic reforms proclaimed by the Central Committee in June 1987. The focus was on the reinvigoration of the economy via the emancipation of enterprises.[6] With the exception of public orders, enterprises are now free to accept and negotiate contracts with partners of their choosing, both within the Soviet Union and abroad. Companies are thus to be considered truly responsible for their day-to-day management and development, which is to lead them to regain their lost sense of initiative and innovation. The inspiration behind these moves is a liberal-patriotic one: the freedom given to companies is to spur them to operate as well as, or better than, foreign firms.

The decrees aimed at immediate implementation, containing in this regard a number of precise specifications. In addition, they account for the numerous constraints accompanying this »period of transition,« stressing the urgent need for an overall economic policy. But the underlying philosophy is to give concrete dimensions to the desire to reduce the extensive foreign dependence. Yuri Ivanov, president of the former Vnechtorgbank, designated three principles in this regard:[7] the development of a Soviet entrepreneurial mind directed towards exports, the improvement of competitiveness in those sectors designated for exports (e.g., the mechanical construction industry), and the determination to use imports more economically. It is from these aspects that we will briefly look at the substance of the above-mentioned decrees.

a) Efforts are under way to revive and extend the traditional practice[8] of allowing firms to dispose of currency funds; this is to be the principal instrument for encouraging exports. The funds represent the »currency revenues« that a company is obliged to earn in a ratio varying with the degree of elaboration of its products. These range from 2-50%, although they generally have a value of 10-30%.[9] The results of the first trimester of 1988 as given by Ivan Ivanov indicate that the proportion of revenues going to the funds are an estimated 25% as far

6 This paragraph is directly inspired by the comments of the decree of 19/8/86 made by the representatives of IMEMO during a meeting with CEPII in October 1986.
7 Ju. Ivanov »Vneštorgbank SSSR i perestrojka mekhanizma vnešneekonomičeskoj dejatel'nosti«. Vnešnjaja torgovlja, 1987,11.
8 »Commerce extérieur et planification en URSS«. Le courrier des pays de l'Est,1969, no 121.
9 A. Ivaščenko, op.cit.

as transactions in transferable rubles are concerned and at least 17 % of operations in strong currencies.[10] Companies do not have direct access to their funds' currencies. These assets are instead credited to their ruble account, after a conversion transaction based on »currency coefficients,« called DVKs; the latter are differentiated according to product, country and kind of currency.[11] This practice has been adopted to compensate for the considerable differences between Soviet and international prices, (hence DVKs ranging from 0.3 to 6.0). The accounting result is virtually the same as that achieved by the previous system, which credited a company's account in terms of internal prices to which an export augmentation had been added. However, the economic result is considerably different: companies are now allowed to reaccess their currency funds in order to acquire equipment (assuming the funds stem from trade activity in convertible currencies) as well as products designed to improve the living conditions of the employees (funds of transferable rubles). Furthermore, the new practice is of pedagogical value, familiarizing companies with the use of currency exchange rates, even though this is still rather restricted. It also teaches them to observe »self-financing in currencies«: goods cannot be imported when they are not covered by equivalent resources.

b) Emphasis has been placed on the improved competitiveness of these products, which are perceived to have the best chances to succeed when exported. To achieve this, the foreign trade monopoly was deconcentrated. Since January 1, 1987, 22 administrations and 77 large industrial groups have been allowed to deal directly with foreign countries. Of these, 8 administrations and 49 industrial groups are found within the mechanical construction sector; others include those administrations and industrial groups traditionally operating in the export field – e.g., the Ministries of the Merchant Fleet, Fishing, etc. This delegation of foreign-trade rights has been accompanied by a transformation of the system of main intermediaries in foreign trade, although the former »centers« continue to exist as Foreign Trade Unions subject to the control of the Ministry of Foreign Economic

10 I. Ivanov »Gosudarstvennaja monopolija vnešnej torgovli, formy i problemy na 70-letnem rubeže«. Vnešnjaja torgovlja, 1988,4.
11 Amongst the many articles devoted to the D.V.K.'s see especially A. Šurkalin »Vnešneekonomičeskie aspekty soveršenstvovanija cenoobrazovanija«. Voprosy ekonomiki, 1988,5.

Relations. In addition, sectoral ministries will have their own foreign-trade organizations, and industrial groups possess their own foreign-trade companies. Exports are thus sought to be promoted by providing not only access to currency resources but also autonomy of action.

c) A more economic use of imports supplements the precited measures. The new rules relating to foreign activities also seek to discourage companies from importing. In this regard, it is not certain that the DVK which allow the industrial groups to access their currency funds in order to import are more unfavourable than the DVK they had received when they exported.[12] It is, however, clear that the funds do not offer sufficient resources. To take into acount this situation, these resources are to be augmented with special loans from the Vnechekononombank. However, the conditions for accessing these loans are so severe that it is hard to imagine how companies might venture to ask for them.[13]

The prevention of imports by the reforms mainly concerns a more general aspect – namely, that now everything will figure under the heading of »foreign economic relations.« The term appears in the new name of the main central institutions: the new State Commission of the Council of Ministers, created in 1986, which is charged with the coordination of the work in the different administrations, with the formulation of a strategy and the implementation of reforms; a new ministry, set up in January 1988, formed by a fusion between the Ministry of Foreign Trade and the GKES; and the Vnechekonombank, which has supplanted the Vnechtorgbank. These formal changes signal a more fundamental reality, in that the variety of paths for entering into relations with foreign markets have been opened up at the cost of strictly commercial operations. The rearrangements are mainly of benefit for mixed companies and for more recent innovations (consortia, free-trade zones, etc.) that are intended to facilitate the functioning of these companies. But in essence, this reflects the wish to find a less expensive alternative to the import of turn-key installations. Savings are expected from the non-disruption of technology transfers and currencies acquired through exports.

In summary, the reforms most certainly are not striving toward autarky.

---

12 I. Doronin »Problemy soveršenstvovanija valjutno-finansovykh instrumentov, čast'1«. Vnešnjaja torgovlja, 1988,4.
13 See: Ju. Ivanov, op. cit.

On the contrary, the increase in the number of potential actors in foreign economic relations – such as local authorities, companies and banks by actions, as well as cooperatives presage a far more open Soviet economy.[14] It is also clear that these moves seek to restore equilibrium in the foreign-exchange balance.

3. Perspectives

a) At the moment, the new principles that have engendered reform are the subject of heated debate, and it is not certain that the reformers will triumph. At times, reform is only old practices with new clothing; for instance, »public orders,« which is applied in both domestic and foreign market strategies, is the most classical instrument of a directed economy, i.e., purchase orders based upon state-guaranteed supplies. On occasion, the new principles are applied contrary to their aims. Sectoral ministries entitled to export to foreign markets thus exploit this ability in order to exercise even tighter control over »their« industries. As was the case with DVKs, a »shock of principles« can lead to a proliferation of administrative instruments. Aside from the internal and international prices, they constitute a new category of evaluations whose number seems for the moment to be up to 4,000, and which combine elements of pure calculation, of encouragement, of negotiation and of a pure arbitrariness.[15] In short, they spell a new chapter in the development of bureaucracy. Furthermore, the fact that the actual process of international transactions is still kept separate from the internal bookkeeping within industries means that an extremely complex, artificial system of accounting is maintained between the budget, the Vnechekonombank, intermediaries in foreign trade and producers.[16] Therefore, the distinction between public finance and foreign accounts is not simplified, and the preparation of managers for macro-economic regulation is not furthered.

14 A.Tiraspolski »Coopération URSS-Ouest: les nouveaux partenaires des firmes occidentales«. Le Courrier des Pays de l'Est, November 1988, no334.
15 The D.V.K's constitute the most questioned aspects of the perestroika of foreign economic relations. Apart the already quoted articles by Surkalin and Doronin, see S. Lavrov and T. Teodorovič »Problemy perestroiki vnešnjkh ekonomičeskikh svjazej«. Voprosy ekonomiki,1988,2.
16 A. Zverev »Valjutnyj mekhanizm vo vnešnetorgovoj rabote promyšlennosti«. Vnešnjaja torgovlja, 1988,8.

The uncertain situation has given rise to two types of proposals. In an article in Pravda, A. Ivaščenko suggested that the reform had engendered disorder and recommended that centralized discipline be readopted. The other proposal, however, seeks to overcome difficulties by leaping forward. For instance, the problems involving DVKs will allegedly disappear once serious price reform and a devaluation of the ruble have been accomplished.[17] Some suggest even further that a market for productive goods be introduced, which would make superfluous an administered reform of prices,[18] or that the ruble be made convertible. The drawback to these latter proposals, however, is that the problems they address are larger than the ones originally sought to be resolved.

b) Due to the problems that the implementation of perestroika is encountering, the reforms tend to aggravate rather than improve the foreign-exchange balance of the Soviet Union. The loans offered by several West European governments will probably not solve the problems. These financial offers represent a general misunderstanding in the West of the type of cooperation needed to promote perestroika from abroad. Nevertheless, a certain amount of crash programs with high Western participation will undoubtedly be necessary to assure a higher degree of domestic popularity.

c) If short- to mid-term difficulties can be overcome and the reforms broadly implemented, then it is conceivable that these reforms contribute to rebalance Soviet external accounts. This result is all the more indispensable in view of the fact that perestroika is currency-consuming. Both the vigor that new forms of foreign economic relations are expected to bring and the essential quality of internal economic mechanisms introduced by the reforms could assist in achieving this result. In short, better control of the economy can be anticipated. But this mechanism alone will not be able to create growth and hence not engender new import needs. The rare Soviet studies on the long-term evolution of external exchanges come to the same conclusion, although based on

---

17 G. Vojtolovskij, P. Zavjalov »Perelomnyj etap.« Pravda, 20/10/1988.
18 N. Astrakhanceva, V. Kuznecov »Ot koefficentov k real'nomu kursu«. Ekonomicveskaja gazeta, 1988, no 35.

different reasoning.[19] These will not be able to be activated before 1995.

d) Mikhail Gorbachev was well advised when he discarded his initial project of an acceleration of growth; he saw that it was contradictory to the reform. At the same time, his critique of »stagnation« turned more institutional – the reigning immobilism – than economic. However, it is inevitable that the economy will be modernized. Soviet economic history demonstrates a number of modernization drives: liberal and then dirigistic, from 1857 to 1877; technocratic, from 1891 to 1902; despotic, from 1929 to 1932; and post-despotic, from 1958 to 1975. These phases were all marked by a high level of internal investment and – in view of the difference in development vis-à-vis the West – the necessary acceptance of foreign economic dependence. The latter continues to exist today, and future economic revival will not aid in reducing it, even if military-industrial activities were to be spectacularly reconverted into civil ones.

The dilemma that will inevitably face the Soviet Union is not reform vs. dependence but rather dependence vs. stagnation. The reforms seek to obviate that both dependence and stagnation recur simultaneously by managing dependence more flexibly and by transforming it into domestic progress. To become effective the reforms require, in the realm of foreign policy, much more than an exhuming of the deplumed phoenix of détente – namely, restoration of Western confidence in Russia as a country principally concerned with its own development. They also require that the Russians free themselves of the traditional double complex of material resignation and spiritual superiority, and accept the true rules of economic behavior.

19 Ju. Šamraj »O tempakh razvitija vnešnej torgovli SSSR v uslovijakh perestrojki vnešneekonomiceskikh svjazej«. Vnešnjaja torgovlja, 1987,7. The study of B. Djakin (op. cit.) also mentions the preparation of a »Conception à long terme du développement des relations économiques de l'URSS pour les années 1991-1995 et jusqu'en l'an 2000« but does only give qualitative informations.

The Soviet Union and World Markets: Implications for the West

Marshall I. Goldman

Because it is the largest country in the world, it is to be expected that the Soviet Union should be more self-sufficient in supplying itself with basic products and raw materials than most other developed countries of the world. That was true as well before the Revolution. The law of averages suggests that at least a little of everything is located on Soviet territory, and in some cases, such as gold, platinum, natural gas, and petroleum, a large quantity of goods is available. But self-sufficiency in raw materials is not the same thing as self-sufficiency or mastery in manufacturing. Traditionally, the Soviet Union and Russia before it has been a net importer of machinery in its dealings with the West. In the pre-Revolutionary period, Russia paid for this machinery with exports of raw materials, particularly with petroleum and grain. Indeed, for many years, Russia was the world's leading exporter of grain. Russia, particularly the Ukraine, was often called the breadbasket of Europe. That was one of the major reasons for Hitler's interest in conquering the Soviet Union. He also had his eye trained on the Soviet Union's crude oil deposits, which were at the time primarily being worked in Azerbaijan.

After the Revolution, there were times, particularly in the 1930s, when Stalin purposely sought to insulate the Soviet Union from foreign world markets. His goal was autarky. In alternating periods, Stalin himself as well as his successors, would sometimes make an effort to increase the Soviet Union's involvement in the world economy and reverse the emphasis on autarky. But even in these more expansive periods, the Soviet Union found itself relatively insular and self-reliant. Estimates of the Soviet ratio of exports to GNP are just necessarily approximate, but the CIA concluded that in 1987, the Soviet ratio of exports to GNP was about 5 % (comparable to the United States) while the Japanese ratio was 18 % and West German was 28 %.

As we noted earlier, size is no guarantee that the Soviet Union will also be self-sufficient in the production of machinery. In both the 18th and 19th centuries, the Russians and Soviets have been dependent on foreigners for much of their machinery. Some observers such as Anthony Sutton insist that in the more recent period the Soviets have found themselves dependent on foreign manufacturers for every new product or technology.[1] Most critics argue that even though the Soviets do rely on foreign suppliers for a disproportionate amount of technology, the situation is in no way as desperate as that. Nonetheless, there are relatively few signs that the Soviet competitiveness will soon improve despite Gorbachev's campaign for *perestroika*.

I.

To gain an appreciation of how difficult it will be for the Soviet Union to change its export profile, it is necessary to consider who the Soviet Union's major non-Communist trading partners are and what kind of goods the Soviets export and import. First let us consider who the major trading partners are. As Table 1 and 2 indicate, Germany is the Soviet Union's main buyer and seller. While the ruble value of its trade is usually second to West Germany, Finland's trade with the Soviet Union as a percentage of total Finnish trade is larger. Thus 16 % of all Finland's exports go to the Soviet Union. Technically Finland should be considered a hard currency trading partner because until recently its trade with the Soviet Union was conducted on a barter or soft currency basis. That situation has now been altered, however, and when the Soviet trade deficit with Finland becomes too large, the Soviet Union must now pay off with convertible currency.

Several countries have become quite dependent on Soviet imports, particularly petroleum and natural gas. For example, 84 % of the oil and 100 % of the gas Finland consumes comes from the Soviet Union. Austria also receives 100 % of its imported natural gas from the Soviet Union, but in contrast to Finland, it also produces about 20 % of what it consumes. Finland has almost no domestic production. No other country, with the exception of Iceland and its relatively small imports of Soviet petroleum, are so dependent. For that matter, oil from the Soviet Union constitutes only 7 % of what Austria imports. Equally typical is Germany which imports 9 % of its petroleum from the Soviet Union. It

---

1 Anthony C. Sutton, *Western Technology and Soviet Economic Development, 1917–1930*, Stanford, Hoover Institution Publications, 1968.

does, however, take 37 % of its imported natural gas via pipeline from the Soviet Union.

Except for its trade with Finland, the Soviet Union's imports and exports play a relatively minor role in the trade of most of the Western world. Almost no one sells more than 1 % of his exports to the Soviet Union. Germany, the Soviet Union's largest trading partner, sells it 1.5 % of all Germany's exports. Moreover, the make-up of Soviet exports to Western Europe consists primarily of raw materials, especially, as we have seen, petroleum. Forty-five percent of the Soviet Union's exports to West Germany consists of petroleum. Natural gas accounts for an additional 35 %. Machinery amounts to only 2 % of what Germany buys from the Soviet Union, a figure typical for most of the West. (Again, an exception is Finland, where Soviet machinery exports constitute 8 % of Finnish imports.)

While the Soviet Union exports relatively little machinery to the West, as part of the historic Russian pattern, it continues to import large quantities. Over 50 % of what Finland exports to the Soviet Union consists of machinery. In a somewhat similar fashion, about 30 % of Germany's and Japan's exports consist of machinery. Not all countries rely so heavily on machinery imports. For example, for the United States, which is primarily a supplier of grain, (it sold about $ 700 million worth of grain in 1987), machinery exports to the Soviet Union amounted to only 10 % of total American exports.

To sum up, just as in the pre-Revolutionary period, the Soviet Union continues to import large quantities of machinery from the West, and export large quantities of raw materials, especially petroleum. One major change is that whereas previously Russia was a major grain exporter, selling 10 million tons or more per year to Western Europe, now it is a major importer, purchasing 30 billion tons in 1987, and as much as 44 billion tons in 1985.

II.

This inability to upgrade its production profile explains why *perestroika* is so necessary in the Soviet Union. If anything, because it must now import so much grain, the Soviet Union's economic competitiveness seems to have deteriorated since the Revolution. General Secretary Mikhail Gorbachev hopes that his program of internal reform will make both Soviet agriculture and industry more competitive. But he recognizes that this will be all but impossible to do if he relies only on internal stimuli. In a break with the recent past and post-Stalinist ideology, he has also decided to turn to the Western community for help. The biggest change is the announcement that as of January 1987, foreign investors, both capitalist and communist, could open up joint ventures in the Soviet Union. While the Soviet Union has participated in joint ventures in Eastern Europe and Western Europe as well as in some Third World countries, there have been no joint ventures inside the Soviet Union since the late 1920s. Ever since then, the Soviet Union has prided itself on the fact that it has freed itself of such exploitation. Obviously, this is a very radical ideological switch.

However, as far-reaching as the ideological implications may be, that in itself is no guarantee that these joint ventures will solve the Soviet Union's problems. There are several reasons for this. For example, even if Soviet authorities have decided to give the new joint ventures an open hand and do whatever they wish, the odds are small that the impact would be large for the very reason that the foreign sector constitutes such a small percentage of the Soviet Union's economy. But equally important, the Soviet bureaucratic approach to joint ventures can hardly be said to be a facilitating one. Because ideologically the return of joint ventures represents such a break with the past, Soviet bureaucrats are nervous that they might suddenly be accused of being too lax toward foreign capitalists and exploiters. Thus, the certification process for joint ventures has been slow. There are miles of red tape to cut through before approval is finally granted. Moreover, foreign investors have been limited to 49 % ownership. Soviet authorities announced in early December 1988 that the 49 % limit was to be abolished and no new limit was set. This should stimulate the formation of new joint ventures but at the same time, because the Soviets announced they plan to devalue the ruble by 50 %, it will make ruble earnings less attractive. For the time being, the repatriation of profits both in rubles and hard currency will not be easy.

Normally convertible currency can only be earned by exporting the joint ventures output to the hard currency world. There are some exceptions, but this is an intentional Soviet decision which is designed to foster exports from the Soviet Union. Of course, most foreign investors have just the opposite aim – that is to gain access to the Soviet market.

162

However, goods sold in the Soviet Union are almost always sold for rubles, which unfortunately cannot be taken out of the country.

In many parts of the world, there is another reason for establishing joint ventures, and that is to take advantage of cheap labor or some other resource available where the joint venture will operate. This explains why several of the new joint ventures are designed to facilitate increased output of raw materials, particularly energy-related products. The joint ventures are typically compensated in kind with those energy products which do indeed enjoy a market in the outside world. But it is hard to see how many prospective joint venturers would be attracted to the Soviet Union because of its cheap labor. The obvious contrast is with China, where cheap labor has become a magnet for joint ventures. As a visit to some of these joint ventures shows, many of those enterprises are old-fashioned sweat-shops, with hundreds and sometimes thousands of young Chinese women working long hours at low pay. This is something that the Soviet workers are not likely to tolerate, much less encourage. Admittedly, China authorized the establishment of joint ventures several years before the Soviet Union did, but it is the attraction of China's cheap labor and more relaxed attitude toward the prerogatives of the joint venture that helps to explain why there are only a hundred or so joint ventures in the Soviet Union and over thirteen thousand in China.

III.

As eager as Gorbachev is to promote his program of *perestroika*, it is hard to see how the Soviet Union can quickly change its foreign trade profile as well as its competitiveness in foreign trade. Before that can happen there will have to be a major transformation of the domestic Soviet economy, that means not only a new and improved manufacturing plant, but new attitudes and standards in a Soviet labor and managerial force. In the meantime, the lack of hard currency reserves and the inconvertibility of the ruble will hamper Soviet efforts to respond to the country's popular as well as its industrial needs.

If anything, Soviet debt is increasing. According to estimates of the CIA, the gross debt of the Soviet Union rose from about $ 22 billion in 1984 to $ 41 billion in 1987. Today the figure is probably closer to $

50 billion. The net debt has increased from about $ 11 billion in 1984 to $ 26 billion in 1987, and about $ 35 billion in 1988.

Among other complications, the Soviet Union had a poor harvest in 1988 which should necessitate higher than expected purchases of hard currency grain. To make matters worse, the price of oil remains far below the prices that prevailed a decade ago.

As serious as the drop in oil prices and the increase in grain purchases may be, these are not new problems. Recently, however, some new complications have arisen that are more in the nature of a structural change and will not go away when the weather improves and petroleum prices rise. The task of developing new foreign markets, while never easy for the Soviet Union has now become even more difficult. Soviet manufacturers are likely to find that almost any product they propose to sell in Western markets is likely to run up against a competing product from East Asia. In the last few years, the countries of East Asia have become a keen competitor in many product lines that a decade or so ago might have proven to be viable export items for the Soviet Union as well as Eastern Europe. In fact, some of the East European countries, such as Hungary and Rumania, had established a foothold for some products such as textiles, bicycles, and shoes only to be pushed out subsequently by more aggressive and cheaper sources of supply in Korea, Taiwan, Hong Kong, and now China. To be successful the Soviet Union will probably have to find some way of outdoing such competition. As even we in the United States have found, it will not be easy.

IV.

While nothing is impossible, and Gorbachev's efforts are sure to bear at least some fruit, acceptance of Soviet products in foreign markets will not come easily. For at least the next five years and conceivably the next decade, the Soviet Union will probably have to continue to depend on raw materials for its exports. At the same time the Soviet Union is likely to find itself coming back to the West for new advanced machinery. Gorbachev's best hope is that sooner or later the size of the harvest will increase. That could mean a drop in grain imports. But despite Gorbachev's best efforts, he is coming to learn that nothing comes easy or fast in the Soviet Union, and that for the next decade or so the Soviet export and import profile will probably stay much the same as it is currently.

164

Table 1.
Balance of Trade 1979, 1980, 1981, 1982, 1983, 1984, 1985, 1986, 1987, 1988
(Millions of Rubles)

Exports from the USSR

	1979	1980	1981	1982	1983	1984	1985	1986	1987	1988
Austria	442	580	854	675	566	761	805	540	431	455
Belgium	533	842	747	1032	991	1198	858	627	738	771
Gr.Brit	1094	859	645	813	1185	1393	1218	1274	1586	1794
Greece	180	409	538	533	533	582	594	219	242	310
Denmark	301	261	252	300	290	334	271	136	137	120
Spain	152	251	274	159	300	333	235	124	498	657
Italy	1292	2101	2484	2821	2998	3156	2468	1581	1804	1691
Netherlands	903	1027	1019	1505	1224	1612	987	576	781	657
Norway	87	49	52	93	80	129	104	64	82	82
Germany	2218	3096	3635	4065	4067	4536	4251	2879	2492	2537
France	1426	2242	2525	2228	2422	2447	2174	1541	1518	1579
Swtzlnd	314	445	331	533	510	541	384	287	344	405
Sweden	554	355	291	409	652	563	492	298	427	463
Japan	944	950	817	757	829	840	928	980	973	1184
Sub Totals	10440	13467	14464	15943	16647	18425	15769	11114	12035	12675
Sub-Balance of Trade										
Argntna	25	30	31	28	26	26	62	53	41	24
Brazil	20	22	16	180	107	95	70	70	46	17
U.S.A.	350	151	183	155	331	306	326	313	279	332
Canada	32	30	50	21	24	19	18	10	47	16
Australia	5	6	11	14	12	22	14	8	12	14
NZ	3	3	7	8	6	8	4	5	6	10
Total	10875	13709	14762	16349	17153	18901	16263	11533	12466	13088
Balance of Trade										
Finland	1469	2024	2290	2581	2483	2421	2299	1595	1707	1529
Balance of Trade with Finland included	12344	15733	17052	18930	19636	21322	18562	14173	14617	14617

Imports to the USSR

	1979	1980	1981	1982	1983	1984	1985	1986	1987	1988
Austria	368	396	507	535	787	891	865	852	600	712
Belgium	286	383	450	573	611	501	581	422	366	376
Gr.Brit	811	953	858	752	632	819	684	515	524	623
Greece	65	92	100	122	155	102	134	65	71	92
Denmark	72	80	208	64	65	115	125	131	76	105
Spain	144	152	375	166	250	307	353	173	159	154
Italy	863	934	1002	1222	1436	1325	1328	1474	1686	1343
Netherlands	243	361	458	359	489	276	313	245	232	278
Norway	51	79	96	72	102	80	73	69	62	83
Germany	2285	2989	2703	2913	3360	3376	3254	2968	2676	3285
France	1198	1510	1665	1268	1728	1777	1603	1130	1090	1190
Swtzlnd	276	403	497	411	345	410	567	456	540	773
Sweden	223	322	347	345	255	272	306	245	225	246
Japan	1654	1773	2213	2926	2176	2054	2287	2205	1628	1951
Sub Totals	8539	10427	11479	11728	12391	12305	12473	10950	9935	11211
Sub-Balance of Trade	+1901	+3040	+2985	+4215	+4256	+6120	+3296	+164	+2100	+1464
Argntna	289	1162	2372	1265	1300	1104	1230	192	417	547
Brazil	160	253	534	416	591	373	380	236	252	151
U.S.A.	2487	1352	1662	2072	1570	2829	2376	1146	919	1773
Canada	453	972	1377	1378	1278	1403	949	624	449	535
Australia	393	775	538	510	404	481	532	509	348	350
NZ	114	167	168	230	179	49	87	89	68	102
Total	12435	15108	18130	17599	17713	18544	18027	13746	12388	14669
Balance of Trade	-1560	-1399	-3368	-1250	-560	+357	-1764	-2213	+78	-1581
Finland	1138	1865	2723	2798	2690	2307	2690	2378	2036	2188
Balance of Trade with Finland included	-1229	-1240	-3801	-1467	-767	+471	-2155	-2996	-251	-2240

165

Table II.
The Soviet Union's Hard Currency Trading Partners
Soviet Exports: Largest Purchasers

1984	1985	1986	1987
Germany	Germany	Germany	Germany
Italy	Italy	Italy	Finland
France	Finland	Finland	Italy
Finland	France	France	U.K.
Netherlands	U.K.	U.K.	France

Soviet Imports: Largest Sellers

1984	1985	1986	1987
Germany	Germany	Germany	Germany
U.S.A.	Finland	Finland	Finland
Finland	U.S.A.	Japan	Italy
Japan	Japan	Italy	Japan
France	France	U.S.A.	France

Table III.
Soviet Union Imports from the United States
1971–1987
(million rubles)

Year	Imports of U.S. Goods	Soviet Imports of U.S. Machinery	Soviet Imports of U.S. Grain	Soviet Exports to the U.S.
1971	129	26	–	54
1972	461	48	318	76
1973	1023	169	707	138
1974	565	189	264	177
1975	1462	454	842	137
1976	2007	621	1185	199
1977	1256	351	594	272
1978	1599	274	1009	253
1979	2487	342	1545	350
1980	1352	311	747	151
1981	1662	201	1163	183
1982	2072	169	1399	155
1983	1570	144	872	331
1984	2829	137	2107	306
1985	2377	121	1632	326
1986	1146	154	319	313
1987	919	93	436	279

Does Gorbachev Need a Breathing Space?

Alec Nove

If this title implies that Gorbachev should halt the reform process to consolidate what has already been achieved, then this would be quite the wrong thing to do. Economic reform has not yet had any serious effect. A series of radical resolutions have been adopted, laws passed, but as of now little has changed. There are three interlinked explanations for this lack of progress: *difficulties of transition, opposition*, and finally, *ambiguities or contradictions* in the reform model itself.

Other papers at this conference have dealt with the measures that have been adopted. That they have so far had little effect is not disputed by anyone, least of all by our Soviet colleagues. It is worth stressing that the more important measures date from 1987 and 1988, and so have had little time to operate. Of course, the reforms were prepared earlier. Indeed they were already under discussion ten and more years ago. Thus in 1977, I wrote an article entitled »The economic problems of Brezhnev's successors«, which was published in the »Washington Papers« in 1978. This article took the form of an imaginary report written by a committee of reforming economists appointed by the (unknown) successor of Brezhnev. Its »chairman« was Aganbegyan. A comparison of this article with the reforms actually adopted in 1987–88 shows many similarities. This is not to be explained by any special far-sightedness on my part. Even in the »stagnant« days of Brezhnev, reform-minded economists did put forward criticisms and proposals for change. What they could not do in published work was to condemn the *system*; their proposals had to appear as aiming at »further perfecting« it. Various reform measures that were adopted were half-hearted and ineffective, because they could not be »systemic«. And partial measures could change nothing, as they did not tackle the basic problem: the incompatibility of centralized planning of the »command« type with the needs of a modern economy and society.

The urgency with which Gorbachev is tackling the task of radical reform is due in large part to the realization that there existed what he has repeatedly called a »pre-crisis situation«. There were and are shortages, inflation pressures, structural imbalances. Yet these very same factors represent major obstacles to a successful transition. For example, how can one abandon the system of material allocation, shift to »trade in means of production«, or relax price controls, when there is excess demand? A recent article in the journal *Kommunist* (No. 17, 1988) has referred to a budget deficit of close to 100 billion roubles, a deficit covered very largely by money creation, thereby fuelling inflation. Yet there are very urgent needs for higher expenditures on housing and health, and for raising the low pay of engineers, technologists, teachers, medical personnel, the service sector generally. The fall in the oil price has reduced export receipts, and to the high cost of the Chernobyl disaster has been added the tragedy of the Armenian earthquake. But even without these added complications the problems of transition would be immense. Few managers have any experience of marketing; they have been accustomed to supply customers designated by the planners. Market-type institutions, and personnel to work in them, are underdeveloped, and so are the needed information flows. Competition is advocated, but again there is lack of experience, and also fear that many suppliers would abuse their position under conditions of shortage (i.e., a sellers' market). Measures intended to stimulate cooperative and private enterprise also become distorted when shortages enable those enterprises to make a great deal of money – or they fail to operate because they cannot obtain needed material inputs. Meanwhile there is much uncertainty and confusion. It can be illustrated with a story, trivial in itself, but symbolic, published last year in *Moskovskie novosti*: a film script writer asked in a big public library to consult the Guinness Book of Records. He was told: together with thousands of other books it had been transferred from the so-called *spetskhran* (closed section of the library) to the open shelves, an obviously desirable change. However – they could not find it! For analagous reasons, many Western businessmen report that they find confusion among Soviet foreign-trade officials; the old arrangements have been swept away, the new ones are not yet functioning.

So it would all be very difficult even if there were no opposition. But of course there *is* opposition. Nor does it come only from »bureaucrats«, who understandably defend their power and privileges. Party and state officials are not well paid. Thus a first secretary of an *obkom* (provincial party committee) has recently published his salary: 550 roubles a month, or (at the official exchange rate) a little less than half of my university pension after tax, and little more than the pay of an experienced Moscow bus driver! Less eminent party officials receive much less, and so they naturally value the legal and less legal »perks« of office. Some Soviet sources speak of »feudal principalities«, sectoral and regional interest groups capable of defying Moscow and blocking or deforming reform measures. But in addition there is ample evidence that many workers are unhappy: redeployment has to be – even unemployment could be – the consequence of a necessary and overdue restructuring of the economy. Millions are accustomed to being paid regularly regardless of the enterprise's economic performance, for little effort. Tightening of discipline, the new quality-acceptance commission, the emphasis on financial results and the end of easy credit cause concern among the labour force. Of course, as consumers they would benefit from higher productivity and improved quality, but meanwhile the shops are still poorly supplied, and so there seems to be little reward for harder work.

Many also lack the widespread belief in a kind of egalitarianism, and there is a long-established, ideology-based belief in the unfairness and basically non-socialist nature of markets. As was recently pointed out by A. Vergeyev in a discussion on a draft of a new textbook of political economy, »it is known that Marx and Engels held that socialism and commodity production were not only contradictory but incompatible. Lenin was of the same opinion. Even today no one has the ›theoretical effrontery‹ to say that Lenin was the creator of the theory of commodity production under socialism. Was the theory of Marx, Engels and Lenin about socialism wrong, or was their theory on commodity production wrong?...« (*Voprosy ekonomiki*, No. 7, 1988). Similar thoughts, formerly regarded as heretical, can be found in the discussion, in No. 10 of the same journal, concerning the 110th anniversary of Engels's *Anti-Dühring*. Of course, »Ideology« is not easy to define, is adaptable to circumstances, indeed is being adapted. However, it does have some effect on genuinely held beliefs. This helps to explain the suspicion with which cooperative and private enterprise are regarded by many ordinary people, not only by »bureaucrats«.

The opposition is able to take advantage of the difficulties of transition. The necessary reforms are interlinked, and need to be introduced

169

together. Thus »full *khozraschyot*«, the enterprises' financial responsibility, cannot be effective until prices are radically reformed; excess demand cannot be curbed unless and until enterprises can be made fully financially responsible; shortages are (in part) generated by the material allocation system, which cannot be abandoned while shortages remain serious, and so on. Meanwhile the five-year plan drafted in 1984 is still current, and enterprises are still judged in relation to various plan-fulfillment targets, despite the decision to abandon them. Nor have prices yet been reformed, but in their present form, they are quite unsuitable for the economic calculations and incentives the reform requires. Partial, step-by-step reform frequently results in contradiction and confusion, which can be made use of by those who prefer to block radical changes. Similarly, political and economic reforms are seen as depending on each other, yet hard to carry out simultaneously, all the more so as political power at the centre is essential to push the process through against opposition. Here, for instance, is the view of E. Ambartsumov: »I think that right now it is impossible to proceed to a democratic society, since we have never had one. It is difficult to imagine the transition without passing through a certain ›authoritarian‹ stage« (*Voprosy ekonomiki*, No. 6, 1988). So the process of *demokratizatsiya*, under conditions in which public opinion is divided, when one sees »the non conformity of current and short-term interests of a sizeable part of the population with the strategic aims of *perestroika*« (S. Tolstikov, in *ibid),* is itself contradictory. One needs a *reform strategy*. It is easier to say this than to devise one that works.

Then one must also consider the ambiguities of the reform model, due partly to necessary political compromises, and partly to differences of view among the reformers themselves.

Thus exactly where *is* the line to be drawn between plan and market? What will be, should be, the content and targets of the next (thirteenth) five-year plan? What is to be the theoretical and practical basis of the reform of prices? What proportion can be, should be, freed of control altogether? If there is to be a capital market, then of what kind? How is wasteful duplication of investments to be avoided? Should wages be a »residual«, i.e. depend on the net revenues of each enterprise, or be based on a tariff rate plus bonus? What precisely is to be the role of the Party in controlling appointments (and supervising elections), what (if anything) is to remain of the *nomenklatura* system by which Party control over personnel has been exercised for sixty and more years? Are economic ministries to survive, if so in what form? What are to be the economic powers of republics and of local soviets? Problems linked with nationalism are already clearly present. How far should one go with family leasing, petty private enterprise, cooperatives? How can the ruble be made convertible? What should be the role of joint ventures, of foreign capital? (»Will foreign capital in joint enterprises exploit our labourpower and create surplus value on our territory?«, to cite a hypothetical question by V. Musatov (*Voprosy ekonomiki*, No. 7, 1988). Some cautious reformers may resemble the Chinese »moderate«, Chen Yun, who is said to have expressed the moderate reform view as follows: »Our managers are in too small a cage; they cannot spread their wings. We must build them a bigger cage. But we must keep them in a cage, otherwise they will fly away.«

The reform process is supposed to move faster in 1989, it having been decided to cut back »state orders« (*goszakazy*) and extend trade in means of production, so that a larger part of the output of enterprises will be subject to negotiation with customers. We shall see if this actually will happen. The reforms must be pushed ahead, since little has yet changed, and a »breathing-space« (*peredyshka*) is the last thing that is now needed. One cannot halt to consolidate when there is as yet so little to consolidate.

However, a breathing space may be helpful if by this is meant temporary relief from the balance of payments constraint. So we should now turn to the *external factor*. The fall in the oil price, problems with oil production, the continued need to import grain, have compelled the Soviets to cut back on hard-currency imports. The idea has been put forward, unofficially that the USSR could borrow large sums in order to provide quickly some visible benefits for the consumer. N. Shmelev argued for the direct import of consumers' goods, but other alternatives are imports of machinery to make such goods (provided it can be effectively used), and, finally, the encouragement of joint ventures which aim to supply the home market. All three require borrowing.

Should we »aid« the USSR? In my view, this is the wrong question. In the first place, no one doubts that the success or failure of the reform will be due primarily to internal factors. Secondly, the USSR is not asking for economic *aid*. Thirdly, there is no good case for some sort of »Marshall plan«, or for making such a plan conditional upon changes

171

in Soviet policy. In any case, there is ample evidence that policy *has* changed, whether in relation to human rights or to intervention abroad. The Soviet leadership is in any case conscious of the fact that too much foreign indebtedness in undesirable, and recalls the sad fate of Poland. No, the correct posture, in my view, is to join in *mutually* profitable exchanges, including the granting of credits, on a non-discriminatory basis. As a commercial risk, the USSR clearly is a more reliable creditor than – say – Mexico, where net debt is five times higher. Not to grant credits would be conscious discrimination against the USSR, based upon the supposition that it is our task to do them harm. This seems to me quite a wrong approach: we should prefer that Gorbachev succeed given that any alternative leadership is likely to be both unstable and unpleasant. Some have urged that the Cocom list be pruned, and indeed it does contain items only remotely connected with military end uses, so I would support this. However, Soviet needs also extend very much into the area of what could be called »low technology«, relatively simple items such as small-scale farm machinery, or equipment for the clothing and food industries or for materials handling.

The USSR is at present overdependent on exports of oil and gas, and her future export earnings should include a wider range of manufactures, though here there is bound to be severe competition from the newly-industrializing third-world countries. It is official policy to incorporate the USSR much more closely into the world market, and this too should be welcomed and facilitated. Closer contact, economic and cultural, cannot harm the West, can help a little in the internal evolution of the Soviet Union.

Is *perestroika* irreversible? No, not yet. To repeat, its progress does not depend primarily on us – though the reversing of the arms race can also help by enabling Gorbachev to devote more resources to cope with the many internal claimants. Meanwhile, voices are heard in the West: a healthier Soviet Union could become a more powerful enemy. A leopard cannot change his spots. We spend too much time persuading the wolf to sign a document promising to be a vegetarian. A well-fed bear is dangerous – and a hungry bear even more dangerous. These analogies are, in my view, misleading. Whatever animal best represented the Stalinist Soviet Union, we now face something different, new, to which »zoological« stereotypes are increasingly inappropriate (unless one views all of *glasnost'* and *perestroika* as an exercise of

dressing the wolf in sheep's clothing, which seems to me contrary to all the evidence).
Instead of or alongside M.A.D. (Mutually Assured Destruction) I would advocate M.A.I.D. (Mutually Advantageous Inter-Dependence). That way lies hope.

The Gorbachev Challenge: Economic Policy Constructive Ideas for a Western Approach

Heinrich Vogel

The term »Gorbachev's challenge« indicates surprise, even embarrassment among Western observers of *perestroika* and »New Thinking«. It is this embarrassment which explains the acrimony from current debates among analysts of diverging schools of belief and among politicians in the Western alliance. The undeniable change in the USSR came about unexpectedly, the need to respond is not welcome to all of them.

The challenge is political rather than economic. The USSR is not an economically competitive great power – on the contrary: the present state of the Soviet economy is dismal; the transition to a more decentralized economic system plus modernization of production, infrastructure and services will deepen the critical situation for the next years rather than boost the economic potential.

The task of developing »constructive ideas« in response to this kind of a »Gorbachev challenge« is not for the economic analyst but for the designers of Western policy. They, however, drift away in the discussion of »to help or not to help« without revealing their set of premises and beliefs.

Discussing constructive ways involves some risk: the very notion smacks of traditional Soviet appeals to the West and the dialogue of the deaf in the old days of »stagnation« and Cold War. It is certainly not advisable to turn the reality of power politics off and to daydream of a new world, lulled in »constructive« East-West harmony. The political bias caused by ideological incompatibility and military confrontation is still constraining the chances for a fundamental detente or normalization. Besides, the conditions of volatile financial markets, unprecedented technological change, and fierce competition on world markets are the most complicated in decades for any newcomer to an unhappy world of economic interdependence. Fancy solutions for all these problems are not available. Grand but inoperable formulas will not work. Still, reasoning about what might be »constructive« offers a chance for identifying the background of current Western disputes in order to reduce controversies over risks and opportunities to the range of realistic options. More than ever before, we are put to the test of explicating our paradigms (in academic terms) or (in less sophisticated language) our ideological prejudices in dealing with one of the world's biggest countries not based on Western values.

Perestroika is for real

In retrospect, it has now become evident to what extent the Western world's political cohesion depends on the very existence of a clearly defined political antagonist and military threat which claimed most of the problem-solving capacities of political actors. True believers in the manichean world outlook are not alone in their hesitation to take the surprising change in the center of world communism for real. Global strategist, too, are not happy to acknowledge after three-and-a-half years that *perestroika* is a serious attempt of the new Soviet leadership at initiating radical change in order only »to reach the new millennium as a great power with dignity«. There is little doubt that the new sober comparison of Soviet achievements and prospects with the outside world undoubtedly has replaced the traditional selfcomplacent boasting. Soviet leaders now openly discuss the situation in terms of the USSR facing inferiority on all the critical accounts of comparative performance: economic growth, structural adaptation, innovative capacity and organizational skills.

Soviet foreign policy of »New Thinking« has realized how risky and counterproductive stressing of the military factor and overextension have been. To be sure, in relations with the outside world xenophobia and the cult of power are features with considerable tradition. Nevertheless, the new language has changed to interdependence, to a demilitarized notion of security, from the notorious zero-sum in »correlation of forces« to peaceful competition. This proclaimed change in the foreign policy outlook is plausible and rational; it makes obvious sense under the prevailing conditions of comparative economic weakness.

True, the relevance of such a change for Western policy after forty years of confrontation depends upon the extent of durable systemic change in domestic policy. But Catonic ignorance, no matter how much has

175

changed or is about to change (because »carthago est delenda« anyway) is jeopardizing the credibility of Western foreign and security policy at home.

Challenge or Risk Assessment?

Perestroika in the Soviet Union is facing handicaps that will not be able to be overcome quickly: the dimensions of the economic aggregates to be moved, the complexity of legislation and organizational change to be designed and implemented, social and political traditions, and behavioural patterns (a.o. risk avoidance, contempt of commercial success, waste of resources deemed to be unlimited) represent a formidable task. At the same time the West is invited to participate in economic cooperation and mutually beneficial cooperation. The call for »normalization« and giving up discrimination is an economic/political challenge, not a call for »help.«

Possible »constructive« responses to *perestroika* and New Thinking depend upon the scenarios considered and the time horizon of such reasoning. It is conventional wisdom, also among Soviet analysts, to assume a transition period of one or two generations necessary for the modernisation of the USSR – even if we accept Gorbachev's bright visions (designs are still missing) of the USSR becoming a competitive industrial power. When applying John M. Keynes's irrefutable political criterion (»In the long run we are all dead«) this is obviously too long a period to be relevant for Western risk assessment: in sociological and economic long-term models too many variables of the Soviet political system and foreign behaviour would have to be considered as open to change. But are they open? What about the »law of unintended consequences«? Adherents of continued confrontation skip this question and simply assume a very short period for successful Soviet adaptation to competitive structures abroad – or they disregard the factor of time altogether in their prophecies of inevitably growing USSR strength.

More realistic are scenarios of a medium-term perspective where obstacles to swift change and reform, as described above, are slowing down the pace of *perestroika*. Less threatening than in fashionable oracular talk of the great gurus of today, »success« of *perestroika* in this perspective is to be seen in keeping the process of painful reform

176

open. »Failure«, on the other hand, would be nothing more than the fading of momentum. It would not (as often is claimed) automatically lead to the »restoration of Stalinism«. Too much has happened already and history is not repetitive. The range of realistic scenarios narrows down to:

1. »Protracted (pre-)crisis management« where social, regional, environmental, and national unrest call for »two-steps ahead/one-step back«-tactics for the sake of survival. The result inevitably is the delay of economic recovery in the short term, with some chance for long-term modernization, though.
2. »Law and Order,« i.e. the repressive response to area-conflagration of simultaneous turmoil: strikes, disruption of production, irridentist, separatist, and fundamentalist activities (sabotage, terrorism, mass riots, large-scale violence). Military (Jaruzelski-type) rule may be in the cards, too, is even more probable than a return to outright Stalinism. The result here again is a slowing down of economic recovery to nil or less. In the long run (as the Polish situation shows) modernization of the country, not to mention competitiveness, would have very little chance.
3. Degeneration of *perestroika* to mere talk, hopeless and total gridlock, reminding of Gorki's notorious negative hero Manilov (the type of the Russian intellectual, full of fancy ideas but constitutionally incapable of acting them out). Modernisation in this scenario is bound to be choked in mismanagement, catastrophes, and disillusionment.

The traditional Soviet great power status defined by military (nuclear) capacities has been wearing thin, degraded in the light of Polish events and defeat in Afghanistan. The economic/political crisis in the USSR and in the empire is beyond military control. Comparative international power today to a diminishing degree is still defined by standard quantitative economic indicators and by military options. But more and more qualitative aspects such as structural adaptation, the »search capacity« of the socio-political system make the difference. Today, innovation rather than expansion, openness and flexibility rather than rigidity and risk avoidance, are describing successful performance.

In the world economy the rules of the game have changed: exports of raw materials and energy will not earn the revenue needed for developing a high-tech infrastructure. Even copying (stealing) Western technology will not do the job. The critical elements are capability to

177

adapt know-how, openness and close-to-equal competence. Obviously these conditions have to be created at home; there is no way of helping by transfer. The Soviet dilemma today is to open an ill-prepared economy to the world market in a time of economic strain: raw materials and energy don't sell, financial markets pose unknown hazards, the NICs are thriving in fierce competition, and protectionist trends prevail on national and regional scales. Becoming a competitive high-tech great power is impossible; a »Japanese« miracle is beyond reach for the Soviet Union.

How to be constructive

To be sure, in Western worst-case analysis the scenario of military rule, even bonapartism, entails the risk of Soviet renewed adventurism based on Marxist or nationalist motivation – in order to dampen internal crisis by invoking (or provoking) an external threat. Military precautions, therefore, have to be maintained by the West, unilateral disarmament is not advisable. But at the same time it is necessary (in order not to miss the chance for real disarmament and for the sake of credibility at home) to respond favourably to propositions of »sufficient« or »defensive« defense – if they are presented in negotiable terms.

But what about longer-term Soviet intentions? With the exception of ritualistic references to Lenin, there is not much to worry about. The declared goal of *perestroika* is the modernization of the industrial state USSR for the sake of its survival as a great power. The new Soviet leadership's understanding of the equation which defines comparative international power gives the priority of political effort to economic viability and competitiveness. The factor of military power is scaled down from its notoriously dominant role to that of a dependent variable. The long-term vision of a modern Soviet Union no longer claims the role of vanguard in an aggressively formulated theory of socialist world revolution actively to be pursued on a global scale. The new aspiration rather is one of being a respected member of the international community, appealing to the non-communist world by the eventual superiority of its economic, social, and political system. Ideology is not irrelevant but under review. Its basis still is the firm belief to stand on the right side of mankind's historical progress. However, this resembles

178

more and more Western-type »Weltanschauung«; the time horizons for some final stage seems to be extended beyond any period of operational relevance.

What can be constructive?

The most widely discussed recommendations for a Western political and economic response are contradictory, corresponding to incompatible ideological premises of confrontation or detente respectively. The extreme positions (»Managing the decline of the Soviet empire« or »Helping Gorbachev«) are based on the unfounded or megalomaniac premise that Western policy has immediate leverage over Soviet domestic and bloc policies. A closer look into the dimensions of Soviet glory and gloom should frustrate such hopes.

Western economic cooperation is not irrelevant. It makes sense for the Soviet economy to open up to the outside world and to transform the stop-gap device of a monopoly-channeled foreign trade system into a veritable link, capable of becoming an auxiliary engine to promote change and growth itself.

Shortage of hard currency caused by the monostructure of Soviet export capacities precludes a strategy of large-scale imports both of capital and consumer goods. And the terms-of-trade are not going to improve in the foreseeable time. Since the partner countries in CMEA are tied down in their own modernization dilemmas and in even tighter hard currency constraints, the OECD countries are a critical source of capital and technology – but under what conditions?

The traditional Soviet approach of large-scale projects or promises of huge volumes in future trade is inadequate to attract major contracts. The dismantling of monopolies in foreign trade organizations and *perestroika* of cadres complicate the ongoing negotiations; current projects are delayed considerably. Apart from the obvious frictions inherent in any reorganization, it is the tendency of policy planners in Soviet foreign economic relations to tackle too much at one time which impairs performance and the optimal use of costly resources. Reforms will have to go a long way before being up to the task of »opening to the world market«.

179

On the other hand, a limited number of financially feasible projects, carried out in due organizational and technological competence, have a chance of producing with decent economies of scale – if the domestic economic system is reformed consistently with a new mechanism of price formation and without central allocation of capital goods (Gossnab). And there is a political side-effect to economic reform and performance: consistent steps are the best way of improving the credibility of political *perestroika*.

Economic *perestroika*, if pursued seriously, poses a challenge to the West, making it more difficult to evade reconsideration of traditional Western attitudes oscillating between blunt denial and wishful cooperation. If only for the sake of credibility at home, the West must be careful

– not to miss a window of opportunity for promoting normalization (demilitarization and de-ideologization) of East-West relations,
– not to frustrate expectations of *perestrochniki* in the USSR whose morale needs encouragement by showing positive interest in what is going on.

Reconsidering does not mean to advocate deliveries of critical resources at all cost. But it is time for sober reassessment, for the reduction of interference of political criteria into economic relations, for relying on economic criteria only – just as they are used in risk assessment for trade with any other countries. If this is the core of Soviet arguments in favour of »economic security« it should be taken as a serious offer. Continued political linkage across the areas of the CSCE process (in the words of Deputy Secretary of State John Whitehead in a statement at the US Chamber of Commerce International Forum on December 6, 1988: »We cannot divorce East-West economic cooperation from the commitments made to human rights in the Helsinki Accords«) will be minimizing feasible progress in the entire process. It did not work in the past nor will it work in the future.

Economic conditions are much more powerful than so called »economic diplomacy,« not least because they imply an element of political linkage for two reasons:

a) Economic reforms are worthless without political reforms,
b) Indispensable risk assessments of Western partners in economic cooperation (banks and large corporations) which involve political elements (e.g. political stability, competence and reliability of eco-

nomic policies, obviously depending on the search capacity of a political system).

In this perspective, it makes sense

1. to encourage strictly commercial lending because it will back up economic rationality in *perestroika*. This argument is not controversial in Western Europe, contrary to the moods in the Congress of the United States where commercial credits to the USSR still are a bone of contention, making US banks shy away from being mentioned in such context.

2. to depoliticize the criteria in national export controls insofar as they exceed the minimal consensus in CoCom, where discussions among the member countries have been complicated over the last 40 years by ambiguous language (»critical«, »militarily relevant«, »sensitive«, »strategic«). This issue is blown out of its real dimensions in propaganda campaigns on both sides: the Soviets claim that it is a major obstacle for expansion of economic exchange while the single most important problem is the lack of competitiveness of Soviet industrial products. US propaganda claims that transfer of Western high-tech is behind a Soviet military threat of increasing technological competence. Yet, serious analytical work shows that such transfer serves other purposes (a.o. comparative assessment), that dependence on Western technologies is carefully avoided and that Soviet R&D is up to the task in areas of critical (military) priority. Since the advanced technologies of today have outgrown traditional control philosophies there is more harm done to intra-Western cooperation than to a potential military adversary. Whatever the measurable effects of CoCom – it is causing delay in project design and negotiation while time is the single most important factor for maintaining the momentum of *perestroika*, not the least because of the uncertainty it creates even for projects which are strictly non-military (environmental protection, nuclear safety etc). In view of these aspects it should be easy to slim down CoCom to the smallest extent advisable, as long as disarmament has not reached the stage of significant cuts in military R&D.

These conclusions will not boost volumes in economic relations to colossal dimensions – contrary to continued talk of a »vast market« or »ogromnye vozmozhnosti.« This has to be stressed in order to reduce the factor of potential frustration looming as a consequence of *perestroiphoria*. Much of the necessary homework is still missing

181

not only on the Soviet side (checking priorities, providing meaningful statistical information, opening up to on-site verification of the dual-capable Western technology utilised in the USSR, sending managers and experts for training abroad in large numbers) but also on the side of the West (sorting out the answerable and the unanswerable issues in the internal debate, reassessing the range of realistic options and risks in cooperation under the new conditions of political change in the USSR, refraining from gigantomania in politically unfeasible projects such as a »Marshall Plan for the East«). The remaining realistic option (a normalization of economic relations at extremely small or no risk), unspectacular as it is, should be worth trying. In a time of dramatic change in international relations on a global scale, it might even be critical for mastering the tasks of a changing East-West agenda.

Part Three:
The Foreign and Strategic Policy Challenge

Soviet Key Terms on International Security: Problems and Issues

Gerhard Wettig

Shifts in terminology – Shifts in Substance?

Under the aegis of Gorbachev's new thinking, the conceptual framework of Soviet foreign policy has changed. The relevant terminology has undergone change as well. This poses a demanding challenge for analysis. To what extent do new terms reflect new substance? New terminology does not necessarily imply new meaning. This becomes clear when one looks at an example from the Brezhnev period.

An Illustrative Case Under Brezhnev's Old Thinking

Until 1976, Soviet spokesmen advocated military superiority and displayed confidence that the USSR possessed it in the European theater. During the negotiations on MBFR, the Kremlin's negotiators insisted that the existing correlation of military forces could not be corrected. It had to maintained, if at a lower level. On 19 January, 1977, however, Brezhnev publicly abandoned this position. He spoke out in favour of military equilibrium and parity and renounced the search for military superiority.[1] Sixteen months later, the commitment to the principle of military parity was included into a Soviet-West German declaration. After the Secretary General had redefined the policy line, all Soviet statements instantly took over the new verbiage.
But no change in practical policy resulted. The Soviet armament process continued unabated. The Kremlin's position in arms negotiations did not change. Advocacy of the existing correlation of military forces was simply replaced by the demand that »existing military parity« had to be preserved. Whatever military potential was added to the

1 Pravda, 20 January 1977.

USSR's arsenals (such as, most notably, increasing numbers of SS-20 missiles), the presumed state of equal military capabilities was portrayed as continuing without reservation. In the meantime, it has become common wisdom in Moscow that Brezhnev's demonstrative armament was excessive in character and could not but provoke the outside world.[2]

Soviet advocacy of military parity since 1977 is a clear case of change which is but verbal in character. It would, however, be misleading to assume that the Soviet leadership simply chose to declare the opposite thing of what it meant. Soviet spokesmen can conceivably resort to arbitrary statements when they exclusively address foreign audiences. But they can't afford to do this when they direct their messages simultaneously at domestic recipients, as they did with military parity. Statements designed for domestic consumption serve the purpose of policy orientation. The cadres and followers at home receive guidance on how they are expected to implement the policies decided upon in the Kremlin. It would be detrimental to the leaders' interests if image-building in the West would have to be bought at the price of wrong guidance given to cadres and followers.

Attaching a New Meaning to Old Terms

It is a traditional Soviet device to seek a solution to the problem by redefinition of crucial words. Key terms which are included into the official terminology in an effort to make a favourable impact on Western audiences, are given a new definition which is communicated to cadres and followers. This is intended to assure that no incorrect meaning is perceived by the supporters of Soviet policy, while foreign audiences can be assumed to grasp the habitual meaning and to neglect internal explanations. What results is bifurcated talk. Cadres and followers are aware of the operational meaning, whereas foreign audiences can be impressed by another meaning which is in the interests of Soviet image building.

2 Cf. Viacheslav Dashichev, »Vostok–Zapad: poisk novykh otnoshenii«, *Literaturnaia gazeta*, 18 May 1988. The argument has been referred to, inter alia, in the official theses for the XIXth CPSU Party Conference (*Pravda*, 27 May 1988) and in Gorbachev's report to the XIXth CPSU Party Conference (*Pravda*, 29 June 1988).

In the military parity case, the cadres and followers were made to understand that the terms of »parity« and »equilibrium« were simply code words for the military status quo attained at the respective moments. At a higher level of sophistication, »renunciation of the search for military superiority« was explained in ideological terms. Accordingly, military superiority must be seen as a »symbol of aggressive aspirations«.[3] That is, military superiority must not be seen as a particular correlation of military forces but as a phenomenon of political intent. Since aggressiveness is invariably associated with the »social nature of imperialism«, it follows that the USSR being a socialist, and hence peace-loving, country can't possibly seek military superiority on grounds of its »social nature«. In consequence of this, it is the United States and its allies which must be blamed for that search for military superiority.

To make the argument come full circle, military superiority was so defined also in positive terms as to fit this purpose. As the crucial criterion, defense of one's own territory was introduced. Since the Soviet Union is located in Europe, any extent of military power can be justified on these grounds as serving requirements of self-defense. On the other hand, the United States, being located outside Europe, cannot claim on this basis that any one of its soldiers and weapons are there for the defense of the national territory. It is the West European allies who are to be protected – but this is a purpose which by definition implies a search for military superiority.[4]

A Different Approach Under Gorbachev's New Thinking?

Brezhnev's professed »renunciation of the search for military superiority« and commitment to »military equilibrium and parity« is a classical example of the traditional Soviet habit of changing verbiage but not substance. At the level specific to the argument, it invites the question whether current advocacy of military parity, which is said to require preservation, continues to be based on the old redefinition. Suspicion

3 N.V. Ogarkov, *Vsegda v gotovnosti k zashchite otechestva*, Moscow: Voenizdat 1982, p. 20.
4 Aleksei Arbatov, *Voenno-strategicheskii paritet i politika SShA*, Moscow: Izd. pol. lit. 1984.

to this effect may result from the persistent argument that parity is both a fact and a postulate and from continuing armament on previous, partially even increased, levels. More generally, the question must be raised whether the technique of redefining key terms newly adopted continues to be practised under Gorbachev's new thinking. If that were the case, this would indicate unwillingness to change substance with words and to abandon old thinking for a really new one.

The Case of Professed Abandonment of a Warfare Orientation

To investigate the problem, let us take a look at one of Gorbachev's new terms. The Soviet leaders have proclaimed a new military doctrine which either has already been adopted or is, at a minimum, in the process of being worked out. It is claimed that, on this basis, a new stance is taken, which leaves behind the old orientation on warfare and on offensive strategy. When asked what has changed in concrete terms, Soviet spokesmen invariably use the only argument that the principle of war prevention has been accorded priority and that it has become the very basis of all military activity. Previous emphasis on warfare, it is added, has been discarded.

To many Western observers, this claim appears to be justified on grounds that the USSR now professes to seek »to deter the aggressor« from war. Previous rejection of NATO's deterrence seems to be a thing of the past. At the same time, it is felt that the traditional concept of »reining-in imperialism«, i.e. seeking war prevention through maximiz-ation of military power against NATO, has been abandoned. At a closer look, however, this expectation meets with the contradictory evidence that, ever since the XXVIIth CPSU Party Congress, Gorbachev and his peers have emphasized that nuclear deterrence is mortally dangerous, morally unacceptable and must be eliminated. So what is the Kremlin's real attitude?

To this day, the Soviet leaders profess that »reliable security« through »reliable defense« is indispensable. In official terminology, this is tantamount to the postulate that the USSR must be as secure in the event of East-West war as in peacetime and that the basis for this is to be capable for successful military action in the defense of the homeland. At the top of the Soviet leadership, it is stated in general terms that the aggressor must be given a »devastating rebuff«. Lower-level Soviet spokesmen tend to posit that the enemy must be confronted with the prospect of a »crushing defeat« and of his being »smashed«. Not infrequently, this perceived need is expressly justified by the principles of new thinking.[5] In contrast to nuclear deterrence as professed by NATO, this concept of safeguarding security is both unilateral and war-waging in character. War prevention must be guaranteed by the defender's sufficient military strength against the aggressor so as to make the prospect of his destruction in the event of war credible.

Underlying Ideas and Assumptions

The aggressor is invariably identified with NATO. It is an essentially ideological argument which justifies the thesis in much the same way as before. Imperialism is ascribed an innate leaning toward war, while the Soviet Union is credited with being a priori unable to initiate aggression. Both allegations are based on the idea of the »social nature«, which the one and the other system are supposed to have based on this ideological premise, »deterring the aggressor« means providing for the strongest possible disincentive for the West to wage war – a disincentive which must be provided unilaterally, since it is only the West which tends to be aggressive. The practical consequence is that peace is the more secure, the greater the military strength of the USSR and its allies.[6] In the last analysis, the forces of the socialist countries are viewed as the guarantors of peace for all mankind.[7]

Soviet rejection of nuclear deterrence can easily be explained on this basis. It is the possibility of escalation to nuclear levels which makes war unacceptable to the Kremlin.[8] This poses a dilemma. In

5 See, inter alia, D.T. Iazov, »Voennaia Doktrina Varshawskogo Dogovora«, *Pravda*, 27 July 1987; P. Skorodenko, »Voennyi paritet i printsip razumnoi dostatochnosti«, *Kommunist vooruzhennykh sil*, 10/1987, p. 15.

6 D. Volkogonov, »Imperativy iadernogo veka«, *Krasnaia zvezda*, 22 May 1987; P. Lushev, »Na strazhe zavoevanii revoliutsii«, *Meždunarodnaia zhizn‹*, 8/1987, p. 68.

7 S.F. Akhromeev, »Velikaia pobeda«, *Krasnaia zvezda*, 9 May 1987.

8 M.S. Gorbachev, *Perestroika dlia nashei strany i vsego mira*, Moscow: Izd. pol. lit. 1987, p. 143; Shevardnadze at the MID Conference on 25 July 1988, *Vestnik MID SSSR*, 15/1988, p. 36. Cf. G. Kostev, »Nasha voennaia doktrina v svete novogo politic-heskogo myshleniia«, *Kommunist vooruzhennykh sil*, 17/1987, p. 12; D. Volkogonov, op. cit.

consequence of presumed political antagonism between East and West, war is seen to be a real contingency all the time, even if its likelihood may greatly vary. There is no way of making permanently sure that Western aggression can be avoided. If, then, war must be reckoned with, it must be made wageable so that the Soviet homeland can be defended if the need should arise. Nuclear warfare, potential or real, is bound to be unacceptable, conventionalization of East-West war must be sought. The practical result is Gorbachev's campaign against nuclear deterrence and for a nuclear-free world. The concrete goal appears to be denuclearization of Europe between the Soviet borders and the Atlantic. The above investigation of the Soviet concept for war prevention does not show much of a difference from previous ideas. In particular, realization of the war prevention purpose is based on a capability for successful warfare. It also implies a perspective of unilateral force maximization which does not appear to result in a defensive attitude. Whether expressly stated or not, the logic of the concept implies the need for confronting the potential adversary as the only possible aggressor with this prospect of military annihilation in the event of war. The crucial point is that prevention of war is sought through anticipated warfare rather than through making war mutually unaffordable. This is essentially traditional Soviet thinking, which persists under the cover of new words.

»Free Choice« and »Elimination of Militarism«

Another key point in Gorbachev's new thinking is the postulate of »free choice« which must be put into practice under conditions of »demilitarization of international relations«. These two ideas have great appeal to Western audiences. Underlying them is the perception that Gorbachev advocates national self-determination and non-use of military means in international politics. Western observers even tend to feel that the USSR whose status as a world power is largely based on its military power, is willing to renounce this instrument to a considerable extent.

The interpretations given by the Soviet leaders indicate a different understanding. The »path of development«, the »way of life« which every country and people is expected to decide upon freely,[9] is defined in social, systemic terms.[10] It is also tied to the »objective course of history itself«,[11] i.e. to history's road from capitalism to socialism as posited by Soviet doctrine.[12] To the extent that this allegedly objective development is impeded, the underlying argument goes on, the military factor enters the scene. To be more precise, Western »militarism« (if resistance comes from within the respective country) and »interventionism« (if unwillingness to accept socialist progress is backed from abroad) have to be invariably seen as the culprits whenever transition to socialism does not go smoothly but entails armed clashes.[13]

More generally, availability of military power is viewed as the very basis which makes it possible for the Western system to continue its political existence for an extended period of time against the onslaught of socialism. Since capitalism allegedly »does not dispose of positive goals and orientations«, it has to rely on force. It is essentially on this fundament that the »social status quo« can be maintained in the long run and »even the possibility of social revenge, of gaining back what had been lost before«, emerges.[14] The centerpiece of such Western reliance on military instruments in an attempt to withstand social change is the nuclear weaponry on which NATO's nuclear deterrence rests.[15] »Gradual demilitarization and humanization of international relations« is to serve the function of eliminating this challenge.[16]

In contrast to the military parity case, Gorbachev's advocacy of »free choice« and »demilitarization of international relations« indicates ideas which do not simply substitute new formulas for old ones. Nonetheless the Soviet verbiage is bound to mislead Western recipients. Against the background of Western language, the Soviet terms contain meanings radically different from what might be expected. That is, the message

---

9 Gorbachev at the XVIIth CPSU Congress, *Pravda*, 26 February 1986.
10 Shevardnadze at the MID Conference on 25 July 1988, *Vestnik MID SSSR*, 15/1988, p. 39; Vadim Zagladin, »Prioritet doveriia«, *Sovetskaia Rossia*, 23 June 1988.
11 Gorbachev at the XIXth CPSU Conference, *Pravda*, 29 June 1988.
12 Cf. L. Mendelevich's remarks as reported in »Press-klub LG«, *Literaturnaia gazeta*, 29 June 1988.
13 Gorbachev at the XIXth CPSU Conference, *Pravda*,, 29 June 1988.
14 Gorbachev at the XVIIth CPSU Congress, *Pravda*, 26 February 1986; Shevardnadze at the XXVIIth CPSU Congress, *Pravda*, 2 March 1986.
15 Ibid.
16 Gorbachev at the XIXth CPSU Conference, *Pravda*, 29 June 1988.

which appears to be conveyed under Gorbachev's new thinking, is not the one understood by its Soviet authors.

Conclusions

In an era of glasnost and perestroika, Soviet political language continues to be phrased along other than Western lines. Both Western analysts of the USSR and the general public should keep this in mind. Otherwise they are likely to be misled time and again. Misunderstandings would inevitably result. To be sure, the argument here is not that the new terminology introduced by Gorbachev is always bound to frustrate Western expectation. But it can – and it does so indeed on occasion as the examples cited here indicate. For this reason one should not simply take note of the general terms used in political discourse by Soviet leaders and spokesmen. It is equally important to take a close look at how generalities are explained in practical detail. It is only on this basis that one can reliably ascertain what the Soviet side really means.

Perestroika and Soviet Foreign Policy

Vadim Zagladin

Discussion of the problems of relations between East and West is a extraordinarily useful thing. We all need to know each other better. Ignorance in itself is a factor that gives rise to suspicion and mistrust. Such meetings allow us to eliminate this factor jointly and, in so doing, to build a new mutual understanding.

Perhaps it is worthwhile to make one more introductory observation. Today's theme is »Gorbachev's challenge in the spheres of foreign policy and world politics.« But is it correct to speak of a challenge? It seems to me that it would be more accurate to say: »Gorbachev's initiatives in the spheres of foreign policy and world politics,« for we do not want to foist a challenge upon anyone. We appeal to the whole world community, and, of course, to the West, with a series of proposals, the goal of which – and the only goal – is to achieve by our collective efforts a turning point in world affairs, or, as Gorbachev said at his speech to the United Nations on December 7, 1988, to achieve the »democratization of the whole world order, to secure the solidarity of the world, its stability and the dynamic character of international relations.«

We in the Soviet Union have termed the present time a turning point. Indeed, the conditions of the existence of mankind have never changed so swiftly and dramatically, as they have in the twentieth century. Never before has mankind achieved such progress in knowledge of the world and its transformation. But never before has the world found itself faced with such a threatening challenge, with the necessity of making such crucial decisions. In politics it is extremely important to take into consideration this uniqueness of the modern age – an age when old conceptions and old solutions no longer fit. And this applies first and foremost to the sphere of East-West relations.

Getting down to the work of *perestroika* within the country, we inevitably should have addressed the sphere of international affairs. Since the foundation of *perestroika* is first of all truth, realism and a realistic

193

vision of problems and of ways to solve them, in the area of foreign affairs we should carefully take into account the real peculiarities of the modern world, its real condition. It should be admitted that in the recent past we approached the evaluation of many phenomena of world development rather schematically. Often we looked at them through the prism of ideological schemes, a part of which had grown old long ago, while others were on the whole untrue. From this have come many of our difficulties in politics, which have brought us, and not only us, considerable harm. But with *perestroika,* Gorbachev observed, »we will completely overcome attempts to be too clever with history, when from time to time these attempts were based not on what is but on what one wished to see.« Having looked at the world with open eyes, without prejudiced and ideological blinders, we saw a completely new picture. What did we see? First of all – *an exceptionally diverse, modern world.* We saw that during the course of the twentieth century, a new pluralism of social, economic and political development had been added to the ancient pluralism of national composition and cultural-historical traditions. In recent decades this has been the pluralism of almost one hundred and fifty independent countries, the political systems in each of these being the fruit of the distinctive choice of its people. The multivarious development of governments of both the socialist and non-socialist worlds, in our view, is an objective characteristic of the contemporary level of the history of human society. Further, we saw that this pluralistic world is deeply contradictory but also *interconnected* and *interdependent.* It is interconnected and interdependent as a result of the vital deepening and continuing intensification of the division of labor and as a result of rapidly expanding economic, scientific-techno-logical, cultural and information exchanges, the wise use of which is capable of enriching all people, every government.

But our world is also interconnected and interdependent because we are all threatened by the same dangers. These are dangers which came about from the unwise use of the colossal achievements of human thought, primarily, with the goal of creating weapons of destruction. These are dangers that have arisen in the sphere of man's relation to nature, in the course of which anthropogenic activity has caused losses to all remaining natural reserves and is beginning to threaten their very existence. These are dangers created as a result of the imperfect relations between various parts of world society, the flaws of the present system of international (political) relations and, in part, the flaws of international economic relations.

The elimination of the dangers that have arisen, the removal of the threat to our entire civilization demands a unification of the efforts of all regardless of faith or ideals. Otherwise, those who profess these faiths and live by these ideals are doomed to perish. As M. S. Gorbachev said at the session of the General Assembly of the UN, »further world progress is possible only through the search for a consensus common to all mankind in the movement toward a new world order.« Analyzing the opportunities for and the paths toward achievement of this consensus, we could not but notice that the »arena« of world politics in the past decade has been noticeably transformed. The actors in world history are now not only peoples, old and new states and their governments but also certain groups of governments. I have in mind here not the traditional political, military-political, or economic associations – they have long existed, and this is a reality which must be noted. I have in mind rather *the gigantic complexes* of peoples and states that have formed in the world, within and among which are in place a set of defined and, as a rule, very complex relations.

This means, first of all, that which we call »West« and »East« or »North« and »South.« The relations within the complex »East« have changed and are changing: new, more flexible links are emerging that are based on genuine independence and, in addition, diversity, but also on cooperation among those who share equal rights. In the complex »West,« interesting changes are also taking place, the character of which is easier for Westerners to judge. As well, new contacts are constantly being created in the complex »South.«

As we know, the relations formed between these complexes are exceptionally important. There is no doubt, for example, that we are on the brink of dramatic changes in the ties between North and South. Far-reaching restructuring of these ties, as well as their harmonization, is urgently needed, taking into account, of course, the interests of both partners. Truly profound changes in the relations between East and West are currently underway. I think that one could hardly doubt that their consequences are vital for both sides and for the world as a whole.

In the course of the past decade, East-West relations have given rise to military-political tensions that are still far from being overcome, which presents serious threats for mankind. We are faced here with the need

195

to take decisive steps along the path toward removing this military threat, in particular, for those people living in the affected countries. Furthermore, this is where the greatest economic potential is amassed, one so great that it can be the source of wealth for an overwhelming part of the world's population. However, this potential is presently in large measure oriented toward the fulfillment of anti-humanitarian, military goals, which can only give rise to new conflicts and problems. A novel direction to industrial development is needed, one which would both serve the interests of all peoples and states and promote the elimination of gaps in the levels of economic maturity between North and South. A transition to new, ecologically safe manufacturing processes is urgently needed. Otherwise, we will all find ourselves facing a catastrophe.

The countries of East and West also possess a huge intellectual and cultural potential, whose rational use, preservation and development can significantly raise the quality of life not only for the people of these countries but also for mankind as a whole.

The foregoing is not meant to disregard the potential, the achievements and the opportunities of the peoples of other parts of our planet. Nevertheless, the specific role and character of the East-West system must be fully taken into account. The peoples, governments and political, social and scientific forces in these countries carry a great responsibility not only for their own future but also for the future of all humanity. In short, there is a manifest need for important changes: East-West relations should be improved and expanded. Only in this way can the existing threat be eliminated, full-blown problems be resolved and new, unavoidable problems be properly dealt with.

At his address before the General Assembly of the United Nations, M. S. Gorbachev said: »We have come to the point where unregulated spontaneity leads to a dead-end. And world fellowship must learn to form and direct processes in such a way as to preserve civilization, make it safe for all and more favorable for normal life. By this I mean cooperation, but it is perhaps better to call it »co-creation« or »co-development.« Although these words were directed to the whole world, I think they apply first and foremost to relations between East and West. However, is such an essential, cardinal change in East-West relations possible? Theoretical and entirely practical proof exists for the realization of such a possibility, for there have already been a number of breakthroughs in common sense regarding these relations. For instance,

196

at the end of the 1950s and beginning of the 1960s, and then again at the beginning of the 1970s, East and West experienced short-term phases of eased international tension, which bore considerable fruit: for example, the Treaty of Non-Proliferation of Nuclear Weapons, the ABM Treaty, treaties of the USSR, Poland, Czechoslovakia and the GDR with the FRG, the Hel Final Act and a series of other important agreements. They spoke substantively on the general condition in the world and demonstrated that international relations can indeed be stabilized. They set a worthy precedent and serve as good lessons.

But the periods of détente in the 1950s and 1970s also taught us a lesson of a different kind: They turned out to be of short duration and did not prevent retrogressive movement. Why did this happen? First of all, these periods of détente proceeded only gropingly and lacked a truly powerful, enlightening strategic idea. So, for example, although both sides acknowledged that the military capabilities amassed by the great powers were sufficient to destroy the entire population of the Earth many times over, the ominous import of this fact failed to give rise to concrete policies. The recognition that the arms race creates a threat to the very existence of humanity is certainly laudable. But can it really be said that everything was done on both sides to brake, stop, or reverse this dangerous process?

It seems to me that there is yet another reason why the thaws in relations were so short-lived in the past. Actions were isolated, confined primarily (and then again only partially) to the military sphere: no real measures aimed at improving relations in other spheres were carried out. The Helsinki Final Act provided the opportunity to make progress in the directions outlined in its three parts, but the opportunity was never seized. Only now are the Act's statutes beginning to find material fulfillment. It is senseless to resort to finger-pointing here. We will leave this to historians. The important thing is not to repeat the mistakes of the past.

The development of world events in past years has created ever more *real opportunities* for improved East-West relations. Where do we see these opportunities?

First, we see them in the fact that in both East and West, the public is coming to understand the need for a change in these relations, the need for a resolution of the problems we spoke about earlier. Just as with individual, group, class or national consciousness, one can see

197

the development of a new global consciousness, reflecting the unity of humanity irrespective of differences in ideological, political, religious and other spheres.

Second, we see new opportunities for the development of East-West relations in the fact that this new consciousness is being increasingly reflected in public policy, in the actions of business, and in political and intellectual forces. There is a growing understanding that East, West, North, and South are all part of one civilization and that all must search for new approaches toward defusing the crisis facing it, toward improving the world situation and toward building a new world. Of course, this process proceeds differently everywhere. But it also has a place everywhere and has already led to real changes in the world arena. These changes have opened a perspective for finding a way out of the vicious circle of power games, in which there must always be »us« and »them,« enemies.

Third, we see opportunities for the establishment of new relations between East and West in the processes of *perestroika,* which are taking place in the Soviet Union and, simultaneously, in different forms in other Eastern countries. This is, of course, not to deny that serious changes are taking place in the West, too, but these are not nearly as radical as those in the East. We are convinced of the fact that *perestroika* possesses a powerful potential for rebuilding world relations substantially broadening international cooperation and stabilizing the world situation.

Why do we think that *perestroika* will emerge as a factor in stabilizing the world situation, eliminating confrontation and establishing an entirely new form of mutual trust?

First, the entire concept of *perestroika* and all related plans have an exclusively peaceful nature. We are now preparing a long-term plan for the development of the country to the year 2005. Three variants of this plan exist; each of them is being carefully worked through. But at their core is the *social reorientation of our economy.* To achieve this we envision cardinal changes in the structure of capital investment, the structure of production in favor of industries producing consumer goods (including the processing of food products), housing construction, health care, etc. All three variants of the plan are clearly based on the prospect of a reduction of military production and a conversion of a part of the military industry to these new purposes (the size of that part will depend on the progress of disarmament negotiations). Our plans also propose that the remaining capacities of the military industry be switched to the production of exclusively peaceful products. The stated changes will begin to be implemented in 1989. It is apparent that such a long-term model for economic development can serve neither as a factor in destabilizing world conditions nor as a factor in increasing military danger.

Second, we believe that *perestroika* promotes the stabilization of the world condition, inasmuch as it signifies the broadest development of democratization and *glasnost* in the sphere of foreign policy, defense and security policies. The process of strengthening *glasnost* is developing ever more swiftly. Our partners from the West have told us time and again, that the supposed threat is created not only by our tanks but also by our secrecy. It seems to me that this thought is fair. One must add, however, that the secrecy and closed nature of our society were a result not only of our well-known internal processes, but also a consequence of the influence of external factors – primarily, confrontation and the »Cold war.« Of course, the negative influences of confrontation were experienced by our country and Western states alike, which had (although to different degrees) their periods of »witch hunts.« Now we are opening up to the world, and to ourselves. Of course, not everything in this sphere has been accomplished. We will need to go quite a bit farther: the tempo depends partly on our Western partners, who at times demonstrate a certain lack of enthusiasm concerning control, verification and their own transparency. It seems as if, with *perestroika,* we have switched roles with the West.

Third, perestroika's role as a stabilizing factor in world affairs is also demonstrated by our striving to be included in a new way in the system of international division of labor to become a partner of the European Economic Community (with which we already have business relations) and in the future to become a partner of GATT, World Bank, and the IMF. If these aspirations of ours have yet to be converted into concrete actions, then by no means is it our fault. But I think, the West will also come to realize in time that including the Soviet Union in the international economic system will contribute to a strengthening of interdependence and trust and remove many of the grounds for mutual suspicion.

Fourth, and finally, *perestroika* increases international stability in that it has changed the course of our foreign policy, our concept of politics in the world arena and our measures directed toward its realization. The most important change in foreign policy was that, on the one hand it was freed of the legacy of the past, the legacy of stagnation; on the other hand, it now adequately reflects the essence of this new phase in the life of our country. Our course in world affairs had to be brought into line with *perestroika's* humanistic orientation. As the resolution of the 19th Party Conference noted, sound foreign political action could contribute to the freeing of the country's resources for peaceful construction. In order to do this, it is necessary to demilitarize world politics, democratize the entire system of our international ties, improve relations with all countries, broaden the geographic scope of these relations, and change the position of these countries in the worldwide division of labor.

In altering our foreign policy, we proceeded in three directions: *First,* a critical analysis of our country's foreign policy activities was needed for the preceding period. *Second,* a realistic assessment of the problems of the modern world had to be made. *Third,* a new foreign policy concept had to be designed that met the demands of *perestroika* and the conditions of modern world development. This work has engendered a broad program of action in the world arena. In addition, it must be said that this work is continuing. From phase to phase, we are deepening our analysis and enriching our theoretical conclusions and practical proposals.

Our analysis of past foreign policy looked at the decade 1975-1985, when the military threat grew. The arms race reached new dimensions, acquiring simultaneously a qualitatively new character. In answer to our sincere appeals for peace we heard ever more blunt accusations about the Soviet threat; public opinion polls showed that our country's prestige had declined to a level similar to that of the early 1970s, even the early 1960s. Clearly, our foreign policy had gotten bogged down. What had happened here? The analysis revealed that although the West itself had contributed significantly to the growing tension, we were in large part also to blame.

In addition, since the mid-1960s, arguments had been raised in our ranks that our foreign policy concept suffered in large part from inconsistency and that it was even contradictory. This had stemmed from our penchant for reducing world events to a struggle between two opposing social systems. As a result, our foreign policy was oriented along the lines of a constant and increasingly rigid confrontation with the other side, and our reaction to activities in the West turned out to be inadequate. In essence, in a considerable number of instances we played into the hands of those who gambled on tension, answering their hostile actions with our own confrontational actions. They provoked us, and we gave in to provocation. Furthermore, although repudiating the idea of nuclear war, we at the same time hoped, if not for victory in nuclear war, then in any case for the survival of socialism and the death of capitalism. This found its reflection in our program documents and our practices. Indeed, our basic forces and our attention were focused on the military aspect of opposing imperialism. However, we often lost sight of the real demands of defense, especially in view of our country's resources. Inadequate consideration was given to the cost to our own people and to other peoples or to what one or another course of action would yield. This, in part, was expressed in the decision to deploy in Europe the SS-20 missiles. This also manifested itself in the protracted, almost fifteen-year growth in the production of chemical weapons. In sum, we allowed ourselves to be dragged into a continually growing and ever more expensive arms race, which could not but take its toll on the socio-economic condition of the country and its international positions. This acquired an ever more alarming character: although military-strategic parity was maintained, with time negative dislocations in the economic and technological correlation of forces between the two social systems were revealed more and more distinctly.

Acting as if hypnotized by the formula of continual and undeviating intensification of the general crisis of capitalism, it must be admitted that we ignored those profound changes that had been occurring in both developed and some developing countries of the non-socialist world, which showed that capitalism had seriously changed – that at each successive turn of the historical spiral, capitalism is able to remove the most dangerous self-contradictions of the moment. In answer to the economic crisis of the 1970s, the leading capitalist states were able to rebuild, to improve the structure of their economies and to achieve an acceleration in the development of technical equipment and a renovation of technology. We were not able to act so effectively. As was noted at the June 1987 Plenum of the Central Committee of the Communist Party of the Soviet Union, »we began to concede one posi-

201

tion after another; in the spheres of efficiency of manufacturing, quality of production and scientific-technical development, the gap between us and the most developed countries began to grow wider.« Thus, power consumption and metals consumption in our manufacturing industries were, toward the end of the 1970s, 1.5 – 2 times higher than in the West. Only 17 – 20 percent (and in a number of branches of industry, only 7 – 8 percent) of our production met the world standard.

However, we failed to draw the obvious conclusions from these facts – that a change in political orientation was clearly called for and that a turn toward disarmament, or at least a halt to the arms race, was desperately needed. We went with the flow, having given in to the will of the current.

Finally, the deficits in our foreign policy brought us serious losses. In this regard, political measures were often suppressed in favor of propagandistic measures and aspirations to »gain points« in an ideological logomachy, which did not achieve concrete political results. I mention here in passing that the West proceeded along a similar path in this area. Thus, in a number of instances, when negotiations started – that is, when political methods began to be used – our representatives acted in accordance with 1950s stereotypes (when we thought, in essence, that we could not expect concrete results from negotiations, inasmuch as we were dealing with imperialism). At the bargaining table, the positions established were irreconcilable with one another, in that each side refused to consider the interests and concerns of the other. And at the beginning of the 1980s, we walked out of missile negotiations entirely, which only played into the hands of the opponents of disarmament.

Fundamental world changes enabled us to be more receptive to actions in the interest of security, but we did not take advantage of this opportunity. For instance, a realistic world view revealed that the role of developing countries was growing. Non-aligned nations became more active, growing in importance as a factor in peace and security. But Soviet diplomacy often reacted passively to this development. We were late in realizing the acuteness of the demand for the creation of a new world economic order. Up to 1985, we lacked independent policies on this issue, including the debt problem, which was taking on an increasingly dramatic character.

Regional conflicts continued, even grew, and new ones appeared. The adversaries continued to remain far from victory, even though they kept on battling stubbornly and persistently. It became clear that a military solution to regional problems could not be effective. This applied also to Afghanistan. Based on the interests of both Afghanistan and our own country, it was necessary to achieve a cessation of the war, to search for an avenue toward political settlement of the Afghanistan problem. But until the beginning of *perestroika,* this had not been possible.

An attentive review of the state of our relations with the countries of the Western world showed that in many cases we were only marking time. The geography of our diplomacy turned out to be entirely limited. With many nations whose role in the world arena was considerable and growing (for example, the countries of the Pacific Ocean basin), we had virtually no contacts. And this, of course, restricted our opportunities. We also failed to take into account the opportunities offered by both interested public opinion and contacts with various political forces that could act as our allies. We did sufficiently estimate the growing anxiety on the part of the majority of the members of the world community regarding the spiraling arms race and international tensions; we did not succeed in converting this anxiety into concrete joint actions.

This all goes to show that a collective spirit was missing for the adoption of responsible decisions, that a comprehensive review and analysis of problems was lacking, and, sometimes, that council with friends was even absent. The leadership of the Communist Party of the Soviet Union has realized that our country needs to withstand such serious foreign economic, political, technological, cultural and humanitarian challenges; to meet them an essential re-evaluation and correction of the international activities of the Party and the Soviet state was in order. The main conclusions that we reached can be summarized in the following basic theses:

The problem of survival is facing mankind. The solution to this problem presupposes not only the removal of the threat of nuclear war but also the creation of such conditions as to prevent the threat from reemerging. The solution presupposes the prevention of ecological catastrophes. It also presupposes the easing of tensions in a series of other systems of a global nature – first and foremost, in the system of North-South relations. If achieved, the resulting situation will mean that *the problems, interests, and demands of all humanity are to be given priority status.* We are convinced that these must become priorities for all members of the world community. Whether one recognizes this or not is another matter.

The realization of this truth has, first of all, shaped our *new approach to the question of nuclear war.* Unlike in the past, we are now firmly convinced that in a nuclear war there can be no winners but only the destruction of all civilization. From this, the logical conclusion is that *security cannot be guaranteed by relying on military-technical means.* The guarantee of security is more and more a political task and can only be solved by political means. These principally include *negotiations with the goal of liquidating all means of mass annihilation and limiting arms.* Unlike in the past, we are now approaching the problem realistically, and we understand that in the modern world no one is ready to forego armaments completely. Therefore, we will not repeat *the proposal for general and total disarmament,* leaving it for a more appropriate time. Instead, we propose disarmament to such a level that each country has the ability to defend itself but not to act aggressively. Taking into account the fact that the modern world is deeply interdependent – in particular, from the point of view of the conditions for guaranteeing security – we hold that *security ought to be guaranteed in equal measure to all countries on the basis of their common, collective strengths.* From this comes our active, constructive approach to the UN, to its institutions, to the Helsinki process and to all other forms of collective diplomacy, as was recently demonstrated with conviction by M.S. Gorbachev's speech before the UN General Assembly.

Our new approach resolutely steps back from the concept of a bipolar world. This concerns, first of all, the question of whether it is possible to boil down all international relations to the confrontation between East and West, as was done by us not too long ago. We are now convinced that to reduce everything to social bipolarity is erroneous. The most diverse factors and forces confront each other in the world arena. A rational policy is called for to take into account the real diversity of countries, their interests and their concerns. This is a signal of a serious change in our approach to peaceful coexistence. Whereas we previously believed that peaceful coexistence concerned only relations between countries with different social orders, we now hold this to be a universal principle. Whereas we formerly thought that peaceful coexistence was a special form of class struggle (what, by the way, diverges completely from the original ideas worked out by Lenin), we how firmly declare that the sphere of interstate relations ought to be delivered from the influence of ideological arguments. The de-ideologization of international relations has become the requirement for a new level of world development. These relations should be based exclusively on principles of international law.

To what has already been said it should be added that in creating support for a legal basis for international relations, we are giving increased attention to the questions of morals and morality in international relations. Suitable norms have been worked out by humanity over the course of centuries. In large part, the understanding, common to all peoples, of the need for humane, civilized approaches to world affairs is expressed in these norms. We share this understanding and rely on it in our concrete actions.

Finally, if we earlier looked on peaceful coexistence only as a defined *policy,* today we think that this policy should serve to create a *new world order,* for which the principles of peaceful coexistence will become the founding law. Speaking of this, it should be stressed that our understanding of these principles follows the precepts set forth in the »ten commandments« of the Helsinki Final Act.

Thus, the change in our foreign policy approach is not so much a reform but a revolution or a profound political-psychological reformation. The renovation of our (and our allies') military doctrine has become one of the most important practical consequences of this reformation. It is true that at some points our Western partners had expressed the following thought: in your words, there is much that is new; but there is little change in Soviet actions. I think that this was always incorrect. It suffices to list our concrete actions directed toward stopping regional conflicts, beginning with Afghanistan. And our proposals for disarmament are not only words but also deeds. If these proposals have so far not been realized, then it is first and foremost because the West, while not rejecting them outright, has thus far not been able to work out an adequate and coordinated response.

M.S. Gorbachev's speech at the UN was the occasion for the announcement of a program of unilateral reduction in our armed forces and a restructuring of our forces remaining in Central Europe on the principles of non-aggressive defense. I think that any doubts about our exclusively practical, concrete and constructive approach to the work of *perestroika* in international relations must now be once and for all dispelled.

The reforms beginning in the Soviet armed forces, which are taking place in accordance with our defensive strategy and concept of reasonable sufficiency and non-aggressive defense, offer obvious evidence of the stabilizing influence of *perestroika* upon international life. *Perestroika* has given our foreign policy significantly greater dynamism and constructiveness and freed it from a score of old stereotypes, which even in the recent past prevented the development of necessary approaches to greater mutual understanding with the West. *Perestroika* has given a new character to our foreign policy initiatives. If before they frequently had the character of improvisations or simple reactions to a given political maneuver or act by the West, they now rely on a well-defined conceptual basis – on a long-term, scientifically determined basis.

Another thing should also be said. The restructuring of the content and concepts of our foreign policy is also accompanied by substantive changes in our country's foreign policy apparatus. The most important change is the far-reaching democratization taking place in this apparatus. Foreign policy has ceased to be a »closed sphere.« Serious public discussions about foreign policy problems are under way, and different points of view are being expressed.

In sincerely trying to understand our policy in the international arena, some Western analysts occasionally seek to »organize« this policy by citing diverse statements by different authors and publications. But, inasmuch as these authors and publications often exhibit divergent, even contradictory, points of view, an inaccurate picture results. With this method, one could »prove« whatever one wished. That is why I would like to give our Western colleagues this advice: judge our policy by official positions and, of course, by concrete actions; the statements of different authors can be used only as an evidence of pluralism in public opinion.

With the election of new government bodies – the Congress of Peoples' Deputies and the Supreme Soviet – their role has greatly increased in, among other things, the preliminary evaluation of foreign policy decisions. The role of the Ministry of Foreign Affairs has changed sharply; it now depends to a much greater degree on the scientific elaboration of issues and is drawn to the work of public opinion. A commission on international affairs has been created in the Central

Committee of the Communist Party of the USSR and is called upon to discuss collectively the most important issues of the international activities of the party.

Our present orientation is toward the search for solutions to problems existing in the balance of interests of all countries, toward the consideration of the concerns of the other side (even in those situations where those concerns seem to us unfounded) and toward the achievement of necessary compromises without violating, but rather by securing, the primary interests of either side. This has made our policy more predictable and understandable for the whole world. And this, it is thought, has facilitated mutual understanding.

Nevertheless there are *obstacles on the road to the establishment of new relations between East and West.* The first stumbling block is mutual *mistrust,* which is based to a significant degree on military confrontation. We are not going to argue about chickens and eggs and whether mistrust or military confrontation came first. But there is no doubt that it is difficult to trust one another if both sides have for decades opposed each other with all sorts of new weapons.

Problems also result from viewing the other side as the enemy. In large part, this image feeds on the notion that differences in the nature of the two social systems must unavoidably carry over into hostility and even conflict between them, including armed conflict. Our Western partners often speak and write frankly about this. It must be admitted that a mistaken identification of peaceful coexistence with class struggle – which, as I said before, we propagandized over quite a long time – did not at all help to overcome this idea. The existence of states with different social systems is a reality of the modern world. But is is not these differences in and of themselves that are dangerous. Rather, danger springs from antagonism, military confrontation and the desire to outstrip each other in strength. States with differing social orders are not at all doomed to arguments and hostility, and especially not to military conflicts. There is no fatalism here. The rivalry between states with different social types, of course, has and will have a place. But it should be more *a competition – a rivalry of ideas, concepts, and the results of their realization.*

The belief of each side in the merits of its system is quite normal. But, on the other hand, we should remember the old aphorism that no one has a monopoly of truth. We do not wish to deny our convictions or our

207

philosophy and traditions, and we do not appeal to anyone else to deny theirs. But we also do not intend to close ourselves off within the circle of our values. This would lead, as experience has already demonstrated, to spiritual impoverishment, for it would mean a rejection of such a powerful source of development as the exchange of all that is original and that makes each nation independent. The rivalry between the two systems is, if you please, a form of collective search for truth, in the process of which each can learn something from his partner.

On the other hand, conviction of the merits of our choice should not at all lead to the conclusion that only one system – »my« system – has a right to exist and that the other is the handiwork of evil forces. The future will show who will develop in what ways. We have already spoken here about the perspectives for cohabitation of the two world social systems. Many interesting things have been said. But it seems to me personally that not one of the hypotheses for possible development thus far proposed will be realized exactly as we have today imagined it. The science of dialectics teaches us that the struggle of opposites leads not to their mutual destruction, and not even to the destruction of one of them, but to their synthesis at a higher level of development. What sort of synthesis this will be is a question for which, as yet, we have no definite answer. However, today – and we are convinced of this – it lies ahead for all of us, regardless of existing differences, cooperatively to seek the road to leadership in ideas common to all humanity by overcoming an innumerable multitude of centrifugal forces and to preserve the viability of civilization.

In addition, the activity of those forces in the West who in 1917 said that the bolshevik child should be smothered in his cradle – and even today say that everything must be done to stop the growth of this child or to remove it from the face of the earth – is an indisputable obstacle on the road toward new relations between East and West. Of course, such ideas are rarely spoken out loud, but their echoes are often heard. Such echoes reinforce pronouncements of the danger that will result should the »image of the enemy« disappear under the influence of *perestroika*. Added to these dangers are the efforts to create a »new image of the enemy,« an enemy who has become attractive on the outside (»concealed« in *perestroika*) and for this reason is all the more dangerous. The appeals to »in no way facilitate *perestroika*« should also be added here. These appeals have different motivations. In some situations, they simply hold that one should not help the »adversary.« In other situations, they argue that if trade with the East, and especially the USSR, were to be expanded, it would be a direct help to the growth of its military potential (although in fact the result of these appeals and the corresponding activity, for example, that of COCOM [Coordinating Committee for East-West Trade Policy], has only created additional difficulties for European and American businessmen in their business contacts with us). In a third case (and this is a more recent phenomenon), they stress that even assistance in the development of light industry and the sphere of services is dangerous, because the Soviet Union would then be able to free additional resources of its own and use these for the growth of its military potential. All of this is nothing other than a blatant cultivation of the »image of the enemy,« an attempt to prevent changes in East-West relations.

What, in our view, can be done to overcome these difficulties, so that relations between East and West can be given a new, genuinely peaceful character? In brief, the following aspects are considered most important:

First, the *absolute demilitarization of relations between East and West* must be achieved with a reduction in the level of armaments of both sides to a minimum, non-aggressive level. In so doing, we should, of course, avoid attempts to »compensate« the reduction of armaments, accomplished in one sphere or another, by increasing or modernizing new weapons. The most correct thing to do would be to agree on a mutual renunciation (under international control) of the use of new scientific discoveries, technical apparatus and technology in military affairs.

Second, not very long ago, international relations were first and foremost relations between East and West and were oriented to prevent war, following the logic of armed conflict and mutual fear. Now they can and should be subordinated to the task of building peace. Given this, the process of improvement of international relations should not be limited to the military sphere. Today the issue should be the *intensification and expansion of political dialogue* on all points of the agenda of East-West relations, including the sphere of disarmament, the liquidation of regional conflicts, the problem of development (including the debt problem), the question of the prevention of ecological threats, and, of course, the exceptionally important sphere of human rights. In

209

addition, none of these issues should be the subject of confrontation. A constructive dialogue in the interests of bringing positions closer together and jointly resolving problems that arise is of vital necessity. We must all practice the political art of finding a balance of interests, the art of searching out mutually acceptable solutions, however complicated the problems may seem. Relations among the existing military-political alliances should also change within this context. Of course, military functions in the foreseeable future will hardly pass away, but these alliances should nevertheless become tools for political dialogue about purely military questions.

Third, broad development of mutually advantageous ties between East and West should be expanded both in the economic area and in the field of ecology, technical equipment and technology, science and culture. Cooperation has now become just as imperative as peace. No area should be closed off from collaboration. The obstacles on both sides should be removed step by step. Integrated institutions from both sides can and should also be included in the general stream of mutually advantageous cooperation. From our side, the way is open. Having taken a course toward active participation in the processes of world development, we are also interested in extending dialogue to those coordination mechanisms in the sphere of economics that are in place in the West. We would like, as has already been mentioned, to participate in their work. We do not exclude contacts with such organizations as the OECD (Organization for Economic Cooperation and Development) and others.

Fourth, both sides should work toward discovering opportunities for more intensive acquaintance and contacts between our peoples, including the youth of the countries of both East and West. There could be many possible channels there, and in each of these directions, tangible results can be achieved.

Fifth, and finally, we must strive with all our collective efforts for the removal of the »image of the enemy.« It is very important to cleanse the ideological discussion of illicit devices. The psychological war and the swelling of mistrust between peoples are incompatible with the norms of a civilized multistate community. In this plan, a truly special role belongs to the mass media.

I would like to conclude with the following. *It is time to bring the policies of all countries to such a level that these policies are not only reactions to changing events but also projections of new international relations based on the principles of humanism and mutual respect.* Such an approach to the formation of policy has already brought the first important practical results. The object now is to develop these results, to reach a qualitatively new stage in the relations between East and West. We are convinced that this is an absolutely realistic goal.

The »Common House«: Gorbachev's Policies Towards Western Europe

Hannes Adomeit

1. Introduction

Since the end of the Second World War, there has never been a separate Soviet-West European policy. There has only been a comprehensive approach vis-à-vis the West – a Soviet *Westpolitik* – in which policies toward both the United States and Western Europe have formed a unified whole.

From Gorbachev's assumption of power in March 1985 until October of the same year, it may have seemed that, in the overall framework of *Westpolitik*, the new Soviet leader was going to give top priority to the improvement of relations with Western Europe. In fact, it appeared as if he were aiming at the encouragement of a common European identity at the expense of U.S. influence and the U.S. presence on the Continent. Such an aim, however, failed to become a matter of practical policies. In the period from Autumn 1985 to Autumn 1988, it was the restructuring of relations with the *United States* that took precedence over relations with Western Europe.

The visit by West German Chancellor Helmut Kohl to the Soviet Union in October 1988, however, may signify a change of tack. Not least because of the election of a new American president and the uncertainty as to his foreign policy course, but also because of certain objective requirements, Soviet relations with Western Europe are likely to become more lively. This change of tack will not establish a »Europe first« approach. But it is likely to lead to a more equal treatment of these two »power centers« in Soviet policy.

2. The »Common European House«: Initial Promises, 1984–85

In Gorbachev's approach to Western Europe several themes can be discerned. The *first* was raised during his visit to London in December 1984. Speaking before the House of Commons, he referred to Europe as »our common house« (*nash obshchii dom*),[1] at that time clearly implying that the United States, as a trans-Atlantic power, really had no business in that house and that, as a *Pravda* editorial put it, »Washington is a stranger to that house.«[2] Another implication of this slogan, then as now, is the idea that the European countries have common interests, which needed to be safeguarded. Such interests, Gorbachev and other spokesmen have asserted, existed above all in the sphere of international security.[3]

A *second* theme, which supplements the first, is the assertion that in addition to geography, »Europe« is bound together by »historical ties« and a »common foundation of European culture,« including a common »political culture.«[4] Its foundation consisted of the »common heritage of the Renaissance and the Enlightenment and the great philosophical and social teachings of the 19th and 20th century,«[5] i.e. mainly socialism. In 1985 this theme was clearly directed against the USA. Gorbachev's supporters were then still to claim that »European political standards are superior to those in the United States« favorably different from the »cowboy attitude to the problems of war and peace« prevalent in Reagan's Washington.[6]

A *third* theme was first put forward by Gorbachev in his speech before the elections to the Supreme Soviet in February 1985. The Soviet Union

---

1 *Pravda*, December 19, 1984.
2 Literally, for Washington it is a »*chuzhoi dom*,« i.e. a house that belongs to others; »Evropa–nash obshchii dom,« *Pravda*, November 13, 1985.
3 Thus, in veiled criticism of the dicussions during Reagan's first term, he added that Europe was, indeed, to be regarded as a home and not simply »a theater of military operations.« *Ibid.*, December 19, 1984; similarly, the above-mentioned *Pravda* editorial claims that, to Washington, Europe is »a battlefield on the maps of [its] strategists;« *ibid.*, November 13, 1985.
4 Alexandr. Bovin, »Evropeiskoe napravlenie,« *Izvestiya*, September 25, 1985. The term »political culture« he used *expressis verbis* in »Evropeiskoe napravlenie,« *ibid.*, July 20, 1986.
5 M.S. Gorbachev, *Perestroika i novoe myshlenie dlia nashei strany i dlia vsego mira* (Moscow: Politizdat, 1988), p. 207.
6 Bovin, »Evropeiskoe napravlenie,« *Izvestiya*, September 25, 1985.

considered »a normalization of relations with the United States to be important.« However, he continued, »we are not for a single moment forgetting that the world is not limited to that country alone.«[7] Later he acknowledged that the relations between the USSR and the USA are »an extremely important part of international politics.« But he then added that »we are far from seeing the world through the prism of these relations. We understand the weight which other countries have in international affairs and take this into account in our assessment of the overall situation in the world.«[8] Such statements could be interpreted to mean that if relations with the United States were to develop unsatisfactorily, the Soviet Union had other options which it could pursue.

A *fourth* theme was sounded by Gorbachev in May 1985. Both in talks with Gianni Cervetti, the chairman of the head of the Communist section of the European parliament and member of the presidium of the Italian Communist Party, and Bettino Craxi, the Italian prime minister, Gorbachev advocated the expansion of economic contacts between the Council for Mutual Economic Assistance (CMEA) and the European Community (EC or EEC), as well as the establishment of official relations between these two organizations. This position taken by Moscow was not new. But Gorbachev continued by saying that »to the extent to which the states of the EEC were acting as one single unit,« the Soviet Union would be prepared »to search for a common language with them on specific international problems.«[9] This was unprecedented. Whereas previously, Soviet interest had extended only to regulating economic relations between the two organizations, Gorbachev for the first time signaled a Soviet interest in coming to some arrangement with the EC at the *political* level.

Fifth, in his talks with Cervetti and Craxi, Gorbachev seemed to view the attempts made by major Western European countries to increase technological cooperation (the *Eureka* programme) as positive and even to express interest in Soviet participation as long as this programme remained confined to civilian research and development.

7 *Pravda*, February 20, 1985.
8 *Pravda*, April 8, 1985. Similar formulations were used by Gorbachev in his speech to the 27th CPSU Congress in February 1986.
9 In his talks with Craxi, *Pravda*, May 30, 1985; see also the report on his discussions with Cervetti, *l'Unita*, May 22, 1985.

Such an interest would fit well with his emphasis on speeding up the »scientific-technological revolution« in the Soviet Union. As if to demonstrate the priority of Soviet-Western European relations, Gorbachev's first visit abroad as party leader was not to Washington but to Paris in October 1985. However, the promise of preferential treatment of Western Europe remained unfulfilled.

3. The Promises Unfulfilled: Autumn 1985-Autumn 1988

In the period from Autumn 1985 until Autumn 1988 the »common house of Europe« turned out to be more of a slogan than a clearly defined concept, and more rhetoric than substance. Both new and traditional elements characterized Soviet policy towards Western Europe. But, on balance, the traditional elements were dominant.

In *trade and economic relations*, »objective« factors continued to limit change. In fact, the overall volume of trade with the EC (despite the addition of Portugal and Spain to the trade statistics) fell from from US $ 28 billion in 1981 to US $ 23 billion in 1986.[10] This was probably the combined result of (1) the substantial lowering of the world market price for oil and gas; (2) the decrease in the demand for energy imports in Western industrialized countries; (3) the significant reduction in the value of the US dollar (the currency in which oil purchases and holdings are denominated); (4) the continued need to import grain on a large scale; and (5) the inability of the USSR effectively to compete with industrial products on the Western European market. Especially dramatic was the deterioration in the export performance of the Soviet Union: in the period from 1981 to 1986, Soviet exports to the EC declined by approximately one-fourth.[11]

The contraction of Soviet-Western European trade continued in 1987. By the end of the year the share of the Soviet Union and the other CMEA countries in overall EC trade amounted to only approximately 3 percent.

Direct investments by Western European countries in CMEA remained practically non-existent (0.1 percent of overall extra-EC investments)

10 Statistisches Bundesamt of the Federal Republic of Germany, ed., *Länderbericht Sowjetunion 1988* (Stuttgart: Kohlhammer, 1988), p. 97.
11 *Ibid.*, p. 98.

215

and, relative to Community investments in other countries and areas, have been declining.

»Subjective« factors also played a role in limiting Soviet-Western European trade and economic relations. Notwithstanding the greater interest expressed by the Soviet leaders in the »international economic division of labour,« until 1988 they remained reluctant to increase the level of indebtedness to the West.

At the *political level*, Soviet diplomats were busy chiefly with playing the traditional game of the utilization of »irreconcilable contradictions« both *among* the Western European countries and *within* these countries. It is quite noticeable, for instance, that although four Soviet-American summit conferences have taken place (Geneva, Reykjavik, Washington and Moscow) and Gorbachev has found the time to visit, in addition to all the Warsaw Pact capitals, New Delhi (November 1986 and November 1988) and Belgrade (March 1988), he considered it expedient to delay time and again a visit to the country that, due to its economic potential and political influence in the Western alliance, is perhaps the most important building block for a »European house«: West Germany. This neglect persisted despite the fact that a succession of West German visitors has been to Moscow: President Richard von Weizsäcker in July 1987; Chancellor Kohl, three times consecutively (July 1983, March 1985 and October 1988); Foreign Minister Genscher, five times; the Bavarian Prime Minister, Franz-Josef Strauss, in December 1987; and the Prime Minister of Baden-Württemberg, Lothar Späth, in February 1988.

Soviet Foreign Minister Shevardnadze's visit to Bonn in mid-January 1988 only produced a vague commitment that the question of a potential visit by Gorbachev to West Germany would »be decided« in the fall of 1988. Only in March 1988 was this vague commitment revised because Chancellor Kohl agreed to visit Moscow for a third time; and only then did the Soviet leadership relent and consent to a Gorbachev visit to Bonn.[12]

Shortly after having assumed power in the USSR, it became obvious that France and Great Britain were treated more favourably and with more respect than West Germany. Thus, during Gorbachev's visit to

12 Chancellery officials have said that firm agreement had been reached with Moscow that Gorbachev's return visit to Bonn will take place within six months after the October 1988 Kohl visit.

France in October 1985, the Soviet Union offered to negotiate separately with France and Britain on nuclear weapons. This may have been conceived in Moscow as a skillful gesture to support inclinations for greater independence in the two countries outside the NATO framework and to make one more step in the direction of eroding nuclear deterrence in Europe. At least it was interpreted in this fashion in Paris and London, and quickly brushed aside.

Utilization of »imperialist contradictions« at the Western European domestic level was evident particularly in the preferential treatment accorded to the Social Democrats, notably those in West Germany.

The limitations inherent in Gorbachev's approach to Western Europe were conspicuous on other political issues. The Soviet political leadership continued to view with unease the processes of vertical and horizontal integration in Western Europe, and vehemently opposed any semblance of military integration, including efforts at French-West German defense cooperation and the strengthening of the role of the Western European Union (WEU).

Nothing came of Gorbachev's hint to establish political links with the European Community. Due to Soviet recalcitrance on the West Berlin problem, it seemed for quite some time – until the spring of 1988 – that even the establishment of legal and organizational ties between Comecon and the EC would not be achieved. As the October 1988 visit by Austrian Chancellor Vranitzky in Moscow showed, the Soviet Union has continued to oppose Austrian inclinations to become a member of the EC.

Western European officials and international relations experts quite unsuccessfully attempted to receive clarification from Moscow as to the substance of the »European house.« Clearly, in the context of Soviet *Westpolitik*, it was the reordering of relations with the United States, rather than with Western Europe, that received top priority in Moscow.

4. New Promises and Prospects

Broadening of Political Contacts. Since October 1988, political contacts with Western European governments have become more frequent, however. Moscow has concluded new trade, scientific, technological and credit agreements with Western European government and private institutions. There has been some movement in cultural affairs. Clearly, a more even-handed approach is emerging in Soviet relations with the USA and Western Europe.

Harbingers of an increased interest by Gorbachev in mending Soviet-Western European relations became visible in the spring of 1988: in June the two economic organizations, the EC and CMEA, finally succeeded in concluding an agreement on mutual diplomatic recognition and trade relations. This step was overdue. Brezhnev, in 1970, had acknowledged the EC to be a »reality.« But it took almost two decades of precedence of politics over economics for the Soviet leadership finally to revise its stand on the Berlin problem and to agree to treat that city as a part of the European Community.

Political contacts with Western European leaders have increased. In mid-October 1988, Shevardnadze went to Paris for the first official visit of a Soviet foreign minister to France since 1980![13] In the same month Italian Prime Minister de Mita, Austrian Chancellor Vranitzky and West German Chancellor Helmut Kohl held talks with Gorbachev in Moscow; French President Mitterrand went at the end of November. Return visits by Gorbachev to the Federal Republic and to France are envisaged for the spring of 1989.

Probably the most important event among the proliferation of contacts between Gorbachev and Western European political leaders has been the visit by Federal Chancellor Kohl. On that occasion a number of agreements were concluded, including cooperation in environmental protection, peaceful uses of space, nuclear energy, prevention of accidents at sea, and food production. A first two-year programme of cultural exchanges was compiled.[14] Projects on the training of Soviet managers in West Germany are to be set up. German enterprises are to build a high-temperature nuclear reactor in the USSR. They are to participate in the expansion of the Soviet food and light industry. For that very purpose a West German banking consortium, led by the Deutsche

13 What is meant here are official visits by the foreign minister. Excluded here are stopovers (such as the two hours of discussion between Gromyko and his French counterpart in 1983) and inclusion of the foreign minister as part of a larger, high-ranking delegation (such as in October 1985 when Shevardnadze merely accompanied Gorbachev).
14 An agreement on cultural exchanges had been in existence since 1973. Nothing had come of it in practical terms, however, because of Soviet-West German disagreements over the inclusion of participants from West Berlin.

Bank, has agreed with the Soviet foreign-trade bank to provide a credit facility of 3 billion German marks. German businessmen accompanying Kohl concluded a number of joint ventures with Soviet enterprises, the total value of the contracts signed by German businessmen reportedly amounting to 2.7 billion German marks (US $ 1.5 billion at the current exchange rate).[15]

Economic Affairs. As these results may serve to show, Soviet-West German and, most likely, Soviet-Western European economic relations are likely to become somewhat more lively. At the very least it would seem that the low point in Soviet-Western European trade has been reached. West German exports to the USSR in the first half of 1988, for instance, increased by 10 percent.[16]

As for credit relations, a compilation of data from European bank sources shows that the Soviet Union intends to borrow approximately US $ 10 billion in Western industrialized countries.[17] That amount is being sought primarily in Western Europe and Japan. So far, US $ 6 billion has been made available in so-called framework credit arrangements (of which US $ 1.7 billion has been granted by West German banks); for the rest of the amount negotiations are continuing.

European Security Affairs. One major East-West arms control agreement has been put in place since Gorbachev's ascendancy to power: the December 1987 agreement for the abolition of intermediate-range nuclear forces (INF). Even though the agreement was concluded between the superpowers it has direct implications for Western Europe. Its noteworthy favorable features are the exclusion of the British and French nuclear forces; the scrapping of an entire category of modern weapons; the acceptance of significant asymmetrical cuts; and a comprehensive regime of on-site verification. It seems that the political leadership accepted the view expressed by civilian analysts, namely that Brezhnev's decision to station the SS-20 missiles was motivated by an erroneous definition of security interests, by a false sense of needing overinsurance and superiority in numbers (»the more missiles,

---

15 *International Herald Tribune*, 28.10.88.
16 *Süddeutsche Zeitung*, October 18, 1988.
17 Credit compilation by Stiftung Wissenschaft und Politik (SWP), Ebenhausen.

the more stable [Soviet] security«),[18] and »by technological advances rather than by political analysis«.[19]

However, in 1987 and 1988 one could legitimately ask whether the Washington agreement was just a different tack on the very same road which Brezhnev had traveled, namely towards the achievement of the de-nuclearization of Europe, the erosion of NATO's doctrine of »Flexible Response« and the separation of Western Europe from the United States, or whether Gorbachev would move towards greater balance and stability of armed forces in Europe and follow suit with significant concessions in conventional armaments.

Gorbachev's announcement of December 7, 1988, at the United Nations concerning unilateral troop cuts is an important step in the latter direction. Reducing the more than 5 million officers and men of the Soviet armed forces by 500,000 is relatively easy, considering that some 3 million of the total, according to Western estimates, are conscripts. Effective cuts can be made simply by shortening the length of compulsory service, currently two years in the army and three in the navy. That this may be the case was indicated by Gorbachev shortly prior to his initiative, when he told members of the Soviet youth organization that he believed »that the length of military service will be reconsidered«.[20]

The most important aspect of Gorbachev's announcement of December 1988 concerns the issues of surprise attack and invasion capability. Definite progress has been made towards a reduction in the Soviet offensive potential. From Czechoslovakia, Hungary and the GDR, 5,000 tanks are to be withdrawn with 50,000 troops, including assault landing formations and river-crossing units which, in the NATO perspective, have been designed for offensive operations in West Germany. Six tank divisions, of the 28 Soviet tank and motorized rifle divisions which Western intelligence says are based in those countries, are to be disbanded, and a further 5,000 tanks pulled out western Soviet

18 Igor Malaschenko, »Warum bauen wir mehr Raketen ab?«, *Neue Zeit* (Moscow), No. 7 (1988), p. 21.
19 Sergei Vybornov, Andrei Gusenkov and Vladimir Leontiev, »Nothing is Simple in Europe«, *International Affairs* (Moscow), No. 3 (March 1988), p. 41.
20 *Pravda*, November 1, 1988.

Union.[21] Also to be withdrawn unilaterally are one in four of Soviet artillery pieces in Europe and one in eight combat aircraft, according to Western estimates of current deployments.[22]

The announcement, if properly implemented, will serve to enhance the credibility of Gorbachev's professed readiness to change from an offensive to a defensive military posture in Europe. It also serves to show that the Soviet party leader is beginning to transfer resources from the military sector so as to improve the chances of the economic reconstruction of the Soviet Union. There are, nevertheless, still ambiguities in the announcement of the cuts. There are also, more broadly, considerable uncertainties and obstacles to a reconstruction of Soviet-Western Europe relations.

5. Ambiguities, Obstacles, and Limitations

Instabilities in Eastern Europe. One of the major problems in Soviet-Western European affairs are not only processes of integration in Western Europe but processes of differentiation, disintegration and decline in Eastern Europe. Gorbachev's assumption for the next five to ten years of Soviet-Eastern European relations appears to be that a lessening of central control and the introduction of pluralist structures will enhance the legitimacy of party rule in Eastern Europe and ameliorate economic performance. He may be wrong. *Perestroika and glasnost'* may fail to improve the economic situation, lead to social and political instability, threaten even further the weak legitimacy of the Communist parties and hence threaten Soviet control in Eastern Europe. It is doubtful whether this would be tolerated by conservative forces in the Soviet leadership. On the other hand, relative success of *perestroika* in Eastern Europe is possible only on the basis of closer cooperation with Western Europe. But this could mean that the reforming Eastern European countries could drift away from the USSR and become the outer rim of an

---

21 As for precise modalities, according to confidential information provided by Soviet arms control experts, the 5,000 tanks to be withdrawn from Eastern Europe are to replace older models in the western parts of the Soviet Union; in this region a total of 10,000 tanks are to be dismantled.

22 As summarized by the *Financial Times*, December 9, 1988.

expanding European Community. This, too, would most likely arouse opposition by party officials in Moscow faithful to the principles of Stalinism and the Brezhnev Doctrine.

From Gorbachev's point of view, the optimal development would be coordinated, gradual and successful *perestroika* in the whole Eastern »bloc«. But what are the chances of this occurring within a relatively short time? Probably very slim. So far, the communist party leaderships are far from agreeing on a comprehensive, let alone coordinated, reform effort. The responses to *perestroika* have been diverse. Only Hungary is moving in the direction indicated by Gorbachev. Poland is making valiant attempts to follow suit but is ideologically, socially and politically so polarized that the implementation of a coherent programme is well nigh impossible. The GDR and Czechoslovakia, probably the two most important countries for a successful modernization of the Eastern bloc as a whole, show no enthusiasm to adopt the full range of change occurring in the Soviet Union. Bulgaria only tampers with reform ideas. And Romania even continues to practise Stalinism in its pure form.

Thus, Gorbachev sees himself faced with a dilemma in his European policy. Any loosening of the reigns and consent to broader East-Western European cooperation is likely to lead to a loss of Soviet influence at the expense of the EC, and, notably, West Germany. But any reimposition of Soviet control is likely to defeat the purposes of *perestroika* in Eastern Europe – and potentially in the USSR itself. This fundamental dilemma explains the reluctance with which the Soviet Union has responded, most clearly and visibly between 1985 and 1988, to persistent West German attempts to embark on a broadening of contacts and exchanges between East and West in Europe.

The German Problem. It is therefore highly unlikely that, as some West German conservatives and neutralists believe, Gorbachev will launch a new initiative on the German problem and perhaps even make an offer for a confederation or reunification of the two parts of Germany. The German problem will remain a major problem limiting substantial changes in the postwar European »system architecture.« If this needed any further proof, it was provided during the Kohl visit in Moscow. On that occasion Gorbachev stated angrily that he had already »spoken several times about the so-called German problem« but that the matter apparently still needed clarification. »The current situation,« he said, »is the result of history. Attempts at overturning what has been created by it or to force things by an unrealistic policy are an incalculable and even dangerous endeavor.«[23]

The problem, then, on the German issue and, more broadly, in Soviet policy towards Europe can be simply put: If the ruling East German Communist party (SED) were ready to embark on comprehensive social, economic and political reform, and if such reform were to lead – by voluntary cooperation of the SED or through popular pressure – to the sharing of power with other political parties and to an increasing orientation towards the West, would Gorbachev still be willing and, domestically, able to renounce the »Brezhnev Doctrine«? Would he, or could he, contemplate a completely new security structure that would in all likelihood spell an end to Soviet domination of Eastern and Central Europe? It is doubtful that the Soviet leader himself has, at this stage of domestic and foreign policy *perestroika*, answers to such fundamental questions of European security.

Ambiguities in Military Security Matters. Despite Gorbachev's announcement of unilateral troop cuts, several ambiguities remain in this sphere, too. Even if optimistic assumptions about the modalities of implementation of the December 7, 1988, announcement were to materialize, Soviet military preponderance in Europe would remain. More cuts, both in the overal size of the Soviet armed forces and of the Soviet troops in Eastern Europe, as well as structural changes, will be necessary to establish a more equitable balance between NATO and the Warsaw Pact forces in Europe.

Another problem is the issue of modernization. As far as is known there has not been a slackening in the comprehensive effort, outlined by the previous (until September 1984) chief of general staff, Nikolai Ogarkov, for the comprehensive modernization of the Soviet conventional forces. Production of modern arms, notably tanks, seems to continue unabated. The end result of the cuts as announced by Gorbachev at the United Nations could, two years after implementation, still be leaner, more modern and more effective armed forces.

Whether or not this will happen depends to some extent on the Western negotiating strategy.

But the fate of »restructuring« in security matters, including in Europe, also depends on the chances of survival of Gorbachev and his

23 At the dinner speech of October 24, 1988, *Pravda*, October 25, 1988.

reform program in the Soviet Union. Large sections of the military establishment cannot be expected to be content with the diminution of their role in politics and society; *glasnost'*, democratization and the sharing of decision-making in security affairs with civilians; shifts in resource allocation from military to civilian uses; conversion of military plants to civilian production; or substantial cuts in the size of the armed forces, withdrawal of forces from Eastern Europe and changes in military doctrine. Their dissatisfaction, particulary if the current trends in national and international security affairs were to continue, could be heightened. If the military were to ally itself with conservative forces in the party apparatus this could spell the end of Gorbachev's rule and the end of *perestroika*.

Such possible changes probably explain the caution with which Gorbachev has proceeded. At the same time they point to limits which Western political leaders and the public have to take into account when they consider the likely scope and pace of change in European affairs.

The German Factor in Future East-West Relations

Renata Fritsch-Bournazel

In the various phases which have marked the evolution of East-West relations since the end of World War II, the German factor has played an important, and sometimes decisive role. Recently, with the implementation of Gorbachev's reforms and foreign policy, East-West relations have entered a new phase, sometimes called »new détente«. Therefore, it is legitimate to ask oneself which place this factor may hold in the diplomatic »new deal« of the late 1980s, given that it involves much more than just the diplomatic aspects of foreign policy.

It is out of question to prophesy or to guess what may happen. But it is possible, and necessary, to think over the multiple elements of a game that is of ever growing complexity and to discover the various trends giving impulses to history in the making, but not always in the same direction. To do this, let us – first of all – analyze the components of East-West relations, as well as of the »German factor« itself.

I. The components of a more and more complex game

After the war, for many years the »German factor« was totally contained in the »German question,« which was the question of a divided or united Germany. After four decades, the two German states have acquired a weight of their own. In the same way, the »Eastern factor« is developing, especially in recent times, towards greater and sometimes contradictory complexity. East-West relations themselves, once dominated by the bilateral dealings between Moscow and Washington, are more and more diversified, with the emergence of Europe, and of Germany.

A. The components of the »German factor«

After the unconditional surrender of Germany, there was no »German

225

factor«, but just a »German question«: should the remaining German body (after the Eastern subtractions) be united or divided? The question was supposed to be solved, legally, by the Four Powers, in fact by the two superpowers. They failed, due to their conflicting views and aims. The Western powers first favored division, to prevent the resurgence of a German threat, and later advocated reunification through free elections in the name of democracy, in order to support the Federal Republic but also to »roll back« eastward the Soviet power. The USSR saw German unity as a means to extend its influence westward and later accepted the division as a safeguard for its wartime conquests. The result was the status quo. In the course of time, the »reserved rights« of the Four Powers became more and more theoretical, and the quadripartite bodies created by them have practically disappeared. There are some significant exceptions, including Berlin and its access, where important parts of the quadripartite status and its rules remain, together with one limited but essential organ: the Berlin Air Safety Center. As a symbol, as a survival kit vital for the West Berliners, or as a »pierre d'attente«? Very soon, as the status quo consolidated, the two German states were created. For a long time, they kept subordinated positions in their respective camps, especially in the political domain. But this is less and less the case. For the Federal Republic, the recovery was more rapid, primarily in the economic field, where after two decades she emerged not only as a European, but also as a world power, whose importance was confirmed and enhanced by the most recent financial crisis. For a long time it was common language to describe the FRG as »an economic giant and a political dwarf.« But this no longer applies. In fact, very soon the Hallstein Doctrine obliged Bonn to become active worldwide, economically and politically, in order to keep the GDR out. But once the Hallstein Doctrine was abandoned, the West German presence continued.

The GDR played a more modest, but not unsignificant, role in the socialist camp, and also outside it, economically and politically. Often described as the most faithful and obedient ally of Moscow, due notably to the lack of national identity, she also in fact developed positions of her own, exerting her influence in Moscow (very likely in 1961 for the construction of the Berlin Wall) and sometimes in conflict with Soviet views (Ulbricht in 1969-71). In the 1980s, East-West tensions brought about a situation where a certain intra-German convergence irritated Moscow; at present, the internal and external policy developed by Gorbachev is met with great reluctance by East Berlin but with sympathy, or even enthusiasm, by Bonn. So the times are gone where the »German factor« was of a purely passive nature: from now on, it remains a problem, but it also includes two – more and more active – actors.

B. The »Soviet« element of the East-West game

For most of these four decades, the Soviet element could be considered as »monolithic,« either internally in the USSR or within the socialist world. This was particularly the case during the Cold War period, during »détente«, and again during the deteriorating East-West relations in the early 1980s. The East European countries had only a small degree of autonomy, and Moscow was eager to control them, if necessary by force (1953, 1956, 1968, 1980-81). Internally, the USSR offered even less margin, except for a few heroic dissidents and some limited bargaining with the Western powers for the release of a few prisoners. In the present Gorbachev era, things have changed considerably. In an attempt to overcome impending economic catastrophe, fundamental political and economic reforms are being introduced; the homeland of secrecy makes an attempt to practice transparency. It is too early to tell what the results will be. But besides these voluntarily introduced changes, the new atmosphere, the new political surroundings, permits the expression of old problems. That applies for the national problems in Armenia, Georgia and the Baltic Republics. Of course, they do not simplify the situation and render more difficult the task of the reformers. Within the socialist community, for decades specific problems have existed, affecting certain countries, so to speak, as part of their singularity. But the economic crisis added new difficulties, even to those considered prosperous, like Hungary or the GDR. The reforms introduced by Gorbachev have complicated the situation even more, creating two categories of allies: those who support and try to apply *perestroika* (Hungary, Poland) and those who reject it (GDR, Czechoslovakia, Rumania). Outside Europe, too, the new Soviet deal has important consequences: first of all in Afghanistan, where the withdrawal of Soviet forces has begun; and in Angola, where the Cuban forces are to withdraw as well. This represents a clear departure from the policy followed since the mid-1970s, when the Soviet Union seized any opportunity to project her power in order to sustain communist regimes. It is certainly part of an effort towards more realism, as well as the consequence of a dramatic economic situation. But is it not, at the same time, a renunciation of one basic »rule,« according to which history was always and necessarily moving towards communism, and a country where a communist regime was established could never go back to capitalism?

C. The three layers of East-West relations

There was a time when East-West relations had only one element of substance, consisting in the relations between the two superpowers; the other elements, i.e. the European countries, played only a subordinate and occasional part. Even the United Kingdom had to recognize this, as early as Yalta; France, which hoped in the immediate postwar period to play the role of an arbiter between East and West, gave up this dream after a few years. In the East, all countries had to accept total submission; for a long time, their attempts to make their own choices ended in confrontations, mostly crushed by force. But even after the European actors begun to play a more active part, the American-Soviet relationship continued to assume a considerable role.

The impossibility of a substantial and active part was even more tangible in the German case: their own will, expressed either by uprising (1953) or by quiet and stubborn choice in favour of the West (1961), only triggered brutal Soviet reactions. The change came in the 1970s with the »Ostpolitik,« an initiative from Bonn. In its implementation, the FRG played a decisive role, almost at parity with the Soviet Union, with the three Western powers having just an episodic, although important role via the Quadripartite Agreement on Berlin. Interesting is the fact that in the 1980s, during the worsening of East-West relations, Bonn and East Berlin developed a kind of intra-German convergence, much to the displeasure of Moscow, giving to German-Soviet relations a real triangular dimension and underlining the substantial aspect of the »German layer« in East-West relations.

The »European layer« in a way preceded the German one, but Western

Europe could not gain real momentum without West Germany. The first elements of strength and an active role appeared in the economic field with the Common Market. An attempt to do the same in the political field, with the »Plan Fouchet,« failed. Efforts were made by individual European states to be more active in the East-West relations, in particular, in the late 1960s by Général de Gaulle, when he launched his policy of »détente«. It was a real success, especially after it was adopted by Bonn in its »Ostpolitik.« Meanwhile, the European Community acquired strength, being recognized by the USSR and its allies. But politically, Europe continues not to exist. Nevertheless, an interesting effort was made, even before the »Ostpolitik,« by de Gaulle to develop a common »German policy,« when, in 1965, he declared: »The German problem is, *par excellence,* the European problem.« Unfortunately, this attempt was not followed with action. But in January 1988, Chancellor Kohl suggested that Bonn and Paris join in a common »Ostpolitik,« which very likely supposes a common approach to the German problem. Will the revival of Franco-German cooperation, especially in the field of security, and the beginning of a *new détente* permit the development of a substantial European layer in East-West relations?

II. The future of East-West relations

Shortly after Gorbachev's designation as the Number 1 in the Soviet regime, some doubts existed concerning the substance of his innovations, internally as well as internationally. After more than three years, most Western governments are convinced of the reality of this new policy. One problem remains, concerning Gorbachev's chances for survival and success. His failure or dismissal would probably mean for the USSR a new era of immobilism. Thus the only case to be studied is the continuation of the Gorbachev era. This should be done by considering successively the various actors involved, or, as previously described, the »three layers« of East-West relations.

A. The Soviet-American relationship and the German factor

The new détente was triggered in Geneva and Reykjavik by the two

229

superpowers. It came as a surprise to many observers, who did not expect President Reagan to introduce such a substantial change in his foreign policy. The first result of this new trend was the INF Treaty. There then developed a multiplicity of political, cultural and economic contacts. These will continue in the field of conventional arms control in Vienna, in a manner (à 23) giving the two leaders of the Alliances the main say on questions concerning, primarily, Europe (the same applied to the INF Treaty). This stands in sharp contrast to the détente of the 1960s and 1970s, where the superpowers' dealings concerned their strategic weapons; European affairs were mainly treated by the Europeans, notably, by the détente policy of France and by Bonn's »Ostpolitik.« This time, and by a concerted effort, Moscow and Washington have taken the lead, and seem willing to keep it.

Will this permit a solution to some of the political problems that have, from the beginning, plagued Europe and are the cause of the accumulation of armaments on the Continent? Up to now, it has not been the case. It is to be noted that in this short period of time, things began to move politically, but outside Europe: in Afghanistan, and more recently in Angola. In both cases, the process of total removal of Soviet or Cuban forces is of great significance, but the real political solutions will depend on what happens after the withdrawal. A similar evolution in Europe is not yet visible; the announcement of unilateral troop and armament reductions is, of course, important but does not imply any political settlement. Have the two superpowers the intention to move in that direction? Is it conceivable that an agreement among them can do more than maintain or consolidate the status quo, since a departure from it would mean a decisive victory for one of them? The Soviet Union has its main interests in Europe, and Gorbachev's new deal includes the abandonment of the various projections of power outside Europe undertaken in the Brezhnev era; on the contrary, the United States is fundamentally interested not only in Europe but also in many other areas (Pacific, Asia, Near East, Latin America, Africa). Is it conceivable that if it comes to political settlements, Moscow may be inclined to make concessions in these outside areas (for example by foregoing its nuisance value) rather than in Europe, where the USSR considers the status quo as essential? Is it not exactly the impression resulting from the deals struck in Afghanistan and Angola, and from what seems to be in the making in the Near East?

B. The triangle Moscow-Bonn-East Berlin

With the worsening of East-West relations in the early 1980s, the relations between Bonn and East Berlin had witnessed a sort of rapprochement, in order to protect the achievements of the Ostpolitik, while Moscow expressed severe criticism. In the Gorbachev era, a completely new configuration has appeared. In West Germany, many politicians express an almost enthusiastic support for *perestroika*. Mr Genscher is considered as one of the most fervent advocates of a positive response to Gorbachev's openings, and he is often criticized for that. But many other members of the federal government share his outlook, and Chancellor Kohl himself, during his visit to Moscow, expressed his willingness to »help« Gorbachev to implement his reforms; and this, despite their divergences on the German problem. On public opinion, too, the impact is considerable: according to opinion polls, Gorbachev is highly popular, considered more highly than President Reagan. The perception of the Soviet threat is diminishing considerably in a population where the fear not only of nuclear aggression but even more of the nuclear weapons stationed in Germany has become an almost irrational, but decisive factor. On the other hand, the enormous economic needs of the Soviet Union, and the attraction, one could say the fascination, exerted by German industry and technology, will constitute in the future an important element in bilateral relations.

At the same time, relations are worsening between Moscow and East Berlin. The GDR is probably the most reluctant ally among the Eastern countries regarding *perestroika*. At the same time, the GDR continues to be interested in developing relations with the Federal Republic, and over the past two years it has made great efforts to give to an increasing number of non-retired citizens the possibility to visit West Germany. In 1987 more than 1 million people benefitted from this. At the same time, the Western influence is increasing, especially among the young people (rock music), who also resent the highly militarised society and adhere to non-official pacifist movements. Is the dispute between East Berlin and Moscow limited to the problem of replacing the Honecker team, or is it more profound? On the substance is there a sort of division of labor, by which Moscow accepts East German resistance towards *perestroika* as a »moindre mal« necessary to keep the exposed GDR under control?

231

In this triangular deal, Moscow can count on West German economic and technological contribution. It can also hope for a favorable attitude by Bonn on many aspects of arms control, and it probably considers that West German feelings about nuclear weapons may hinder certain Allied moves (modernization of tactical weapons) and help, directly or indirectly, Soviet efforts towards denuclearization of Europe, at least in the tactical field. But this is not certain: Chancellor Kohl has already clearly rejected the zero-option for tactical weapons.

To make the deal more attractive, can Moscow offer some concessions in the political sphere, especially where the FRG is »demandeur,« e.g., on the German question? The question has been reiterated in Moscow by President von Weizsäcker (July 1987) and by Chancellor Kohl (October 1988). Gorbachev's answers are well known. To declare that history will decide what will happen in hundred years, to suggest building the common European house, to live in it and to see what happens is not just a »réponse d'attente« but also a rather defensive attitude. It stands in contrast to previous formulas, which flatly stated that the problem had been solved once for all and no longer existed. But can a solution be expected in this triangular context? Many ameliorations are conceivable, and many are already under way, as, for instance, the greater possibilities for travel (although these are conducted along the »hostage system«: one member of a family is allowed to travel while the others stay at home). Improvements can also take place in Berlin, where Eastern and Western susceptibilities have often hampered progress; but the necessity to maintain those aspects of the status vital to the survival of West Berlin and its access will remain, and the Wall, even if it can be made more permeable, will probably stay for a long time.

Many improvements will be feasible, but with precise limits in each case: the limits beyond which the regime would be in jeopardy. Much will depend on the internal evolution of the GDR, especially concerning the youth, which, totally formed and educated by the regime, seems far from being unconditionally attracted by communism. On the other hand, speculations and accusations that the FRG could accept neutralism in order to achieve reunification are inaccurate, since they ignore the strength of the multiple links binding West Germany with the West, especially the United States and the European Community. Moreover, the common European home is not meant just to house the

232

German-Russian triangle, and the German part of the house is precisely the one that creates problems.

C. The European dimension of the German factor

Efforts were often made to intertwine European undertakings with the German question. 23 years ago (press conference of February 4th, 1965) Général de Gaulle emphasized the European nature of this problem, inviting the Europeans, East and West, to work on it. Of course it was a long-term goal, necessitating profound changes in the Soviet Union. When, in January 1988, Chancellor Kohl suggested Paris and Bonn should practice a common »Ostpolitik«, which is at present on its way, did he not reopen such a perspective, not in the short but in the long term? And at a time where the USSR is precisely undergoing a process of deep change?

Would the emergence of a more autonomous Western Europe incite Moscow to be more flexible on the German problem itself, without tempting her to take control of the western part of the Continent? These are very speculative considerations. One could also argue that the German question is on its way to be »desingularized« as a »national problem,« due to the emergence, in and around the Soviet Union, of a series of national problems of various types and urgencies (Armenia, Georgia, Baltic Republics, Rumania, Afghanistan, etc.). In such a surrounding, there is much less chance for the German case just simply to fade away, as the East hoped in the early 1970s.

But can it be solved, in one way or another? Either by reunification, or by rendering »permeable« the inter-German boundaries, as well as other inter European boundaries? And how to deal with the Berlin Wall? One thing is certain: although West European interests outside Europe are important, it is difficult to imagine that Moscow could offer compensations abroad, in exchange for a confirmation of the status quo in Central Europe. On the other hand, the attraction for the economic, financial and technological capabilities of a united European Community can only increase after the establishment of the single market. At present, on the German question, Moscow's reaction is negative: can it remain so in the long run? Within such a variety of national problems, could a European approach to the German problem be eased, or made more difficult?

Of course, Germany is the only case of a nation divided between two alliances, two systems and two ideologies. Faced with demands to open the boundaries and to abandon the GDR regime, Moscow would evidently refuse. But which are the points considered as essential by the USSR: The boundaries and the Berlin Wall? The regime? The stationing of its forces? Could it be conceivable to grant to the USSR some form of guarantees for these essential points, provided that extended liberalization could be achieved on the other aspects? In that context, could the concept of an »Austrian status,« once suggested by Adenauer, be considered? Could a common West European approach, a common »Ostpolitik«, tackle the division of Germany in liaison with the division of Europe? Could such an approach constitute the Western version of the »common home,« i.e., a home without barbed wire and »Schießbefehl« and of course with rooms for the American cousin?

This is exactly why one should not confine this analysis to the question of what the European context could contribute towards solutions of the German problem and what role the German actors could play in this process, but also ask what the German factor could bring for Europe. In the early 1980s, during the deterioration of East-West relations, the two German states developed between themselves a sort of mini-détente and positive cooperation, in order to »limit the damages« and to protect the results of the »Ostpolitik«, despite Moscow's anger and various Western countries' suspicions. In the future the two German states could again take a similar attitude, in the event of new East-West tensions. But couldn't this also apply in a phase of continuing détente, as a factor of progress, and as a contribution to the »European order of peace« often invoked in West Germany? This time, Moscow would probably not show the Germans the cold shoulder! And the West, if it rallies to a realistic détente policy, should also welcome and support such an »entente,« which could efficiently promote progress in the most central, but also most tense area of Europe.

The first détente in East-West relations was essentially based on the status quo, and as early as 1968, the West was reminded of this by the invasion of Czechoslovakia. The »Ostpolitik« was mainly considered, and not only in the East, as a total recognition of the status quo in and around Germany; later on, it proved to be much more and much less than that. But, after all, the mood was for immobilism on the European stage, in the post-Khrushchev Soviet Union as well as in Western Europe after the unrests of 1968, while the USA tried to get rid of the Vietnam War and was more and more inward-looking. The most active and substantial factor was brought by the »Ostpolitik«: a West German contribution.

To which extent a German »model« could play a role elsewhere in Europe remains to be seen, because the intra-German relationship is largely »sui generis«; but by helping to provide more normalcy in this area, it would constitute an important factor of amelioration, both in the daily life and in the atmosphere, which would have its repercussion in the rest of Europe. Moreover, since the German question is the most extreme case and most vivid example of the division of Europe, its evolution, even toward a partial solution, will serve in measuring the evolution of the European question and constitute the best indicator of real détente, i.e., a détente not merely a mixture of improvement in certain domains and of stubborn refusal of progress in others. This supposes a clear consciousness in the West and in the East, especially from those who advocate the »common European home,« that the European question remains open as long as the Brandenburg gate remains closed.

Gorbachev and the Eastern European Countries

François Fejtö

In a speech just before Christmas 1988, the right hand of Gorbachev, Yakovlev, spoke of »the worldwide maturity-crisis of socialism«. Making a cautious reference to Lenin, he said that Marx and Engels had made an error concerning the building of a non-commercial production system. »Life has not confirmed this hypothesis, War Communism has been an error«. Gorbachev who represents the historic change in the eyes of the West has stressed at the recent Party conference that »the Soviet people remains faithful to 1917 and the human values of socialism«. At the same time, he proclaimed that »there cannot be socialism without democracy«.

The Revolution of October 1917, however, had nothing to do with democracy and the declarations of Gorbachev lead us directly to the problem of the two phases of the Revolution of 1917 which from February to October was inspired by the French ideals of 1789 but which adopted already in October the principles of the »Terreur« of 1793. There were two Russian revolutions which no more constituted a »seul bloc« (the term used by Clémenceau) than the French Revolution did, as recently reinterpreted by François Furet and many others of the new French generation of historians.

So far as Gorbachev is concerned, these contradictions, which are strongly felt in a Central Europe subject to Soviet hegemony, come from the fact that he intends to reform the system inherited from Stalin and Brezhnev without changing its foundations. As Michel Tatu has put it, he attacks the walls in which he tries to make holes but still wants to preserve the building. The failure of semi-reformist communism in Yugoslavia, the sick man of Europe, should however have shown him that a reform based upon half-measures could but lead to failure.

This is what we should keep in mind when examining the »Gorbachev effect« on the other socialist countries in Europe. Above all we should not forget that the political class and the intelligentsia of these countries are well informed of the problems encountered by Gorbachev inside his own country, if not by the national press, at least by foreign radio stations such as Free Europe, B.B.C., R.T.L., Austrian and German radio which are no longer jammed. The comments of Yuri Afanassiev, rector of the Institute of Archives of the Soviet Union, have been noted, according to whom »a relatively high number of intellectuals consider the momentary thaw as stimulating but of short duration, because they think it will inevitably be followed by a renewed frost.« In Budapest, Warsaw and Prague people have taken into consideration the statement of the sociologist Zaslavskaya (June 1988) saying that Gorbachev cannot definitively impose his ideas »without risking a battle with conservatives and after abandoning the idea of a homogeneous society«. Hence this hesitation, this caution which can be observed with respect to the »Gorbachev effect« in the behaviour of all the communist leaders in Central Europe with the exception of Ceausescu who overtly attacks the Soviet leader's infidelity to the pure Marxist-Leninist doctrine.

Gorbachev formulated the main lines of his Central-European policy on the occasion of the 70th anniversary of the Bolshevik Revolution. As Khrushchev had already done before, he stressed that »there is no unique model of socialism for all countries« adding that »each communist party in office is responsible to its own country«. This last sentence marks a certain distance towards the Brezhnev doctrine as proclaimed in 1968 when Brezhnev added to the old formula the following: »and to international communism«. This addition served as a basis for the intervention in Czechoslovakia. The political writer and French judge of Hungarian origin Béla Faragó describes a recent visit to Hungary in the December issue of the review »Commentaire«. He relates a statement of »a relatively high official« according to whom »the tolerance limits of the Soviet Union towards the other socialist countries have been broadened, even insofar as the reforms envisaged by the Hungarian leaders are concerned« and who added that in any case the »Soviet Union is solely concerned with the fact that no politically hostile countries exist in its neighbourhood«. This is probably a true statement although the tolerance limits remain uncertain. There is for example no indication whether Gorbachev would or would not admit the replacement of the monopoly of the communist parties by a multi-party system or whether he would accept a true pluralism including free

237

trade unions. On the other hand, it seems more certain that Gorbachev seems to wish that the leaders of the other communist countries follow his example of cautious *perestroika* and *glasnost* thereby avoiding a destabilization caused either by a slack attitude or one of extreme rigour. It also appears that he admits criticism and refusal to follow his policy, as demonstrated not only by Ceausescu but also by Honecker and Jakeš – provided that this behaviour does not complicate his foreign policy. This might explain the fact that he is tolerating the behaviour of Ceausescu although it must certainly concern him and although even the Western countries would probably pardon an intervention aimed at putting an end to this pathological behaviour just as they would have pardoned Vietnam for having put an end to the terror of the Khmer Rouge in Cambodia, provided they would have withdrawn their troops after a police action.

I think that Leonid Yagodovsky, the deputy head of the Institute of the World Socialist System in Moscow gave the most precise definition of the Central-European policy of Gorbachev when he stated that »if the process of reforms stopped or even became reversed – which may happen – in one of the Eastern European countries, we would of course not be pleased. But this would not mean that the Soviet Union would force these countries to follow a policy of reforms by using its tanks. You can use tanks to stop reforms but not to introduce them«. One might see in this statement a disapproval of Soviet interventions in Hungary and in Czechoslovakia where Soviet tanks stopped a pursuit of reform but it has been noticed that Gorbachev has never admitted real affinities with reformers such as Imre Nagy and Dubček. It is true that in April 1987, Academician Smirnov stated that »new thought should be given to the events of 1968« but as far as I know, nobody in the Soviet Union came back to this question. It still is almost utopian to hope that the process of de-Stalinisation and de-Brezhnevisation could lead Soviet leaders to a revision of the policy of imposed bolshevising as practiced by Stalin in the countries liberated in 1945 by the Red Army in favour of a greater independence – close to the status of Finland or Austria. Such a change would however be in the very interest of the Soviet Union if it really wanted to be surrounded by non-hostile countries, and it is the task of the West to make this known to the Soviet Government. Awaiting this change, it is important to remember Churchill's statement: »No Soviet leader, especially if he is serious about reforming Russia, can afford to preside over the liquidation of the last Empire in the heart of Europe«.[1]

Let us come back to the countries of Central Europe: in my book on the »History of Popular Democracies«, I stressed the fact that the first signs of independence from the Soviet Union came from countries where the communist leaders were opposed to the policy of de-Stalinisation launched by Khrushchev: Czechoslovakia, East Germany and Rumania. Today these are the countries that show the greatest opposition against Gorbachev's reforms. Certainly, one can say that in general all the communist parties, even his own, are worried about the consequences of *perestroika* and *glasnost* and see Gorbachev as a potential »sorcerer's apprentice.« However, the most overt and strong opposition to Gorbachev's policy comes from the afore-mentioned countries.

One might think of the Jaruzelski of the December 1981 coup as not being very enthusiastic either about the reformist policy of Gorbachev. But proving himself very astute, together with his right hand, the intelligent Rakovski, Jaruzelski claims to be gorbachevian hoping thereby to achieve legitimacy in the eyes of public opinion. Furthermore, insofar as *glasnost* is concerned, Poland did not wait for the advent of Gorbachev. The military dictatorship has paradoxically admitted a certain freedom of expression and relatively large contacts with Western countries. Even without the advent of Gorbachev, Jaruzelski would have been pushed by the course of events in his own country to look for a normalization of his relations with the civil society and to open dialogue with Solidarnosc.

In Czechoslovakia, the departure of Gustav Husak, Brezhnev's man, is perhaps not independent from advice given by the Kremlin. Following his departure, the battle between Strougal, who wanted to be the number one gorbachevian of his country and the arch-conservative Vasil Bilak led to the success of a more flexible conservative, Miloš Jakeš. His participation in the repression after 1968 does not prevent him from realising reforms which had anyway become inevitable. Like his German collegue Honecker, Jakeš seems to be convinced that economic efficiency can be improved without necessary reforms of the political

1 Jacques Rupnik, *The Other Europe*, Weidenfeld and Nicolson, London 1988

institutions in the sense of a greater democracy. His intention is to perform *perestroika* without *glasnost*.

With a certain air of impertinence the journal of East Germany's Communist Youth *Die Junge Welt* expressed the East German leader's ideas about the Gorbachev effect. This journal wrote recently that the Soviet Union should be thanked for the services rendered in favour of the Revolution but that insofar as the organisation of economy and technological progress are concerned, East Germany »has no lessons to learn from anybody«.

Hungary is an exception. The retirement of Kàdàr in May 1988, who served Brezhnev as devotedly as his former boss, Khrushchev, might not have taken place so quickly without the arrival of Gorbachev. On the other hand, *glasnost*, the intellectual effervescence which finally led to the replacement of the political personnel in Hungary happened before the arrival of Gorbachev. At present one might say that, within the communist world, Hungary has the most open government, and that claims for liberty and democracy are most clearly articulated in this country. Kàroly Grosz, the successor of Kàdàr, modelled the new Political Bureau in the image of the Soviet Union by accepting the membership of moderate reformists such as Jànos Pozsgay, who is very popular among intellectuals as well as the economists Rezsö Nyers and Miklos Németh, the latter having been chosen last May as President of the Council. But »kadarists« still remain in the Political Bureau as well as in Government. They have a dominating position in the apparatus and Kàroly Grosz who sees himself in the centre, is often accused of practicing Orwellian »double-talk« by behaving as a reformer when addressing himself to intellectuals and speaking a ligachevian language to reassure the party activists upset by the degree of agitation in the country.

Some of the statements of the new reformist leaders, which are largely covered by the press, the radio and the television which are at least provisionally free of censorship, depict promising perspectives. There is much question of pluralism, that is to say of a recognition of the autonomous existence of the civil society, as well as the growth of the market economy and the reorientation of exchanges with capitalist countries.

The adoption on January 11th 1989, after several months of discussions of two laws concerning respectively the freedom of assembly and the right of association, constitutes an important step although the question of a possible organisation of other parties and henceforth the abolishment of the monopoly of the communist party will not be tackled before August 1989.

It should be noted that in Hungary as well as in Poland the intellectuals did not wait for the green light of the authorities before creating independent organisations be they political or trade unions. Contrary to what happened in Poland, however, the working class still remains passive. During 1988 a real associationist fever filled the country. Amongst the hundreds of associations created, the most important on a national basis are the »Democratic Forum« which benefits from the discrete protection of Jànos Pozsgay; the »Union of Free Democrats,« previously called »the Network of Initiatives,« which includes several existing groups, amongst them ecologists and conscientious objectors and which places itself clearly in opposition; the »Federation of Young Democrats« which is also in favour of radical changes; and finally the »Free Trade-union of Scientific Researchers,« which has more than 1,000 members. The most dedicated members of the party apparatus, who follow with anxiety the development of all these movements, which publish journals and magazines, have created a circle of their own. This circle is called Ferenc Münich in honour of the former companion of Kàdàr and the former Ambassador in Moscow also, and whose role in 1956 during the call for the Soviet intervention is ignored by nobody. There is however a contradiction between the effervescence of intellectual life and the economic situation, which is constantly deteriorating. The Grosz Government tries to overcome the crisis by adopting the austerity measures recommended by the International Monetary Fund but people in Hungary are questioning the effects which a decrease in the standard of living may have upon the population although such a decrease is indispensable for the reorganisation of an economy which had given raise to a certain artificial prosperity in the eighties.

In conclusion and to slightly simplify things, one can say that Hungary as well as – to different degrees – the other socialist countries (except Rumania, which is presently completely blocked) reflects for the moment a battle between two lines: The conservatives on the one hand who can mainly be characterized by their fear of *glasnost*, and the reformist leaders who hope to be able to reform economy and

241

the political institutions, and, at the same time, keep the single-party system. As the editor of the »Wall Street Journal«, D. Satter, stated, the conservatives have the advantage in this battle to remind the population of a past whose disadvantages it has already forgotten, where the atmosphere had not been disrupted by the clamours of the intellectuals and where, as a kind of social contract between the party and the population, »people could exchange their obedience for the security and liberty of not being obliged to work too hard.« This is true for the Soviet Union and mutatis mutandis for the other socialist countries except East Germany. This situation is uncomfortable, and in the long run it will be impossible for the socialist leaders to live with two contradictory logics: It will not be sufficient to recognise verbally that the success of economic reforms depends upon a political reform; one has to work on it. If this is not done, conservatives will come back in one form or another, and the model they may adopt may perhaps be the one of East Germany.

The European Dimension of Soviet Foreign Policy

Vitaly Zhurkin

Many have noticed the more European slant taken by Soviet foreign policy in the past few years. This tendency will likely continue through the 1980s and 1990s. Yet the following reservation should be made: this change is by no means made at the expense of other aspects of Soviet foreign policy. Relations between the USSR and the United States have been, are and will continue to be extremely important. In addition, it is difficult to overestimate the current and potential importance of relations with Asia and the region of the Pacific Ocean.

Nevertheless, the European element of Soviet foreign policy is playing an increasingly important role and is particularly dynamic in the Soviet Union's rapidly expanding activity in contemporary international affairs, i.e., in a series of Soviet initiatives in the sphere of security, arms control and arms reduction. Many examples of this could be mentioned. Some of the most notable include:

– a series of summit meetings held in 1988 between the Soviet and West European leaders (not to mention the drastic activation of contacts with Eastern Europe) and the clear determination to continue this tradition in 1989 and the following years;

– the idea of a »common European house,« which has been put forth recently and is gaining strength; and

– the important decision of the Soviet Union unilaterally to reduce its armed forces and weapons in Europe.

It can be said with assurance that the relations between the Soviet Union and the rest of Europe will expand in all spheres – security, political, economic, humanitarian, human rights and many others.

What has caused this change in the approach of the Soviet Union? It seems to me that in short this question can be answered as follows: Europe is the most suitable region of the world for this, since it is Europe where particularly favorable conditions exist for the realization of new political thinking and which has called for an expansion of constructive cooperation. Conditions also exist there for creative interaction

243

of cultures and systems and for joint efforts in developing initiatives built upon the priority of common human values and freedom of choice. Historically, politically and economically, Europe is a particularly favorable field for the realization at the end of the twentieth century of, if you will, a gigantic experiment in cooperation and interaction between East and West.

There are many reasons for this; for example, one need only consider the common history of Europe and the particularly advanced infrastructure of negotiations, agreements and contacts between the governments of Eastern and Western Europe. The most notable accomplishment of these governments is the process of cooperation and security, in which for over fifteen years 33 European nations, as well as the United States and Canada, have participated; this has laid a firm foundation for progress. Europe has had wide experience with economic cooperation between East and West, beginning with the traditional forms of trade and ending with the particularly advanced and modern systems of joint ventures. As far as culture is concerned, in many regions of Europe a commonality has formed in the course of history.

Fundamentally, there are a number of generally accepted factors leading to improved relations, such as the inconceivability of war in Europe, either nuclear or conventional. Others include the need for all countries and social systems to ensure survival, the necessity of creating reliable safeguards against the military threat, and the need for a system that ensures security and cooperation. To this list of factors that further the favorable development of cooperation between nations and systems in Europe, I would add the fact that the system of military-political blocs that have formed on the Continent has finished its historical role and will become obsolete, making way for a more modern, civilized and collective system of security. It is not an accident that in both Eastern and Western Europe, more and more thought is being given to how to transform the military-political structure of Europe, how to ensure survival, and moreover, how to strengthen security in the new historical conditions of the late twentieth and early twenty-first centuries. It is clear, however, that this is not a simple matter, since the potential for mutual mistrust is great, and both sides differ sharply in their evaluations of balance, the correlation of forces, the role of nuclear arms.

What basis do we have to think that the West will react positively to the new European dimensions of Soviet foreign policy and that this attitude will be stable and will last? Where is the guarantee that mutual trust will increase and that the situation in Europe will become more constructive? It seems to me that in every dimension of pan-European cooperation, there are spheres of long-term mutual interest. In the political arena, the new initiatives of the Soviet Union are directed toward strengthening stability in Europe. This includes the progressive stabilization of relations between East and West; it is precisely in this direction that they will move in the process of future negotiations on the reduction of armed forces and armaments from the Atlantic Ocean to the Ural Mountains. New Soviet initiatives also include the continuation of the dialogue on confidence- and security-building measures, as well as on disarmament in Europe and the normalization of relations between NATO and the Warsaw Pact in the process of other joint actions designed to strengthen security in Europe.

When speaking about the building of stability in inter-governmental relations in Europe, we cannot avoid the problem of applying it to the two fundamental European systems – East and West. Stability in the system of relations in the West is an important element of overall stability in Europe. Therefore the Eastern side should conduct itself in such a way as to ensure that stability will not be broken, and it should proceed from the assumption that the condition and development of inter-Atlantic relations is the concern of the West. To an equal degree, stability in Eastern Europe is an important element of both the constructive and stable nature of the general European situation and pan-European cooperation. We should be confident that the West will be sensible and restrained in these matters. In other words, concern over stability should be reciprocal. As far as stability itself is concerned, it is in the interest of all: the East, the West, non-aligned and neutral nations.

An important requirement for the uninterrupted development of the international situation in Europe is the growth of mutual trust regarding the other's actions, called »credibility« in English. This means that the conduct and actions of each of the participants in the pan-European process should be carried out in a manner that allows the other side to be sure that announced goals are trustworthy, that sensible methods will be used to carry them out and that foreign policy is conducted constructively. This requires constant care in avoiding anything that

245

could give rise to anxiety or apprehension on the part of the other side. It also requires thorough analysis of the arguments upon which the other side bases its position, its approach to problems and the whole of its politics. Such mutual trust is of vital importance to both Western and Eastern Europe, no matter how difficult it is to achieve this in our world, with its decades of mutual suspicions.

As trust increases, arms levels shrink and stability grows, one of modern Europe's most often discussed questions will again and again be raised: the fate of the military-political alliances into which Europe is divided. The question can be put in a different way: how will confrontation between the military blocs be able to be overcome? Or, how will the schism of Europe be able to be surmounted? It seems that there emerges here the possibility of a carefully thought through compromise between Eastern and Western approaches. In the West there exists a significant consensus on the expediency of surmounting the schism of Europe. In the East the opinion is that military-political alliances should wither away to make room for a common European system of security and cooperation. Although it is difficult to predict in concrete terms just how this process will develop, it is likely that as both sides become confident that European security is growing stronger, reliable and irreversible, the military element of the blocs will become blunted and wane. The blocs will remain purely political alliances, uniting groups of participants in a common European system of security; we will see between the blocs consultations and contacts on a Europe-wide basis, the establishment of more permanent ties, and the emergence of pan-European institutions. If allowed to develop, this process will steadily reduce the role played by the military-political blocs in ensuring the security of the states within it, with a new, pan-European system taking their place in this area. The most important ingredient of this protracted process has been and will remain not only stability in Europe, but also, to the greatest extent possible, its reinforcement and expansion.

At the core of the process of strengthening stability is the working toward a reduction of arms and forces, i.e. a reduction of the level of military confrontation. It is difficult at this point to judge how quickly and energetically Europe will move in this area. The Soviet Union has taken a number of far-reaching measures that both invite the other side to make constructive responses and create favorable conditions for reciprocal, dramatic cuts in the levels of military forces.

246

These measures include the Soviet Union's unilateral decision to reduce over two years its armed forces by 500,000 and to eliminate 10,000 tanks, 8,500 artillery systems and 800 airplanes. Also scheduled are the withdrawal of 50,000 Soviet troops and 5,000 tanks from East Germany, Czechoslovakia and Hungary and the structural realignment of Soviet armed forces stationed on the territory of Soviet allies.

It seems to me that all of the participants in this process are deeply interested in a basic dialogue on the problems connected with nuclear arms. If such a dialogue permits the arguments, concerns and interests of both sides to be taken into account, it could become possible to analyze jointly the concepts of, among others, a non-nuclear Europe and minimal deterrence and to examine whether these concepts can serve as steps along a common path toward lasting peace in Europe.

As for the armed forces, both sides in Europe could realign them along the principle of reasonable sufficiency, that is, retain enough forces for defense but not enough for an attack. A restructuring of the security system in Europe according to this principle would, in the final analysis, be of universal interest.

In the sphere of economics, it seems that there has long existed a consensus in Europe that developing trade and various forms of cooperation between East and West is both expedient and of mutual benefit. However, there are also a number of questions arising from the rapid development of the single internal market in the European Communities (EC), which is to be formed by the end of 1992. The most urgent issue is the degree to which the EC will be interested in the development of economic cooperation with Eastern Europe once this market is established. In answering this, one must also consider, more generally, how the EC will interact with the rest of the world after 1992. It is difficult to imagine that its internal market will enable the EC to cut itself off from either the North Atlantic economic zone (particularly, the United States) or the Pacific economic zone (particularly, Japan), because, among other reasons, it will be impossible for it to break ties with the centers of dynamic scientific-technological development. In addition, the European Communities will not be able to avoid reordering its relations with developing countries, since many of them also feel uneasy about the formation of the internal market. Under these conditions, it is more reasonable to expect that the fathers of this market will develop a reasonable basis for cooperation with the EC's traditional

247

partners in Eastern Europe, though one cannot exclude the possibility of difficulties in regulating such cooperation. Much will depend on whether the East will be active and on how quickly *perestroika* will progress in the Soviet Union and the Council of Mutual Economic Assistance (CMEA). In any event, the formation of the single internal market is fundamentally a positive development, one whose potential is not to be ignored; it is capable of furthering the development of both economic and political relations in Europe. Various forms of cooperation are certainly possible between European economic groups – CMEA, EC and EFTA (European Free Trade Association).

The European dimension of Soviet foreign policy is steadily taking up humanitarian problems and issues of human rights. Within the framework of the pan-European process, along with the common European house presently under construction, East and West will become more open to one another. This will lead to generally accepted, common ideas on human rights, including political, social and other rights. In short, there exist in this sphere broad opportunities for cooperation on the basis of a large number of converging interests in both Eastern and Western Europe.

I would like to emphasize that the concept of a common European house – that is, common European development – is not to be taken as an exclusion of the rest of the world; it is an open concept. Indeed, the countries of North America – the United States and Canada – already participate in the pan-European process. It is entirely possible that the future will see this process spread to other regions with similar historical phenomena, such as Asia or the Pacific Ocean. The survival of humanity and the cause of international cooperation in an ever increasing number of areas – first and foremost, in ecology – undeniably require the globalization of international processes that are developing in our planet's diverse civilizations.

The Soviet Union and the Integration of Western Europe

Christoph Bertram

1.   I do not want to talk about the Soviet perspective of West European integration; others in this colloquium are more qualified to do that. My own feeling is that the Soviet Union is still not quite clear of what to think, and this is indeed understandable: after all, integration in Western Europe is an experiment without precedent. However, the Soviets seem to be more convinced than many in Western Europe that economic integration begets political integration in the end. The idea of a »Common European House«, so dear to Soviet politicians, is probably addressed more to their own citizens than to those of the West. It is less a foreign policy concept (for that it is too vague to be taken seriously) but more a modernisation device for internal use.

However, there are two concerns for the Soviet Union. The first is that West European integration is not destabilising for Eastern Europe – in other words, that the sucking-in effect of successful West European integration is held in check; hence their opposition to neutral states like Austria or Sweden joining the West European enterprise. The other Soviet concern is that Western Europe should not become a counter-power; hence the reservations over the prospect of West European defence integration. Whatever the West Europeans do will have to take these two Soviet concerns into account.

2.   The main question I want to concentrate on is the effect of the Gorbachev challenge on West European integration and the response that Western Europe will have to consider. It is tempting to think that this challenge does not really affect the Community – particularly when one sees it primarily as a device for the economic, and possibly political, modernisation of the backward Soviet superpower. But there are two ways of looking at developments in the Soviet Union: the cautious one – nothing much will change for long, let us wait and see; and the imaginative one – what could be a new relationship with the Soviet Union once the ambitious reforms in Moscow are well under way?

249

Western analysts should look at both these possibilities, not just, as they have largely done, at the first, the cautious one. Moreover, the effects of »the Gorbachev challenge« are *political*; they therefore must be assessed both in their more immediate implications and in their possible dynamic repercussions on European politics over the next decades.

3. Because these effects are first and foremost political, they directly concern the emerging West European Community. This is particularly marked in three aspects:
– the future relationship of the European Community with Eastern Europe;
– the effect of greater security in Europe on the emergence of greater security cooperation in Western Europe;
– the impact of Soviet policy and evolution on the West German role in Western Europe.
Please note that I emphazise *Western* Europe. This is both a clarification and a choice. I do want a distinct *Western* Europe, because only here do I see the possibility for a long-term European contribution to stability on our own continent. And only here do I find the conditions for a political union that deserves that name.

4. The relationship between the Community and Eastern Europe:
Eastern Europe is in a different category of power and in a very different economic and political situation from the Soviet Union. While, of course, the Community has to have a relationship of regular contact, exchange of ideas, development of trade, etc. with the Soviet Union, the Community has a particular responsibility towards Eastern Europe – in the sense of owing it to itself to assist stability in that region.
Of course, all these countries are very different. But despite their differences, they have a few disturbing features in common:
– they belong inside the security periphery of the Soviet Union; any fundamental change in their foreign policy would raise the security question for Moscow;
– they reflect to various degrees a profound endemic instability, given the decline of ideology as a legitimator for power and, in most cases, a clouded economic future. Eastern Europe is a collection of under-developing countries. Yet, instability in Eastern Europe, if it breaks out and

spreads, would cause a major East-West crisis in Europe and beyond. This must remain a problem of profound security concern for all of us. What can help in this situation? I would like to see the European Community as a stabiliser. It has a unique possibility (which the Soviet Union does not have, nor the United States): it can, without challenging the essence of political stability in Europe, provide a horizon of expectation and hope for the economic future of Eastern Europe.

Let me explain what I mean by this. I am probably not the only one to be impressed by the European Community's 1992 exercise: it has taught West Europeans to look forward to something. But what has Eastern Europe to look forward to? The prospects are rather bleak – unless one sets a target date at which things can turn better. The only body that can credibly do this is the West European Community.

A Marshall Plan from, say, 1995, provided that certain reforms have been implemented by then? Perhaps. We need to remember that the Marshall Plan was not imposed by the United States but that it proposed American assistance if European governments made requests which would then be sympathetically examined. This should also be the approach of the European Community. One of the ways to meet it would be, perhaps, to give the special status that the GDR currently enjoys in having access to the Common Market to other East European countries by, say, 1995.

Of course, this can only be a very sketchy proposal. The important consideration is this: the ability of the European Community to formulate a comprehensive policy towards Eastern Europe will also define its ability to play a role on the international stage. Can anyone imagine that Sweden, Austria, Morocco, Israel or Turkey will be associated with the European Community but not Eastern Europe?

There is another consideration that needs to be kept in mind: When the Community deals with applications for memberships from neutral countries, such as Austria, it has to see this in the context of its East European strategy. To meet Soviet concerns, the Community must create a special type of associateship, which involves other countries in the formulation of economic policy without sucking them into a political (and strategic) union. To offer full membership to Austria is, therefore, exactly what the Community should not do, neither in the interest of Austria nor in that of Eastern Europe or of itself.

251

5. This is important, not least because of the second aspect: West European defense integration.

It is, after all, the natural outflow of political existence to look after one's own security. Without it, there cannot be a political union in Western Europe. What is significant is that the Gorbachev impact will make it easier for Western Europe to go down the road towards closer defence integration.

The main reason for this lies in the fact that as long as Europeans give priority to their security over the creation of a political union, that union will not come about. There is no way in which, for the foreseeable future, the kind of security arrangement conceivable within Western Europe can compete with NATO.

As long as NATO exists in its present form, however, Western Europe cannot seriously develop its own defence identity. There has been, for almost thirty years, much talk of a »European Pillar« within the Alliance. But progress has been meagre – apart from some cosmetic exercises primarily designed to impress the U.S. Congress that »Europe carries its share of the burden«. But there is no specifically West European coordination of strategic priorities, no specifically West European cooperation in training or crisis management. And if there is, as in the case of the Franco-German brigade created in 1988, a modest melding of forces, these are taken from that section not integrated in NATO.

There can be only one explanation for this remarkable cleavage between rhetoric and fact: the NATO Alliance simply does not allow that kind of evolution; and West European political leaders, their speeches notwithstanding, know this only too well. NATO is, after all, not just a traditional, 19th century type of alliance but the first nuclear pact in history. Nuclear deterrence determines its structure. NATO is based on the assumption that nuclear deterrence by the United States is essential for the security of Western Europe – not as a result of America imposing her will, but of West Europeans welcoming this extraordinary US involvement.

But what follows from this involvement is, by necessity, a hierarchical alliance structure. Since the nuclear decision lies with the American President, he has to know what is going on on the ground, he has to be sure that American officers can control events, he has to be certain that a small ally cannot force America into a world war. The credibility of American nuclear deterrence and its very acceptability to Americans require American control. This is the basic law of the Alliance, and West European countries have, through their successive governments, recognized that basic law.

So far, they have not wanted to change it, because their concern over security was always much stronger than their ambition for more independant West European action. But now, because of the changes in the foreign policy of the Soviet Union, West Europeans can afford to reconsider the security priority.

Of course, Mr. Gorbachev has not suddenly turned the world into a peaceful one, nor has he shed the superpower status of the Soviet Union. Conflicts will errupt – in Eastern Europe, in the Middle East, within states and between states. And the Soviet Union will remain, in terms of military resources, the first power in Europe. Yet, there is evident desire in Moscow – made credible by a series of arms control proposals and significant initial cut-backs in military forces – to change the East-West relationship from one of cooperative confrontation to constructive cooperation. The »threat« is diminishing.

As a result, West Europeans can now afford to take risks which they hitherto refused to entertain, namely, to give priority to the establishment of a political West European Community over the maintenance of an inflexible NATO structure. This would not mean a severing of ties between Europe and the United States; indeed a new West European defense organisation will continue to require firm security ties with the United States. But it would imply less dependence on American nuclear deterrence and, therefore, more independence in choosing a special West European structure of military integration.

Clearly, such a change would require careful study and preparation. It must not be seen as an expression of distrust vis-à-vis the American ally; on the contrary, American support for such a reformulation of security cooperation is vital, not least to overcome intra-European obstacles, particularly in Britain and West Germany. But the point here is to underline that perhaps for the first time since NATO was founded almost 40 years ago, the changes in Moscow have offered a chance for Western Europe to develop its own security identity. This is part of the Gorbachev challenge. The question, here as in other fields, is whether Western Europe will have the courage and will to meet this challenge.

6. Finally, the West German aspect.

West Germany will play the decisive role in the formation of a future West European entity – not by its concepts (they will have to come from others) but by its sheer economic and monetary weight. The Federal Republic is today the economic and monetary superpower in Europe. Unless it accepts the responsibility of a superpower – namely to smooth, through financial efforts, the difficult passage towards a common West European economic region – that region will not come about. But for that to happen, it is imperative that the West Germans see their only sensible future in West European integration.

The Soviet Union is the only power to make that choice more difficult for West Germany by suggesting that there might be another future, namely, German reunification. Even then the end result would probably remain the inseparability of West Germany from Western Europe. But Soviet »playing the German card« could deprive Western Europe of the momentum it needs to move to political union in the foreseeable future.

The question is, therefore, what notion of European stability will evolve in Moscow. Is it the traditional one of a superpower that likes to avoid power centers nearby in order to control events better and to operate by that old device »divide and rule«? Or is there emerging in Moscow an »internationalist« notion of relations between countries, welcoming structures of order as conditions for international cooperation?

That, too, is why, in thinking about the »Gorbachev challenge«, we have to distinguish between the near-term, cautious approach and the longer, more imaginative one. And why, in its relationship with Western Europe, the Soviet Union has to make up its mind on how it wants the German situation to evolve – and the structure of Western Europe with it.

Building the »Common European House«: The Political and Economic Aspects

Vladimir Baranovsky

The idea of a »common European house« exists simultaneously in a number of different dimensions. It is understood as a propagandistic slogan, as a political metaphor, and as a reference point for concrete diplomatic activity. In addition, the need is growing to rework this idea as a scientific concept. Our point here is to reveal the sources of this idea, to substantiate clearly its content, and to outline the way to its practical realization.

The very appearance of this formula seems to be caused by the erosion of the existing European system of relations between states, primarily along the East-West axis. Such an assertion at first glance could seem unfounded, since over the course of some forty-plus years Europe has known no major wars, which, it would seem, convincingly testifies to the persistency of the international-political system that has taken shape here. But let us not forget that this system, fortunately, has not faced any real test of its stability, and so it is unclear how vigorous it would turn out to be in a serious political crisis.

Meanwhile, neither side has felt very confident in matters concerning security. Otherwise, there would hardly have been continual upgrades in weapons, increases in military power, and the working out of new military-strategic concepts. This process in and of itself is fraught with destabilizing consequences.

We cannot avoid taking into account that support of the existing system is becoming a more and more onerous task. It is not by accident that the problem of defense allocations has, in the majority of Western European nations, acquired a very painful character. Even in the United States, the necessity to direct half of all military expenditures for the »defense of Europe,« evidently, is being looked at with less and less enthusiasm. This theme has been raised recently in the Soviet Union as well, since *perestroika* of the economy unavoidably requires, among other things,

255

a reduction in the financial, material and intellectual resources being directed toward the military.

Finally, one can hardly regard as acceptable for European nations and peoples the price, in the broader sense of the word, that must be paid to support the international-political system that has taken shape on the Continent. This price, reduced to a short formula, has become the division of Europe; in other words, the violation of Europe's natural economic, political, cultural and other ties. It is bitterly ironic that European civilization, now scattered far beyond the boundaries of the Old World, turned out to be severed into sections precisely where it arose. It is severed and therefore weakened in its capability to occupy a fitting place in the world and to answer worthily the challenges of the contemporary world.

Any social system, including a regional system of relations between states, acquires a momentum of its own. It can preserve itself for a period of time even after it has become useless. But in Europe favorable conditions for change are gradually taking shape.

First, becoming more and more obvious is the obsolescence of the path to security, along which primary interest is being given to military means. Progress along this path is reminiscent of a pursuit after a mirage. Let us say that for a long time the West hoped to compensate for the conventional superiority of the Warsaw Treaty Organization with unconditional dominance in the area of nuclear weapons. First, strategic parity was formed on the level of Soviet-American relations, and the nuclear guarantees of the United States to its allies were fundamentally undermined. Then, the balance changed in short-range nuclear missile systems and in battlefield nuclear weapons, and the scheme of escalation dominance came crashing down. And if skepticism with relation particularly to the military guarantees of security is becoming more noticeable, then this, perhaps, is most evident in Europe, where public opinion recognizes the absolute unacceptability of a large-scale armed conflict.

Second, in some way, the issue of the Cold War has lost its importance. The debate of who began the Cold War and who won it would be pointless. Rather, both sides suffered defeat. The social revolution in Western Europe did not take place, nor did the restoration of capitalism in Eastern Europe. If one can speak of radical changes within the USSR, then they ripened within Soviet society itself and by no means were the result of pressure from the outside. On the contrary, the Cold War was always an obstacle to reform; it is quite possible that without it change in the Soviet Union could have begun earlier and would have been deeper.

Third, the security policy has begun to acquire a more democratic character. In this sphere, broader social forces are being included, and their influence has become more essential than before. This is happening both in the West and the East and in general is becoming a healthy process.

Fourth, a change of generations is occurring. In both the West and the East, the voices of those who reached adult age after the first peak of the Cold War – at the end of the 1940s and in the early 1950s – are influencing political decisions more and more. These people feel less of an association with stereotypes and ideological dogmas and therefore are capable of making serious innovations.

In such conditions, the transformation of relations between the European states is becoming not only desirable but also possible. This is the source« of the vitality of the idea of the »common European house« as an attractive and viable alternative.

If one can speak about this alternative's general contours without referring to the current day, but above all keeping in mind the direction in which it is expedient to move, then the fundamental parameters of the alternative model for Europe could be described in the following way:

– in the political sphere: the absence of both the elements of confrontation, as well as the elements of domination in relations between states;
– in the military sphere: demilitarization of these relations, the minimal level of military preparations, ensuring military security on a collective basis;
– in the economic sphere: a qualitatively new state of economic ties, progress toward a common regional economic complex;
– mobilization of society's internal resources and society's relation with nature: the joint resolution by all states in the region of their common problems (ecology, scientific-technological progress, etc.);
– in the humanitarian sphere: the restoration of the unity of European culture (of course, together with the preservation and even the development of its variety); the compatibility of ideas on individual human rights and freedoms – and possibly, the progress towards common

257

concepts in this area; provisions for the most broad relations between people of different nations.

Of course, this is only a rather schematic description of what the »common European house« could become and not a detailed design with carefully worked out details. Maybe such a design is not needed now – it might deprive us of the flexibility needed to build the »common European house.« It is also important to bear in mind that no one can predict what this detailed design is to become. On the contrary, its working out must be an act of joint creativity. In the Federal Republic of Germany, for example, there has arisen the idea of a »European peace order,« and in France, the idea of a »European legal state«; ideas such as these seem to enrich the concept of a »common European house« and can be with full justification incorporated into it. No matter what kind of ambitious plans are connected with the construction of the »common European house,« they should not be the basis for building paper castles or for destroying that which already exists. Over the past forty years there have been built in Europe no small number of buildings in this common home – both in the West and in the East. Possibly their architectural style is not always perfect, and together they clearly do not form some sort of whole complex. Maybe they should be rebuilt; they certainly need to be made to fit with one another. But the construction of the »common European house« cannot and should not be compared to the realities already existing in Europe.

This point should be discussed more concretely. One of the obvious realities of political developments in post-war Europe is the palpable presence of the United States in Europe. Some people have seen in the formula of the »common European house« only an attempt by the Soviet Union to »remove« the United States from Europe in order to achieve hegemony on the Continent. It seems obvious that such a goal would be, first, unrealistic and, second, destructive. Let us not try to guess what course American-Soviet relations will take in the future or how the elements of rivalry and cooperation will be combined in those relations. But today the United States is an organic part of the European political landscape, and any attempt to change that landscape must be made with US cooperation.

And with the participation of the Soviet Union, for that matter – which is something that we would not even have to be reminded of if it were not for occasional illusions that the »common European house« would

258

be more comfortable and secure without the Soviet Union, which is too big for such a house. Of course, geopolitical factors cannot be ignored – but they cannot be seen as an insurmountable barrier to the »common European house,« especially since in the given instance, the geopolitical factor is not strength but rather weakens the case of the Soviet Union, which must constantly prove that it poses no threat to the rest of Europe.

Let me mention another inappropriate juxtaposition – that between the »common European house« and Western European integration. Some have seen in the Soviet challenge to busy ourselves with the construction of the »common European house« only a reaction to the magical date of 1992, and believe the Soviet challenge to be an attempt to prevent the creation of the »single European market« within the European Community. On the other hand, some declare that the Community itself is the »common house,« and the occupants of it somehow do not need a new, more spacious building.

Yet, in the development of Western European integration there clearly have been achievements. And this experience, naturally, would be useful in the development of economic ties that will cover the whole of the Continent. On the other hand, it is important that these developing processes of integration (not only in Western, by the way, but also in Eastern Europe, albeit not equally and with unequal results) have not deepened the trench between these two systems and have not increased the economic disunity on the Continent. In order to do this, it is necessary at the very least to take steps to make efficacious the agreement between the Council of Mutual Economic Assistance (CMEA) and the European Economic Community (EEC). In this matter, much depends upon CMEA and on how it can overcome its lethargy and acquire dynamism and flexibility. But the European Community as well should not simply be a passive observer, for upon it depends whether the year 1992 will become a symbol of what has been called the »European fortress« (meaning, of course, Western Europe) or whether provisions will now be made to activate relations between West and East.

Relations between CMEA and the EEC are by no means the only aspect of common European development in this area. Activating ties of individual socialist nations with the European Community can contribute to the formation of an economic structure that would extend

259

to both Western and Eastern Europe. And finally, within this structure, the European Free Trade Association [EFTA] must find its place.

It is important here to realize that the formation of the structure of Europe-wide economic ties is a process both beneficial and necessary for the East as well as for the West. This is by no means a situation in which one side stands with an outstretched palm and collects charity from the other side. Yet, it is extremely important for the Soviet economy to overcome its withdrawn nature and to join up with world markets so that it can learn how to meet their demands. This is far from an easy task, but all of the conditions for its accomplishment are more favorable with respect to Western Europe.

However, even for Western Europe, development of economic ties with the Soviet Union is attractive. It is getting crowded in Western Europe; all calculations show that in the near future there will just barely be enough room for three or four large producers of identical products. But the successful development of economic ties with the Soviet Union will allow the market to double in size. It is not only the market that is important here but also the perspectives for economic partnership in the broader sense of the word. There definitely are possibilities for partnership, since the Soviet Union has at its disposal much of what is vital for such partnership: space for expansion, labor (including skilled labor), and scientific and technical ingenuity. It is another matter that we are still too frequently not in the condition to manage these resources. But the Soviet economy is awaking – it possesses gigantic potential – and the effect of this awakening will eventually be much stronger than is the case of newly industrialized countries.

Therefore, it is expedient now to turn our thoughts on the economic dimensions of the »common European house« into something of a more practical nature. For example, it is clear that if agreements are not made soon on standards, it will soon be impossible for us to »dock« our markets and technologies. We must solve also those problems that have to do with products of high technology. Of course, as long as there is military confrontation and as long as political relations are far from idyllic, limitations in what both sides can do are unavoidable. But at least we can try to find mutually acceptable criteria for those limitations, and to provide for their gradual reduction. This, by the way, could help transform »Eureka« into a truly all-European project.

Finally, I would like to discuss the relationship between the Helsinki process and the construction of the »common European house.« The Helsinki process is a unique achievement that demonstrated the possibility of long-term and large-scale joint measures between the states belonging to different social systems in Europe. It is precisely along this course and on this basis that the construction of the »common European house« should be carried out. However, it would be proper to ask how the one differs from the other, and whether or not something new need be thought up if the Helsinki process produces its own results anyway.

One can say that there are differences – at least in two respects. First, the greatest political work of the Helsinki Final Act was to ensure that the international political order formed after World War II and, in particular, international borders were accepted by all. The high pathos of the Helsinki process, as far as political genesis is concerned, is the affirmation, confirmation and reproduction of the status quo.

At the time this was absolutely necessary. Today, however, it no longer suffices. Therefore it would be useful to make the idea of change one of the key parameters of the »common European house,« especially as changes are obviously imminent both in the East and the West, within governments and between allies. No one wants these changes to have destabilizing consequences. Therefore, the idea of joint guarantee of stability through economic, social and political changes could become the driving spirit of the »common European house.«

Second, the Helsinki process is developing primarily on the level of interstate relations, and its primary agent is the government of each nation. The process of building the »common European house« should have a wider framework; it should develop on levels both higher and lower than that of the government. By the words »higher level« I mean the possibility to form a supranational, suprastate structure. Of course, one must not overindulge his illusions or run faster that he has strength. Even within the framework of the European Community, this process is proceeding slowly and with difficulty. But this does not mean that the process is impossible in the »common European house« – it is enough for it to begin in separate spheres and with concrete, individual issues. The experience of IAEA [International Atomic Energy Agency] shows how politically independent, unpoliticized organizations can be useful and productive. Can't this experience, for example, be used to verify agreements on disarmament in Europe – especially in light of the imminent negotiations on deep reductions in conventional forces? Or this experience could be used to solve other problems of a common European nature – for example, problems of the environment, energy, and transportation. No one can doubt that a common European approach would be useful. But maybe it would make sense to think of this approach not only in terms of traditional intergovernmental decision making, which often leads to overly general decisions or turns out to be overloaded with a great number of individual issues and details. We can proceed along another path – delegate plenary powers to functionally oriented organizations, grant them financial resources, and give them the right to carry out concrete plans.

The construction of the »common European house« must also be carried out on a lower level. I refer here to the inclusion of ordinary people, social organizations, etc. in trans-European relations. Here, there are great opportunities that can be exploited with relative ease – for example, extensive student exchanges between European countries can be organized, the barriers for trips from country to country can be liquidated, etc. The humanitarian dimension of the »common European house« includes the free exchange of information, much broader circulation of cultural values, and other steps directed toward the formation of a European consciousness.

Finally, let me say that the political infrastructure of the »common European house« by no means must be formed only through the formation of new mechanisms. From a practical point of view another path may be more, not less, promising – activating already existing mechanisms that have a common European dimension – both national as well as multi-lateral. For example, ties between the national parliaments of Europe could be expanded, or ongoing activities could be established between the parliaments of Eastern European nations and the parliaments and assemblies in Western Europe (within the framework of the European Community, the Western European Union and the Council of Europe) – including the North Atlantic Assembly. Contacts with these organizations can be more extensive. The Western European Union, for example, which has clearly become more active in the past few years, will likely give increasing attention to the problem of arms limitation. Why couldn't the alliance establish some sort of exchange of opinions on these issues and maybe get the agreement of the Warsaw Treaty Organization? This, by the way, could weaken existing suspicions held by Warsaw Treaty nations that the formation of a new Western European military-political bloc is afoot.

In principle, there are also opportunities to weaken suspicions by means of »European political cooperation.« It is well known that this mechanism of international coordination calls forth a guarded reaction from neutral countries, which sense the economic attractiveness of the EC. But this matter can be examined from another point of view – it can be made an open system, and in one form or another the other European nations can be included.

As far as the Council of Europe is concerned, the idea of turning it into a truly universal European organization has become very popular. It is quite possible that it is here that the first major breakthrough toward the »common European house« will be made.

Gorbachev – New Era, New Perspective?

Lothar Rühl

The changes in the Soviet Union since 1985 are considerable by all standards. In fact, the world is witnessing the first fundamental change of the Soviet system since the establishment of Stalin's dictatorship, indeed »a revolution within the revolution,« as Gorbachev himself has called the movement set into motion by his »perestroika« and »glasnost« initiative. One can, of course, object that the Russian Revolution came to an end many decades ago and that the political system of the Soviet Union is a post-revolutionary order with strong conservative forces at work. However, the social and political order established after Lenin's death and Trotzki's eviction from Russia represents the results of the communist revolution in Russia as well as later achievements and deviations of the »socialist« régime forced upon Russia and the Russian empire by the communists. The Soviet system was extended to other countries, albeit with national variations. Whether truly »revolutionary« in the historical sense or »revisionist« by classical communist standards, Gorbachev's policies are changing at least the conditions for the exercise of Soviet power if not the essence of this particular brand of political power itself.

The experiment is still in its first stage, and while much seems to have been changed in the top layers of Soviet society, much more remains to be changed in the depth of Russia and Soviet Asia. Success is not certain yet. The movement of »perestroika« may be »irreversible,« as many politicians in the West say, but this does not say much about the ultimate result. It is part of the character of revolutions that their development, even protracted as it has been in the Russian case, is unpredictable and that they may produce contradictory results in the end, including a negation of their original principles and objectives.

Gorbachev claims to restore Leninism and »socialist democracy,« although Lenin did not stand for any kind of democracy but indeed for the dictatorship of the Communist party as the organised political vanguard of »the proletariate.« Whatever the rhetorics and the ideological justification, Gorbachev's programme of reforms and changes seems to be inspired by a rational humanitarian concept of politics and of social relations in a developing socialist society. His main problem is that this society in the Soviet Union has been frozen solid under the cold pressure of the totalitarian state ruled arbitrarily by a post-revolutionary bureaucratic class, organised in a minority party, enjoying the monopoly of power. He must mobilise the constructive forces of Soviet society, provoke the adversaries of change into open opposition in order to be able to crush them with the popular power he tries to activate and to win the support of the people. Whether he will succeed, remains to be seen. He does not have much time, and hence he cannot afford to play for time and to overcome the resistance of the privileged »apparatchiks« at the various Soviet bureaucracies gradually by intrigue, persuasion and indirect strategies. The impatience of the people with the dire living conditions, the lack of confidence in the Party and its leadership, the general distrust of the authorities and the general opportunism of workers everywhere, seeking to preserve their mediocre but relatively convenient and secure arrangements with the Party and the state, seeking not to work too much and to make gains on the side, all work against real reform.

But for all of this, Gorbachev's appeal is the first genuine signal for change in the Soviet Union and in the relations between the Soviet Union and the world. It is, therefore, in the interest of all peoples to support – as much as can be done from the outside – Gorbachev's experiment and to use the time Gorbachev has to bring his experiment to success as well as his personal situation to make all the gains possible for international security and cooperation. This is the paramount interest of the West and in particular both of North America and of Western Europe.

Since 1947-48, East-West relations have been determined by the politics of confrontation and strategic competition. There is no serious doubt that this confrontation in Europe and in Asia was originally caused by the incompatibility of Soviet and Western political objectives for the postwar international order and in particular by the aggressive attitude and the expansive foreign policy of Stalin's Soviet Russia. Stalin's determination to consolidate Russia's territorial gains from the war and to force Soviet communism on the conquered people, »liberated« by the Red Army in 1944-45, led to the division of Europe. Stalin's

265

successors maintained this ambition and tried to uphold Soviet political control – if necessary by military force and by the intervention of the Soviet political police in the »socialist countries« – over Eastern Europe. They looked upon the peoples of Eastern Europe as an integral part of the Soviet Russian empire and defined the security of the Soviet Union in terms of imperial possession of the East and of hegemonial power in Europe. The last manifestations of this imperial concept were the military intervention in Afghanistan in 1979-80, with the ensuing warfare against the Afghan people, and the threat to Poland in 1981-82 during the heyday of the Polish democratic trade union movement, which was a form of socialist counter-revolution against the political and social order established by the Polish communists and the Soviet Union after the war.

The Polish case, however, already pointed to a certain change in Moscow: The Brezhnev régime did not want to use military force against Poland as it had done in 1968 against Czechoslovakia. Although the threat of military intervention was massive and quite convincing, Moscow preferred the indirect intervention by the Polish army with the help of martial law. Polish national sovereignty and territorial integrity were respected, and a peaceful solution was sought, albeit by means of massive pressure and coercion.

In its dealings with the West, the Soviet leadership of the Brezhnev period tried to obtain advantages in the strategic-military and economic relationship without offering an appropriate counterpart. Concessions offered were always small and conditional upon larger Western concessions. Compromise was never sought on the middle ground, and negotiations were protracted propaganda campaigns, such as SALT and START and the negotiations on conventional force reductions in Central Europe or on medium-range missiles. Outside Europe Soviet policy tried to mobilise opposition against the West in Africa, Latin America and Asia. Soviet arms and influence were spread over the world in a global political-strategic competition with the West. Revolutionary situations and civil strife were used as detonators by Soviet policy to destroy Western interests. Podgorny, at the time President of the Supreme Soviet, stood at the East African Victoria Lake and proclaimed that here were »the battlefields of the future«.

Will »the new thinking« in Moscow change all that? There are signs in Soviet policy and in the Soviet discussions on policy that point to

266

such a change. But nothing has been accomplished yet. However, the extraordinary events taking place in the Soviet Union since Gorbachev was named secretary general of the Party offer new opportunities for a profound change in East-West relations and for stable international security.

The first gain that can be made is related to Europe, where the East-West conflict originated and where the passive but massive military confrontation still exists, organised in the two opposing alliances across the Continent.

The essential problem for European security is the imbalance of forces between East and West and the offensive structure of the Warsaw Pact in Central Europe. If the Soviet domestic reform programme is to succeed, then the order of domestic priorities must be changed in favour of productive investment in the Soviet economy, improvement of consumer-goods supply and innovation in the fields of technology, management and the organisation of production. This, in turn, demands that more talent, more knowledge and more capital products be made available to the civilian economy. Gorbachev's first unilateral decisions concerning reductions of the armed forces point in this direction. If the Soviet Union has to reduce its armed forces and armaments substantially – which remains to be seen – then it must have an interest in mutual arms reductions by arms control with the West. For the first time since negotiations began on mutual force reductions in (central) Europe in 1973, a prospect for meaningful agreements appears. No agreement is in view yet, but the new negotiations, prepared in Vienna, may well lead to considerable reductions of Warsaw Pact forces in Europe if an acceptable Western counterpart can be negotiated. The difficulty lies in the fact that the West, i.e., NATO, has only a small margin of safety facing the superior forces of the Warsaw Pact, in particular in Central Europe. NATO forces cannot, for this reason, be considerably reduced as long as an approximate balance of forces has not been reached – which means that more unilateral or anyhow much larger Eastern reductions are needed. But this difficulty could be surmounted if the Soviet Union had a real interest in the reduction of its own forces. Gorbachev's policy could both serve Soviet national economic and European security interests and meet international requirements for stability and cooperation, as well as national requirements for change and progress in rejuvenating Soviet society.

267

The Soviet concept of a »European House« in which all European nations would find their appropriate place in peaceful cohabitation is a summary and vague one. It needs specifications. Above all it needs a solid foundation in terms of European security, a balanced force relationship, national independence and the recognition of the special links between countries such as the members of the European Communities. It also needs a solid American connection, since there is no question that an all-European security and cooperation system could replace the North Atlantic Alliance, which is and will remain the guarantor of the security of Western Europe. The Soviet Union has a vested interest in Eastern Europe and in maintaining the Socialist cooperation framework with its allies. Therefore on both sides there will be conditions to be met by an all-European construction. The general framework would best be the CSCE, in which both the United States and Canada participate in the process of East-West détente and in military security arrangements for Europe. The successful conclusion of the CSCE phase in Vienna and the common decision to continue the CBM conference, begun at Stockholm, on the basis of the Stockholm documents have created the necessary conditions. North America will therefore not be excluded from the European security and cooperation process but can participate fully and with constructive initiatives. On such a foundation, which would be balanced and stable, a European construction would not separate Western Europe from North America nor would it make the Soviet Union the predominant partner and create Soviet supremacy. A stable postwar order for Europe could not be ruled by Soviet power, and Soviet policy could not expect to exercise hegemony as long as the North Atlantic Alliance exists and American military power is present on the continent of Europe, backed by the strategic commitment of the United States.

Such a situation would be compatible with arms control and mutual force reductions. Both are necessary since the level of forces is much too high throughout Europe under conditions of peace. Arms and forces will be necessary to guard the peace, but the present level of military confrontation between East and West far exceeds what is needed to safeguard defense. In order to lower the level of forces and ease the military confrontation without losing stability between East and West, the imbalance favouring the Warsaw Pact must be eliminated together with the structural invasion capacity of Warsaw Pact forces in their present strength and deployment. Once the Eastern military posture in Europe changes to a purely defensive one, the military posture of NATO in Western Europe can be reduced and adapted accordingly. This will be a difficult operation on both sides, but it could be accomplished if the political determination is sufficient on both sides.

In this respect, Gorbachev's announcements and declared intensions bear a promise of progress in the right direction. There is genuine Western interest in exploiting the opportunities offered in negotiations and lending assistance to Gorbachev's programme's where these could be used to mutual advantage in common efforts for military stability at reduced levels of forces and reduced military expenditure. It is the excessive weight of Soviet military power in Europe that has placed the heavy defense burdens on Western Europe and the United States. Once the cause for superarmament will have been eliminated, a lower level of forces and of military readiness including large exercises can be reached by reductions and confidence-building measures. Mutual security can be negotiated on the basis of a balanced and stable military force relationship. Political allegiances must not change for this purpose. Western Europe can and will remain a distinct part of the European political structure, and it will continue its own process of economic and political unification. Relations between European countries across the dividing line between East and West can and will probably improve to an extent not imaginable only a decade ago. Hungary is the first candidate for such a rapprochement with the West, but it is not the only one.

The Soviet Union will, however, preserve its influence in Eastern Europe, which is the main political result of the war together with the territorial changes. The CSCE Final Act of Helsinki in 1975 was signed on this basis. What change may occur in the future will have to be compatible with Soviet security interests – but these can be redefined in the light of an over-all change in the East-West relationship as well as in the relations between Socialist countries, as will be necessary in the Polish case.

The margin of possibilities is as large as the considerable ambiguity around the relations between the Soviet Union and its East European neighbours, which are at the same time its allies and dominated vassals with noticeable tendencies towards more national independence.

All in all, European politics will develop on both sides and tend to change the East-West relationship further. Gorbachev will need to accommodate such development if he is to obtain external economic co-operation and political agreement permitting the Soviet Union to change long-term priorities in favour of internal reform and a revitalisation of Soviet society.

The second great opportunity that may arise from Gorbachev's response to global change lies in the field of creative and constructive international cooperation. Military security and armaments have gained too much over civilian investment everywhere, in the United States and in Western Europe as in the Soviet Union and in many countries of Asia, Africa and above all the Middle East. The post-colonial development in large parts of the world was accompanied if not even determined by confrontation and armed conflict. Arms sales have played a great role, and the Soviet Union has become the main source of armament in the Middle East – mainly to Syria and Iraq – as in Africa – mainly Angola and Ethiopia – and in Central America. Soviet technology has proven itself to be at its best in modern arms and in the aerospace industry. It is no exaggeration to say that Soviet military power and the Soviet armaments industries are the foundation and the main characteristics of the Great Power status of the Soviet Union; they also have become the chief instruments of Soviet foreign policy.

Lately Gorbachev has operated a strategic withdrawal from regional conflicts, a cost-and-damage-limiting policy, designed apparently to save resources and to rebuild international political credit for the Soviet Union as a responsible and constructive world power. The effects of this new international policy can be observed in Angola, in Ethiopia, in the moderation of Soviet attitude towards the Arab-Israel conflict, in Indochina and in Afghanistan. A new relationship with the United States as with China and perhaps with Japan seems to be possible on the basis of Soviet moderation. In his speech at Wladiwostok in 1986, Gorbachev offered Asia an international system of mutual security and cooperation following the example of the CSCE system of Helsinki. Withdrawal from Afghanistan, where the Soviet army accomplished nothing in eight years of military occupation and warfare, and from Outer Mongolia, by all political standards a Soviet protectorate, influence on Vietnam to evacuate Cambodia and Laos, pressure on Angola and Cuba to end the Cuban military involvement – which was originally engineered and organised by the Soviet Union in 1975 – and on Ethiopia

270

to end the devastating civil war all are signs of this strategic withdrawal. If this retreat from adventurist enterprises of the Brezhnev era were to be completed as can be expected today, then international cooperation free from expansive power projection could become possible.

Such an evolution would have two aspects: the US-Soviet power relationship and multilateral cooperation. As in Europe, a global strategic balance could be achieved by negotiations such as renewed START talks. Geopolitical arrangements could be negotiated between the Soviet Union and the United States, China and Western Europe. Such arrangements would have to respect the territorial integrity and national sovereignty of all countries concerned. A strengthening of the United Nations and of international organisations would be the result. The example of Great Power cooperation for the restoration of peace in a regional conflict has been given by the policies of the United States, the Soviet Union and the UN in bringing about the cease-fire in the Gulf War between Iraq and Iran. Without American-Soviet understandings, the UN could not have operated with success.

But such relative achievements, as yet incomplete and fragile, can only be considered as first trials for responsible policies needed to build a new international order with a stable security and growing cooperation. Gorbachev has pointed out that the global requirements for the survival of mankind have to be met by a »new historical thinking,« which is the admission on his part that Soviet policies have been determined by classical power politics and the ideology of the class struggle, to which everything had been subjected in and by Moscow. Therefore, the enlightened and generous offers of the West in the postwar era for universal peaceful cooperation can be renewed.

There are fields, where such cooperation already exists, such as medical and scientific research, space exploration, meteorology, cultural exchange. But this cooperation is still limited and constrained by strategic conditions posed in the spirit of confrontation. If the world were indeed to witness the end of the ideological era – which is possible but still highly doubtful – and certainly the end of the era of confrontation – already announced by President Richard Nixon in 1969 – new prospects would appear for economic and technological as well as for scientific and environmental cooperation. Environment protection on a global scale, the moderation of human exploitation of the natural resources, global birth control and health and welfare policies are the tasks of the

271

future beginning with the present for international cooperation. This demands the understanding of all nations, highly developed ones as well as underdeveloped ones, as can be seen in South America, Africa and Asia, where the national resources for the survival of mankind in a tolerable climate and environment are at risk as they are in the polar regions and on the seas. But without a special understanding between the United States and Canada, the Soviet Union, China, Japan, Australia and Western Europe, no international agreement of significance for the solution of the global economic, environmental and human problems could be reached or would last. A responsible and efficient management of global resources, international economic relations, nuclear energy, chemical and biological technologies and of the electronics revolution in process, of global communications, transports, information and travel can only be developed on the basic of such understanding. The competition of ideas, philosophies and political systems will always limit such cooperation as it will fire rivalries between countries and cause conflict. Complete peace will never be the reality of the world. But a reasonable measure of universal cooperation should be possible above the present level, if the Great Powers at the end of the 20th century are to work together in the spirit of internationalism and with a cosmopolitan attitude in order to limit and to settle national conflicts and differences of national or regional interests. This is the lesson of this century, so full of promise and progress as of turmoil and destruction. If this were the new message from Moscow, as it has long been the message from Washington during »the American century,« if this were the meaning of Gorbachev's »new thinking« and if it were translated into political deeds, then an era of universalist construction could dawn at the turn of the century.

The Construction of Europe in the Context of a Changing Transatlantic Relationship, Developments in East-West Relations and in the Overall Situation

Alfred Cahen

Introduction

What is called the process of European construction began almost immediately after the Second World War some forty years ago.
It developed first through the Treaty of Brussels (17 March 1948) creating the Brussels Treaty Organization – later the Western European Union – the Treaty of Paris (16 April 1948) establishing the Organization for European Economic Cooperation and the Treaty of London (5 May 1949) setting up the Council of Europe. Subsequently, it has progressed through the Europe of the Six, the Nine, the Ten, and today the Twelve.[1] This Europe of the Twelve has, with its economic communities (Coal and Steel Community – Treaty of Paris, 18 April 1951; the European Economic Community and Euratom – Treaties of Rome, 25 March 1957), an economic dimension and, with its European Political Cooperation, increasing concertation in the field of foreign policy.
The Single European Act, adopted by the »Twelve« in December 1985, provides for the establishment in 1992–93 of a fully integrated market among the member countries.
As the »Twelve«, therefore, are preparing an important leap forward, the world around them is rapidly changing, particularly as regards transatlantic relations and the East-West relations.

A Changing Environment

The problems relating to the process of building Europe go back to the end of the 1970s and the early 1980s, to what was in fact a static period

---

1 Belgium, Denmark, France, Federal Republic of Germany, Greece, Italy, Ireland, Luxembourg, the Netherlands, Portugal, Spain, the United Kingdom.

273

as regards the situation in the USSR and in the Warsaw Pact and with regard to East-West relations and the transatlantic relationship.

In Moscow, the end of the Brezhnev era and – following the brief leadership of Andropov – the government of Chernenko bore the hallmarks of a rigidity both domestically and in terms of foreign policy. This situation was not particularly conducive to a positive development in East-West relations. In fact, the characteristic feature of these relations at the time was not progress in what has been called – with some justification – détente, but rather a rise in tension. Nevertheless, this rigidity in Soviet policy – though not constructive – did give a certain amount of predictability to East-West relations which was of some help, particularly for Western decision-makers and negotiators.

Admittedly, this rigidity did not extend to the whole range of East-West relations. Movements were under way in some Warsaw Pact countries which were to culminate in the events in Poland and, for some of the states involved, in a greater assertion of their national identity vis-à-vis the USSR.

As for the Atlantic Alliance, this period was marked by the status quo. Its political doctrines – enshrined in the Harmel report in particular – were not challenging in any way. (I am not, however, saying that they should be, because I believe that the Harmel doctrine is essentially just as right today as it was when it was presented to the Alliance in 1967 with its twin aspects of the need for a strong defence and dialogue with the East. Moreover, when in 1984, on the initiative of the Belgian Foreign Minister, Tindemans, it was decided to re-examine this doctrine, the Allies finally agreed at their ministerial meeting in Washington to endorse its content, even if this meant adapting some aspects of its implementation to a situation characterized more by growing confrontation than by deepening détente.)

Similarly, Alliance strategies were not called into question. When they were discussed, it was merely to identify new ways of making their application more effective.

Indeed, problems which were acute at the time – and which have since become even more acute – such as defence burden-sharing or the possibility of American troops stationed in Europe being recalled to the United States, had, with the exception of defence burden-sharing, on which attention was focused for some months in 1980, lost their intensity and become more a matter of routine.

But now all that has changed. Three or four years ago, this static period ended and events have proceeded so quickly that one has the impression that it has been like this for some decades.

In the Soviet Union, rigidity has given way to a policy of intense movement. Doubtless some aspects of this policy, notably external relations and security, are of a tactical nature. There is indeed a major debate going on in the West about the significance, extent and even the substance of the reforms proclaimed in Moscow. Questions were being asked about how long they will last, and this debate is undeniably useful.

That said, it is hard to deny that something important, especially internally, though with inevitable repercussions on external relations, is happening in the Soviet Union, which we cannot fail to heed. Gorbachev's speech at the General Assembly at the United Nations on 7 December 1988 is proof of this point.

It is a fact that since the end of the Second World War, Soviet forces have adopted an offensive posture. While this was generally denied by his predecessors, Gorbachev has recognized the fact and has proclaimed his government's intention of changing definitively to a defensive posture.

So far, however, there is no concrete evidence of this new policy. Nothing has changed in the deployment of the Soviet forces, the training given to its troops, the nature of their manoeuvres – which remain as offensive as in the past – the type and production rate of its weapons. This is understandable. This kind of situation does not change overnight. But it is now time for action to back up the words. With the decisions announced at the United Nations Organization, a first significant step should be taken in this direction, consisting of a change in the number and deployment of Soviet troops stationed in Europe and a reduction in its essentially offensive weapons such as artillery and armoured vehicles.

While it remains to be seen how all this will come about, it must nevertheless be recognized that it is an important step. If indeed both the Atlantic Alliance and the Warsaw Pact were to adopt a defensive military posture this would be the supreme »confidence-building measure« which would profoundly change – in a positive direction – the trend in East-West relations. In its own interests, as well as in the interests of peace and economic development the Atlantic World should take this into account. In fact, it is doing so increasingly.

Clearly, this movement has implications for the other states in the Warsaw Pact, though these are far from obvious. These countries are also tending to become more assertive – tempered though this is with caution because the lessons of history (Hungary, Czechoslovakia) have not been forgotten. This increased assertiveness is being shown at the national level, in East-East relations, at the European level and even at a wider international level. There is also a combination of very limited liberalization measures and hard-line reactions caused by the unease of governments which feel under threat such as those in Czechoslovakia and in the German Democratic Republic, to say nothing about the special case of Roumania. Hungary, on the other hand, seems to be moving with calculated but undeniable resolution towards more openness.

In any event, the impact of this movement on East-West relations is clear. The tensions have probably not entirely disappeared, but dialogue, which is now on the agenda, and negotiations, particularly on arms control, have acquired a pace which they have not had for a long time. This alone would be enough to explain the end of the status quo within the Atlantic Alliance. There is, however, another reason and it is not less significant. It is the debate which is evolving on both sides of the Atlantic on the future of the transatlantic relationship.

In the United States, this debate is fuelled by books such as the one by Professor Paul Kennedy entitled »The Rise and Fall of the Great Powers« or the one by Professor David Calleo entitled »Beyond American Hegemony«. On our side of the Atlantic contributors to the debate include John Palmer, the European correspondent of the »Guardian« in a book entitled »Europe without America« in which he says: »The economic, military and political world of the Atlantic Alliance, in which two generations of Americans and Europeans have grown to adulthood since 1945, is visibly crumbling ..... even the most sober of all observers now openly discuss the crisis in the Atlantic partnership and how long it can survive in anything like its present form«. I do not in any way subscribe to Palmer's analysis, but I have to acknowledge that the issue exists.

Facing us today, therefore, is a rapidly changing pattern of East-West relations and a transatlantic relationship in transition, the seriousness of which must not be exaggerated nor its importance underplayed.

While the Pacific area is becoming of increasing importance politically and economically, our attention is still drawn to the Third World. Admittedly, this Third World – so described after the 1955 Bandong Conference in contrast with the First World (the West) and the Second World (the socialist world) – is by no means a universe of identical situations. It is a multipolar world of almost infinite variations.

It is nevertheless a fact that the present international economic and financial crisis has had a severe impact on the vast majority of Third World countries.

The fall in the price of basic products, accumulation of debts and the servicing of the external debt of many of these countries – out of all proportion with their potential and their economic structures – have led to a disturbing regression in their economies. Added to this in many cases is the impact of local conflicts (with the consequent problem of refugees) and natural disasters (followed logically by famines). Such situations constitute a threat to the overall stability of the world.

Indeed, it is now perfectly clear that the states of the world increasingly depend on each other. Up to the First World War, each state could carry out, through its own resources, the essential tasks for which it was responsible, namely the provision of physical security and a minimum of economic security for each citizen. Nowadays much more is expected of these states. Their economies have become much more complex and very much depend on international relations. For his part, the citizen expects the state to guarantee for him not only a general framework of security, but also, especially in the industrialized countries, a reasonably satisfactory standard of living. Any major disturbance in the relationship between states, wherever it may occur, constitutes a threat to the prosperity and even the security of each country. Hence a much greater need than in the past for the cooperation of others in order to achieve a minimum assurance about the essential international stability. It is in these changing contexts that the process of constructing Europe is taking place today.

The misadventures of history and the various and many obstacles which the process of European construction has encountered along the way have combined to make it a complex and multi-faceted enterprise.

In this connection, I like to make two types of comparisons.

For the first, I use the image of one of those ancient cathedrals that are the glory of the Old Continent. They were built in many stages; an 11th-century romanesque part, a 12th-century gothic part, a 16th-century flamboyant gothic part and also perhaps a renaissance or baroque part or even a classical part. Nevertheless, these cathedrals have a remarkable unity through the faith that inspired them and their mellowing over the years.

The edifice of Europe resembles one of these cathedrals, but as it would have been in the 11th century. One romanesque part has been built, that is, the Communities. A gothic part is under construction and this is Political Cooperation. Then there is a tract of land available for other buildings but strewn with stones, which are the aborted remains of projects such as the European Defence Community and the European Political Community. And in the corner of this site there is a building which belongs to the whole edifice without quite forming an integral part of it: this is Western European Union, which one day perhaps will merge into the edifice as the European security dimension.

In the second image, I compare the process to a plant on which, just as it is beginning to grow, an evil spirit has placed heavy stones to thwart its growth. In order to grow, therefore, the unfortunate plant has to put out shoots in different directions, directions which nature – and in this instance, the logic of European growth – had not intended.

So it is that we now have:

- with the Council of Europe, a Europe of Twenty-one;
- with the European Communities and Political Cooperation, a Europe of Twelve;
- with the European members of the Atlantic Alliance we have the Fourteen which come together notably in the Independent European Programme Group – though Iceland is not a member – and also the more restricted Eurogroup which does not include either France or Iceland;

278

- with the Western European Union, a Europe of what was Seven and is now Nine;
- this is not to mention the growing number of bilateral relationships which the European Allies are forging.

In addition, there is of course the Europe of the CSCE among whose participants are two North American states which have historical links with Europe. And then there is this »common European house« which Gorbachev invites us to build.

Michel Rocard, French Prime Minister, neatly described this situation in his address at the opening of the first European Advanced Defence Studies Session on 15 November 1988 when he said, with respect to the building of Europe: ». . . though much has been achieved, there is still a long way to go. Difficulties remain which may be traced to the difference in statute between our countries, to the different courses their histories have taken and which have often brought them into conflict and to the more recent decisions they have made in both the political and military fields; they may also be traced to the harshness of our economic and technological environment in particular, which fuels fears and sharpens competition. But, as President François Mitterrand said a short time ago at the same rostrum, these difficulties must prompt us to act. After all, did anyone think just over thirty years ago that the building of the Common Market would be easy? Was this a reason for abandoning the whole idea?«

From so many Europes can one emerge which is unique and which reconciles geopolitical vision with cultural, economic and institutional vision?

Which Europe then?

In reality, this Europe has a number of component parts: the Council of Europe, the Europe of the Twelve, the European part of the Alliance and also WEU.

In a way, it is a multi-fora edifice whose common foundations are the democratic and human values to which all its occupants subscribe. This building is open to all who already share or who in future decide to share these values. Furthermore, its occupants are ready for dialogue with others who do not share the same vision and the same values. It is

279

in this perspective that its occupants view the project of the »common European house« suggested by Gorbachev. This project, undoubtedly, corresponds to realities, above all, the division of our continent and the need to overcome this.

The Platform on European Security Interests adopted by WEU Ministers in The Hague on 27 October 1987 states in its introduction that »Europe remains at the centre of East-West relations, and forty years after the end of the Second World War, a divided continent. The human consequences of this division remain unacceptable, although certain concrete improvements have been made on a bilateral level and on the basis of the Helsinki Final Act. We owe it to our people to overcome this situation and to exploit in the interest of all Europeans the opportunities for further improvements which may present themselves.«

The »common European house« also corresponds to the reality of the historical and cultural ties that have developed between the states of Eastern Europe and those of Western Europe.

The plans for that joint house do not seem to me to be entirely clear even though I have read with great care the relevant passage in Gorbachev's book »Perestroika«.[2]

I wonder whether, looking at the European edifice being erected around the Council of Europe, the Twelve, the European part of the Alliance and WEU it would not be desirable at this stage to create a common garden where the West and the East could walk together and speak of the means of building, for all of them, a better future where their children could play together as they await this future? This garden should also belong to the North American Allies of the Atlantic Alliance, the United States and Canada, which were born of Europe, which share its culture, which are the Allies of the fourteen European countries and which, in this respect, unequivocally belong to our Old Continent.

The Europe of the Twelve and the World

This European edifice may be considerably strengthened by what will

2 This address was made before the one made at the same colloquium on the subject »the common European house« by Professor Baranovsky, which entirely clarified the problem at issue.

happen in 1992, provided that the Twelve remain outward-looking, not only in their relations with the participants in the other parts of European enterprise, notably in the Council of Europe, but also in their relations with their Allies, with the other part of our continent and finally with the world as a whole, in particular the Third World.

But let us beware – only a European Community which has a global vision and vocation, as desired by its Founding Fathers, will be able to meet these challenges. If this European House is no more than a single market – however large it may be – it may soon become a mercantile entity with an increasingly inward-looking vision of its interests, open to all forms of protectionist temptation and ultimately hostile to outsiders and exposed to their hostility, a Europe increasingly reluctant to shoulder the vital responsibilities, be they in connection with its security, the East-West dialogue or the development of emerging states. On the contrary, if it takes a political perspective leading to a Union with all the required competences – not only economic but social, cultural, foreign policy and security – it will inevitably be outward-looking because it will not be able to forget neither its partners of the Council of Europe, nor its Allies, nor its interlocutors of the other part of our continent, nor the Third World and its development.

How can such a Europe, conscious of the problems of its security, forget the Atlantic Alliance? Conscious of the role that it must play in international relations, could it forget the neutral and non-aligned European countries, on the one hand, and the socialist countries of Europe, on the other? How, with a dimension that is not only economic, but political, could it forget both its interests and responsibilities with respect to the Third World? In a word, how could it lose sight of the rights and interests of others?

Conclusions

This Europe, which is taking shape in a changing world, is not developing according to a specific architect's plan. This is why it is so pointless to hold theoretical discussions on what it must become in its final form. One of the greatest Europeans, Jean Monnet, understood this well when, at the end of his Mémoires, he wrote that »those unwilling to undertake anything because they have no guarantee that things will

281

turn out as planned are doomed to paralysis. No one today can predict the shape of the Europe of tomorrow, for it is impossible to foretell what changes will be begotten by change. . . .«. But he added: »the path ahead must be opened up a day at a time, the most important thing being to have an objective clear enough not to be lost from sight.« This is indeed the global vision which must guide the building of Europe and define its relationships with the other parts of the world.

The New Challenge of Europe*

Michael MccGwire

Negotiations about force reductions in Europe have been underway, at least nominally, for over fifteen years. Today, however, we face a situation that is radically different from that which pertained in the 1970s. We have been presented with an unusual opportunity and we need to recognize the broader challenge this poses.

The Opportunity

In May 1987 the Soviets announced the objective of reducing forces in the area extending from the Atlantic to the Urals to a level that would deny both sides the capability for surprise attack or offensive operations in general. This objective was included in the Berlin statement that articulated the newly revised Warsaw Pact doctrine. If the Soviets operationalize that doctrine, they will have given up the capability to launch a successful offensive into Western Europe, a capability they have striven to maintain for the last forty years. In doing so, they will also forego the capability to fight a world war, of the kind they have prepared for in the past.

The new objective stemmed from decisions taken in late 1986, early 1987. Two years later, having had time to work through the practical implications, members of the Warsaw Pact announced unilateral force reductions in Eastern Europe totaling almost 110,000 troops and about 7,250 tanks. Of these, 50,000 men and 5,000 tanks would be Soviet. The latter were part of the unilateral force reduction of 500,000 Soviet troops that was to be completed by 1991.

---

* This essay draws on the analysis in *Military Objectives in Soviet Foreign Policy* (Brookings, 1987) and *Perestroika and Soviet National Security* (Brookings, forthcoming 1989), and *The Genesis of Soviet Threat Perceptions* (Brookings, forthcoming).

NATO is having difficulty in assimilating these Soviet initiatives, but the immediate implications become clear when these developments are viewed in the context of long-standing Western threat perceptions.

The Threat of Soviet Invasion

In 1947–48 the West perceived a threat from the Soviet Union that combined internal subversion by national communist parties with external aggression by the Red Army. As the fear of internal subversion waned, the focus shifted to the military threat and, throughout the 1950s and much of the 1960s, NATO considered that the Soviet Union posed both an »intentions« and a »capabilities« threat to Western Europe. However, it became increasingly difficult to conceive how Soviet interests could possibly be served by invading Europe, and Western perceptions of a Soviet intentions threat steadily diminished during the 1960s and 1970s. The capabilities threat persisted, of course, and significantly increased in the 1970s, when the Soviets restructured their forces so as to be able to implement their new strategy that relied primarily on conventional means.

In the 1987 Berlin statement, the Soviets offered, in effect, to negotiate the removal of that capabilities threat and to restructure their forces so that the military invasion of Europe would no longer be a physical possibility without a major mobilization. At the end of 1988, they publicly committed themselves to taking a major step in this direction, unilaterally.

It is hard to exaggerate the catalytic potential of this development. For forty years, the threat of Soviet invasion has defined the context of East-West relations worldwide, has justified Western defense budgets and has provided the backdrop to all negotiations. Lifting this threat would bring immediate advantage in three areas.

First, negotiations about arms reductions in Europe, which previously were zero sum (because one side's gain was the other's loss) could now be expanding sum, with agreement benefiting both sides. Second, it would now be possible to achieve a stable military balance, whereas previously the zero-sum nature of the two sides' strategic concepts made it inherently unstable. Furthermore, non-offensive means of defense would assume a new importance, whereas they had been irrelevant in a situation where the Soviets saw no real offensive threat from NATO ground forces, but were themselves postured for a conventional blitzkrieg. And third, the conflict between objectives could be resolved. Previously, as both sides pursued the military objective of being able to prevail should war be inescapable, they increased tension and undermined the more important political objective of avoiding world war. Now both sides would be able to focus on averting world war.

An obstacle to reaping these advantages is the attitude among many Westerners that unilateral Soviet concessions are its due entitlement. The West has always assumed a communist urge to aggression; it therefore sees itself as the injured party. The Soviets are now prepared to admit that NATO had reason to view their offensive military posture as threatening and are taking unilateral measures to mitigate that problem. But they do not see themselves as the only ones at fault; nor do they see themselves as the root cause of the confrontation in Europe.

It tends to be forgotten that as World War II drew to a close the universal concern of the Allies was to prevent a resurgence of German and Japanese aggression. In 1944–45 Stalin saw the primary threat to Russia as a restored Germany in 15–20 years time, with perhaps Japan in the rear, and he sought to preserve the collaborative relationship with the United States in part as a means of containing that threat. He also set out to establish a glacis of pro-Soviet regimes on Russia's western borders and saw punitive reparations as a way of delaying the German resurgence while helping to rebuild Russia's shattered economy.

The threat of a resurgent Germany persisted as the focus of Soviet policy. By the fall of 1945, however, U.S. policy towards the western parts of Germany had swung from repression to rehabilitation, and the primary concern was to prevent Germany from being a charge on the American taxpayer. The Soviets were not, however, prepared to make major concessions on the vital issue of German reparations or on the political complexion of Eastern Europe, issues they considered to have been settled at the wartime summits.

This stubbornness was a source of increasing friction with the English-speaking partners, and by mid–1946, the U.S. administration had concluded privately that the Western democracies were effectively at war with the Soviet Union, an assessment that was articulated publicly in the »Truman Doctrine« of March 1947. Stalin was at first unwilling to acknowledge this historical trend, and retreated reluctantly from the wartime entente with Roosevelt to the rapidly deteriorating detente of 1945–47. He only began to accept the inevitability of armed confrontation in mid–1947.

In 1947–48 the Soviets reassessed the threat and concluded that rather than Germany in 15–20 years time, they faced the more immediate danger of a capitalist coalition led by the English-speaking powers that would be ready for war by 1953. This coalition would include the erstwhile opponents of the wartime Grand Alliance – Italy, Germany and Japan – two of them long-standing enemies of Russia and all three members of the Anti-Comintern Pact. At its core would be a radical new partnership between France and Germany, the recognized proponents of large ground forces.

Judging from pronouncements by leading Americans and from U.S. initiatives in the military field, the coalition's objectives seemed clear: to prevent the Soviet Union from acquiring an atomic delivery capability, to contain the influence of Soviet communism within the borders of Russia and to effect a fundamental change in the nature of the Soviet state. None of these objectives could be achieved without resort to force.

In the 1948–53 period, East and West mirrored and fulfilled each other's threat perceptions. Without going into details or seeking to apportion blame, it can be confidently asserted that there was ample evidence to fuel the apprehensions of *both* sides.

On the basis of this evidence the Soviets had good reason to fear premeditated capitalist aggression, and their response was a projection of their experience in World War II. The basic principles, strategy and tactics that had proven so successful in driving the Germans out of Russia and back across the eastern half of Europe could be used to repulse a future aggressor and drive him back across the other half of Europe. This thrust into Western Europe would be primarily a by-product of offensive operations to destroy the enemy's forces rather than an end in itself.

The pattern of military confrontation was thus established. And while the Soviets progressively discounted the threat of a premeditated Western attack, there still remained the danger of war, precipitated in some way by the imperialists. Soviet forces were therefore structured to cover the worst-case contingency of world war, a war the Soviets absolutely wanted to avoid but couldn't afford to lose. And notwithstanding the successive adjustments to the underlying strategy, if the Soviets were not to lose such a war, they would have to defeat NATO in Europe. This required military superiority, an offensive posture and surprise.

It is important to appreciate the military logic of the existing Soviet posture facing Europe. If the Gorbachev leadership is to achieve the kind of mutual security regime it now proposes, the Soviets will have to make disproportionate concessions. It will be harder for the Soviet military to stomach these concessions if the West adopts a self-righteous approach or implies that the Soviets are responding to *force majeure*. We must recognize that the threat posed by Soviet ground forces facing Europe in the 1950s was in essence comparable to the threat posed to the Soviet Union by the 1,700 U.S. strategic bombers targeted on Russia. That threat was signalled by the Congressional decision in 1948 to fund an air force of 70 wings and by the steady acquisition of U.S. rights to use foreign bases encircling Russia, a process that was well advanced by the end of 1947. It is in this wider context that we must judge the »legitimacy« of Soviet security concerns and military requirements.

We must also acknowledge that it is Soviet threat assessments that have evolved over the years, while NATO has remained stuck in the mold of 1948–53, with all the blame for the military confrontation attributed to the Soviet Union. And we must recognize the radical nature of the doctrinal change that is implied by the Soviet proposal to give up the capability for offensive operations in general. In foregoing the possibility of evicting U.S. forces from Europe in the event of a world war, the Soviets would be foregoing the possibility of prevailing in such a war. This is a politically audacious concept which the United States has yet to contemplate. But the Soviets are proposing to go beyond that and to relinquish the option of being able to fight such a war.

Rethinking the Worst Case

The essence of this shift in Soviet military doctrine can be expressed as follows. From the late 1940s through 1986, Soviet security concerns were centered on the worst-case contingency of world war. They are now proposing to recenter their plans on the lesser contingency of limited war on the periphery of the Soviet bloc. From 1948 through 1986, Soviet military requirements were driven by the increasingly open-ended objective of »not losing« a world war. They are now moving to adopt the lesser objective of ensuring the territorial integrity and internal cohesion of the Soviet bloc. This objective does not require military superiority or surprise. And a westwards offensive, which previously had been a strategic imperative, is now excluded since it would precipitate world war.

This most recent change in military doctrine and strategy is the outcome of an evolutionary process that has been under way since the early 1950s. Just as gradually lowering the temperature of water will change its state from liquid to solid, so too can an evolutionary change in doctrine result in a completely new approach to national security. Prior to 1956 Soviet military doctrine assumed that war between the two social systems was ultimately inevitable. In 1956 it was ruled that such a war was no longer inevitable, but of course the possibility of world war remained inherent in the prevailing structure of international relations and must therefore be prepared for.

The likely implications of nuclear missile warfare led to a radical reassessment of both the nature of war and the way it would be fought. In the late 1950s the Soviets concluded that a world war would inevitably be nuclear and involve massive strikes on the Soviet Union. In such a circumstance the optimum Soviet strategy was to launch a preventive nuclear attack, if war seemed inescapable. The difficulty of making such a determination and the political constraints on launching such strikes were obvious, but an offensive, damage-limiting strategy was the least of all evils, particularly in the face of their opponents' overwhelming nuclear superiority.

This nuclear strategy did not eliminate the need for a land offensive westward, which had the twin objectives of destroying NATO's military capability and gaining access to Western Europe's economic resources. The latter would be essential to rebuilding the devastated economies of the Soviet bloc and to ensuring the survival of the socialist system.

Military doctrine underwent another sea change in the late 1960s, when the Soviets decided that a world war would not necessarily be nuclear or involve massive strikes on the Soviet Union. It thus became logically possible, and therefore necessary, for the Soviets to adopt the wartime objective of »avoiding the nuclear devastation of Russia,«

288

a corollary being that they would have to forego nuclear strikes on America, because that would invite retaliation against Russia. The U.S. military-industrial base would therefore remain intact, which made it essential that America be denied a bridgehead in Europe from which to mount an offensive once it had built up its forces, as it had in World War II.

The military problem was how to evict U.S. troops from the Continent without precipitating intercontinental nuclear escalation. One part of the answer was to restructure Soviet ground and air forces so that with conventional means only, they could disrupt NATO's means of nuclear delivery and mount a blitzkrieg offensive into Western Europe. This assault would hamper, perhaps even avert, NATO'S resort to nuclear weapons and would reduce the momentum toward escalation. The other part was to deter escalation by threatening retaliation against North America with Soviet intercontinental ballistic missiles. It was this emerging capability, in conjunction with the U.S. adoption of »flexible« and »assured response,« that had justified the doctrinal shift.

The need to restructure and increase Soviet ground and air forces to provide the superiority required for a successful conventional offensive meant that the Soviets could not engage in serious negotiations to reduce force levels in Europe in the 1970s. But the very opposite considerations applied to negotiations on strategic nuclear arms. During the 1960s the Soviets still lagged behind the U.S. intercontinental capability and their ultimate objective was superiority; hence arms limitations were not in their interests. But the logic of the 1970s strategy decreed that Soviet interests would now be served best by nuclear parity at as low a level , or not at all. And if escalation did occur, the smaller the number of U.S. strategic weapons, the less the nuclear devastation of Russia.

The only way to get the United States to reduce its arsenal was to negotiate strategic arms reductions. This military rationale clinched the argument of those Soviets advocating arms control as a means of promoting détente. The proposals put forward by Gorbachev at Reykjavik were a straight line projection of the decisions taken at the end of the 1960s.

This most recent change was forced on the Soviet leadership by the logic of events. In 1983 the Soviets had finally acknowledged that the assumptions that had shaped foreign policy since 1971 were no longer valid and embarked on a major reassessment of policy. In the course of this reassessment the Soviets faced up to the fact that in restructuring their forces in the 1970s to improve the chances of »not losing« a world war, they had fostered distrust and sharply raised international tension. In 1971–73 the Soviets had thought that war was most unlikely; 10 years later they considered it a distinct possibility. Meanwhile, in covering the ever more remote contingency of world war, the Soviets had incurred heavy political and military costs in the form of NATO's response to what the West saw as an increase in threat. These political and military costs came on top of the economic burden of maintaining the military capability required to implement their contingency plans for world war.

The Soviets initial diagnosis of this unfavorable situation focused on the symptoms of the problem rather than the cause. They concluded that if they relaxed their offensive posture facing NATO and embarked on active negotiations in Europe, this would reduce tension and improve political relations with the countries of Western Europe, while yielding major savings in defense expenditure. At the same time, this should allow the anti-war movements in the West to achieve their full political potential in the struggle to avert war.

Of course, Soviet military doctrine at the political level had always been defensive, and avoiding world war had always been a first order national objective. But by mid–1984 the Soviets had decided to develop a defensive doctrine at the military-technical level. It was also recognized that the problem of averting world war would have to be addressed at that level. The implications of these decisions were worked out over the next two years, and publicized in the Warsaw Pact statement of June 1986, that became known as the Budapest Appeal. It proposed major mutual reductions in forces in the region lying between the Atlantic and the Urals, and accepted the need for intrusive verification.

The Soviets were forced to focus on the roots of the problem in the final months of 1986, largely under the pressure of economic duress. The bizarre experience of the Reykjavik summit and its turbulent aftermath seems to have formalized the conclusion that Soviet policy had been unduly impressed by U.S. military threats and capabilities, and overly reactive to changes in U.S. behavior. By allowing the United States to set the terms of the competition and by responding in kind, the

Soviet Union had provided »aggressive circles« in the United States and the U.S. military-industrial complex with the external threat that was needed to fuel continually high levels of defense production. By allowing itself to be drawn into a ruinous arms race, the Soviet Union had played into the hands of those who sought to bring about its downfall by economic rather than military means.

The critical diagnosis of past policy blended with Gorbachev's new political thinking about international relations to yield clear-cut policy prescriptions, reflecting three interlocking principles: (1) deny the United States a threat by de-demonizing the Soviet Union in Western eyes; (2) extricate the Soviet Union from the arms race, if necessary sacrificing national pride or what was »fair« to more important interests; and (3) provide the military with no more than was essential for the security of the Soviet Union. Underpinning the three principles was the central assumption that world war could and would be averted by political means.

By adopting that assumption, the Soviets finally addressed the root of the problem that faced them. Only by ceasing to plan for the contingency of world war would it be possible to move significant human and material resources out of defense and into the civilian sector. The assumption of »no world war« was essential if the Soviets were to prime the pump of mutual force reductions by making major unilateral cuts in their own forces.

These initiatives were the key to changing the Western image of the Soviet Union, a change that would ensure a calm international environment as the Soviets embarked on the perilous course of engaging the energies of their people through political democratization. A change that would make it more likely that the West would be willing to assist actively in the daunting process of restructuring the Soviet political economy.

The Wider Context

In May 1987, the Soviets expressed their readiness to negotiate the restructuring of forces in Europe so that neither side would have the capacity for a surprise attack or for mounting offensive operations in general. In making that proposal, they were implicitly indicating their readiness to renounce their long-standing strategic requirement to be able to launch a successful offensive against Western Europe and their readiness to forego the capacity to wage world war.

This was made explicit by Marshal Akhromeev, the chief of General Staff, in the December 1987 issue of *Problems of Peace and Socialism*, an authoritative Party journal that is published in 40 languages and circulates in 145 countries. He explained that whereas, traditionally, military doctrine had concerned the nature of a likely war and the way to fight it, it now concerned the prevention of war. He stressed that doctrine was now »aimed against war ... instead of preparation for war.« The revised doctrine was designed first of all, to prevent and avert war, and only secondly to provide socialism with a reliable defense. In December-January 1988–89, the members of the Warsaw Pact announced *unilateral* cuts that totaled the number they had proposed in the 1986 Budapest Appeal for *mutual* force reductions.

These developments opened up the prospect of a completely new approach to arms control in Europe. But the full scope of these opportunities only becomes apparent when placed in the context of the Soviets' »new political thinking« about international relations, at the center of which lies the question of national security. The Soviets claim that the traditional approach to national security is outmoded, that a state that unilaterally seeks to improve its security will automatically increase the insecurity of others, and that reliance on military power will actually reduce security by increasing the danger of war. National security, the Soviets now say, can be achieved only by cooperating with other nations to provide mutual security. Guaranteeing national security has »become above all a political task and not a military one.« There is nothing very original in these ideas, which echo the report of the Palme Commission. The underlying principles are embodied in the Charter of the United Nations and have been regularly advocated by former Western political leaders – albeit, once they had left office. What is novel is for a superpower to espouse these ideas as government policy on the grounds that they serve its national interests as well as the common interests of mankind. And the Gorbachev leadership has gone one step further regarding the age-old adage that if you seek peace, then prepare for war: in the nuclear age, to prepare for world war is to make it more likely.

There is a tendency in the West to interpret these developments through

292

the narrow lens of the East-West confrontation. It is acknowledged that the Soviets have a genuine interest in peace at this period, since a benign and tranquil international environment is important to the success of domestic perestroika. But the broader goals of the new political thinking are seen as empty propaganda designed to give the Soviets the breathing space they need to restructure their economy. A significant body of American opinion sees such economic restructuring as being against U.S. interests and is disinclined to facilitate the process. Others in the West who favor such restructuring worry that the Soviet peace offensive will breed complacency in NATO and provide the Soviets with the opportunity to gain a military advantage.

These Western reactions are shaped by the »realist« view of international relations, which dismissed the new thinking as utopian. It is deeply skeptical of the underlying premises, although lip service must be paid to them because they appeal to Western electorates and to the broader international community.

This instinctive response ignores the evidence of a fundamental redefinition of Soviet military requirements. Such a redefinition is a prerequisite for negotiating a mutual security regime extending from the Atlantic to the Urals, without which the goals of the new thinking would be so much pipe smoke. The Soviets are not only talking about the catastrophic effects of a nuclear war; they have embarked on positive steps intended to neutralize the danger of such a war. These policy initiatives carry high political costs and risks for the new leadership and provide persuasive evidence that the new thinking is more than propaganda. We must therefore take account of this new thinking when we assess the wider implications of the shift in Soviet military requirements.

The Challenge

The opportunity presented by the redefinition of Soviet security requirements and the call for a new approach to international relations present the dual challenge of timeliness and vision. If the West does not respond contructively to the Soviet proposal, the opportunity for major arms reductions may be lost to the vagaries of U.S.-Soviet relations. If, however, the West focuses exclusively on the military balance, it may

293

lose sight of this unprecedented opportunity for a new political approach to the problems of Europe. There is the possibility of developing a new kind of politico-legal regime covering inter-state relations from the Atlantic to the Urals, a regime that the peoples of Europe have been groping towards since the Napoleonic wars.

Timeliness

There is compelling evidence that in mid-1984, work started on developing a defensive doctrine for Soviet forces facing NATO, and it was also acknowledged that the problem of averting world war had to be addressed at the military-technical level of applied strategy. By the end of 1986, it was recognized that it was essential to take the next logical step and plan on the assumption that world war could and would be averted. Only by focusing all efforts on averting war rather than preparing to fight it (should it be inescapable), was there a reasonable certainty of avoiding that catastrophe. And only by ceasing to prepare for the contingency of world war would it be possible to redirect sufficient resources from the Soviet defense industries to the civilian economy.

In the wake of these decisions, a general discussion of defense issues emerged in the professional literature, beginning in mid-1987. This was not a debate about what should be done, but an airing of views and an exploration of issues, a well-established method of shaping opinion prior to implementing a change of policy. The extent to which civilian analysts were involved as advocates of the new policy was, however, unprecedented.

Although largely predictable, the discussion about what was »sufficient« to ensure the secure defense of the Soviet Union is important in highlighting the role of the West in the Soviet decision on how much is enough, a final decision that has yet to be made. The two sides of the discussion, which can be characterized as favoring »defensive« versus »reasonable« sufficiency, attach differing importance to a counteroffensive capability. One can postulate a more concrete fourfold division of opinion on that score that overlays the somewhat nebulous twofold distinction between the two kinds of sufficiency.

294

At the high end of the scale is a full counteroffensive capability, analogous to what the Soviets had at Kursk in 1943, one that would not differ significantly from the present Soviet capability for offensive operations in Europe. At the low end of the scale is the absence of any offensive capability, and complete reliance on non-offensive means of defense and the aggressor's voluntary withdrawal. In between these two extremes is a limited counter-attack capability, able to clear the defender's territory and restore the *status quo ante*, and a significant counteroffensive capability, capable of repulsing an aggressor and defeating him on his own territory.

These various distinctions reflect underlying attitudes and beliefs about the relative potential of military and political instruments of policy, about what drives the East-West conflict and the possibility of change, and about the nature of the future threat environment. The West is, of course, the main component of that threat environment. Our interests clearly lie in a decision that favours reasonable sufficiency, biased heavily towards non-offensive means of defense. But that means convincing the Soviets that the West will cooperate in developing a mutual security regime that relies more on political than military means. Western officialdom appears insensitive to its inevitable involvement in this Soviet decision-making process. With a few exceptions, the response of NATO governments to Gorbachev's initiatives on Europe could have been deliberately designed to reinforce the Soviet military's arguments for defensive sufficiency and for the most expansive definition of a counteroffensive capability. There is widespread skepticism in NATO circles that the Soviet proposals are anything more than rhetoric intended to confuse Western electorates. Among those who do admit the evidence that a wrenching reappraisal of Soviet military requirements is under way, two attitudes are prevalent. One is the assumption that the confrontation in Europe stems entirely from the Soviet military posture, hence unilateral Soviet concessions are the West's due entitlement. The other is the belief that the Soviet Union's economic problems will lead to major force reductions in Europe, so NATO has nothing to do but sit back and wait.

These attitudes foster self-righteousness and complacency, and a NATO approach to the ongoing arms negotiations that differs little from that of the 1970s. Commitment to the negotiations is half-hearted, and participation is seen more as an aspect of alliance management than a means of changing the nature of the confrontation in Europe. The tendency is to pocket Soviet concessions and then press for more, while resisting Soviet proposals for comparable asymmetrical reductions by NATO. Meanwhile the primary preoccupation of NATO's political-military establishment is not the mutual reduction of arms in Europe, but how to compensate for the unforeseen outcome of the INF negotiations and how to ensure that NATO force modernization plans are not set back. In defending this approach of self-righteous disinterest, NATO official-dom has taken refuge in the fact that the Soviets had yet to halt their weapons replacement programs or reduce their forces facing NATO. That was true, in the past, but Soviets have now committed themselves to adjusting their posture in Europe. Meanwhile realism cuts both ways. It was unrealistic of NATO to expect the Soviets to curtail their production programs or to make sweeping changes in force structure before they had reached some conclusion concerning the direction in which their military requirements were likely to move.

The larger question of how best to provide for the security of the Soviet Union has yet to be finally resolved. What reliance should be placed on political means, rather than military strength? What are the chances of negotiating a satisfactory mutual security regime extending from the Atlantic to the Urals, and how effective would such a regime be in protecting Soviet interests? These are portentous questions, and the answer must depend in large part on estimates of Western behavior. If NATO stands aloof from this reassessment process, then Gorbachev is likely to be proven wrong, and the argument will prevail that when dealing with the West, security can only be achieved through military strength.

What is needed from NATO is official recognition of the military concessions and the reversals of long-held positions that have become apparent since the generational change in the Soviet leadership, and acknowledgement that those initiatives are consistent with the mounting evidence of a fundamental shift in Soviet security policy. NATO should express formal interest in the idea of a new kind of mutual security regime for Europe, and emphasize its readiness to engage in exploratory discussions on that score. It should acknowledge that there is persuasive evidence that the Soviet Union has recentered its security concerns, and no longer has the strategic requirement to seize Western Europe. And it should specify what changes in the structure and posture of Soviet forces facing Europe would be needed to finally convince NATO that this was indeed the case.

No one is suggesting that NATO should »drop its guard.« All that is being asked for is a modicum of vision.

Vision

Embedded in the various Soviet proposals and pronouncements about security in general and the European situation in particular is the concept of a mutual security regime extending from the Atlantic to the Urals. It is not clear whether the new leadership has developed a detailed blueprint of this concept or whether it is just an idea that has to be fleshed out through negotiations with other parties. The general thrust is, however, clear. It would require major force reductions so that neither side had the capability for a surprise attack or sustained offensive; there would be an emphasis on non-offensive means of defense and each side's defensive capability would outweigh the other's offense; and both sides would be open to extensive intrusive verification, and advance notice would be required for military movements above a fairly low level.

This is a far cry from the present military confrontation or the focus of current negotiations on force reductions in Europe, and in responding to these new ideas, we must keep three different requirements conceptually distinct. One (labeled A) is to maintain our capacity to defend NATO against the existing capabilities threat posed by Soviet forces facing Western Europe. Another (B) is to define the parameters and flesh out the details of a future mutual security regime. The third requirement (C) is to identify the steps needed to get from A to B.

Minimum criteria for B have already been suggested by the Soviets in successive Warsaw Pact statements, and their proposals to hold discussions on military doctrine should be seen as an invitation for military staffs to come up with a mutually acceptable regime. This is an important opportunity, because there is still a wide range of possible outcomes, and the final situation could well be not so very different from what exists today. Alternative regimes can extend from those that still rely on the most modern weapons and existing force structures to those that rely primarily on non-offensive means of defense and greatly

297

modified force structures. These different military postures would bring with them different political implications.

Meanwhile, we still lack any real idea of how the Soviets envisage the political-military situation developing in Eastern Europe. This will obviously be a key consideration as we move from A to B, particularly its final stages, and may well determine the Soviet Union's minimum force requirements in the region. It is not, however, essential to provide full specifications for the nature of B at this early stage. What is important is that both East and West should accept the principle of a mutual security regime at as low a level of force as possible, and should adopt it as a common goal. Formal and informal negotiations will be needed to achieve this acceptance.

Providing for A, the defense of NATO, requires realism as well as vision. The traditional approach has been to press for steady improvements in NATO's military capability by increasing the number of forces, modernizing their equipment, and introducing new weapon systems. It is unlikely that the Warsaw Pact countries will renege on their publicly announced reduction and reposturing of forces in Eastern Europe, and it is therefore doubtful that such Western improvements are still necessary, even allowing they were justified before. But should it be decided that it is still desirable to go ahead with such improvements, then the larger goal of a mutual security regime must be kept in mind. We must ensure that the process of moving from A to B is not complicated or prevented by the attempt to improve NATO's immediate capability. MIRVed ICBMs and SLCMs provide telling examples of the long-term costs of seeking short-term military advantage.

A different approach to A is to increase NATO's security by reducing the opposing threat of a blitzkrieg offensive. The West has legitimate grounds for arguing that the Soviets should make unilateral concessions to lift this specific threat, and by announcing unilateral force reductions, the Soviets have tacitly accepted that argument. But NATO seems to think it is entitled to concessions in relation to all aspects of the Soviet threat, which it depicts as ranging from premeditated attack to inadvertent war, and from a standing-start offensive to a sustained mobilization build-up. NATO fails to see that by treating the full range of Soviet capabilities as an undifferentiated military threat, it diminishes the likelihood of concessions in areas that really matter.

We must recognize that the new Soviet willingness to negotiate arms reductions has two distinct justifications. One is the renouncement of the requirement to be able to fight a world war and hence the need for an offensive posture facing Europe; this allows unilateral concessions that would reinforce A. The other justification is the new political-military objective of a mutual security regime; this requires mutual force reductions that can only be negotiated as part of the move from A to B. By ignoring this distinction, NATO undermines legitimate Western demands and provides substance for Soviet claims that the United States is still pursuing the goal of military superiority.

How we define A is more important at this stage than the details of B. If NATO's security requirements are pitched at an unrealistic level that ignores legitimate Soviet concerns, the negotiations are likely to bog down in mutual recriminations. Equally important is our readiness to redefine A, should there be progress in moving towards B. Up to now, the Soviet offensive capability facing NATO has justified our ignoring the factor of Soviet intentions. But if (or when) this offensive capability is reduced or eliminated, the West will have to start factoring intentions into their calculus of the Soviet threat, and will have to decide ahead of time what criteria it will use, and then abide by them.

The West has established such criteria in the past, but as soon as Soviet behavior measured up to them, they were replaced by more demanding benchmarks of Soviet good intentions. The results were foreseeable. By excluding the factor of intentions and interests from our calculus of the Soviet threat, we have ensured a worst-case assessment that implicitly assumes a Soviet urge to aggression while ignoring the costs of such action to the Soviets. Worst-case assessments demand a zero-sum approach to negotiations that would make it difficult if not impossible to achieve a mutual security regime in Europe.

Having defined A and B, the third requirement is to work out the best way of getting from one to the other. It is natural to envisage this as a downward process involving successive reductions in forces, but conceptually it is important to see B as being displaced laterally from A rather than lying somewhere below it. This reflects the facts that B will be qualitatively different from A, rather than a watered-down version of the present situation.

The trajectory between A and B will not be direct, and it helps to envisage C as a series of doglegs, involving three main stages. The difference between the first two stages reflects an important distinction between two aspects of the existing Soviet force structure and posture in Europe. To use the analogy of a public utility, a large part of this Soviet military capability can be seen as the base-load capacity that is required to meet the military demand created by the very presence of Western forces in and around Europe, irrespective of the reasons justifying that presence. Reductions in this base-load capacity will require the mutual adjustment of demand and supply. Another part of the Soviet military capability is responding to the special demands of Soviet plans for the contingency of world war, most notably the requirement for a blitzkrieg offensive. If this demand (requirement) is reduced or cancelled, supply (and generating capacity) can be adjusted accordingly.

There is no way of determining exactly where the division lies between these different requirements, but the analogy indicates where it is realistic to expect unilateral Soviet concessions and where it is not.The West needs to acknowledge that mutual misperceptions in the 1948–53 period drew both sides into a military cul-de-sac, and to escape this dangerous situation will require mutual cooperation and concessions. But the West is entitled to require, at an early stage in that process, the Soviets to eliminate the threat of a blitzkrieg offensive that was added in the 1970s.

The first stage of reducing the immediate offensive threat to Western Europe is a prerequisite for further progress, and the Warsaw Pact took a major step in this direction when it announced substantial unilateral reductions and its intention to redispose the remainder of its forces in an unambiguously defensive posture. The second stage of C will be considerably more protracted and involve the mutual (although probably asymmetrical) reduction of forces. During this stage we may find that the Soviet requirement to retain political control in Eastern Europe can no longer be subsumed under the base-load, but has to be treated as a separate category of demand. The third stage of C will involve the introduction of non-offensive means of defense, and that will require the major restructuring of forces on both sides.

These three stages of C can also be characterized in terms of dismantling the threat: remove the surplus of Soviet capability over their revised requirements, thus eliminating the threat of a blitzkrieg offensive; reduce the size of both sides' forces and adjust their structures so that neither can mount a surprise attack or general offensive, thus eliminating the threat of premeditated war; and restructure the opposing

300

forces so that neither side has the capability to wage war on the other's territory, thus eliminating the threat of force as an instrument of policy. Although it is useful to keep these three stages conceptually distinct, in practice they will overlap. In the case of negotiations (as distinct from implementation), it is important that work on all three stages of C should proceed concurrently, albeit at different tempos and levels of detail. However, general agreement is needed on the broad principles that will shape the later stages of C, since those principles will affect the climate and trade-offs of the detailed negotiations at the earlier stages.

The Historical Perspective

I have talked so far in terms of a mutual security regime for Europe and a time horizon of 5–10–15 years, but that vision is too limited. The opportunity and the challenge that faces us in the last decade of the 20th century is to bring to fruition something that the peoples of Europe have been striving towards since a Europe of nation states first took form in the second half of the 17th century, after a hundred years of convulsive war. During the 18th century a collection of Great Powers emerged, among which it was possible to maintain a fluctuating balance, and this European state system prevailed for over two hundred years. It was also in the 18th century that an interest emerged in the preservation of peace, and, in the 19th century, the prevention of war became an increasingly important aspect of international relations.

This goal was first pursued through the Congress system (1814–30), which was followed by the less ambitious and less effective Concert of Europe, but that had collapsed by 1880. The second half of the 19th century saw an upsurge in wars but also the rise of peace movements, and in 1899 and 1907 the Hague Peace Conferences were held. These were the first international conferences to focus on preserving peace, rather than terminating a war that was then in progress. As we know, the conferences did not achieve their objective, but the search for peace intensified in the wake of what was then called »The Great War« of 1914–18. This search justified dismantling the German, Austro-Hungarian and Ottoman empires, and led to the concept of collective security, to the League of Nations, and to President Wilson's Fourteen Points,

301

of which national self-determination was particularly relevant to the European remnants of empire.

This pattern of a persistent, if largely unsuccessful pursuit of peace in Europe might seem to have been broken by the history of intra-European relations since World War II, but in a paradoxical fashion this turns out not to be true. For more than forty years, the enforced division of Europe into opposing blocs has imposed peace on its quarrelsome states. During that period, states within the two blocs have learned to live peaceably together, if not always to like each other. In several cases, particularly in Western Europe, traditional enmities have been muted and may have largely evaporated. Besides their own historical experiences, the people of Europe have had the spectacle of war in Southeast Asia, the Indian subcontinent, and the Middle East to keep fresh in their minds the destructive costs of conflict. There has meanwhile emerged an overlapping series of ongoing conferences and negotiations on arms limitations and confidence-building measures. These have now been under way for 15 years and more, embracing all the nations of Europe in one way or another.

This forty-year period of enforced peace and limited but growing diplomatic interaction has served as an incubation period that may allow the emergence of a completely new kind of politico-legal regime, now that the underlying reasons for inter-bloc military confrontation are dissolving. To negotiate such a regime will be a daunting enterprise, but we already have the successful experience of the Law of the Sea negotiations to show what is possible in present-day circumstances.

The Law of the Sea is an analogy that extends beyond an example of successful international treaty-making. Like modern Europe, the concept goes back to the 17th century, and, like Europe, that law was determined and enforced by the Great Powers (who also fought among themselves), while military strength (naval force) was the ultimate arbiter. However, starting in 1948, when the United States claimed rights to its continental shelf, customary law of the sea began to crumble and has subsequently undergone revolutionary change. This was the unforeseen outcome of the protracted negotiations at the Third Law of the Sea Conference, negotiations that ran from 1967 through 1984, and involved over 160 nation states plus countless non-governmental organizations.

It is not important that the United States refused to sign the Treaty (as did Britain and Germany), reversing the policy it had pursued for 15 years. Most of the provisions of the Treaty are fast becoming customary law, including those that affect most closely the security interests of the superpowers. Of course, negotiations on a new politico-legal regime covering Europe will impinge far more seriously on superpower vital interests. But if the negotiations on a mutual security regime for Europe engender a new climate of international relations, that could lead to a redefinition of superpower interests in the region. There is no *a priori* reason why such interests could not be accommodated by the provisions of an innovative politico-legal regime in Europe. The more daunting problem will be how to accommodate German aspirations, while avoiding German domination.

Besides the precedent of the Law of the Sea negotiations, lessons can be drawn (and encouragement taken) from the array of overlapping intra-European institutions that already exist in both Eastern and Western Europe. And beyond that are the various regional organizations throughout the world, including the Organization of African Unity. Although the OAU has not been particularly successful in preventing conflict in the region, it made an important decision on national borders at the time it was constituted. Despite the arbitrariness of the colonial boundaries, it was agreed that the lesser evil was to accept those borders as inviolate, rather than embark on the conflictual process of restructuring Africa according to ethnic or historical criteria.

When we join these worldwide precedents to the more direct experience of intra-European negotiation that has been gained during the last twenty years, and then add to this mixture the radical »new thinking« on international relations that is being advocated in Moscow, the concept of a completely new kind of European politico-legal regime is less utopian than might at first appear.

And that is the new challenge of Europe!

East-West: Problems of Security, Confidence and Disarmament

Oleg A. Grinevsky

Revolutionary internal change in the Soviet Union has made it imperative that Soviet foreign policy, too, be renewed rather than simply improved. And this stands to reason. Foreign-policy priorities are dictated by international priorities: foreign policy must adequately reflect the requirements of the internal development of a state as well as its social system, rather than merely ensure the best possible conditions for achieving its internal goals. That is why as early as in April 1985 we asked ourselves straightforwardly just what foreign policies *perestroika* must pursue. To answer that question, we took an honest and unbiased look at the past, compared it with the present and looked into the future. Since the Decree of Peace, a build-up of strength has never been conceived of by the Soviet state as the means for ensuring its security. Just one fact will give food for thought: over a three-year period up to 1924, the Soviet Union unilaterally reduced its armed forces by a factor of twelve. And, with regard to *glasnost,* it should be noted that the USSR was the first to publish detailed data about its armed forces – all this at a time when our country was only beginning to break out of enemy encirclement.

It was Lenin's vision that precisely the progress towards socialism through democracy ensured not merely coexistence but active interaction with the outside world, thus countering the plans of the forces hostile to Soviet Russia. At that time, our diplomacy was actively engaged in the establishment of a system of international relations that would provide favourable external conditions for socialist transformation within the country.

Such have been the rationales behind the foreign policy concepts of *perestroika:*

In the field of security: renounce the fixation on a search for parity at any cost and in all conceivable areas, which in practice has resulted in a debilitating military competition; embrace the principle of reasonable defense sufficiency to free the country from the excessive cost of arms race and confrontation and to channel the resources thus released toward peaceful activities and *perestroika*.

In the field of politics: renounce the excessive emphasis on polemics and propaganda, where we virtually followed the lead of those in NATO who would polemicize with us on any subject and for any length of time as long as urgent international problems were not being practically addressed; proceed to an intensive search for arms control agreements and for the settlement of conflicts and crises in the world on the basis of a balance of interests and compromise, naturally, without abandoning our principles, interests and ideals.

In the field of ideology: revise the concept of increasing ideological confrontation molded on Stalinist theories of aggravation of class struggle, as transposed to the international policies of a nuclear age; focus attention on the need for a joint solution to the problems facing mankind.

None of these changes has been imposed on us. We embraced them as an indispensable prerequisite of change in the world around us. Just like any other country, we would like to live in an environment conducive to our internal development. I would argue that this also serves the interests of all nations.

This rethinking of the realities of international development found its conceptual expression in the set of policy guidelines known as new political thinking, which is not a sudden revelation but rather a logical result of the development of philosophic as well as political thought and of the moral and ethical rules of the second half of the twentieth century. In that sense, new thinking is a result of objective historical processes. It is, as it were, a combination, a synthesis of the recollections of the past, and an analysis of the future and of the prospects that scientific and technical change opens up before mankind today.

However, it was *perestroika* and internal renewal that gave an impetus to the ideas of new thinking and promoted its wide acceptance in international relations. I will not seek to discuss all the aspects and applications of the philosophy of new thinking in this brief presentation. However I will address in detail what I believe are some of the most important aspects of this issue.

Under the concept of new political thinking, mankind and the world represent a diverse and multiform single whole, which is indivisible,

305

above all, in terms of security. Security itself has a variety of aspects – from the military and political to the humanitarian ones. Having embraced the idea of a single world, one realizes sooner or later that it is impossible to ensure national interests unless they are placed in the context of universal human values. Ensuring the survival of humanity, delivering it from the risk of nuclear war, ecological disaster, hunger and whatever may pose a threat of annihilation of paramount importance. Universal human priorities prevail over differences in social systems, world outlooks, ways of life and traditions. There is no getting out of this maze of problems alone. In the final analysis, we all share one destiny. And precisely those »intertwined destinies«, as our poet Pasternak put it, require concerted action and joint efforts. New thinking requires mutual openness and predictability. Those are today among the universal human priorities stemming from the world Community's objective need for universal, mutual security.

From the times of Marquis de Custine up to the present day, Russia has frequently been portrayed as a savage giant overshadowing smaller Europe and harboring secret designs to strangle it in its powerful embrace. It should be noted that our country had no trust in the West either, and not without reason, for over the past five hundred years, military threats have always emanated from it. In general, while the West painted a nightmarish picture of Soviet tanks rolling toward the English Channel, we have always been mindful of the lessons of 1941 and continued to do everything not to be caught off guard by the adversary. There is hardly anything that divides and antagonizes people more than to look at each other through a gunsight, even if that gun does not fire. The same holds true for nations. Virtually all areas of international relations – both political, economic, and humanitarian – have been deformed by the arms race and militarized mentality. This begs the question: for how long will East and West continue to crouch uncomfortably over their gunsights? Is it not now time to cast away the blindfolds of old and often ridiculous stereotypes, to look straight at each other and face today's realities of war, peace and the scientific, technological and intellectual development of humanity?

Apparently this is where reciprocal openness and transparency are needed, without which it is impossible to overcome stereotypes of the »enemy image«, to arrive at a balance of interests or to ensure mutual confidence – not a blind confidence but one based on the knowledge of each other and predictability of actions. There is in essence a direct relationship here – the more openness, the more trust, and vice versa. Naturally, all problems cannot be solved at once. But we could start with equal openness in the military, political, economic and humanitarian affairs of states.

Take the example of military and political affairs. Openness and predictability of each other's actions in this field could be ensured by the publication and comparison of defense expenditures, as well as the publication by countries of data on their armed forces and their activities, naturally, under appropriate international observation and verification. In addition, we could encourage a broad dialogue among military officials and the practice of visits to military and military-industrial facilities. This is a new field in international politics and gives much food for joint thought.

Hardly anyone today will dispute the fact that imbalances and asymmetries exist in the two sides' force structures. They were formed throughout history, often under the influence of geography and the two alliances' different force structures; of course, they were not unaffected by the stereotypes of mutual suspicion. And if NATO countries are understandably concerned over the Warsaw Treaty advantage in some types of weaponry, the Warsaw Pact is, conversely, justified in its concern over NATO's superiority in some areas of military power. To mark a beginning, we proposed to NATO countries back in March 1988 an exchange of numerical data on armed forces and conventional armaments – not a simple exchange of data but also inspection to verify those data, in order to exclude any suspicion of possible cheating. NATO did not accept that proposal and failed to provide an articulate explanation, although in November 1988 it did unilaterally publish numerical data on certain types of its armaments.

Well, we could only welcome this step just like any other unilateral step toward openness and *glasnost,* if only that step had clarified rather then confused the true picture of armaments in Europe. For instance, it is not clear why certain types of weaponry are included on that NATO list and on what basis others are excluded. Nor is it clear what criteria were used to calculate the number of weapons. And finally, how can one be sure that these are the true figures? Frankly speaking, I believe that the NATO publication was basically motivated by propaganda rather than by the desire to clarify the military situation in Europe. The balance of forces in Europe requires a comprehensive rather than a selective assessment.

I am sure I shall be asked why the Soviet Union has not made such an assessment, why it has not yet made public its data. We do not have any problem with making our data public, hence our proposal to NATO to exchange such data. The point is how best to do it in order to avoid fruitless bickering and not to complicate the issue of starting European conventional stability negotiations. In the past, we had the unfortunate experience of unilateral data publication at the Vienna MBFR talks. At that time, both NATO and the Warsaw Treaty each defended ferociously their own sets of data. The result is well known: the figure juggle sounded the death knell for the negotiations. I think we need a different approach. Why couldn't NATO and Warsaw Treaty officials first identify criteria according to which each side will issue its data? Later, after the exchange, it could be checked through international verification and inspection. However, the public data exchange, despite its significance, is but a prelude to stability and disarmament. Here, *perestroika* and new thinking made significant changes in Soviet policies. I agree with Academician Sakharov, who believes that disarmament is a necessary, integral element of *perestroika* in the Soviet Union. It is not time-serving and represents one of its main elements. The January 15, 1986 programme for a stage-by-stage elimination of nuclear arms by the year 2000 was one of the first steps of *perestroika*. Then the idea of establishing a comprehensive system of international security was launched and put on a practical track. We put forth specific ideas regarding the lowering of the level of military confrontation in Europe and the restructuring of relations in Asia and the Pacific. We adopted bold decisions regarding verification, confidence-building measures and openness in the military field. Our concepts of freedom of choice, balance of interests, defense sufficiency and non-offensive doctrine, and of a »common European house« are indeed intended to find a fresh, radical solution to all those problems. And I would say that such a broad approach is far more effective from the standpoint of starting a dialogue and engaging the collective thinking of the world Community. I do not think it would be an exaggeration to say that new approaches to foreign policy problems have produced important qualitative breakthroughs.

No one in the world disputes the conclusion that the risk of war has been pushed back. Furthermore, a conclusion that the Cold War receded into the past was made in the West. This reality is felt by all in a tangible decrease in tension and confrontation. A big step was made toward actual disarmament by reducing military and, above all, nuclear confrontation. The European territory is covered by the system of measures regarding the prevention of surprise attack and confidence-building measures, which was established by the Stockholm accords. Generally speaking, a new reality is being born right before our eyes: a turn away from overabundance of weapons toward reasonable defense sufficiency.

I will be candid. Mankind has never before faced such an impressive range of opportunities. Today, the main challenge facing the human civilization is, probably, not to miss them:

– A treaty on a 50-percent reduction in strategic offensive arms is in the works. There exist all the necessary conditions for that treaty to become a reality, including the strategic stability ensured by the ABM Treaty.

– A convention on the cessation of production and elimination of chemical weapons is at an advanced stage of development. This should be facilitated by the strengthening of the regime of their non-use, which will be discussed in full at the Paris Conference in January.

– Agreements on the limitation of nuclear explosions are about to come into force. This will open the way to a further reduction in the number and yield of nuclear tests, and, eventually, to their complete prohibition.

– Early next year, new, large-scale negotiations on the reduction of conventional weapons in Europe will begin. The mandate for these negotiations has virtually been drafted in Vienna.

– An active search is going on for approaches to strengthening confidence and security in Asia and the Pacific.

If we are to find a common denominator for all these emerging changes, we could say that a new model of interstate relations is being created in which security is ensured not through arms build-up, as in the past, but through their reduction, and not by force but through negotiation and mutually acceptable compromise. And in this process the impact of *perestroika* on disarmament was very strong in the area of verification.

I'll be frank. In the past three years we have considerably revised our approach to verification. We have done away with all kinds of contrived taboos that constrained our negotiating positions. The rationale behind our new approach to verification is based on the following: We advocate disarmament and therefore wish to have credible guarantees of our own security in the context of disarmament; we want to be confident that agreements are implemented in good faith by all. Acting on this assumption we are in favour of the most stringent and effective verification based on the use of national technical means and international procedures, including on-site inspections. For us there are no longer any political difficulties to verification. We are prepared to go as far in the area of verification as appropriate to have a guarantee that agreements are strictly complied with. For example, during the INF negotiations we proposed an all-embracing verification regime establishing the highest standards of openness, *glasnost* and mutual verification. In many respects that regime provided for a more deep and intrusive verification than measures proposed by the US side. This is also true of the START negotiations, as well as of CW and conventional talks.

Obviously, negotiation of mutual and balanced reductions in the armed forces and armaments has been and continues to be central to ensuring security. However, one should not reject possible anticipatory steps, naturally, to a degree not inconsistent with the objective of maintaining national security. The decision by the Soviet Union unilaterally to reduce its armed forces and conventional weapons announced by Mikhail Gorbachev in his address to the forty-third session of the UN General Assembly is one such example. This decision has many aspects. It is not a cosmetic finish applied to reality, not a desire to please the public or an adjustment to our negotiating position in the prelude to the conventional arms talks. This decision involves deep and very serious changes in the structure and posture of our armed forces necessitated above all by the imperatives of our own internal development.

Judge for yourselves. Soviet armed forces are being reduced by five hundred thousand troops, which equals the numerical strength of the entire West German Bundeswehr. The ten thousand tanks that we are eliminating in Europe equal the number of tanks in West Germany, Turkey and Italy together. 25 percent of Soviet troops are being withdrawn from Hungary. And the list of these examples could be continued.

Naturally, the question arises as to why the Soviet Union decided to make such deep and unilateral reductions. I believe that the answer should be sought in the policies of *perestroika,* which I discussed earlier. Let us now address the logical consistency of the steps proposed by Mikhail Gorbachev. By effecting these reductions, we will withdraw from Europe and disband six tank divisions, assault and some other units, including assault craft. And the Soviet divisions that still remain on the territories of our allies are being reconfigured. They will be assigned a structure different from that of today; following a major reduction of the number of tanks, that structure will become strictly defensive. These steps are consistent with our proclaimed defensive doctrine. Furthermore, they will entail an appropriate reorganization of armed forces on the basis of the principles of defense sufficiency. Not infrequently, we used to be told with reproach: We welcome your new doctrine, but what about its implementation in the force structure and location? Well, now you have the answer.

Naturally, we expect our decision to give additional impetus to the whole process of disarmament and, above all, conventional disarmament. Today, reductions in these very weapons come clearly to the forefront of European politics. Leaving aside propaganda here, common interests of the West and East will become obvious. The NATO position, stated in December, regarding conventional arms negotiations and the Warsaw Treaty proposals have in this respect much in common, despite serious differences. Both sides – NATO and the Warsaw Treaty – advocate stability at lower levels of arms through the elimination of existing asymmetries and imbalances and the reduction of the armed forces and armaments, above all those that have the capability of surprise attack and large-scale offensive operations. And another aspect: under these conditions any talk about supplementary armament, rearmament or modernization, particularly against the back-dsupplementary armament, rearmament or modernization, particularly against the backdrop of deep unilateral cuts by the Soviet Union, looks like a poor production coming out of the theatre of the absurd. After all the tremendous effort that went into the difficult decision to scrap INF missiles, the script of that theatre production seems to call for replacing them with new systems with capabilities similar to those of INF missiles. This applies, for instance, to the Lance missiles, whose range would be increased from 120 to nearly 500 kilometres and, of course, to remote-controlled systems launched from aircraft. This begs the question: what is to be compensated and how? This would merely

311

substitute one way of annihilating Europe for another. Then again, will this lower the level of military confrontation? There would be a patent contradiction in this NATO position, should the Alliance start down this road.

The shift toward reasonable defense sufficiency raises in a different manner the issue of tactical nuclear weapons. It is difficult to imagine a modern equation of European security that would not take into account nuclear weapons. The military potential of the two alliances is based on a combination of conventional and nuclear systems. Therefore, disarmament the way NATO conceives it, where troops and some weapons would be reduced while missiles and their nuclear warheads would continue to be deployed at their sites, would present a surrealistic picture. The role of the nuclear factor in the European military balance would increase, and the probability of nuclear weapons being used in a conflict would grow. Will this make the situation in Europe more stable or predictable?

In practical terms, too, such a position is absurd, as the majority of tactical nuclear systems located in Europe form an integral part of army units (divisions) or formations (corps, army) of land forces. The very proposition of leaving tactical nuclear weapons intact would produce inequalities among European countries in terms of security. The range of these weapons does not exceed 500 kilometres. This will breed a race of nuclear aristocrats – namely, those whom these weapons will not reach – and a race of nuclear pariahs, i.e. those who can be hit by these weapons. Small wonder that the issue of tactical nuclear weapons is heatedly debated in West Germany, for it is mainly on its territory that Lance missiles and other tactical nuclear systems are located. And if the irreparable should happen, its territory will become a nuclear battlefield. Of course, arms reductions are not easy to accomplish. That is why we are in favour of implementing confidence-building and other measures promoting progress toward disarmament concurrently or in parallel with those reductions. But this is obviously a different subject.

So there is no shortage of problems. And our approaches to them in all areas, including security and disarmament, can be perceived and understood only by perceiving and understanding the essence of new thinking. I do not know whether, as Dostojevsky predicted, beauty will save the world. I am not certain it will. But I am certain of the omnipotence of reason, and I am sure that thought is capable of renewing itself and the world. Europe gave birth to the classical Carthesian maxim »cogito ergo sum« (I think therefore I am). Today it could be formulated as »I think in a new way therefore I shall exist,« because today only the ability of new thinking to abandon past fetishes and old prejudices will give mankind a singular chance for survival.

Are the Nuclear Superpowers Moving Toward New Strategic Policies and a New Strategic Relationship?

Thomas C. Schelling

The answer is obviously yes. But this movement is not new; it has been going on for four decades. And for the past twenty-five years the movement has been toward a better strategic relationship. I consider the apparent worsening of relations that started in the Carter Administration with the invasion of Afghanistan and that was aggravated during the first five years of the Reagan Administration to have been a matter of rhetoric more than a matter of substance; the strategic relationship did not seriously worsen during that process, as witnessed by the ease with which the atmosphere clarified as soon as both sides elected to abandon the hostility.[1]

The greatest change in the strategic relationship has been the evolution of expectations. In 1960 the distinguished novelist C.P. Snow was reported on the front page of the *New York Times* to have predicted nuclear conflagration as a »mathematical certainty« within ten years unless the world drastically disarmed itself and revised its fundamental security arrangements. His prediction received attention not because it was preposterous but because it voiced a widespread feeling of apprehension. That was the year that advertisements for backyard fallout shelters began to appear in American newspapers. Berlin was the focus of most of the apprehension, and when the wall went up

---

1 Whether or not in retrospect my readers will agree with me, evidently at the time there were those who felt quite the contrary about retrogression in East-West relations. The Palme Commission – the Independent Commission on Disarmament and Security Issues – published its report on *Common Security* in 1962, and said in the first sentence of the first chapter, »Less than two generations after the carnage of the Second World War, the world seems to be marching toward the brink of a new abyss ...« And in the second paragraph of Chapter 2, »Although the Commission does not wish to appear excessively alarmist, we are deeply concerned, believing that for several years the trends have been moving in the wrong direction, toward a growing risk of war.« »The threat of war – even nuclear war – is more ominous today than it has been for many years.« I think they took the posturing of the Soviet and American governments too seriously.

in the late summer of 1961, people held their breath in Europe and North America. Each side in the Cold War was apprehensive about the other's intentions; each felt that every move on the other side was a challenge and a test of resolve; each had what appeared to be good grounds for expecting the other to exploit the most dangerous form of brinksmanship.

It is now, a quarter century after the Cuban crisis and the end of atmospheric testing, confidently understood on both sides that neither side will risk nuclear war over anything currently in dispute or likely to come into dispute. Not every move has to be construed as a test and challenge. There has been no experience of being on the brink of something dreadfully dangerous in the past twenty-five years. The »nuclear alert« during the October war of 1973 was not even, at the time, taken as an indication of nuclear danger.

This change in expectations deserves emphasis not only because it may be reassuring evidence that war is much less likely than anything like that »mathematical certainty« of which C.P. Snow spoke. It deserves emphasis also because it is a genuine development in the strategic relationship. Nothing is more important in that relationship between the nuclear superpowers than their expectations about the likelihood of nuclear war. The most dangerous characteristic of nuclear weapons and their delivery systems has always been the importance, in the event of nuclear war, of striking first or being a very close second. In the absence of preemptive instability it is exceedingly difficult to imagine – I would say impossible, but there are those who claim they can imagine it – a sequence of steps by which a decision to launch intercontinental nuclear weapons could be brought about. And nothing is more conducive to preemptive stability than a confidently shared understanding that nuclear war is so unlikely that even in some kind of crisis, patience will be preferred to the urgency of nuclear attack. It is not an exaggeration to say that preemptive stability or instability is largely a matter of expectations; and since the close of the Cuban crisis the relevant expectations have improved markedly and steadily.

Another dramatic development in expectations has been the evolution of the almost universal conviction that nuclear weapons are not like other weapons. President Truman did not hesitate to use the first two nuclear weapons in warfare as soon as they were available. By the time of the Korean War, following a gestation period of five years since Hiroshima,

315

there was a great outcry at the prospect of atomic bombs being used in Korea, and the Prime Minister of Great Britain flew dramatically to Washington to urge the President not to contemplate any such thing. President Eisenhower occasionally spoke of nuclear weapons as capable of being used like any other ammunition, but he clearly didn't believe it; his Secretary of State considered the widespread inhibition against nuclear weapons to be a severe inconvenience, and even contemplated that their use in the Formosa Strait would terminate the taboo. The Kennedy Administration, in contrast, energetically campaigned against the automatic use of nuclear weapons in the event of war in Europe; and President Johnson said in 1964, »Make no mistake. There is no such thing as a conventional nuclear weapon ... For nineteen peril-filled years no nation has loosed the atom against another. To do so now is a political decision of the highest order.« The nineteen years were part of the reason why; and the nineteen years have now stretched to more than forty.

It made no difference that nuclear weapons could be made small enough for a man to carry, or could be given yields lower than those of the largest high explosives that could be delivered by aircraft or missiles. And the difference is not in the physics and chemistry of high explosives and nuclear fission. The difference is symbolic, psychological – a matter of convention, a universally shared belief *in* a universally shared belief that nuclear weapons are different. They came under a curse, a taboo, even while inspiring awe and being a symbol of power and technological advance.

For a long period the Soviet Union expressed the official doctrine that any »limited war« would inevitably escalate into general nuclear war (e.g. the Soviet publication, *Military Strategy*, edited by Marshal Sokolovskii in 1962). But by the end of the 1960s it was clear beyond any doubt that Soviet military planners agreed with American military planners that a war in Europe might be confined to conventional weapons and ought to be if it could. The evidence was simply the tens of billions of dollars spent on both sides on weapons, such as aircraft designed for delivering conventional weapons, that were of no use if the war were going to be nuclear from the outset, and of no use if conventional war were bound to escalate to nuclear weapons.

This acknowledged understanding that a line must be drawn between conventional and nuclear weapons has to be recognized as genuine arms

316

control. A treaty that would have obliged the NATO and Warsaw Pact countries to make this distinction and to spend money on a capability to keep a war from becoming nuclear would certainly be considered arms control; and such a treaty could not have accomplished more than has been accomplished without a treaty. Restraints on the *use* of weapons, as well as on their possession and deployment, I count as arms control; and the restraints need not be embodied in formal agreements.

I have emphasized the forty years' evolution of the strategic relationship between the nuclear superpowers not to detract from but to provide a context for the dramatic changes in that strategic relationship during these past twenty-four months. The question has been raised at this conference whether the world is different now. The world is different. The Soviet Union is different, the Soviet Union is a large part of that world, and relations between the Soviet Union and the rest of the world are changing dramatically. There is no better evidence than the words spoken by the distinguished Soviet participants in this conference. And in that respect this conference is not unique: Soviet officials in recent months have been saying publicly things that I believe a few years ago would have cost them their jobs, and perhaps more than their jobs. One might try to argue that words do not count, that words are cheap, that the Soviet government has changed its »line« on earlier occasions and is merely revising once again the doctrine with which it addresses the foreign public. But when important people, large numbers of them, speak in a way that until very recently would have been a violation of official doctrine, that doctrine must no longer be governing.

I'd like to give a brief personal experience to illustrate. Five years ago I spent a week in a workshop on military crisis management; it was oriented toward things like the hot line, confidence-building measures, crisis management centers, and the other institutional arrangements that were becoming popular fare for conferences at that time. A day was spent on the Cuban crisis of 1962, and the two Soviet participants in this workshop were by far the most knowledgeable in the group about decision-making at the highest level of government during that crisis – but of my government, not theirs. Not the slightest glimpse could we obtain from them about what Khrushchev or others in the Soviet government expected or believed, or even who the main participants may have been in the crucial decisions. One of those two Soviet participants visited Harvard University at the end of 1988, and in company with three of his colleagues he engaged in an exceptionally candid, knowledgeable, insightful analysis of Soviet decision-making in the Cuban crisis, the Berlin crisis and even the Suez crisis. I am convinced that this kind of *glasnost* is irreversible. The world has changed.

But, in its own regular way, the United States is changing too; the man who has been President for eight years is being replaced. And fortunately the new President inherits a brief tradition of exceeding goodwill between the U.S.A. and the U.S.S.R., a recent tradition that may facilitate the continuation of those greatly improved relations in public between the two nuclear superpowers. But we do not have much basis yet for predicting how the Bush Administration will respond to the *glasnost*, the *perestroika*, and what at this conference has been called, by our Soviet colleagues, the »new thinking« on defense in the U.S.S.R. But since I am the one who was allotted this topic, I must at least address the possibilities, whether or not I make any good guesses. What will be the new Administration's interpretation of what is so dramatically going on within the Soviet Union?

One possibility, perfectly consistent with what some of our Soviet colleagues have said at this conference, is that the Soviet Union needs a period of calm in its foreign affairs in order to give its undivided attention to *perestroika*. Just as the Soviet Union may have used Berlin as a way to generate anxiety in the West it may now restrain itself from any foreign adventures and even participate in arms reduction in order that troubles outside its borders not interfere with its coping with troubles inside its borders. According to this interpretation, one should welcome but not trust the new calm that comes out of the new thinking; once the Soviet Union has consolidated itself internally, it will be even stronger to face whatever opposition it chooses to engender abroad. While I would not consider this interpretation entirely unreasonable, it would not be my interpretation. As I mentioned earlier, much of what we are told under the »new thinking« could not be said under the »old thinking,« so I take the new thinking to be genuine. I also believe that *perestroika* is not something to be neatly accomplished in a very few years so that attention can then be turned elsewhere; this is a restructuring that, if not a permement effort, will require a period long enough to provide a new historical era.

A second possible interpretation will be that the Soviet Union has been »contained« after forty years, contained in the sense in which George Kennan is still quoted from his *Foreign Affairs* article of forty years ago. When Kennan called for a »long term, patient but firm and vigilant containment of Russian expansive tendencies« in 1947, he looked forward not to some kind of American military, economic, political or diplomatic victory but to some moderation, at a time distant in the future, in the motives and the behavior of the Soviet government toward the outside world. I expect that President Bush will have some advisors who, while welcoming the recent changes and acknowledging them as genuine, will claim credit for a policy of containment that has been, even if not altogether patiently and regularly, implemented over four decades, and will argue that too much relaxation of the containment pressure may undo what has already been accomplished. One of the policy implications could even be to keep up the pressure on the Soviet military budget.

A third possible interpretation of the Soviet government's more recent attitude may be that a combination of MX and SDI exerted the kind of pressure that it was hoped they would exert and forced the Soviet government into a more accommodating posture. A central argument of the Scowcroft Commission in favor of proceeding with at least limited procurement of the MX missile was that the United States had to demonstrate its readiness and willingness to procure a large modern ground-based multiple-warhead missile in the face of the Soviet deployments, to make clear the determination of the United States not to fall significantly behind, and thus to persuade the Soviet government of the futility and the economic unwisdom of continuing the arms race. It was not clear to me, from the Scowcroft Commission Report, whether it was the MX missiles themselves that were supposed to exert the pressure or instead just the demonstration of the U.S. willingness to spend the money. The modesty of the ultimate MX deployment suggests to me that the missiles themselves are unlikely to have had much effect on Soviet perceptions of the strategic relationship. Perhaps SDI exerted a significant influence. I never thought SDI to be sufficiently promising of results and thus to be a likely major concern of the Soviet government, but the Soviet government surprised me by making an issue of it. I know many thoughtful people who believe that SDI was perceived by the Soviet government as an enormous challenge and that

319

it therefore may have been substantially responsible for the turn toward the new détente. A Bush Administration may credit that interpretation. Besides trying to determine what lies behind the new Soviet strategic attitude, the Bush Administration will have to give thought to some of its consequences, especially its effect on the NATO alliance. There is a tendency for many in the U.S. government to read good news as bad news. Reduced tension may lead to reduced commitment. Easier East-West relations relax the NATO alliance. I do not doubt that the new administration will welcome the easier East-West relations; the gains clearly outweigh the problems. But American officials usually expect Europeans to go too far in response in the better relations, and can be expected to be publicly more cautious and skeptical than in private.

I hesitate to predict, but I shall make a few guesses. I think SDI will fade away. SDI was President Reagan's dream, and Secretary Weinberger shared that dream. There is little support for SDI within the scientific community and little support within the military services. I believe a significant part of the research done in support of SDI was research that would have gone forward anyway, and another part competes for scarce resources for which there are more urgent needs. The damage to U.S. military space activities occasioned by the shuttle disaster and subsequent rocket disasters probably put SDI in the position of a competitor with other space programs, not a complement.

If SDI slowly fades into history, as I expect it will, much of the recently expressed dissatisfaction with the ABM Treaty may disappear. The prospects for that Treaty's survival in its original interpretation I think are good.

I expect serious but unhurried negotiation toward deep cuts in strategic weaponry. The somewhat frantic activity of the past eighteen months was due to the impending change in the presidency. A Bush Administration should be just as serious but not as much in a hurry. I think it important, in negotiating »deep cuts,« to avoid the linguistic and doctrinal trap of thirty years ago, belief in the goal of »general and complete disarmament,« a nuclear-free world, the removal of nuclear deterrence. Whatever the reasons, and there are probably many, for substantial reductions in strategic nuclear weapons, a reason that should not be adduced is that deep cuts are a step toward complete elimination of the weapons. I believe nobody seriously has in mind eliminating strategic nuclear weapons and eliminating dependence on nuclear deterrence; and it would be a mistake to speak as if we did. President Reagan's dream of an impenetrable shield that could make nuclear offensive weapons obsolete should be treated for what it was, a dream.

But what about the elimination of nuclear weapons as an »ultimate goal«? Should we not at least dedicate ourselves to that ultimate objective? My answer is no. The only purpose of identifying an ultimate goal would be the guidance it gives us in choosing immediate steps. And it gives us none. The reason for reducing weapons now is not that that is the direction toward zero. We may be entering a new era of candor in strategic relations between the nuclear superpowers, and pledges of allegiance to a goal that neither side believes in would only interfere.

Conditions and Criteria for a Regime for Conventional Stability in Europe

Andrei A. Kokoshin

Both East and West are becoming aware of an increasingly pressing need to work out common understandings and criteria for strategic stability in Europe, taking into account all major parameters of this issue – political, military (strategic, operational tactical) and technological. Nevertheless, there are many obstacles facing the Warsaw Treaty Organization (WTO) and NATO in developing such criteria and strengthening strategic stability at reduced levels of opposing general purpose forces and conventional arms. These obstacles are in many respects greater than those existing in the area of strategic nuclear forces. The traditions and patterns of using conventional forces are much more deeply rooted in the minds of political leaders and military commanders. These traditions run counter to the objectives of a system designed to strengthen stability on the basis of mutual security, since the principles of military art and military thinking are oriented not to joint, cooperative actions but to trials of strength and to misleading the other side.

At the tactical (company, battalion, regiment, perhaps even division) level, the traditional provisos of military art cannot but hold sway for the foreseeable future. But at the strategic and operational levels, the requirements for ensuring mutual security demand a radical revision of these principles. The less uncertainty about the composition and structure of the opposing groupings, their degree of readiness and their ability to start immediate combat actions in peacetime, the greater the chance to reduce the possibility of war. Worst-case analyses – one of the most important factors stimulating the arms race – will also disappear. The task of providing reliable mutual security, however, is not confined to maintaining balance, asymmetrical or not. The continued development of military hardware and strategy, both in general-purpose (conventional, chemical and battlefield nuclear) forces and in strategic nuclear forces, will not provide stability, even if the overall balance is

322

preserved. The current balance is maintained at very high and dangerous levels. The armaments of the two alliances are continuously being modernized and are becoming more sophisticated and more powerful. General-purpose forces and conventional armaments are reaching a new stage of development. Some of the new weapons' combat characteristics are approaching those of weapons of mass destruction. The range of conventional forces enables them to engage in combat actions not only in frontline regions but also over a great part of the territory of the countries and their allies. Such capabilities were much more limited in past wars. This qualitative leap in the development of conventional means of destruction has led to changes in the nature of training and waging warfare. And it makes conventional forces employable in newer, more destructive ways than before.

The tendency toward offensive or defensive actions and methods to converge must also be taken into consideration. Contemporary offense and defense combine fire strikes, rapid advances by tanks and armored infantry supported by air forces and combat helicopters, and the deposition of airborne troops far behind enemy lines and at the flanks of opposing groupings. Accordingly, removing or considerably reducing each side's offensive capabilities would lead to establishing more clearcut distinctions between offensive and defensive military actions. This is essential for providing strategic stability at the general-purpose and conventional arms level.

A very important impulse towards the new approach to strategic stability in Europe was given by the Warsaw Treaty member states in their Budapest Appeal of June 1986, which was underestimated by many Western analysts. Later it was even strengthened with the Berlin Declaration by the WTO states in May 1987. This approach, worked out with the contribution of scholars and nongovernmental experts, calls not only for far greater quantitative reductions than are being discussed in the Vienna talks on mutual force reductions in central Europe but also for measures aimed at qualitative structural changes that, along with the reductions, would strengthen strategic stability.

These changes must be oriented to mutually reducing the threat of surprise attack and large-scale offensive operations. Under present conditions, surprise is becoming more and more a necessity to the success of offensive as well as defensive operations. A most important precondition and a decisive factor in achieving surprise is the ability

323

to group forces secretly and quickly and to keep them on the alert. At the same time, achieving surprise is becoming more difficult and costly, due to a combination of factors. Today's armies, compared with those of World War II, are saturated with more diverse armaments and hardware. This necessitates greater efforts to conceal the preparation and conduct of operations. Reconnaissance units are also equipped with advanced technical means, which greatly increase their abilities and make concealment difficult. These factors should be taken into full consideration when working out joint or parallel measures aimed at establishing strategic stability at reduced levels of balance. With regard to the aims of achieving reductions in weapons and forces and strengthening strategic stability, the analysis of the WTO-NATO balance should however not be confined to simply comparing numbers of divisions, tanks, aircraft and so forth.

In order to prevent large-scale surprise offensives, the combat capabilities and purposes of opposing formation units and armaments must be defined. This, in turn, will call for a definition of basic parameters to be used in assessing such capabilities. It seems worthwhile to work out beforehand such agreed methods of comparison. In addition, effective and reliable verification, including on-site inspection, must accompany any agreements on conventional force reductions. The capabilities of technical means of verification are now far greater than those of 30-40 years ago. A number of such methods have been worked out and are successfully used in other fields. At the same time, additional new means and methods, designed for conventional forces, are needed. Some progress was made with the full implementation of the decisions of the Stockholm Conference on Security- and Confidence-Building Measures and with the U.S.-Soviet INF Treaty of 1987 eliminating medium- and shorter-range missiles.

Confidence-building measures should be used more widely and extended to air forces and navies. The Stockholm results certainly have lessened mistrust in each side's permanent military activity and political and military intentions. Timely notification of large-scale exercises and of the relocation, concentration or transportation of troops above certain levels as well as the introduction of certain limits on maneuvers, have reduced the possibility that concealed, concentrated troops might launch surprise offensive operations. This enhances defense. The agreement to exchange information on annual planned military activities is also very

324

important. Such an exchange is sure to contribute to eliminating mutual mistrust. This measure will also help each side to understand the other's military doctrines and strategic and operational concepts.

The idea of bringing a definitely defensive character into military doctrines and operational planning, making them develop strictly in this direction, is an important factor in providing reliable mutual security and in strengthening stability. It is necessary to get rid of mutual suspicion and mistrust, accumulated over the years, and to sort out each other's concerns caused by military doctrines and concepts. Convergence in the direction of strictly defensive force structures and strategies on both sides would create a synthesis of conditions that could reduce political and military tension in Europe and in the world as a whole, opening the way to a nuclear-free world.

Frank and concrete discussion of military doctrines and concepts would contribute to mutual, agreed rejection of the most dangerous dogmas of military thinking still existing on both sides. Such work should be done keeping in mind the recent joint declarations of Soviet and U. S. leaders that there can be no winners in nuclear war and that the two sides will seek to prevent nuclear as well as conventional war. In such a new political-military context, the very notion of »military victory« should be reexamined – especially on strategic (operational-strategic) and operational levels.

The Warsaw Pact's contemporary military doctrine, declared in May 1987, as well as the military doctrines of each of its member states have the following major characteristic, according to Soviet Defense Minister Dmitri T. Yazov: they are geared to solving a cardinal problem facing humanity, the prevention of nuclear and conventional war. »Under present conditions«, General Yazov emphasizes, »when huge arsenals of nuclear weapons are accumulated that pose a threat to the future of all of humanity, nuclear war cannot be a means of achieving political goals.«

The problems of war prevention have never before been so exhaustively considered as in the WTO's strategic and military doctrine. The essence of Soviet understanding of military doctrine was considerably expanded in the process. Prior to May 1987, Soviet doctrine had centered on the nature, goals and character of a possible future war, how to prepare the country and train armed forces for it, and what capabilities would be needed to wage it. This doctrine had been adopted by the state for a given period of time. The Warsaw Pact and Soviet military doctrine, as the Soviet government and military leaders have emphasized, is aimed at providing sufficient defense in accordance with the principle of reasonable sufficiency in military arsenals, a principle put forward at the twenty-seventh Soviet Communist Party Congress in 1986. Warsaw Pact states propose mutually to reduce conventional forces and armaments to levels that preclude either side from having the means to undertake offensive actions, while leaving enough for defense.

The idea of non-offensive defense has become prominent in Soviet political, diplomatic and military circles. Only 5-6 years ago, career military officials in the USSR and other countries of the WTO were mostly very sceptical about non-offensive defense. But they had forgotten that in the 1920s, the concept of non-offensive defense was actually pretty well developed by several leading Soviet military intellectuals, among whom A. Svechin was the most outstanding. One result of the discrediting of A. Svechin and a number of like-minded theorists in the late 1920s was that Soviet military theory had failed before the Great Patriotic War 1941-1945 to evolve proper ways and means of holding the strategic defense line. This understandably took its toll on the preparedness of both our troops and, in general, theatres of operations deep in our territory.

A strategic offensive by a superior enemy force cannot be repulsed in passing, as if this were an intermediate task. To do this, it is necessary to carry out a whole series of prolonged and bitter defensive operations. Had plans for them been laid, it would have been possible to deploy forces in the districts concerned in an entirely different manner – namely, with due regard to defense tasks – and to organise differently the control of operations and the in-depth distribution of materials and other mobilisation resources. Being oriented to an immediate counter-offensive developing into a general offensive and unprotected in proper measure by defenses distributed in depth, our forces turned out to be highly vulnerable to powerful surprise attacks from the aggressor. Mistakes of a military-political, strategic and operational character led to heavy setbacks for the Red Army, many millions of deaths and the loss of a substantial part of our territory; huge material losses were also incurred, including a considerable part of our industrial potential strenuously brought into being by the people and the Party under the prewar five-year plans.

Until recently, Soviet postwar literature on the strategy and campaign tactics of the Great Patriotic War confined itself mainly to the conduct of successful strategic offensive operations in the second half of the 1943–1945 period. Many authors failed to note that these operations were only made possible after a series of strategic defensive operations. Psychologically, this disregard of the early period of the Great Patriotic War is quite understandable. But seen from the standpoint of our present-day policy and strategy, it is as harmful as was our failure in the 1920s and 1930s to take proper account of the Red Army's reverses and defensive operations during the Civil War.

This orientation to primarily offensive operations determined the development of Soviet military thought not only in the 1940s and 1950s but also in later decades. It is only recently, in particular, with the announcement of the WTO military doctrine at the Berlin meeting of the Political Consultative Committee (May 1987), that the situation has begun to change. But there is reason to feel concerned about a certain absolutising of the experience of the Great Patriotic War (for all its unquestionable value) to the detriment of full consideration of all the new political, economic, scientific, technological and strategic factors that are now thoroughly changing the entire »strategic landscape,« to use Svechin's expression.

In assessing the military-political situation in the world today, many Soviet authors are still influenced by the syndrome of June 22, 1941, the day of Nazi invasion in the USSR. This is quite understandable and in many ways justified. The bourgeois democratic regimes existing in the leading Western countries today, even where power is in the hands of conservative governments, of course differ greatly from Hitler's and Mussolini's dictatorships. Nevertheless, when estimating the likelihood of war, some of our authors virtually fail to take account of these qualitative differences or the deep imprint left by the results of World War II on the social consciousness of the majority of developed capitalist countries, including the Federal Republic of Germany and Japan. Still, bearing all this in mind, we must continue to watch carefully the activities of various extreme right-wing alignments and organisations capable of reversing the political and hence the military-political situation – all the more so, since the West has created and is building up the technical and organisational prerequisites for attack in a number of fields.

327

In addition, in view of the increased interdependence of countries, the very character of the struggle by capitalist countries for markets and raw material sources must change in comparison to the situation between the two World Wars and in the early postwar decades. Most indicative in this respect is the policy of Japan, which lacks many raw materials (beginning with energy resources) and lags far behind other capitalist countries in military power. We should also remember that the period of liberation of colonial and dependent countries is essentially over. At present, more and more conflicts in this zone occur between newly liberated countries themselves in an effort to shape their national and multinational (multitribal) statehood. This obviously calls for a different answer to the question of just and unjust wars.

Political and military-technical components of military doctrine must be in complete harmony if strategic stability is to be strengthened according to the idea of mutual security. The Warsaw Pact doctrine sets up theoretical and practical guidelines (which are binding) for building Soviet and allied military forces, for defense planning, command bodies and troop training, for working out military concepts, and, particularly, for choosing a war-fighting mode if war were to come. Gen. Makhmud A. Gareyev, deputy chief of the Soviet General Staff, declared on June 22, 1987 that the Soviet armed forces would operate mainly in a defensive mode to repel aggression. This was probably one of the most important changes in Soviet military doctrine and strategy since the 1920s. This change resolved the contradiction beween defensive-oriented political goals, stated in military doctrine, and the operational-strategic side.

Soviet leader Mikhail Gorbachev, in his speech to the UN General Assembly on December 7, 1988, announced several unilateral Soviet steps in the military sphere in accordance with the principle of reasonable sufficiency. Soviet armed forces in Europe will be decreased by 500,000 over the next two years; a substantial number of conventional arms will be reduced, including 10,000 main battle tanks, 8,500 artillery pieces and 800 combat aircraft. Six Soviet divisions will be withdrawn from the GDR, Czechoslovakia, Hungary. Also, Soviet special assault and bridging formations and units will be withdrawn from the territories of these WTO countries. The structure of the remaining Soviet divisions on the territory of the USSR's WTO allies will be changed in such a way that these divisions will have a definitively defensive orientation.

Following the Budapest Declaration and the opening of the Vienna meeting, strategic stability in the conventional arms sphere at reduced levels of confrontation has been a subject of intense discussion at various unofficial multilateral forums. Discussions with representatives from the NATO countries were quite heated at times. We frankly voiced our complaints about structure and composition, deployment, military doctrines and concepts for armed forces. Our partners voiced their traditional reproaches with regard to the superiority possessed by Warsaw Treaty countries in tanks, armoured personnel carriers, artillery, pontoon bridge fleets, anti-aircraft forces and facilities. Furthermore, they expressed their displeasure with the configuration of WTO troop deployment in Central Europe. In the course of the discussions, Soviet scientists and experts drew attention to NATO's superiority in strike aviation, combat helicopters and naval forces. We also mentioned the fact that as far as we had been able to gather, the deployment and composition of NATO forces did not correspond to the principles proclaimed in NATO documents, according to which counterstrikes on a tactical and operational scale were to be the main form of combat action. Criticism was levelled against the U.S. Army's destabilizing Air-Land Battle concept, the NATO Follow-on-Forces Attack (FOFA) concept, the U.S. maritime strategy (associated with the names of ex-Navy Secretary John Lehman and ex-Chief of Naval Operations Admiral James Watkins) and the character of NATO troop exercises.

It appears that of all three arts of warfare – strategy, operational art and tactics – operational art will play the key role in bringing about stability at the level of general-purpose forces and conventional arms. Great importance is therefore attached today to the elaboration of the principles of operational defense, its stability and ways of ensuring its predominance over the other side's offensive operations.

It is extremely difficult to work out a universal criterion for comparing the quantitative and qualitative parameters of armed forces and armaments. There do exist, nonetheless, certain indices and characteristics that make it possible to qualify with an adequate degree of certainty a given system or facility as predominantly offensive or defensive. For instance, some Soviet and Western experts regard as predominantly defensive such weapons as guided anti-tank missiles, mobile anti-aircraft missile complexes, mine-detonating facilities, various obstacles, truck-drawn artillery systems and interceptor fighter planes that are

329

non-refuellable in flight. Tactical-technical characteristics – including speed, mobility, the degree of a system's universality, protection and vulnerability, and whether it is equipped with combat facilities for use in all types of weather and at night – are seen as important qualitative indices which make it possible to distinguish clearly between defensive and offensive weapons. Other factors must also be taken into consideration, such as the character of the forces' deployment, their distance from the front and the number of systems in service. If small and stationed well away from the likely combat area, an offensive weapons system is not considered too dangerous.

In the course of discussions, the two sides have approached a common, if schematic, concept of stability. Stability presupposes that neither side can conduct major offensive (strategic) operations or mount a surprise attack (on a strategic scale, chiefly) following a secret, massive concentration of air and sea forces, including missiles. Agreement has been reached on the following issues:

– Tight restrictions are to be imposed on the possibilities for a rapid buildup of forces deployed in peacetime. The transferring of troop contingents and combat-ready reserves from other areas and mobilization are prohibited.

– Outside the zones in which measures are being taken to ensure strategic stability at lower levels of confrontation military activities should not endanger overall equilibrium.

– A regime is to be established making it impossible to change the balance of forces through the development (modernization) of weapon systems, both those that are covered by restricting agreements and those that are not.

– Observation (intelligence), control and communications systems, as well as the structure and facilities of forces, should be set up in such a way that in the event of a conflict, heads of state and the supreme army commands of both sides are able to obtain in a timely fashion essential and sufficient information on the state of the conflict, so as to terminate it at the lowest possible level.

– The mechanism for interaction between the two sides should contain »inbuilt« elements that would localize an armed conflict if political and diplomatic »safeguards« failed. Paradoxical as it sounds, the effort to prevent war should not be restricted to the period immediately preceding actual combat.

330

The goal is that WTO's defense potential should considerably exceed NATO's attack capability, and vice versa. The result would be a shift of emphasis from the offensive to the defensive in the military doctrines of both sides. Military-political objectives and strategic concepts are to be formulated in exclusively defensive terms.

This regime has been devised in such a way as to cause enormous material expense and moral damage for the side that attempts to upset the equilibrium. Although the proposed conditions and criteria for stability in the sphere of general-purpose forces and conventional arms at a reduced level of confrontation are far from exhaustive, they can be recommended as a complete formula. But in coming years, this discussion must be set forth with members of the general public as well as with experts who will have to become more involved.

Conventional Stability 2000
How NATO Could Regain the Initiative

Albrecht A.C. von Müller

I. The Overall Political Setting of the 1990s

After decades of conventional superiority, the WTO seems to be moving seriously in the direction of conventional stability. This change is based on a fundamental rethinking of long-term political goals on the side of the Soviet Union. One can only speculate about the motivation, but there are two plausible explanations. The first relates to savings in the federal budget urgently needed for the economic reform process. The second argument is a bit more complicated and relates to maintaining a major say in world politics.

The status of a world power has traditionally been based on the accumulation of military power and/or on techno-economic superiority. For the Soviet Union, the second is not at hand for the foreseeable future, even if the reforms will be successful. At the same time, the relevance of the first factor, military power, is fading, due to both the nuclear stalemate and the increasing difficulty to project power (see Vietnam, Afghanistan).

In this situation, Gorbachev opted for a very intelligent and courageous approach: According to his assessment, a paradigm shift in world politics is inevitable. By this, the traditional pattern of hegemony-oriented power politics will be superseded by new, global challenges, such as ecological issues, North-South relations, etc., which can be solved only by reaching international cooperation. Since coming to power, Gorbachev has tried to gain a leading role for the Soviet Union in this paradigm shift, thus maintaining or regaining international reputation and sympathy, allies and impact.

Up to now, this strategy of substituting the two traditional factors of world power by the new third factor of conceptual innovativeness worked extremely well.

This »Machiavellistic« reconstruction of the reasonableness of Gorbachev's policy is not meant as a critique. On the contrary, it is to the advantage of the West if the new reasonableness is not just based on good intentions or idealism but on a very thorough and comprehensive analysis of the long-term interests of the Soviet Union.

The West should try to utilize this window of opportunity and join in a constructive transformation of the international setting, without compromising at all on security interests. We should offer a global security regime with three components:

(a) robust minimum deterrence (as proposed by Richard Garwin), combined with an enhanced ABM and ASAT Treaty,

(b) a global non-intervention regime, comprising both direct military involvment and the financial and logistical support of subversion;

(c) an arms control regime for Central Europe, that achieves increased stability at reduced force levels.

A comprehensive proposal of this kind, proposed by the United States and its Western allies, would probably not be rejected, and it could be an unprecedented step in protecting the survival of mankind for the next centuries.

Unfortunately the reaction of the West to the challenges and chances posed by Gorbachev were fairly meager up to now. At the beginning, we were taken by surprise, but after half a decade, we should try to get our acts together. To make it clear, the proposition here is not to convert to irresponsible optimism, compromise on security or mere hope that Gorbachev is serious and that his reforms will be successful. On the contrary, in such a transition phase we should be more vigilant than ever, but we also should come up with a far-reaching, comprehensive and fair proposal on how to reshape the international setting for the 21st century.

In the following, we will focus only on the third component of such a comprehensive approach by asking how a regime of conventional stability at substantially reduced force levels in Europe could be achieved.

II. The Basic Features of a Conventional Stability Regime for Europe

To begin with, it is important to have a clear idea of what conventional

333

stability is not. Unfortunately the debate is still dominated by a mixing up of the notions of symmetry and stability. All arms control regimes will opt for certain forms of symmetry. But symmetry is not enough. The best, and by now quite well-known example of this are the two cowboys, slowly approaching each other in the dusty mainroad of Dodge City for the final shoot-out. Despite perfect symmetry, there exists maximum instability. It is caused by the ratio of offensive to defensive capabilities, which in this case constitutes a regime of clear offense dominance combined with a high bonus for pre-emption.

Exactly the opposite is needed for conventional stability: a regime in which the defensive capabilities of both sides clearly exceed the offensive capabilities of the opponent, the bonuses for pre-emption not being large enough to topple this regime.

Operationally speaking, lasting conventional stability requires the fulfillment of four different criteria:

(1) Pre-Emption Stability

For this purpose, the possible bonuses for pre-emption must be systematically minimized. This can be achieved by three means: (a) reduction of the number and relevance of targets for pre-emption, (b) improved protection for the remaining, inevitable targets, (c) limitation of weapon systems that can be used for pre-emptive missions.

(2) Battlefield Stability

For this goal, the exploitation of the advantages of the aggressor on the battlefield must be inhibited. This means that especially surprise effects and local superiority must be denied. It can be achieved by limiting offense-prone mobility, massing and momentum. It also can be achieved by geographical and/or numerical limitations of munition stockpiles, mobile bridging equipment, autonomous logistics, etc. At the same time, the structural advantages of the defender must be systematically exploited. This means that there should be no limitations on attrition-oriented weapon systems and units that do not possess strategic mobility. This includes especially modern mine technology, barriers, terrain preparation and anti-tank and anti-air PGMs, as long as they are not mounted on strategically mobile platforms.

(3) Force Generation Stability

In this regard, it is essential that the potentials for force generation

334

be controlled and shaped in such a way that no significant superiority can be achieved at any time or by any mobilization pattern.

(4) Arms Race Stability

Here, finally, the overall military setting must make sure that the acquisition of additional offensive capabilities is more expensive than the means to compensate them.

These four criteria refer to different time horizons. In the pre-emption calculus, the units of measurement are minutes and hours: the battlefield calculus draws more on days and weeks: the force generation calculus, on weeks and months; and the arms race calculus, finally, relates to developments that are to be counted in years and decades.

If we evaluate NATO's opening position in Vienna against this matrix of criteria, we find some serious insufficiencies. They are not caused by incompetence or unwillingness but by the need to find compromises between various national positions and perceptions that in some cases are fairly heterogenous up to now.

NATO is proposing a symmetry of today's land forces, just a bit below the present force levels of NATO. But this would mean that NATO militarily is confronted with sort of its own mirror image. Such a regime would not at all be stable, both due to the present characteristics of the land forces and due to the enormous pre-emption bonuses in the realm of air forces. They are by far the most destabilizing factor in case of crisis yet were completely neglected in the NATO opening position.

In the realm of the air forces, a pre-emption bonus of up to 50 % could be achieved at present. At the same time, today's land forces are very dependent on avoiding air superiority for the opponent. Thus, systems effects would even increase at the expense of the defender, affecting seriously his land capabilities, too.

As NATO is a defensive alliance, it will never be the attacker. This means that we will not be the one to gain the pre-emption bonus. Therefore, it is most unwise and counter-productive for NATO to exclude exactly the most pre-emption-prone components from its arms control approach. This holds true for conventionally tipped missile systems, too, which are also absent from the NATO opening position. But even regarding land forces per se, the picture is uncomfortable. At present the emphasis on both sides is on heavily armoured, highly mobile units. Those units can be used for delaying and for defense battles.

335

But they can also be used, and due to their characteristics probably even more effectively, for massing and breakthrough operations.

Assuming that a successful attack requires local superiorities of more than 3:1, the attacker could deploy roughly 50 % of his land forces in defensive modes and could utilize the other half to build two formidable axes of attack. With these axes, he could then achieve local superiorities of up to 8:1.

The crucial point is that even a perfect symmetry of today's land forces would be inherently instable due to the very characteristics of these forces. In order to achieve conventional stability, we have to change not only quantities and go for equal ceilings but also the quality of the force ratio as such.

If, for example, both sides possess 15 modern infantry and barrier units (without strategic mobility) and only 7 heavily armoured, highly mobile units (with strategic mobility), the picture would change completely. For strategic offenses, only the latter could be used effectively. This means that the attacker would be confronted with a very disadvantageous force ratio as soon as he crosses the border: He would face a twofold superiority of modern infantry and barrier units backed by an equal number of heavily armoured units.

As this logic would apply for both sides, it means that even in case of an acute crisis, the general staffs of both sides would have to tell their political decision makers that there are no problems as defender but that one would maneuver oneself into a devastatingly inferior position by deciding to attack. And those mandatory incentives to stay home even in the most acute of crises are exactly what striving for conventional stability is all about.

There are two reasons why one should not give up the heavily armoured units altogether. The first relates to the complexity of the threat for the possible attacker. If he would be confronted only with a monoculture of infantry of barrier units he might counter-optimize. This becomes much more difficult if he has to be prepared for both, fighting against modern infantry and barrier units *and* for fighting in a mobile warfare of the traditional kind. The second argument relates to the capability to restore territorial integrity. For this functions, mobile units that possess at least operational counter-attack capabilities are needed.

For these two reasons it seems advisable to go for a mixed force structure, which is not at all a purely »defensive defense« but which nevertheless provides an overall regime in which the defensive capabilities of both sides clearly dominate the offensive capabilities of the opponent. (Such a regime would even fulfill the criterion favoured by the Soviet military, namely, to be able to provide a »crushing defeat« for the attacker.)

So much for land forces, but what to do about the air forces? One big advantage is that in such a scheme the dependence of the land forces on air support would be drastically reduced and that modern barrier and infantry units do not provide attractive targets for a pre-emptive attack. In addition to this, one should try to achieve an arms control regime for the air force in which the interceptor capabilities of both sides dominate the penetration capabilities of the opponent.

Today, NATO could not afford such a position, because it needs its penetrations - capable, ground-attack airplanes to engage second-echelon forces. But the prize for our formidable air-strike capabilities is that we cannot deny similar capabilities to the WTO. Given the fact already mentioned that NATO will never be the attacker and given also the enormous vulnerabilities of our air forces, this constitutes a most serious disadvantage for NATO.

In the regime proposed here, the sheer mass required for strategic echeloning would disappear and thus the related tasks for our air force to engage them. Under these circumstances, it would be advisable to go for a regime of defense dominance also regarding the air force. This could be achieved by focusing on interceptor capabilities, by hardening shelters and by shifting the emphasis to vertical take-off planes as much as possible. Their characteristics fit quite well with this modified role of air forces, as deep penetration is no longer the task but rather to survive and to maintain air superiority over one's own territory.

Obviously all these questions have to be studied thoroughly and in great detail. But in principle, it should be possible to contain and reduce the pre-emption bonus also in the realm of the air forces to such an extent that it no longer destabilizes the overall regime of conventional stability.

III. What NATO Should Propose in Vienna

We are in the process of reshaping the postwar military realities in Europe. It would be a pity if NATO were to continue to restrict itself to short-term, small-step proposals, leaving all the initiative and thus the public support to Gorbachov.

NATO should come up with a far-reaching proposal that describes a comprehensive regime of conventional stability at drastically reduced force levels. This transformation of the military setting in Europe will not be completed before the next century, but it is important that we know quite soon in which direction we want to steer the process.

Those who are more skeptical about the long-term prospects of the present reform process should be especially keen to taking advantage of the present »window of opportunity« for a fundamental reshaping of the postwar military setting in Europe. If we achieve a regime of a robust, mutual defense dominance at substantially reduced force levels, it would be very difficult for any future Kremlin leadership to turn back to the old hostile and threatening attitudes and military postures.

NATO should therefore come up with a proposal describing the military setting we want to achieve by the year 2000. It could have roughly the following core elements:

(1) Selective Reductions of the Most Offense-Capable Components
E.g., equal ceilings at roughly 50 % of the present NATO force levels for main battle tanks, infantry fighting vehicles, artillery, attack helicopters and combat aircraft, combined with density limits that prohibit attack-capable force concentrations.

(2) Defense Dominance Rooted in the Force Composition
E.g., a ratio of 2:1 on both sides between modern barrier and infantry units and the traditional heavily armoured, highly mobile units with counter-attack capabilities.

(3) Complementary Minimization of Pre-Emptive Capabilities
In addition to aircraft ceilings, a range limitation of 50 km for all unmanned weapon systems should be achieved, with the exception of a few hundred missile systems that are specifically allowed. (See below.)

(4) Complementary Restrictions of Offensive Mobility
This can be achieved through geographical and quantitative limitations on munition stockpiles, bridging equipment and mobile logistics, making sure that even the remaining heavily armoured units are logistically incapable of strategic offensive missions.

Beyond these four core elements, there exist four more problems that have to be tackled in a conventional arms control regime. They relate to the questions of (a) what to do with surpluses, (b) how to verify compliance effectively without making the verification process more costly than the military capabilities to be reduced, (c) how to regulate the modernization process in order to make sure that it does not undermine the regime of conventional stability, and finally (d) what to do about the nuclear weapons in Europe.

(a) Dismantling

Regarding surpluses, it should be agreed not just to redeploy them geographically (e.g., behind the Urals) but to dismantle them and to dissolve the related units. (This should be acceptable to the WTO, as major redeployments would be very costly and substantial savings are crucial for the success of the economic reform process.)

(b) Verification

Regarding land forces, the best solution might be to have an officer of the opposing alliance as permanent guest of every brigade or regiment. Through him, the equipment, the personnel, the training patterns and possible force concentrations could be verified on a day-to-day basis by a relatively small number of arms control officers on both sides.

The restrictions on combat aircraft will pose specific problems. One option might be to leave the planes that are to be reduced in the ATTU area but to disaggregate them, meaning, e.g., that the engines are brought to Spain, the wings, to Denmark, the chassis, to Great Britain, etc. This would facilitate verification and would be a most reliable hedge against sudden redeployment. In addition, all air bases between the Atlantic and the Urals should be supervised by officers from the opposing alliance.

Combined with the existing technical means, this should add up to a very reliable and comprehensive verification regime that does not cost too much and that would not interfere with the legitimate defense interests of both sides.

(c) Modernization

Here again we face a very difficult task. On the one hand, it is not realistic and probably not even desirable to stop modernization altogether, as technological progress can also be utilized to enhance stability and a regime of defense dominance. On the other hand there obviously exists the danger that all concrete arms control provisions could be circumvented or undermined by specifically

339

offense-oriented utilizations of technological progress. The task, therefore, is to harmonize modernization with the regime of defense dominance.

In principle, there exist two ways to do that. One would be to list all possible destabilizing developments and prohibit them one by one. In practice, however, this is impossible due to the fact that we can not know today the inventions of tomorrow. The other approach is to allow modernization but to set the rule that it must be announced in detail from the very beginning and that the initiator automatically concedes twofold reciprocity to the opponent.

What does that mean? If, e.g., NATO considers introducing a new, highly efficient mine system, it could not prevent the WTO from introducing two times as many. On the contrary, it would be to the advantage of the West if the East rechannels its investments in this direction. On the other hand, one would hesitate to introduce a new main battle tank, as in this case the »2:1 rule« would probably lead to a net deterioration of one's own security.

In general, this means that one has not to engage in meaningless definitions of what is an »offensive« or a »defensive« weapon, and one also avoids the complexities of in-advance listed prohibitions. Instead, one can leave it to the self-interest of both actors that they will opt only for those modernizations that specifically favour defense. (Technically speaking: Only if the decoupling factor is greater than 2, a modernization leads to a net improvement of one's own security.)

With such a regulation, it should become possible to harmonize modernization and stability, i.e., to make sure that modernization does not undermine but rather enhances the regime of a robust, mutual defense dominance.

(d) Nuclear Weapons in Europe

For the foreseeable future, the existence of nuclear weapons in Europe will contribute to stability and war prevention by being a factor in the ultimate incalculability of any war. But, if we get to a regime of conventional stability, including the abolition of offense-capable echeloning, the size and features of the nuclear component can be changed drastically.

In combination with the above provisions for the conventional realm, NATO should propose the following regime for the nuclear realm: Both sides are allowed to have up to 400 mobile, single-warhead missiles with ranges below 500 km (according to INF agreement) and without terminal guidance. No other nuclear systems are allowed in the ATTU area.

Such a regime would fulfill the function of enhancing war prevention and would even enable both sides to intervene in the most unlikely case of an emerging conventional defeat. At the same time, all the destabilizing side-effects of today's nuclear arsenals in Europe that fuel the arms race would be avoided, as well as all thinking in terms of extended nuclear warfare.

The Military Dimension of European Security

Anatoly V. Bolyatko

The process of *perestroika* underway in our country is a complex, versatile and all-enveloping phenomenon. It has inevitably affected the issues of war and peace, military policy and the structural organization of the armed forces. The acuteness of issues inherent in the present stage of world development persistently demands new political and, hence, new military-political thinking; stereotypes of past years, which exist today in international relations, must be overcome.

A creative analysis of the issues of war and peace, taking into consideration the nature of modern times and the profound changes in the tools of war and its potential after-effects, has led to a reworking of ideas on how to improve military-political thinking and of approaches to improving international problems. New approaches to the problem are necessitated by the nuclear confrontation between the United States and the USSR, NATO and the Warsaw Treaty Organization, the real danger of nuclear war and its catastrophic consequences for world civilization. »New political thinking« in the military sphere requires all nations to adopt exclusively defensive doctrines.

The military doctrine of the Soviet Union is clearly defensive in nature, and its primary tenet is to prevent the outbreak of war. The approach consists of a new attitude to violence, particularly within the military sphere, as a factor of international politics. To attempt to resolve problems between nations by means of force is, in the nuclear age, tantamount to creating a threat to mankind's very existence. Thus, the need for mastering the art and science of restraint in international relations and for settling conflicts by political means is of top priority. The new military-political thinking combines social optimism and stringent realism in assessing the extent of threat and its origins, as well as the prospects for preventing war.

Lengthy talks on strategic nuclear arms have borne fruit. The INF Treaty was signed. The talks on 50 percent reduction of strategic offensive weapons are going on intensively. The determination to reduce the

342

level of nuclear confrontation is apparent. In these conditions, the task at hand is to reduce the level of confrontation in conventional arms and armed forces, especially on the European continent. The military confrontation in Europe is far too great and therefore too dangerous. Immense armed forces of NATO and the Warsaw Treaty Organization face each other there. In addition, the build-up of non-nuclear arms is continuing. Conventional weapons are becoming much more sophisticated in their power, accuracy, speed, state of alert and range. It is becoming more difficult to restrict the after-effects and the scope of casualties brought about by a conventional war. It is becoming more difficult to hope to win such a war. The destructive consequences of a conventional war have become comparable to those of a nuclear war, and therefore the notion of strategic stability now embraces both nuclear and conventional arms and forces. It has become important to seek conditions that make a surprise attack and offensive operations impossible. The idea of »nonprovocative defense« (otherwise known as »non-offensive defense« in the USSR) fits the new military-political thinking because it proscribes the use of force to solve international problems. It also conforms to the military doctrine of the Warsaw Treaty Organization in that it is exclusively defensive in orientation.

The program of European disarmament put forward by the Warsaw Treaty states in their 1986 Budapest Appeal is aimed at a radical reduction of arms and armed forces in Europe from the Atlantic to the Urals and at establishing a level of military potential that would secure for the two opposing sides the means for defense but deny them the possibility of offensive operations. We view it as a way to a safer military and political situation in Europe. The leaders of the Warsaw Treaty states suggested that over one or two years, NATO and Warsaw Treaty forces be reduced by 100,000 to 150,000 men on each side, and that in the early 1990s a one-fourth reduction be carried out – that is, over one million servicemen on both sides, this process continuing in the future. The following two years saw no reductions, though the idea of reducing forces from the Atlantic to the Urals was supported by NATO. Since February 1987 the consultations of the 23 on the mandate of negotiations have been going on.

We must make way for new trends and not just mark time. Above all, this means more openness. Speaking at a press conference in Washington in December 1987, M.S. Gorbachev said: »We must lay our cards on the table face up, exchange all information, assess it, reveal asymmetry in weapons and troops and get down to practical solutions... We are prepared to make the most radical cuts... This is likely to be a phased process. Not all problems can be solved at once. But this process must be begun by beginning serious negotiations and by eliminating asymmetries and imbalances so that confrontation can be radically reduced.« Alongside the proposals aimed at reducing military confrontation in Europe, the USSR and other socialist nations are putting forward a package of confidence-building measures, including measures that would prohibit the sudden initiation of war in Europe. Particularly, this means a reduction of arms and forces in the zone of contact between the two military alliances down to the lowest agreed level, the removal of the most dangerous offensive weapons out of this zone, and the establishment of a nuclear-free corridor between NATO and the WTO [Warsaw Treaty Organization], each side removing all nuclear weapons.

In response to the peace-oriented initiatives of the USSR and the ongoing process of nuclear arms limitation, Gen. Galvin, Supreme Allied Commander of NATO forces in Europe, said that as soon as the medium- and shorter-range nuclear missiles are liquidated, »weapons available to NATO will be insufficient to destroy potential threats.« He spoke in favour of an all-embracing modernization, including air-to-surface stand-off missiles with a range of about 400 km and surface-to-surface missiles with a range of about 450 km, which would replace the Lance missile. This »modernization« would also include the additional deployment of the strike aircraft F-15, F-16, and F-111, as well as moving sea-launched cruise missiles closer to Europe. A number of Western European leaders have spoken out in favor of this so-called »modernization« of US nuclear weapons positioned in Europe. The main argument of those who support the modernization is the idea that as soon as the American and Soviet missiles are removed from Europe, the superiority of WTO over NATO in conventional arms and forces will create a situation unfavorable for the West.

Assessment of the military balance, while not an easy thing to do, is not, however, hopeless if the contracting parties would sit down to negotiate and work out a mutual understanding with regard to the actual overall balance of their armed forces. Specifically, the WTO nations have offered to discuss the problem of imbalances and asymmetries.

344

Also offered is a thorough verification of all submitted data, including on-site inspections. No one denies that the WTO nations have more tanks. However, there are serious imbalances that favor NATO as well, for example, in tactical strike aircraft. Even according to US figures, the superiority of NATO in this kind of weapon amounts to 1,150 aircraft (excluding the air forces of France and Spain). Soviet estimates place that figure at 1,400 aircraft. NATO experts argue that tanks have a higher offensive capability than any other type of weapon. If one examines the history of World War II and post-war conflicts, he will see that it was air strikes that secured success at the initial stage of war, and that it was aircraft that cleared the way for tanks.

Another NATO argument is that WTO is superior in the number of divisions. NATO estimates of WTO superiority vary from one and a half to twice the number of NATO divisions. However, it is never mentioned that there is approximately the same difference in the number of personnel in those divisions in favor of NATO. For example, an American division numbers from about sixteen to nineteen thousand men, and a West German division numbers as much as twenty-four thousand men. In contrast, a WTO army division numbers at maximum eleven to twelve thousand men. Putting the total number of divisions aside, and considering only combat-ready divisions, NATO has ninety-four such divisions and WTO only seventy-eight. Moreover, the total number of NATO and WTO forces are about the same.

Even if NATO representatives decided to give an unbiased assessment of individual types of weapons or forces that they selected themselves, such a discriminatory approach would be unacceptable. It is impossible to assess the balance of the two sides without taking into account such offensive weapons types as tactical strike aircraft or disregarding an entire branch, such as the navy, with all its weapons intended for land targets.

At present, NATO has, in comparison to WTO:
- 7.6 times as many large high-seas surface ships;
- 3 times as much tonnage in military fleets;
- 2.4 times as many navy aircraft.

NATO marines forces are also several times more numerous than [comparable] WTO forces.

In the Atlantic alone, the joint forces of NATO can deploy up to 500 combat ships and over 2,500 combat-carrier based and shore-based

345

planes and helicopters. The combat capabilities, including capabilities for action against land targets, of the American fleet of surface ships and submarines are constantly growing. The United States is persistently building up its aircraft carrier force (there are already 15 carriers, and of these, five are nuclear powered). Battleships are being reactivated and equipped with Tomahawk cruise missiles. Similar missiles are put on ships of other types.

Evidently, because the United States and NATO are superior to the USSR and WTO in naval strength, NATO representatives do not want to include naval forces in the negotiations and prefer to limit the said function of these forces to »protection of naval communications« and »rapid sea lift of forces.«

The present parity in conventional arms could be violated by long-range, high-accuracy weapons, as well as by electronic warfare (EW). Lately EW has grown from being a type of combat support and has become an inherent part of small- and large-scale operations. The local conflicts of the 1980s reveal that EW is now a relatively independent and specific form of armed struggle.

The balance estimate must also rely on the abilities and skills of soldiers, especially those who operate modern sophisticated equipment. We must see the difference between a young man drafted for two years straight from school and an enlisted long-term professional soldier.

The seriousness of the balance of forces requires a serious approach that takes into account all its peculiarities. However, one cannot say this about the NATO decision to publish the report »Armed Forces and Conventional Weapons in Europe: Facts.« Unfortunately, after becoming acquainted with the text, one comes to the conclusion that the information set forth in the report is selected in such a way so as to distort the real relation of forces between NATO and WTO by using calculation techniques that favor NATO. The figures published by NATO do not allow the reader to assess the combat strength of the two alliances or their military potential. In place of an objective assessment, a tendentious, selective approach is taken. The authors juggle the figures in order to show the superiority of the USSR and WTO and to hush up whatever NATO has more of. In the published data, there is no information about the military-naval forces of the US and NATO, not even about the European NATO navies and the US Atlantic Fleet targeted directly at Europe. The reference to the

346

number of planes and their types hides the real picture of the air forces. Combat-ready divisions are not shown. Anti-aircraft defense forces are not properly considered. Information about artillery has been tendentiously selected. As for the goal that haunts the publication of the given document, it could never be called constructive: This is sheer propaganda. The propagandistic goals are clear – to convince public opinion of the authors' devotion to the cause of disarmament, to secure support for their position at the upcoming talks, and to achieve a one-sided reduction of WTO forces in view of WTO's supposed superiority.

However, as serious politicians and specialists in the West will acknowledge, WTO has no superiority; approximate military parity exists between NATO and WTO.

At the same time, the Soviet government set out unilaterally to reduce its armed forces and weapons. It proceeded from the new political thinking, the defensive nature of the Soviet military doctrine, and the desire to avoid a deadlock in conventional arms reduction. In the next two years, the strength of the Soviet armed forces will be reduced by 500,000 men. These reductions will be unilateral, not connected with the coming talks on reduction of armed forces and conventional arms in Europe. From the GDR [East Germany], Czechoslovakia and Hungary, six tank divisions will be withdrawn and disbanded, in accordance with the agreement with the Warsaw Treaty nations. This withdrawal includes air assault and a number of other units, including river-crossing units together with their weapons and combat equipment. The Soviet troops stationed in the GDR, Czechoslovakia and Hungary will be reduced by 50,000 men and 5,000 tanks.

All Soviet divisions remaining on the territory of our allies will have a new organizational structure, which will be clearly defensive in nature. This will be accompanied by a reduction in the number of military personnel and weapons in the European territory of the USSR. The Soviet armed forces in Europe, both within the USSR and on the territory of our Warsaw Treaty allies, will be reduced by 10,000 tanks, 8,500 artillery pieces and 800 combat airplanes. The armed forces deployed in the Asian part of the USSR will also be significantly reduced. A significant portion of Soviet troops temporarily stationed in the Mongolian People's Republic will return home.

These decisions have been made on the basis of the new military-

347

political thinking of the Soviet Union, which states that military means are no longer practicable and that any military presence must be limited by national borders. These principles are supported by our practical steps in military policies, including those measures announced in New York. Western political and military leaders have said that they would welcome the new defensive military doctrine of the USSR but claim that the words are not being supported by actions. The latest unilateral action taken by the Soviet Union is a reply to these skeptics. It is a voluntary and unilateral contribution to the cause of disarmament and a step toward a safer Europe and a more secure world.

The Gorbachev Proposals: Western Responses or Western Initiatives?

Eberhard Schulz

When Mikhail Gorbachev on December 7 addressed the General Assembly of the United Nations, everybody agreed that he is definitely a formidable leader. His announcements of considerable military reductions were widely reported and taken seriously. But the philosophical framework of his remarks and his non-military observations largely escaped public attention. A different Western reaction was hardly to be expected: People had become accustomed to Lenin's shrewdness, Stalin's cynicism, Khrushchev's erratic outbursts and Brezhnev's idle talk and fraud. While Gorbachev personally enjoys worldwide an extraordinary reputation, trust in Soviet political overtures is still hampered by painful experiences. Still few would agree that Communist Russia left behind its totalitarian past of mass extermination and subjugation of her own and other peoples. Or was there indeed evidence that the »revolutionary perestroika« Gorbachev mentioned in his presentation again so profoundly changed Soviet attitude as to introduce an era of as he put it an entire world doomed to common survival or catastrophy? Wasn't this a cheap propaganda phrase, and didn't the enthusiastic echo in the Western world indicate that his real aim was to cast the Atlantic Alliance into disarray?

And even if Gorbachev meant what he said, why did he choose the show on the stage of the United Nations which so often proved not to be on friendly terms with the United States, why did he pronounce his initiatives on American soil? Didn't he want to humiliate the rival superpower? Didn't he hit Washington at a time when the leader of the Western alliance was put out of action by the change of administration? Was he, on the other hand, in full control of his own country? Wasn't there a chain of troubles from Eltsin over Ligachev to Akhromeev's resignation just upon Gorbachev's speech on unilateral force reductions?

Whatever the merits of the substance in Gorbachev's proposals, one thing is beyond doubt. He regained the initiative in East-West relations the Soviet Union had lost some two decades ago. Now the West is grudgingly reacting to what Gorbachev chooses to table. Some feel that this situation, uncomfortable for the West, is inevitable, as a totalitarian dictator is in a position to do what he wants to, while in the West, there is an alliance of free nations that always need a complicated process of harmonizing views before they arrive at a common line. I submit that this is an excuse that is far from compelling. What makes Gorbachev strong is not a crude dictatorship as it was exercised by Uncle Joe half a century ago, but a fascinating leadership the logic of which seems to correspond to the best interests of the whole of mankind.

Having said this, I hasten to add that I do not recommend a blue-eyed confidence in Gorbachev's words, but a careful examination of what is behind these words, i.e. of the facts which characterize the present situation in the world, including the developments within the Soviet Union since Gorbachev took over. Such a scrutiny might help us to evade the traps of a possible Soviet hoax or perhaps of our own prejudice and to redefine our own attitude. During my professional military life I was taught that it is inexcusable to leave the initiative to the other side. What I am aiming at then is regaining the initiative in East-West relations. Thus after my analysis, I will try to draw some conclusions on how the West might proceed.

Gorbachev told us in New York that by 1991 six armoured divisions in the GDR, in Czechoslovakia and in Hungary will be disbanded. Whether he lives up to this promise is relatively easy to verify. The same is true for the restructuring of the remaining Soviet forces. Whether the indigenous East European armies will follow suit remains to be seen. The Hungarians already announced that they plan to cut down their defence budget for 1989 by 17 percent. Perhaps they will provide the evidence that they have done so. They also reported that Soviet military training flights had been reduced effective from December 1 of this year. If this is not realized protests from the population are likely to be raised. Gorbachev's further announcements were rather vague. The dismantlement of half a million troops affords some time in order not to repeat the social hardships Khrushchev inflicted upon the dismissed army people in the early 1960s. As for the 10,000 tanks Gorbachev said that they will be removed. He did not indicate whether they will be destroyed. Anyway, the penetration and invasion capability of Soviet troops in Central Europe will certainly be diminished if it formerly existed.

As for to the invasion capability, a certain proviso is in order. The United States was the first power to develop nuclear weapons, which were meant for warfighting. But the Americans were also the first to realize that the devastating characteristics of nuclear weapons went far beyond traditional arms. For the first time in history weapons were developed which would not only decide wars, but reliably exclude wars. Nuclear weapons thus had the primary task to deter, not to win, wars. And, indeed, during the 43 years after the first use of nuclear weapons many wars were fought throughout the world, but none of them between nuclear powers. Obviously, this does not prove that such wars cannot arise, at least unintentionally. But past experience very strongly indicates that between nuclear powers the famous Clausewitz dictum that war is a continuation of politics by other means no longer holds true. Unfortunately, in the West this experience was more and more neglected, while the Soviet military doctrine flatly discarded it.

It was not before the »new political thinking« came up that in the Soviet Union that this basic experience was accepted. During the ensuing heated debate, Soviet theorists reinvented the idea of »sufficiency« rather than parity. This idea had originally been developed in the U.S., but was dismissed there in the early 1970s. The core of this idea is that parity is too complex in operational politics to became an applicable criterion and that the striving for parity in all of its many facets just nourishes the arms race. Much more reasonable is a sufficiency of military arsenals, which maintains a second strike capability. Under its umbrella the incalculability of risks deters a potential aggressor even from waging a »conventional« war. If this is true, then the ivory-tower idea of »escalation control,« which presupposes a certain military superiority and thus also feeds the arms race, becomes dispensable.

To be sure, this learning process in the Soviet Union was enhanced when the Soviet leadership realized that the Soviet economy was threatened with collapse if the military budget could not be reduced. In this respect, the extraordinary military spending of the Reagan administration contributed to the »new political thinking.« Thanks to the new »glasnost« in the Soviet Union Western experts had a chance to pursue the sharp debate which evolved around the principle of »reasonable sufficiency«. When the army newspaper »Red Star« in

October 1987 praised the Chinese experience, it became visible that the Soviet leadership considered following this example in unilaterally cutting down the size in order to improve or maintain the quality of the armed forces. Perhaps the fact that Colonel General Moiseev, the commander of the Far Eastern Military District, which is close to China, was chosen to succeed Marshall Akhromeev is an indication of Gorbachev's intentions.

Another indication of a very profound change in the Soviet Union is the debate about ideology in general and foreign policy in particular. This is not the place to reproduce the argument. Thes gist of the »new political thinking« is that ideology must not interfere in international relations. Now, after so many decades of purposeful Soviet disinformation – is the new departure trustworthy? I submit that it is, and there are strong indications for this view. Vladimir Shlapentokh explained how difficult it is for Kremlin leaders to change »party ideology« as opposed to »public ideology.« I cannot elaborate here on that. Suffice is to say that the publication of discussions at a large conference in the Soviet Foreign Ministry as well as of the address given by Foreign Minister Shevardnadze at an election meeting in the party organization of his ministry give evidence that what is at stake now is »party ideology«. As the legitimation of the present Soviet system is based on this part of the ideology, it is not easily manipulated. Thus, the change in Soviet foreign policy is profound, much more profound than the actual behaviour of Soviet diplomats hitherto could prove. This is not to say that we just can lean back and believe. In politics caution is always indispensable. But this time we have a fair chance to try.

This leads me to my final question: what should the West do in order to protect its interests. The present moment seems propitious for regaining the initiative. In the United States, President Reagan, at the end of his tenure, set the stage for a new relationship with the Soviet Union. Many of his demands were fulfilled by Gorbachev, e.g., that Soviet occupation forces move out of Afghanistan. In all major regional conflicts the Soviet Union ceased as a matter of principle to back the forces hostile to the U.S. In arms control negotiations the Soviets acknowledge the need of verification. Human rights are being improved in socialist countries. On this basis the new American administration will not lack public support if it tries to normalize relations with Moscow. President-elect George Bush's first steps look promising: By choosing

General Brent Scowcroft as his national security advisor he signaled to the Soviets that SDI will not be given priority in American defence programmes, and the nomination of John Tower for secretary of defence will reassure those Americans who fear that defence might be neglected. It is precisely in this preparatory phase that new ideas on the security relationship with the Soviet Union can be elaborated.

If my analysis is appropriate, the military threat in East-West relations has ceased to be the problem number one. For many reasons, NATO has never been in a position to occupy large territories in Eastern Europe in a way which threatened the integrity of the Soviet Union. Western Europe, on the other hand, while facing a strong conventional and nuclear superiority of the Warsaw Pact, had always been protected by the incalculability of the risk a potential aggressor would incur. Military parity did not play the decisive role in guaranteeing stability and integrity of European countries. Much more important are the domestic acceptancy and the international cohesiveness of the Atlantic Alliance. Political rather than strategic factors occupy first place. It would be unwise simply to rely on change in the Soviet Union and create a military vacuum next to the frontiers of the Warsaw Pact. It would, however, likewise be shortsighted to neglect developments in the Soviet Union and not to respond in kind. If we continue to promise our alliance partners increasing defence efforts and fail to live up to our commitments (as we did in the Long Term Defence Programme) we threaten our credibility with our partners. Politically strengthening the alliance by reconsidering alliance strategies, force structures, weapons procurements and military exercises according to the principle of reasonable sufficiency for deterrence rather than numerical parity for warfighting is our primary security task.

Much of that task is a psychological one. We must avoid misunderstandings which undermine confidence. There is the issue of modernisation. Abstaining from modernizing our defensive forces at a time when in the Warsaw Pact modernizing goes on would be a misleading signal. So we have to modernize our forces at a proper pace. What we should avoid, however, is double-dealing. We made this mistake during the missile debate in the late 1970s when we talked of »modernizing« the Pershing IA while, in reality, we prepared for the deployment of missiles with a much larger range offering new military options. We should not repeat this performance with the replacement of the Lance missiles, thereby putting at risk the acceptancy of our security policy and the Alliance at large.

In addition, from a psychological point of view, Gorbachev's unilateral move impresses people in Germany and elsewhere. They wouldn't understand if we just swallowed his concession. They do not believe any more in the threat of an imminent war. They instead believe that it is now our turn. What Gorbachev will remove from Eastern Europe is not essential for Soviet security. If we now want to attract attention we should act, not wait. We might decide to remove short-range nuclear systems whose usefulness is anyway highly controversial – to say the least. To be sure, this would give disarmament new momentum and whet the appetite for more. Such a decision should, therefore, not be taken before the next steps are considered. But this process would certainly add to the confidence of most Europeans in Western security policy and perhaps, at the same time, lessen pressures on the American president to reduce the burden of American forces in Europe.

Some will argue that a sequence of unilateral steps would take the steam out of multilateral disarmament negotiations. This is a dangerous contention. Whoever soberly watches the preparations for the Vienna talks and keeps in mind the more than 13 years of MBFR talks will agree that substantial reductions, negotiated by the 23 actors, are not likely to be attained in a forseeable span of time. During the 1970s, when détente was at a recess, one could argue that talking was better than shooting, but this is not at all convincing under present circumstances when people sense what is now essential is not a volatile and ambivalent détente but a profound change in international relations. At this stage, mankind is threatened much more by the lack of vision in North-South relations and by the rapidly worsening natural environment than by an East-West conflict. Gorbachev, in his New York speech, was aware of this sentiment, but the Soviet Union has no leverage whatsoever to tackling these issues. It is NATO and the OECD countries that are expected to deal with these issues. Admittedly, this is a terrible task. But if we decide to address these questions and call upon Gorbachev for cooperation, the Soviet Union will hardly be able to side step this, and again, the initiative would return to our side. This would be a meaningful and credible contribution to peace.

But what about the threat of an inadvertent outbreak of war? Miscalculation, nervousness and similar factors still are dangerous. They cannot be neutralized by relying ad hoc on rational behaviour. Much more promising is a policy which generally keeps tensions at a low level. Since the political and ideological character of the Soviet system actually is changing, a policy fostering cooperation between East and West on a permanent basis provides the best chances for preserving peace. In this respect, the levers of the West are much longer and stronger than those of the East. Regaining the initiative is easiest in this field.

Remember how successfully the West acted in fostering human rights. Gorbachev has not only addressed this problem in his country and freed Sacharov and others, but he has learned that he will not achieve stability in his country unless he does justice to the legitimate demands of his people. This is the basis on which solid peace and fruitful cooperation between East and West can be constructed.

A Western Response to Gorbachev's Proposals

Willem F. van Eekelen

Wide attention was garnered by Mikhail Gorbachev's address to the United Nations in December 1988. To begin with, there was a distinct absence of an ideological bias, with no mention being made of Lenin. Gorbachev appealed for the »de-ideologizing« of international relations, which seems to indicate that he has gained the upper hand in the debate over whether the class struggle should play a dominant role in international affairs. In addition, there was no trumpeting of past or expected Soviet achievements and no Khrushchev-esque talk of burying the West. Gorbachev deftly adopted United Nations vernacular in discussing such issues as co-development and solutions to the Third World's debt problems. But his speech also contained some rather peculiar references, such as singling out the French and Russian revolutions as the greatest moments of history; it seems odd to compare the triumph of individual freedom at the Bastille with the upheaval in 1917, which led to the world's most authoritarian regime.

Perhaps the most significant aspect of Gorbachev's speech was his announcement of a general reduction of the Soviet military establishment, a reduction more substantial than had been expected. In particular, he proposed the withdrawal of 6 tank divisions and 5,000 tanks from three countries bordering the Iron Curtain; since 6 divisions are equipped with less than 5,000 tanks, other units will probably have to be thinned out as well.

During a visit to Moscow in October 1988, I became aware of a debate raging between academicians and the military over the next move in the arms-control process. The former advocated unilateral reductions in order to lessen some of the more striking asymmetries in the conventional balance of forces in Europe; the military maintained that any reduction – even the application of a new defense doctrine – should be put to negotiation in Vienna. Although it is now clear that the unilateralists won the debate, the victory took its toll: the replacement of General Akhromeyev as the top military officer on the day of Gorbachev's address is a sign that there is strong opposition to these measures.

356

Thus, the level of support that Gorbachev can expect from the military for perestroika is by no means resolved. To date, they have seemed to back his efforts to get the Soviet economy moving again, which is hardly surprising given the importance such individuals attach to efficiency and modern technology. Nevertheless, their support might wane if the role of the military is retrenched too severely. Although the INF agreement can be seen as a success for Moscow, in that it eliminates a threat to Soviet territory, the approval of new weapons systems might be essential in order to assuage the defense establishment.

The tank withdrawal, to take place over the next two years in East Germany, Czechoslovakia and Hungary, will reduce the strength to roughly the level maintained by NATO in Europe. However, the Warsaw Pact will, overall, continue to hold a 2:1 superiority in this area. Although this measure is a meaningful step in the right direction, the aim of conventional stability is still far from being reached. Its importance lies in the signal given by Gorbachev that he is seriously pursuing the ongoing negotiations. It seems that he has come to the conclusion that the forces in Eastern Europe are far larger than is required for defense purposes – or, for that matter, for underpinning the regimes in the satellite countries. It might also be that he is questioning the cost effectiveness of military expenditures from the aspect of the political power and influence to be expected in return. It is in any case undoubtedly clear to him that the continued improvement of relations with Western Europe depend on a build-down of the capabilities for large-scale offensive action.

In the long term, decreased military power might affect the Soviet Union's status as a superpower, as this is primarily measured in military strength. Whether this will transpire turns, of course, on the Soviets' position vis-à-vis the United States, which for its part would also prefer to reduce its expenditures for defense. If the Soviets continue their policy of curtailing foreign commitments –which began with Afghanistan and has now become apparent in other regional conflicts as well – the relations between the superpowers might become less virulent. By concentrating on internal reforms and economic development, the Soviet Union is a less frightening actor in the international arena, but also a less important one. With the easing of Third World tensions, the unhappy situation in Eastern Europe will once again move into the foreground. We can assume that reform here will only be tolerated to the extent that the leading role of the Communist party is maintained. How, then, will the citizens of these countries react? They will likely find it hard to accept the assertions of their leaders that *perestroika* has already advanced to a stage beyond that in the Soviet Union or that further glasnost would lead to anarchy. Thus the crucial question in the coming decades will be the management of change in Eastern Europe. In recent speeches, General Galvin, the Supreme Allied Commander in Europe, has warned that change may create new instabilities and, consequently, that caution and vigilance are called for. This brings me to the concept of stability, a term often batted about but seldom defined. Stability means that neither side has an incentive (through capabilities or force posture) to start a war and that both can afford to wait. From the standpoint of the strategic equation, stability is only able to be reached when the level of central systems is much lower. The European theater is still in need of appropriate criteria; one must take into account not only numbers of forces but also the readiness to fight and the ability to mobilize. The Soviet Union's long-standing argument was that because no war has broken out since 1945, stability exists. But this ignores a crucial factor: Although the establishment of approximate parity in major weapons systems, like tanks and artillery, would clearly be the most desirable outcome of the Vienna negotiations, the positioning of these forces and the opportunity for quick reinforcement are of equal significance.

In addition, a distinction will have to be made between measures that increase warning time and those that equalize capabilities. Thus far, emphasis has been placed almost exclusively on confidence-building measures, such as the announcement of major maneuvers. Although these measures are not unimportant, they consistently raise a decisive question: in the event of a violation, is the increased time provided for sufficient for mounting an adequate defense? The possible limitation on bridge-laying equipment illustrates the complexity of these calculations. This restriction would clearly impede an aggressor, but depending on the terrain, it could hamper defense even more. Furthermore, with regard to the time needed to bring such equipment to the front, a U.S. analyst demonstrated that the transportation of all Soviet bridge-laying equipment in Eastern Europe requires fewer trains than that for a single division.

The Conventional Stability Talks are expected to commence in 1989 for an undetermined duration. In view of fifteen years of MBFR, one should be cautious in estimating success here. The most immediate danger to the negotiations is getting bogged down in endless data discussions, although the unilateral Soviet move will make asymmetries somewhat less glaring. The objective should be common ceilings with a credible system for verifying them. If this can be achieved, then it will be unnecessary to focus on precise figures for reductions.

However, should the Conventional Stability Talks result in agreement on common ceilings, this will have to be embodied in a formal document, which could take years to draft. My suggestion is that unilateral measures be defined within the framework of the negotiations; in addition, unilateral reductions during the negotiations would serve as a stimulant and increase confidence in the outcome. Such steps would also lead to enhanced transparency and predictability of the other side's policy. In »Setting the Record Straight,« Carnesale and Haass pointed out that these two aspects have been the major achievements of the arms-control process, even more significant than the treaties that resulted.

Nevertheless, if the Warsaw Pact were further to reduce asymmetries, NATO would find it difficult to respond, since we should not effect conventional reductions until the Soviets have reached our levels. Action could, however, be taken in the nuclear sphere – not because we possess superiority in this field, for the Soviets have overtaken us here as well, but because by modernizing our force posture, we could simultaneously reduce the number of tactical nuclear warheads substantially. A modest number of nuclear missiles replacing the Lance system would be able to fulfill the minimum requirements for NATO ground forces and allow the number of very short-range artillery warheads to be slashed. The argument that such a move would violate the INF Treaty cannot be sustained, for the agreement does not cover missiles with a range of less than 500 km. Moreover, the Soviets have already undertaken the sort of modernization measures now being discussed by NATO.

Although the positive climate currently being experienced in East-West relations may make new nuclear decisions less than propitious, obsolete weapons must nevertheless be replaced in due course if we hope to avoid unilateral structural disarmament. Disarmament would certainly not enhance stability, since conventional forces alone are an insufficient deterrent; war would once again become calculable. Further agreements on reducing nuclear forces in Europe should be tabled until rough parity is reached in conventional forces. A decision in principle on the successor to Lance and a stand-off weapon for aircraft would suffice, as these weapons systems are not yet available; however, when production is to begin, Washington could justifiably demand assurances that the weapons will be able to be deployed in Europe.

In addition, NATO should as soon as possible complete its comprehensive concept. I began advocating this some two years ago as providing a framework for dovetailing our defense requirements with arms-control objectives. It also offers a common backdrop against which all NATO members could formulate their reactions to developments in East-West relations. The concept seems presently to have gotten hung up in the relationship between the two pillars of NATO established by the invaluable Harmel Report: defense and détente. The debate centers on two questions: Do events in the Soviet Union constitute an irreversible process? Should NATO at this point formulate a negotiating position on short-range nuclear forces? More than getting its nuclear thinking straight, the West will have to determine the minimum level of forces needed to address the various scenarios of Soviet capabilities and deployments. In the past, we used the word »threat« to describe this potential, a term with two connotations: from a technical standpoint, it describes the other side's capabilities, and politically, it denotes the danger of war. Since today's Soviet leadership is widely viewed as being devoid of aggressive intentions, we will need to put our defense efforts in a different perspective – as more of an insurance policy against possible dangers.

We should also temper our expectations regarding our ability to influence developments in the East. This is a process that must take its own course; we should not hinder it and can hardly assist it. For me, détente signifies cooperation in those fields where it is possible and moderation where cooperation is not (yet) feasible. Ambitions of aiding Gorbachev could easily lead to illusory policies and even to counterproductive effects. We should instead demonstrate a willingness to pursue new possibilities consistent with our own interests. In the economic field as well, our actions should be more precisely coordinated within a framework of common objectives. The stream of potential money-lenders toward Moscow should not turn into a flood of »fools rushing in.«

Finally, we should resist such attractive, but empty, concepts as »a common European house.« The notion of building a common house suggests something cosy and exclusively European, with the Soviet Union inside the house and the U.S. outside. It goes without saying that in Europe we have common interests and share certain common experiences. Nevertheless, the many differences cannot be ignored. Europe would therefore not be comfortable with only one superpower in the house. For this reason, it is far better to continue the CSCE process with both superpowers playing a role in European security and cooperation.

As 1992 and the European Community's free internal market approaches, efforts are underway to develop a European pillar within NATO. At the same time, however, we should also explore Soviet attitudes toward European integration. Far from cherishing the idea, Moscow has thus far targeted its foreign-policy objectives not only at the withdrawal of U.S. forces from Europe but also at the prevention of a consolidated Western Europe. In the long run, it will not be able to pursue both avenues. The Soviet Union has recently agreed to the further normalization of its relations with the European Community, albeit under the guise of various direct contacts between the EC and Comecon. It has also been attempting to strengthen the bonds within Comecon, although the prospects for success appear dim. For its part, Western Europe should continue its efforts to create a proper union, as this is the only way to remain competitive with the U.S. and Japan. But the inclusion of Eastern European countries in such a union is out of the question, although I can foresee more substantial agreements with them. Conversely, I am not in favor of self-denying declaration by the West – a sort of Yalta in reverse. NATO has no aggressive options and is not capable of holding territory, but it nevertheless cannot forsake its championing of individual freedoms and human rights. For the foreseeable future, it does not seem realistic to expect that the satellite countries will become neutral, and it is not up to the West to offer this. The same goes for the reunification of Germany. Any overtures in this direction can only hamper the existing opportunities for step-by-step progress. I mentioned earlier on that the management of change is the main problem in Eastern Europe. Although the West has little to manage here, it must show a willingness to explore while coordinating its policies and keeping up its guard.

Part Four:
Conversation between
John Kenneth Galbraith and
Leonid I. Abalkin

»Capitalism and Socialism: Coexistence or Convergence?«

Ed A. Hewett, Brookings Institution:
We are indeed fortunate today to have a conversation between two of the world's most prominent economists. On my right, John Kenneth Galbraith, professor emeritus of Economics at Harvard University, former ambassador to India, former president of the American Economic Association, one of the world's most distinguished and original analysts of capitalism, who has through his life's work provided testimony of the fact that it is possible to talk about economics with clarity and even with humour and to talk about the most important issues on economics without resorting to obscure language and mathematics. On my left, Leonid Ivanovich Abalkin, a member of the Soviet Academy of Sciences, director of the Institute of Economics, increasingly establishing himself in the Soviet Union as one of the most prominent spokesmen for *perestroika* and one of the most prominent theorists developing the foundations of economic reform in the Soviet Union and of the new system to which they are now moving. Today these two will talk about these issues and Professor Galbraith has kindly agreed to begin the conversation.

John Kenneth Galbraith:
I should explain that I come, as I think my economic colleagues are aware, not as one of the distinguished specialists on the Soviet Union who have been with us here in these days and not as one of those who have talked so competently and even eloquently this morning out of a lifetime of work on the grave problems of the Soviet Union. I do come as an intensely interested observer and one in pursuit of my own instruction on these matters. I would point out something which I think we should all have in mind, Academician Abalkin, that while there have been many discussions, decades even centuries of discussion of the change and reform operations needed in a capitalist world and a non-socialist world, we have here a subject of some novelty. We are talking about reform and change in the socialist world, not nearly so accustomed as a topic of conversation. This is a reform which I think all of us in the non-socialist world, all of us of any intelligence,

365

of any integrity wish to see succeed. The first topic I would like to hear discussed is recognizing the problems in the socialist world and not alone in the Soviet Union, but in Eastern Europe and China: By what steps can we help to ensure the success of this effort, by what steps can we help to ensure the success of an effort which will be extremely important for the peace and tranquility of the world? I think everybody in the Soviet Union and I hope also in the West is aware of the extent to which the horrors of fifty years ago, the horrors of World War Two were born out of the failure of capitalism, out of the failure of the non-socialist economies. I think we are all aware that peace and tranquility in the world depend in no small part on the successful performance both of the non-socialist and the socialist world, and this in turn suggests that there should be all possible help extended between them and particularly any help that will seek to make *perestroika* and the great changes in your country more successful.

Leonid I. Abalkin:
I would like to begin by saying some words in regard of Professor Galbraith, who is well known in the USSR. Many of his works are translated into the Russian language and are therefore available for students, professors, and even to those who do not know the English language. Quite recently, in addition to his many other titles, he was made an honorary doctor of the Moscow State University. I would like to take this opportunity in front of this auditory to congratulate him on yet another honorable title. Now with regard to how *perestroika* can be helped. I would like to answer this in a non-traditional fashion. The greatest help can consist of the fact that you exist: That the Soviet people can imagine an economy in which there is a market which has all the goods you want on it, from food to micro electronics, to automobiles, to housing, and the very fact that such an economy can exist is an incredible stimulus for *perestroika*, because people can clearly see how they could live. This is a very substantial aid. I must also admit a simple fact, namely, that we are different. And that is also good. Perhaps it is a big stimulus for capitalism that there is another system with which capitalism can be compared, contrasted to. I would also like to add that help has not necessarily to be direct. It can consist of a wealth of experience. Our *perestroika* is an open model, an open system. We are now open to suggestions. We would

like to take the best that has been learned in the world, in the United States and Japan, Sweden and People's Republic of China, Hungary, FRG and other countries, and this openness to learning from others is a very pragmatic approach. This is not an ideological study of other countries. We are looking for pragmatic things, such as methods of fighting monopolies, i.e., the trust laws, the development of the cooperative movement, in collaboration with the wide experience of individual ownership and individual business ownership. As far as the direct assistance is concerned we are looking forward to mutual and beneficial collaboration: we have very clear priorities in which kinds of things we can cooperate. We look towards taking away artificial barriers and other hindrances to free trade. We can provide a substantial market for Western exports and imports, and it is important to arrive at both these markets early in order not to be last. Of course we would like to receive those kinds of things with which we can directly improve the life of the Soviet people and also the tools with which to make additional items, to be given help in acquiring and mastering modern technologies, and also to learn how to organize production. This perhaps is the most important thing both for us and for you. This perhaps is how one could answer such a complicated question. To continue the discussion, I would like to pose a question myself. How do you assess our *perestroika*? Perhaps a specialist is humble to say he is not an expert, but please give me a view: Are we travelling in the right direction? What is your view as to the balance of different sectors of our economy – and you have studied the problems of such a balance in your works in the 1960s – the problems of a balance between a free market and a state-controlled economy? How do you see this relationship now and what could be its perspectives today? What do you think is the possibility for its development in the USSR?

John Kenneth Galbraith:
Let me say one other thing. First, I must thank you for the most pleasant comments and tell you how great was my pleasure in receiving an honorary degree from the Moscow State University, in the company of Graham Green, and the extraordinary audience I enjoyed that day. And it has caused me to reflect on the fact that the world does improve. If I had received that degree thirty years ago, I would have returned to endless questioning by the Congress of the United States as to how my

patriotism was being sacrificed to evil purpose. This time I returned only to great approval. As I say, the world does improve. I would certainly endorse one thing particularly that you mention: the time has come, for example, the time has long past for the elimination of the Jackson-Vanik Amendment and to accord the Soviet Union most-favored-nation treatment, as we call it. And I would very much like to see, on the part of the Western European countries and of the U.S., such steps translatable into consumer goods, which would give in the Soviet Union eventually, I think, an atmosphere of promptness to change and would contribute to the success of *perestroika*. As to your question, I think that the informed view in the West and in the United States of the perspectives for *perestroika* is a combination of hope and also of a sense of the real difficulty. And if I were expressing my own view as to the problem, it would be that we must always in this world think of the sources of power in any economy, in any society. In the Soviet Union there exists the established power of the vast bureaucratic apparatus of the ministries – a counterpart of the power that we see in the United States in the Pentagon. We have a certain appreciation of the rigidity, the stubbornness with which great organizations, inevitable in both modern capitalism and modern socialism, – the stubbornness with which they adhere to their power. If I were asked, as I have been asked to say, what seems to me to be the greatest difficulty of *perestroika*, it is the power structure which for so long has accorded so much authority to the ministerial bureaucratic apparatus of the Soviet Union. Let me now return the question to you. Do you see this as one of the great problems?

Leonid I. Abalkin:
We have a great number of complicated problems, and it is very difficult for me to say which one is the most difficult. But this is certainly one of the most difficult. It has to do with the process which we are currently analysing and the one we are looking to for solutions. Yes, the bureaucratic process has tremendous power. On what is it based? We, as economists, we must consider things from the economics perspective, and if we can find this basis and the roots for it, we can then resolve the problem. The attempt to solve the problem by replacing bad bureaucrats by good ones – younger ones, more educated in Europe – does not solve the problem. Once they land in the chair of bureaucracy, they get used

to it. So there must be an economic basis for this change. We hope that we have found it, and I speak about the research done at our Institute. We have identified one of the most profound deformations in socialism and in our perceptions of socialism – the deformation of property. It is based, first of all, on the separation of the worker, of the working class from the property. The proletariate, which we used to call the owners and which turned out not to be the owner, was separated, alienated from it. I often use the following expression: Our people seem to think that the property is not theirs and they seem to think that it is nobody's. In Russian, this formulation sounds very nice and often produces nods when people hear it in Russian. But once my colleagues in my Institute told me: Why do you speak about nobody's property? Property cannot be nobody's. But if the owner is not the working collective, the working class which we used to declare to be the owner, which we used to declare as the ultimate owner, then who in reality is the owner? The one who has all the power to control the property. Who is he? And it turned out that the apparatus which was created was in fact this owner, this tremendously overgrown apparatus with a tremendous economic basis. It turned out that unless it was possible to give the appropriate rights to use this property to republics, regions, workers, cooperatives, nothing can be accomplished. The question is: Is it even possible to get rid of a bureaucracy anywhere? Once there is a government, there is a bureaucracy. But we intend to act very decisively here and take very revolutionary measures to reform and rebuild the economy, to remove this deformations and to create a dynamic, growing economy, an economy which we hope will also be quite efficient. But this is only one of the problems, because it is possible to take the property from one and give it to somebody else. The question is: Are those others able to assume the powers and the responsibilities connected with this property? This is just one of the very many problems which we are working on right now. A return question: Are you in agreement with this analysis of connection between property and power: are they really inseparable? And how do you look at the analysis of property and power in today's complicated world?

John Kenneth Galbraith:
I don't regard that as inevitable. I think there can be motivation apart from the private ownership of property and that Marx is too important

369

a figure on such matters to be entirely left to socialists. I think that the possibility of non-property motivation in all societies is possible and also a virtue. Let me ask a larger question, one that I think has not come up yet in this discussion. We take for granted that the norm in economic achievement is the Western consumer economy, that the measure of economic success in any country, is the standard of living, the variety of products, designs, services that are common to bourgeois middle-class life in New York, London, Paris, Luxembourg. This is a design which, I think we would agree, is very difficult in the socialist economy to meet with the enormous variety of consumer requirements that that imposes on the socialist structure. Why would it not be possible in the Soviet Union to think of another design for living which involves a less complicated display of goods, a less complicated variety of goods? I remember once many years ago on my first visit to the Soviet Union – this was in the exuberant days of the late 1950s, when everything seemed to be going well – a distinguished Soviet economist said to me and to my American colleagues: »Do you realize that we are going to catch up with you?« And I said to him: »You are not going to do that, are you?« He said, »Yes.« He said, »Do not underestimate us.« »Well,« I said, »look here at the streets of Moscow, the widest in the world. Already, it is as much as your life costs to cross them. Have you realized what those streets are going to be like if you have as many automobiles per capita as New York, let alone Los Angeles? What are you doing to the air? How many people you are going to have running parking lots and service stations? Why should the objective of a planned economy be the greatest insanity of an unplanned economy?« I am sorry to say that my point did not go over very well. All he said was: »Do you realize we are going to catch up with you in everything but automobiles?« But is it possible (I must not make a speech, this is a conversation), is it possible for a socialist economy to have a different design from the automatic commitment to the multiplication of goods and services of the modern bourgeois economy?

Leonid I. Abalkin:
To return to the 1950s and our designs to catch up with the West, I must say we really did catch up and even exceeded by such criteria as

production of steel, of oil, of tractors and field equipment and many other criteria which seemed essential and unattainable. We now produce two-and-a-half times more steel than the United States, we make six-and-a-half times more tractors than the USA, we have one-and-a-half times more mineral production, fertilizer production. But this has not made us happier. Profound changes have occurred in our societies – perhaps within a lifetime of a single generation or, maybe, a generation and a half – in our values, in our approach to the problem of the catching up. I think quite a lot about the question you have raised on how to combine the consumer society with the spiritual and moral values of humans, with the solution of ecological problems. One must realize that even when there are many cars in the streets and the shops are full of goods, people are not always happy. It is not enough just to have enough goods. Perhaps this hinders even, but it is certainly not sufficient to make humans happy, to make the human have a happy life, to understand himself and his children, to be happy with his relatives. These are very deep reflections. Why do we not talk about this in the USSR now? Why do we talk very little about this and think about this very little? Well, there are many reasons. I would name just two of them. Primarily, the majority thinks about the deeds and the work of the moment, of one or two years. Not everybody likes to think about global problems, such as the fate of the nation, of mankind. Mankind should be happy that people like you exist, who constantly raise these issues and direct our attention to such deep philosophical thoughts. Number two: How would now in our country a doctor's lecture sound on the usefulness of a restrictive diet? We eat a lot – perhaps not what we want to eat, but a lot of it. By average weight, we probably exceed the West: in fatness, we exceed the West. But that is not it. That is not what counts. It would be nice for doctors to discuss nutrition, about the balance between vegetables and meat. All this is very important, but to go to people who do not have enough meat with such discussions is not very ethical. Such conversations are often therefore delayed, even though I do feel this is a very important problem. The question is how to avoid being buried under the debris of a consumer society, how to retain enough free time for human contacts, to have culture, culture which makes the people a nation, so it is important to search for such ideas. There are of course models here which must be considered and proposed. I don't discount certain national cultures and certain

371

traditions which are important here. But the task is to think now while there is still time.

John Kenneth Galbraith:
I think that it is very interesting, very appropriate to our discussion and very much to the point. I would like now to change the subject of our discussion. I must interpret a personal recollection from a recent visit to the Soviet Union: I went out to see one of the great figures of the Soviet Union, Dr. Chazov, then the great cardiologist and now the Minister of Health. I was taken around that enormous institute of his outside of Moscow. It is impossible to believe how large it is. I was led to ask him why so much money was spent on cardiological remedy when I noticed that in Moscow everybody smoked much too much and quite a few are overweight? He informed me very sternly that remedy was much easier than prevention. Let me pass, however, to a much more serious question. Here I again have Marx on my side. Marx would have been outraged at the thought of a Communist Ethiopia or Mozambique or Afghanistan. As anyone should have been outraged – I am equal-handed on this matter – by the notion that capitalism was a relevant concept in Vietnam. Can we assume, is it possible to assume that the Soviet Union is or will give up on the notion of socialist countries such as Ethiopia, Mozambique, which in the words of Marx have not yet had the socializing influence of capitalism?

Leonid I. Abalkin:
I would like to begin with the cardiological center. I also would like to remember my last trip to your country, to the United States. This was in March of this year. I was at Harvard, I was always inconvenienced, which forced me to ask provocative questions, because I smoke myself. The strong and stringent laws which you have in the United States! I was always forced to the back seat of a plane, the last place to smoke. At Harvard I broke all Cambridge ordinances, and the standard joke was when I came to a restaurant where I couldn't smoke, I was always asking what about how the human rights are in your country. When they asked what I meant I answered: »Well, can I smoke here?« America took a great step in this respect. When I look at the anti-smoking campaign in your country, when I saw people of all ages jogging around in Maryland, – I was impressed. I know the assessments of our

372

specialists about how the problems with heart attacks have diminished in your country. Even the dentists are telling me a great deal about the huge progress you have had in your country. I think this is more impressive than the number of cars in your country. As far as some African and Asian countries that you mentioned are concerned, I will speak my own mind. We become different people now. We now think differently of the world. We have declared two things. The first – and I consider this as an historical event: the signing two years ago of the Delhi Declaration, in which we supported the idea of a non-violent world. We feel this was a document in which two philosophies were united: the European and the Asian. We shall yet have time to assess the importance of this document, the concept of peace without force, under which there is the signature of our Party and State leader. This is not propaganda. This is our current thinking, our current philosophy. In the speech by Mr. Gorbachev at the United Nations in New York, we declared our program for free choice. This is our new philosophy, our new world view: free choice given to each country, to each people. We are ready for this and of course ask other countries to respect our choice and the choice of any other people. I feel this should be applied to all countries, to all countries in Asia, Africa, Latin America and so on. This is our new world view. Perhaps things in reality do not follow these programs as quickly as we would like, but in this respect our *perestroika* is irreversible. This is not a tactic, this is our world view, this is our approach to the world, grasping the complexity and cohesion of this world and all other things. So this is how I see, for myself as a citizen, as a scientist, how I appreciate these countries you mentioned, – Mozambique, Ethiopia, Nicaragua and so on.

John Kenneth Galbraith:
I do not plead perfect innocence on these matters. I share the distress of many of my countrymen – including, I assume, most of the people over here – on the past tendency and the present tendency by the United States government, by my government, to identify democracy not with democratic government but with private ownership of private property, forgiving however dictatorial a regime may be that has that particular virtue.
I wonder if I might change the subject once more and come back to a field that has long greatly interested me, and that is agriculture. I

think for most of my life I have been the only senior member of the Harvard Faculty in Economics with no degree in Economics, only in Agricultural Economics, with earlier specialization in the production of animals, animal husbandry. It has long been my impression that the only, or at least the most successful, structure of agriculture is that of the individual cultivator, where to a quite extraordinary degree he exploits himself and his family and he is for some curious reason quite happy in doing it. This is the sort of agricultural system that in the United States we celebrate almost prayerfully as the family farm. I am puzzled in the Soviet Union as to why at the kolkhoz or the state farms an orderly pleasant life with defined hours, pleasant community should give way, as now proposed, to long leases in which the farmer would have this curious responsibility of working himself from dawn to dusk and similarily overworking his family. Why that should be accepted after now some fifty years of the relatively orderly and possibly more civilized if considerably less productive life of the state farm or the collective farm? I was born and brought up on a farm in Canada. I have been a refugee from manual work all my life. If I were on a Soviet state farm as a worker or a member of a collective farm, I wouldn't dream of going back to the hard exploit of work of the individual entrepreneur. I would want to stay with this comfortable life. Is that not a problem that you foresee – that some of your fellow Russians will opt for the easy life and reject Mr. Gorbachev's proposals for long leases for self-exploitation?

Leonid I. Abalkin:
Sixty years ago we put farmers in the kolkhozes, collective farms. The next year should be the jubilee, but we will probably not celebrate this jubilee. 1929 was the year of the so-called great break. Yes, we broke indeed a great deal of things. Now, in the sixtieth year of the kolkhozes, in the seventy-second year of the existence of the Soviet power, we still have to face the food problem. You need not be a great expert to agree that a system which has over so many years failed to solve the problem is a system that must be radically improved. One of the ways to do it is to introduce the renting of land. But the problem which you have described, however, is indeed a real problem. Not everybody wants to become independent. This summer, in August, I was in one of the kolkhozes, a very good kolkhoz, a strong kolkhoz,

indeed a quite productive kolkhoz: it is in the Ukraine, in Chernigov region, the region itself is also quite productive. The region produces meat, 191 kilogrammes per person, which is a high standard result. I spoke with the workers, with the leader of the kolkhoz. The leader is a famous man, he has visited Moscow, listened to the speeches about the renting of land, returned back to his workers and told his workers: »We are going to rent land.« And they said: »No way,« and this should not work here. In western Ukraine it will work. They have a different agricultural structure, a different structure of cultivating the land, different historical traditions. The small farms will need a very different technology. Well, what is a Soviet tractor (you may call it a sort of tank)? It is a very big tractor. All our tractors are made to cultivate very large pieces of land, it is not possible for an individual farmer to use it. So I started thinking, and I can tell you the results of my thought. Well, there is no absolute truth, but I am just searching for the truth. I think we must leave the choice to the peasants. We should not force them with the same stick out of the kolkhozes just as we used to put them in the kolkhoze by the stick. If they want to leave, let them leave. If they want to take the land, let them take the land. If they want to take credit, let them take credit. But one should not force them out. The feeling of choice should be recognized here as well.

What is the greatest danger in our country? It is an eternal problem with us. It is our habit to direct everybody and everything from Moscow. To give directives on how to cultivate land in the Baltic republics, in Uzbekistan, in Siberia or Ukraine. We think that there will be different requirements for those regions. Likewise it is the same with industrial production. You need different kinds of production facilities in the same way you need different farming facilities – big and small, state-owned, private, or cooperative. And only under real competition, real serious competition, the strongest will win, the strongest, those who take the most competitive path. And life will give the final answer as to which forms are the most acceptable. It is very dangerous for us to invert the parameter, to use exactly the same methods as those we used before to create a new structure by coercion. This is a new danger, and the tendency to use these old methods is a very strong one, so we must avoid it. We have not yet forgotten how to give orders. We must look for freer means, freer methods of creating change. We must look for the most rational ways of work. I think we will use different means, and history therefore will be different.

I have some ideas on how America came to be, how it became populated, how its laws were created. It is a tremendous history of how things came about, and that is why America came to be what it is. Therefore there can never be a kolkhoz in America. It is impossible no matter what government you have. But we came through a different path. Long before the kolkhoz we had a very strong cooperative system in our land, even before the revolution. There was a cooperation at all levels, which is starting from a peasant community. A famous Russian thinker, Herzen, saw in this peasant community the key to the future of Russia, of socialism. We say that he was misled in his views. However, these communities were a fact of real life. We should also start from the real life, from peasants' tradition, their habits. If some forms will not survive, so be it. One thing is clear, however: The modern kolkhoz is a dead-end on the road of social development. Each country has its own ways of doing things, things are different in each country. There shall be different kinds of competition which will be necessary. Each person should choose; people can leave if they choose to.

Ed. A. Hewett:

We change the topic one more time. We ask a question. I suppose Academician Abalkin might be the first to answer about the role of economists in the great reform, such as the one that is now going on in the Soviet Union. Frequently, at least in the West, we have regarded economics as far too important to be trusted to economists, for example, in an area such as tax reform. And I think that has also been true in the Soviet Union. But my question is whether it is changing now. I know that Academician Abalkin this summer at the Party conference, the very important 19th Party conference, gave a speech in which he seemed to be saying to President Gorbachev that it was important to pay attention to economists and to economics. My question is whether economists in the Soviet Union feel that they are being paid attention to now and whether they feel the role is changed?

Leonid I. Abalkin:

Well I think all those present here can guess what I shall start with, and that will be the thesis that economists are the most important people in the world. And of course that is the case with *perestroika*. Well, how does the situation change? It depends on which angle you look from. From yesterday or from tomorrow. If you look from yesterday, then the situation has transformed dramatically and fundamentally. Having spent in this science of economics dozens of years, I do have a base for comparisons. At no time in our history has there been such an attention paid to economics by all levels of the government as it is paid now, never has there been such an attention to economics. Never has the government listened so carefully to us, never has it asked us to look at specific problems and various questions. Tremendous changes have occurred just in three years. Of course the job became more difficult, more responsible. It's one thing when you simply write an article. But is another way around when laws are approved on the basis of your recommendations. Compared to tomorrow, we are not satisfied. Economists claim that people don't listen to them well, that their advice is not listened to, that they are not consulted well, that the State Planning Committee (Gosplan) makes decisions without due account of our recommendations. Compared to yesterday, everything is much better. Look at how many economists we have today, let's say in our highest lawmaking body – the Supreme Soviet. From one-and-a-half thousand people, there are one, two, perhaps three. That is not sufficient, we are not satisfied. Of course, changes happen. We are very happy for these changes. This is like free fresh air, as if the windows opened, we can breathe more easily, we can work better. But in comparison to what we want, it is not enough: we are not happy, we are not satisfied.

Ed A. Hewett:
Professor Galbraith, would you say that the role of the economists of the United States is a model that the Soviet Union should emulate?

John Kenneth Galbraith:
Eventually. There is no question about that, because as economies develop, as education institutions proliferate, as institutions like Brookings multiply, not to mention the American Enterprise Institute, more and more economists are trained, more and more economists are participating in the tasks of teaching, and there are far more economists then who can possibly be heard on economic policy, on the policy of the government. And our design is one which I strongly recommend to the

Soviet Union, that is, to have a very large number of the economists engaged in mathematical, technical irreleventia, communicating with each other, avoiding any policy discussions and that allows the few of us who are concerned with public policy to have a voice. If in the United States all economists spoke on public policy, our position would be hopeless. So as the economists proliferate in the Soviet Union, I strongly recommend that you encourage a very large number of them to engage in irrelevant technical discussion.

Ed A. Hewett:
Let me as a final question start with Academician Abalkin, to ask him, to press him a little bit further on the future, as one of those people who does think more than two or three years ahead. Tell me a little bit about the Soviet Union in the year 2010 or 2020. What will be the difference between socialism as we now know it and socialism of that time? And more importantly what will be the distinctions, the important distinctions, the most fundamental distinctions between socialism and capitalism? We understand those distinctions now, some of them have to do with much greater inefficiency under socialism, but also much greater economic security. Presumably you are searching for some new trade-off between economic security and efficiency, but what would that look like and will I be able to tell the difference between, let's say, the Soviet Union and Sweden or for that matter the United States?

Leonid I. Abalkin:
I think to resemble Sweden is not that bad. I have visited that country on several occasions, specially studied this experience, studied how it has dealt with social and economic problems and have realized that it is a very interesting experience. They have solved in a very interesting fashion the social protection problem. It is very impressive how they have solved this problem, and on top of that, they have a quite efficient economy. It is a different model than that used in the United States, and therefore it is a bit difficult to compare those two. When you speak to American economists, the moment you say the word Sweden they all become a little tense and begin to complain and argue. If it were a bit difficult for me to make certain arguments for socialism, then I would cite Sweden as an example. Well, I would say after all in Sweden they take three times more grain from an acre of land as in the USSR,

378

but it is also one-and-a-half times more than it is in the United States, and per cow they get seven thousand liters of milk, not five-and-a-half or six. If the cow does not provide seven thousand, they eat it. Such a cow is not necessary in Sweden. They have social protection and high productivity, and they sell always in America. One per cent of the United States market is Volvo. Three percent of the British market is Volvo. They have very efficient production lines – conveyors, though they eliminate them as a pattern of production now.

When you ask us: What will your economy look like?, I will answer that of course it depends on the economists. It depends on whether the economists will be involved in making decisions. Near 2010 we hope that we shall be able to solve a number of problems, primarily by creating a different structure of economy. We hope that by the year 2010 we shall not import grain, we shall produce as much as we need. I don't know if we will have a problem of overproducing, but we shall not import. We shall be a different trade partner, because in twenty-two years we shall be able to alter the structure of exports. We shall not be any longer a country which only sells its raw materials. But rather we shall have a spectacular representation at the world's industrial markets. We shall have a strong consumer economy, a very different infrastructure for service industry. Let me tell what we have calculated in this sphere: By the year 2000, perhaps slightly later, by the year 2005, we intend to move fifteen million people from the production sector to the service sector. In this short time we shall make this tremendous transformation. Fifteen to sixteen million work places will be eliminated in the production sphere, and an adequate number of jobs will be created in the sphere of services. This will be a very different structure for our economy. By then we hope to have solved financial and monetary problems. Ours will be a multi-sector economy, with a high proportion of cooperatives. This will be done by introducing cooperatives and giving them power. We hope that in some sectors, fifty percent of production will come by cooperaters and in others even up to one hundred percent. There are various kinds of cooperatives, whether rental of land or others, substantial balanced market of consumer goods and a multi-layered system with a developed economic competition. If this does not happen by the year 2010, that would mean that our generation has not fulfilled its historical duty toward succeeding generations. We must do this, we do not have any other choice. Perhaps I made this a little bit too optimistic. There will be problems, the path will not be an easy one. There shall be lateral movements, difficulties, conflicts, but I hope that within twenty-two years after all, we shall be able to celebrate the 25th anniversary of the April (1985) Plenum of the Central Committee of the CPSU. We shall compare notes and calculate the results: We have done a lot, but we shall of course say that this is not enough. We will of course still criticize, say this is not enough, we shall criticize ourselves, we shall strive for more, but this is characteristic.

Ed A. Hewett:
Mr. Galbraith?

John Kenneth Galbraith:
This is indeed a very brief final word, which expresses my very, very profound pleasure in having the opportunity for this discussion, and I must add one word. A country that is in the hands, that has the guidance of people such as we have heard this morning and particularly Academician Abalkin, whom we just heard, a country that has that guidance is indeed very fortunate. Those of us who wish *perestroika* well, wish the Soviet people well, wish the Soviet Union well, can only be encouraged by the quality of the people that we have been hearing at this conference and the quality of my colleague's comments here this morning.

Leonid I. Abalkin:
Thank you very much.

Ed A. Hewett:
It is only left to me to thank both John Kenneth Galbraith and Leonid Ivanovich Abalkin for a very interesting conversation, which I enjoyed simply listening to.

Part Five:
Round Table

»Soviet Studies in the United States and in Western Europe: A Critical Assessment«

Armand Clesse:

Most of you sitting here are experts in the field of Soviet studies, teaching or researching in that field. I am not, some others here are not. The idea for a round table came to me as I was preparing this conference. At that time, I was in the United States visiting several institutions and university institutes. Of course, I had only a superficial look at what was being done in the field of Soviet studies on the East coast – for example, in Washington, New York, Boston and Cambridge. I noticed what an enormous output and, especially, what extraordinary quality very small structures, very small institutes, achieved with very few people. Then I thought about what was going on in Western Europe, and I tried to inform myself about it. I discovered – perhaps my impressions or my findings are wrong – that in some Western European countries, Soviet studies are rather well developed, having reached a good scientific level – for example in West Germany, where they have also the necessary structures. I also had a look at what was going on in France. There are some very good people there, but I also got the impression that Soviet studies are dispersed, such that the one researcher was not really aware of what the other was doing. Results thus do not always match input. In Great Britain, there are also a few institutes, things are happening in the universities, and there are eminent people. But still I think, compared to the United States, they are somewhat behind. Even further behind are other European countries, like Italy, Spain, Portugal, the Scandinavian countries, the Netherlands or Belgium. Based on these observations, I got the idea of this round table. Several experts, sovietologists, also thought that it was a good idea and that one should come together to exchange experiences and views and to have a critical look at what is going on in the United States and in Western Europe in this field. One could then determine what could be improved academically, structurally or, perhaps in reverse, structurally and then scientifically, intellectually.

383

So, without further remarks by a non-specialist, I ask who would like to comment on this or who would like to start the discussion.

Marshall I. Goldman:
You asked me to prepare some thoughts beforehand, and I have tried to put together some ideas about the fate of Soviet studies, at least as we see them at the Russian Research Center. I should say, among other things, that Gorbachev is not only interesting because he it doing some interesting things inside the Soviet Union, but he is also a godsend, so to speak, for those of us in the field of Soviet studies in the United States. I think in part the field of Soviet studies has been revived and probably is stronger now than it has ever been, largely because of the developments inside the Soviet Union. It may very well have begun with the death of Brezhnev, but that seemed to have unleashed an interest in the Soviet Union that was dying before. For those of you in Europe, you may be well aware of the fact that in the mid-1960s, interest in the field of Soviet studies began to diminish: Interest is measured in the United States, as so many things are, by the ability to attract funding to the field, and many of the foundations that had been providing support with regularity switched their interest to other fields, particularly the Ford Foundation, which had been one of the main sources of support for the Russian Research Center at Harvard. Now that was also due in part to the fact that many of the foundations began to have some problems with their own portfolios, and their income diminished, at least temporarily. They also began to support new studies: urban studies, work in the Third World, work in Asia. And so, specifically in the case of Harvard, the money dried up.

There finally came a point in the mid-1970s, when the situation was so serious that the Dean of Harvard indicated that unless things improved, the Russian Research Center would be closed down, because at Harvard there is the principle that every facility must support itself financially. So this was a very low point, and indeed there was real concern as to what was to happen. There may be some who say it should have died, but there are others who were a little more charitable. Just to give you an idea in terms of figures, the Russian Research Center had been giving out fellowship money, and the fellowship money in 1976-77 had been reduced to about $ 25,000, which was really not enough to support one individual.

384

Anyway, things changed, and even before Gorbachev came on the scene, there was a realization that the United States should continue to produce scholars. We were worried that people like Abram Bergson would retire and there would be no one to take his place; the situation, then, became rather serious. The funding began to come back in, partly through hard work, partly through the realization by foundations that they had to do something, led by the Rockefeller Foundation and the Mellon Foundation. Today, the Russian Research Center is able to give out fellowships on the order of $ 350,000 a year, which indicates just how far we have come. Much of it is indeed endowed income that has come about. We have now received funding for three chairs in Soviet studies in the Center. This coming year, we will have a new professor of government. We will also have a new economist working in that area. It has been particularly difficult to find people, because the Economics Departments are always interested in theory, whereas most of the people trained in the Soviet Union are trained in institutional analysis. Fortunately, we found somebody who we think will satisfy both needs. There are not many Bergsons in the world who can satisfy both needs. In addition to which, of course, the most important thing is students. All the money and all the faculty positions are for naught if you are not training students and if you are not attracting students to the field. Well, the money attracts the faculty for fellowships and for teaching; the students, when they see the option is there, begin to take the courses, and again Gorbachev has made it so much more interesting. And so now we find ourselves with very large enrollments, very large interest among the students. Indeed it is a brand-new world, in many ways more exciting even than it was in the 1950s, when Soviet studies were so strong.

Let me just conclude by saying that in the process of attracting the funding, we find then that other schools throughout the country also become interested. Once they discover that places like Harvard and Columbia are bringing new members to the faculty, the smaller schools then begin to do the same kind of thing. There is one drawback to that, and that is that in our effort to expand, we sometimes draw heavily from people in Europe – particularly in England – and the United States to some extent now is raiding the work and the scholars who have been trained in Europe. That benefits us enormously. I am not sure it benefits the Europeans that way, and I mean particularly Great Britain.

We have established, at least in principle, exchange relationships with three or four institutions in the Soviet Union. At one point, when Soviet scholars would come to the Cambridge area, they did everything they could to skirt the Russian Research Center. Now we are one of the first ports of call. After they visit Galbraith, they come to us, and I have been told indeed by some Soviet officials who have nothing to do with American studies of the Soviet Union that they cannot go home unless they have been able to report that they have visited the Russian Research Center and have met with the sovietologists. At one time we were viewed as anti-Soviet; now we are viewed as those who see through the thicket of the political concerns that so often blinded Soviet scholars in their own country. In that process, we do not only have Soviet scholars doing research with us for the semester or the year; we have Chinese scholars, we have scholars from all over the world, and we probably will be embarking on some joint projects as well. Let me end by saying that we have gone through an enormous transformation. We think we are producing some very good students for the future. We have learned a lesson from what happens when the foundations withdraw their support. We have sought to endow that research and those positions for the future. Should there come another time, good or bad, we think we will be able to continue that work not on a seasonal basis or a cyclical basis, but basically for eternity.

Armand Clesse:
Thank you Marshall Goldman. You said that there are not many Abram Bergsons in this world. But there is at least one, since we have one with us sitting next to me. Professor Bergson.

Abram Bergson:
Marshall Goldman is correct: Not all has been roses all the way in the evolution of the study of the Soviet Union and of Russia in the United States. There have been lean years as well as fat years and genuinely lean years at different times. I recall vividly when I was serving as director of the Russian Research Center being sidetracked in my efforts to raise some funds for the Center at the Ford Foundation, which turned its attention entirely to China (which was quite popular at that time), whereas Russia was a sort of sleeping country not going anywhere. So the problem of fund raising was rather difficult. But we

386

are now in a period where Soviet studies are flourishing in the United States. One wonders whether this is to be succeeded by another lean period.

It may be of interest to cite a few data that have been compiled on the quantitative state of Soviet studies in the United States. They are just data, and they say nothing about the qualitative aspects. I am citing some figures from a survey that was recently published in the Journal of the American Association for the Advancement of Slavic Studies, an article reporting the results of a survey put out by Dorothy Atkinson. According to this survey (and this relates to the Soviet Union and Eastern Europe together), there are approximately 11,000 specialist positions – I interpret this to mean professional as distinct from clerical positions – in the Soviet and East European fields in academic institutions, in government and in business enterprises. There are 250 institutions of higher education: universities and colleges that are offering programs and courses in more than one discipline in the field of Soviet-East European studies. Approximately 2,000 faculty members are teaching about 7,000 courses in these areas. At 98 institutions with graduate programs, there are 2,542 graduate students working for advanced degrees at this time. Now this includes language instruction and literature as well as the social sciences and history, but the greater part of the faculty that I have just referred to and of the courses is concerned with the social sciences and history.

Despite this quantitative abundance, there exist some limitations. Economics has been one of the weakest fields from a numerical point of view in this whole range of studies. It is an interesting question why economics has not flourished as other fields have flourished. As things stand, only 7 percent (139 persons) of the more than 2,000 faculty members who are teaching courses on the Soviet Union and Eastern Europe are in economics. As I see it, the major reason is that economics is not organized in terms of areas, and it is therefore very difficult to get graduate students to concentrate in economics. Graduate students in economics must become qualified in a number of quite technical fields: econometrics and statistics, mathematical economics, theory generally, economic history. At Harvard these are all required of all the graduate students in economics; and to undertake in addition to that a study in an esoteric area, like Russian economy, involving the use of Russian-language materials is asking a great deal. So up to now,

387

not so many students have responded to that. Sociology, by the way, in the United States is even worse off: it is not even listed in the survey among the separate disciplines that were recorded.

As I look at the development of the field of Russian studies and East European studies in the United States, I feel that in addition to the limitations in economics and sociology, there is reason to be uneasy about the development of work on Eastern Europe. The great effort in the U.S. and the great bulk of the funding that has been available has gone to Russian and Soviet studies, and that is for fairly obvious reasons. But I think the upshot is that through the years there has not been as much of an effort on Eastern European countries as would be appropriate. If you consider merely the problem of quantifying the growth of the Eastern European countries, there has been one research project conducted through the years in New York that has been grinding out data on the growth of national income in different Eastern European countries, and I think that this has been competently handled. But nevertheless, this project has never really been integrated into the field: the people who were engaged in this work were pretty much off by themselves; there has been very little serious and searching review of what they do. The upshot is that the people who are doing research on the Eastern European economies, who wish to have some quantitative representation of what has been happening, will either use the official data that are published in Eastern European countries or, alternatively, these independent computations. The growth rates in question are often quite different.

As I think about the field, not merely from the standpoint of what is going on in the U.S. but what is going on more generally, one of the things that seems to me might merit a discussion here – a matter of a momentous importance – is the changing situation in the Soviet Union and, among other things, glasnost, which opens up possibilities for research that we never might have imagined in the past. There is a question what these opportunities are like and how we might respond to them. Ed Hewett, I was pleased to see this morning, took the opportunity to chastise the Russians regarding the state of their work in statistics. This seems to me just a dreadful situation, and right now you have official data published in the Soviet Union that are attacked by various, somewhat dissident elements in the sharpest terms as being wholly discredited. At the same time, you have very prominent people, like Aganbegyan, quoting data on the rate of growth that are entirely different from the official data. You know, the official figure on the growth of national income for 1981-1985 is around 3.5 percent. Aganbegyan, in his book on perestroika, quietly says: »Maybe the growth was zero.« And he actually goes beyond saying »maybe.« No elucidation, no documentation, no details on how they got the figure zero. And as I say, you have the various dissidents in the background, who have been attacking the Soviet official data through the years, Russian dissidents, and you have to ask what do the Russians themselves know about this. Of course, it also raised the question, a very important question, as to how we react to what is going on.

I have wondered whether the time is not approaching where there should be some joint research in this area, Russian and Western, that would carefully consider the methodologies that are to be used, examine what data are to be examined. I should think that a good deal on this could be done without invading the innermost areas of security. Well, that may be a bit of a dream, but it does seem to me that in a large way, we are confronted with a very new situation on which some quite serious reflection would be appropriate – how we react not only to the new development generally in the Soviet Union but also the very specific fact of glasnost and what it means regarding the release of information, opportunities to meet with Russian scholars, possibly doing research in Russia in areas that have been off limits in the past, and so on.

Armand Clesse:
Thank you Professor Bergson. I think that was very interesting and certainly even further stimulated the upcoming discussion. The next on the list is Alex Pravda.

Alex Pravda:
You did ask me to say a few words about the situation in Britain. Basically, it is a small community, I don't know the exact numbers. We do have a national association. I would guess the number of people involved in Soviet studies, in social sciences – leaving out the prerevolutionary historians and the linguists and the literature people – is about 200 – 300, and nearly all of them (as opposed to the apparent

figure in the U.S.) are teaching in universities. Relatively few people work full-time in any sense on the Soviet Union outside the university sector. We have no state-supported institutes, although there have been various words about the idea of creating one. I don't think this will come about. We do have dedicated centers, major centers at various universities, and there are five or six of these centers, some of them on the way down, some of them well-established and specializing in particular areas of Soviet studies. So this is a small community, a teaching community for the most part. Surveys have shown that the average age of the social scientist working in the Soviet field was 47, as opposed to 42 for the average social scientist in British universities. We are an aging profession in that sense. We have a major problem – a generation gap – in that in the lean years, in the 1970s in British universities, I think everyone with a degree of conscience discouraged good graduate students from doing Soviet studies, since there would be no posts available for them at the end of their PhDs. Therefore, we are now faced with the familiar situation where the government is saying that we have a great deal of interest in studying the Soviet Union, but there are no or very few people in the right position at the right time. There is a certain danger here – given the resurgence of interest in the Soviet Union now – that we may get a lot of people coming to the field, that some teaching positions will open, and then when the excitement about the Soviet Union becomes more normal, government and general interest will decline, and those people will be in a difficult position, too. So feast and famine is a particular problem, because governments and funding organizations follow fashions as much here as in any other field.

The other problem we have is a familiar one (Marshall Goldman indicated this for the States, and it exists in Britain as well): there is a difficulty in getting people in the fields of economics and sociology. This sort of disciplinary ghettoism is a familiar phenomenon. I don't think it strikes quite as badly as it does in the United States, but nevertheless it is a fact. I think last year there was one graduate student in economics dealing with the Soviet Union; I think this year there are none. This is an amazing figure, which shocks the government when one tells them. But it doesn't actually convince them to bring money into the field, to create posts that are earmarked for the study of economics and economy in the Soviet Union and Eastern Europe. There is a career problem here: it is not just a matter of student demand. I don't think that demands on the students themselves is the only reason for this, although they are heavy. It is a fact that career prospects are so uncertain if you are going to the Soviet fields, as opposed to choosing any number of other fields and area studies to go into. So we do have a problem here. When I look to the strengths and weaknesses, I think Britain is particularly strong in history, politics and political science, weak in law, weak in international relations, weak in sociology. And certainly if we are going to the area of Eastern European studies, it is also weak for the very reasons you enumerated because of the lack of interest of foundations in universities in what is a collection of minor states rather than a giant one. So there is a problem: there is a problem of recruitment, there is a problem of graduate-student interest. Now the interest is there, but as I said before, it is a problem of career prospects. In terms of losing people to the U.S., this is, as Marshall Goldman indicated, a serious problem for us. We are a small community, a relatively small generation of people who are trained and teaching. Many of those, for both reasons of finance and also support and morale (and it is another question of British university morale at the moment), have gone to the U.S. in recent years, are going to continue to go to the U.S. And this does deplete us quite severely. We can't do anything about it, except to shout to our own government to do something about it, and they on the whole say, »So be it: market forces.« Incidentally, when confronted with the similar question – Why is there more Japanese funding coming in to the United Kingdom in the moment in many fields, including the Soviet? – I would say in some areas then there are British who say, »That's fine. As long as they pay enough, let them come in.« They have no understanding, in other words, of the long-term consequences of this kind of situation. We are in a problem with funding. The major body, which is the ESRC (Economic Social Research Council) in Britain, does an analysis in perestroika itself, and it is just about getting out of that, does pay some attention to the Soviet field and has made some awards recently to Oxford to do a study on the relationship between the economic and political reform, for example. But generally speaking, we are not particularly favorably regarded by that organization. U.S. funding is diminishing for the reasons again given. Japanese funding, as I indicated, is increasing; interest is increasing. And I wouldn't want to denigrate that. There is, however, I think, a shortage of any kind of coordination of the West European funding, except for (and it is generally West German foundations who are named here) on an Anglo-German cooperative basis, and they usually are interested in particular issues rather than in the Soviet field.

This brings me to an even more serious question that has long bothered me and I think concerns many people in Britain. It is that although we have good communications with our colleagues in the United States and a good deal of cooperative projects go on, we have very little with our colleagues in Western Europe (we are part of Western Europe, so we must not say in Western Europe but rather in other parts of Western Europe). Some West Germans, particularly, have long come to our annual conferences. There were few joint conferences, I think, but I can't recall (Alec Nove would correct me) many actual joint research projects, people who have cooperated in projects, let's say, based in Britain and the other way round, based in West Germany. As for formulating a project, I don't think this is happening in a way it should, and perhaps it is something we should look at as West Europeans.

Generally speaking, I have also been worried (leaving aside the national cooperation question) about the way in which research areas are concentrated in Britain in Soviet studies, and also in the United States and everywhere. Perhaps this is a larger reflection of academic studies. Grants are usually tied to projects that are large, which have quantitative elements to them, a lot of research assistance. I am no way denigrating those kinds of projects. But it means there is a neglect of projects that need maybe two or three people with pencils. It is difficult for those people to establish themselves in a center or a university.

There is also a problem in terms of what we study. We have in Britain, at least until very recently, not devoted much attention at all to looking at gaps in our research vis-à-vis the Soviet Union. For example, *nothing* (I stand to be corrected) proper or substantial was done on Soviet bureaucracy, government or the ministries; on how they operated, even on a quantitative basis; on how many they were, apart from looking at career patterns or career structures within the whole elite. Very little was done on this. Relatively little was done on the interaction of interest groups after the initial sort of studies in the early 1970s. This brings to mind the possibility whether we shall in Britain have an

R&D committee to look out for areas that should be investigated and to encourage people to undertake investigations.

But encouragement is not very effective without money, and therefore it comes back to funding. We have a very small amount of money at the moment to do that. So although the interest is greatly revived, the basic structure is still poor, and the prospects for getting new posts in Soviet studies are very low. Although Mrs. Thatcher says she wants more, she is not ready to put money behind her particular interest. The depletion to the U.S. is increasing; Western European cooperation is not rising. Therefore the general verdict has to be one of a very cautious optimism in terms of possible future funding resulting from the Gorbachev phenomenon.

Armand Clesse:
I was hardly able to refrain Alec Nove from interrupting – and that only by promising him (I think tacitly) that he would be the next discussant. I think it is high time for a Scottish variant of a view of the situation, and perhaps Alec will tell us something about culture, also about cultural imperialism, in that field.

Alec Nove:
I want merely to say that we did have two projects with the Germans: one funded by Ford, one by Volkswagen. The latter alas fell apart because in the end, the participants couldn't agree on a final version. Nothing joint has ever been done with the French, as far as I know. But I think the picture in Britain is slightly gloomier, possibly because of the closing down in recent years – due to financial stringency – of a whole number of places where both Russian language and Russian studies were being carried on. The degree of financial pressure on universities being what it is, we have an additional phenomenon to be mentioned here (in economics, which indeed is serious) that the area specialist is not given adequate reward but is simply under pressure. The sheer need for the bread-and-butter departments to go on providing bread and butter makes it in fact impossible for universities to make specialized appointments at all. We once had four people on China: we now have none. None of the departments where they worked felt it could afford a specialist on China.

I think that on top of all that, we have the further problem of the

393

abolition by order of the government of the guarantee of tenure. No British professor now appointed will not be subject to instant dismissal if by any chance the order is given for the subject to be no longer taught. This is a unique phenomenon in the Western world, as far as I know. It is in the context of all of this that the brain-drain to America begins to be rather serious. I think we are not in any difference here, because on top of everything else, even those people who are studying the subject – possibly with distinction – may find under the new regulations an instruction that their university should stop teaching it. This could happen to any subject, by the way. It has already happened to philosophy; several British universities have stopped teaching philosophy. As extraordinary as this may seem, if this can happen to philosophy, it can easily happen to Soviet studies. Any potential victim being offered a job – not just at Harvard but also at less prestigious universities – would look at it with considerable temptation. I think this is probably worth mentioning.

Of course, we do have some centers, all trying to do their best. Our institute does its best and will continue to do so. But it is shrinking: my own outfit in Glasgow is, in terms of staff, at least 30 percent smaller. Two more people are retiring, and we still do not know if we will be able to replace them. So the prospects are a bit gloomy, I think. But there is to be a committee, now sitting, that may recommend some earmarked funding for Soviet studies. We think that this we can thank Gorbachev for. Let's be hopeful. Of course, all of us try to get funding from outside, we have a number of projects, including Soviet visitors, Hungarians, two Chinese in Glasgow now, usually through the noble efforts of my successor in Glasgow, who is very good at raising money. But its very much a hand-to-mouth operation.

Armand Clesse:
Thank you Alec. Let's cross the Channel. Georges Sokoloff is next on the list.

Georges Sokoloff:
Mr. Chairman, you said that the French system is very dispersed. You are certainly right. I myself am dispersed, between my functions in the university, where we have some research, and the public-sector side that we have on economic studies in France. My personal experience is

mostly in the second type of research: I am somewhere in the middle of this special system we have in France (which is very French) of small agencies working on the economics of the Soviet Union, of Eastern Europe and of China. The main centers as you know are the one in CEPII, where we have a small department on socialist countries, especially on the U.S.S.R.; a big center in La Documentation Française, with about twenty people working on economics (and working pretty well I think); and a very strong center in La Maison des Sciences de l'Homme for China, where good people are working. My personal remarks, generally speaking, about the subject are the following: First, from time to time and more often, actually, I hear that we must change our methods of work, since the Soviet Union is becoming an open economy, a market economy and since glasnost gives everyone access to Soviet economic information. Second, we have a general problem, a terrible problem, not because of the lack of information, of course, but because of the lack of time to absorb all that information. I see no solution to that. Maybe the only solution is organizing high-level professional meetings in order to exchange information and views. At least we need something like mutual consultancy, improved mutual consultancy, better communication among specialists, because I think that oral information is simply easier to absorb than written information. A third point is a rejoinder to Alex Pravda. I think that such an action would be particularly useful among West European specialists, because we have to prepare ourselves to be more European. One of these days, of course, the European Communities will really need a specialist on Soviet-type economics and, more importantly, future specialists, I mean students educated with a good professional background. My final remark is just to know something. Finally, I would like to point out that there is a Soviet move to organize common research in all fields, especially on the famous European Common House. Something of that type is starting in France between La Maison des Sciences de l'Homme and the IMEMO. I was asked to participate in that. But I didn't give an answer yet, because I don't now know exactly what I am supposed to agree with or to disagree with, and this is a new problem.

Armand Clesse:
Thank you Georges Sokoloff. Next would be Heinrich Vogel.

Heinrich Vogel:
Actually it is with some embarrassment that I have been listening to the bleak picture as described specifically by our British colleagues, who are really in trouble. The embarrassment is that in terms of adequately funded institutionalized research in think tanks, I think Germany is quite well off. We really don't have to worry about continuity or minimal coverage of what is going on. That is at hand.

But this is not to say that we don't have any problems. We have weak fields, first of all, in training the next generation. Those who hold chairs in applied Soviet social sciences are, with the exception of economics, having trouble finding adequate numbers of students, who don't have much of a career chance. At the same time, the bread-and-butter competition is very hard. So if by some accident there would be a need to fill one or two positions outside the very central fields of research on the Soviet Union – trained historians or trained economists – I would be extremely hard put to find adequate candidates. They are just not around. This does not mean that there is not a general demand, but it is just not funded where it ought to be, namely at the universities. Now, we do have a problem in Germany, which is the opposite of the situation in Britain: We have, practically, a total tenure system. Whoever has a job is pretty much safe until the end of his days, such that a lot of good jobs are being filled by people who may lose the motivation, no matter what Gorbachev is doing or not doing. Quite frankly, this is a derivative of the Soviet-style tenure system, and I hate it. But there is nothing that we can do about.

Flexibility is a problem we have, and it is also reflected in something that I would call parochialism. By far, not all those who would be invited or have a chance or the funding would go abroad; by far, not all who would have a chance to learn adequate English would spend the time for doing so. The German market is large enough to be self-complacent, but it is too small really to bring academic research and policy-related research to the level of excellency where we would certainly want to have it.

So the answer is (and also indeed a critical factor) an international division of labour in Europe. This is where I am really concerned about how little we are actually doing. We have been trying to install something like (and Alec is the next candidate) an advanced-studies program, where we invite foreign scholars from East and West along

396

the lines of something like the Kennan program. This works very nicely, but is very hard to support for a protracted time; it is only being funded until 1991, and there is little chance for having it extended. There is only one (or one and a half) foundation that would be willing to spend money for such an exotic field like Soviet studies or Soviet and Eastern European studies, but we can't always go to Volkswagen, even if we can show that we are cooperating in a joint project with a British or French institution.

What we also need is some response in terms of finance for internationally defined and executed projects in France, in Britain or elsewhere. We can't do it all alone. But when it comes to the task to which we are all put – the Gorbachev challenge to the profession – I think we should think twice before ending up in demanding extensive growth only. Not just for the sake of facing up to the hardships of this situation, I think we should maybe try to address the issues in a better way, in a more economical way. In other words, we should try to avoid duplicating or triplicating certain research in one or the other field in one or the other country. I think we could do a lot more by coming together in some rhythmic fashion, say once a year. We should not seek to give answers or to exchange papers, which we can do by mailing them. Rather, we should attempt to ask the proper questions and to define not simply those issues that are relevant for answering current questions or writing up the next article for a newspaper. So I think within the range of financial resources (unequally distributed as they are), we can do better. I think it is about time that we really think about something like a conferencing scheme to bring together a very limited number of professionals at a not excessive cost in order to discuss the issues that we really ought to look into. Then maybe we can do a little about telecommunications and easing ways of working together.

Armand Clesse:
Thank you Dr. Vogel. In one sense, you anticipated the second part of this round table. But tomorrow, when I hope we will once again meet for one hour to discuss outlooks and perspectives, you and some others will no longer be here with us. So I think we are grateful for these very constructive, forward-looking and operational ideas. Remaining on my list are Jerry Hough and then Ed Hewett.

Jerry F. Hough:
I would like to follow up on the comments of Dr. Vogel. It does seem to me that often in discussing the Soviet Union, we don't raise the questions of extensive versus intensive, of the discipline impact on the market, and so forth. One looks at the experience in the United States and Great Britain with sadness in both directions. From a human point of view, one is sad about the situation in Great Britain. But the fact of the matter is that in the fields that I know, adversity has produced productivity. It seems to me that in general with a much smaller size, Great Britain has done a far better job of studying the contemporary Soviet Union than the United States has. What we have is large numbers of people who strike me as being probably quite productive among the historians, but if you look at any other field, it is essentially a disaster. We have talked about economics and the problems there, sociology, law, anthropology. Political science is no better. We have large numbers of people teaching at universities, but in terms of the number of people doing research, it is *extremely* small. The reason we are raiding the universities of other countries is because we don't have the cadres ourselves. Harvard selected a Canadian to fill a position. There was no American candidate who was in the ballpark. Columbia is also trying to fill a post at the present time. If one talks about the junior level, Harvard had a search for a junior post last year, but they could not find anyone satisfactory. This year they are having another search with a different group of people; it looks like the outcome is going to be the same, unless they go in the direction of international relations.

The fact of the matter is that we have *extremely* few people studying the Soviet Union. We have a number of senior people commenting on Soviet affairs, but with regard to research on Soviet foreign policy (let alone, research on domestic policy), there is virtually nobody in the age group between 25 and 40. I think Harvard has turned out one PhD in the last ten years in domestic politics.

The problem of research on the Soviet Union has become a disaster with glasnost. In other words, if it is in Moscow News, in Ogonyok, or in a few other places, then we know about it. But there is a vast amount of information that perhaps is being examined in the government but that is certainly not part of the academic situation. We have a most severe problem with that which we would call research. We do not have an Institute of the U.S.A.; in other words, we do not have an

398

Arbatov Institute. My own sense is that there are ways of solving this: at Duke, we are creating a center with 10–15 persons doing research on the politics of reform, the politics of the entering of Russia into the West.

But it seems to me that what one really needs is a series of equivalents to natural-science laboratories working on more narrowly defined projects. Again, the problem of a Russian research center (or a Harriman or Kennan Institute) is that if you must distribute fellowships among history, literature, politics, economics and sociology, the whole problem of getting some kind of critical mass – the kind of situation in Birmingham, with a series of people working on it – is very difficult. Of course, I would not say that one should deny Americans tenure, although it would be a wonderful thing if we didn't have tenure. But the whole problem how to get product out – product in terms of students who actually publish, product in terms of senior professors who publish – is a problem the United States has not begun to solve, at least in political science, which is normally considered a discipline in which we have a lot people.

Armand Clesse:
Thank you Jerry for this certainly challenging view. If nobody wants to challenge that challenging view, the floor would be to Ed Hewett.

Ed A. Hewett:
I just have a few comments based upon listening to what has been for me a very interesting discussion. First of all, it is certainly true that funding for Soviet studies is far better in the U.S. than anywhere else in the world, other than possibly the Soviet Union, although we are better off than our Soviet colleagues in many ways. One thing that should be mentioned is that this is not just because funding fell on us; we fought hard for it. For example over a decade ago, a number of individuals from several universities, including Harvard and Columbia, got together, lobbied for and created the National Council for Soviet and East European Research. The fund advanced research on the Soviet Union. We are now well over a decade in giving grants. But they don't tend to be large grants. The average size of the grant is well under $ 50,000, and a lot of people are just using pencils. Indeed, as of this year, the rule is that the grant – excepting extraordinary circumstances

399

– can only be for one year and has to be under $ 50,000. Although it was begun with Department of Defense funding, the National Council has consistently maintained the rule (I think quite successfully) that the decisions on grants are only academic decisions. Even now, when the funding has shifted to congressional funds under Title 8, the Council also insists that there be no interference from the source of the money in the decisions. I think that has worked rather well, and it is something very important in any venture of this sort.

In the mid-1980s, we began as a profession to push for congressional funding for Soviet studies and received it. The first act was, as I recall, passed in 1984 – Title 8 Act to the State Department Appropriations Bill – and every year on average since then we have received somewhere in the neighborhood of $ 4–5 million, which go to the National Council, to the joint committees for Soviet and East European studies (those are separate committees), to the Kennan and to the New East European Program at the Wilson Center. That has been a fairly stable source, although under that stability is a good deal of fighting. In addition to foundations, the universities and business have provided a stable source of funding. None of us is so complacent as to believe that apparent stability is long-term, and all of us are concerned in trying to create more of a source of endowment income for the field. Some things are going into that direction.

I would say the main problem we have now is not money but cadres – i.e., people who are doing work. I watched the flow of applications coming to the National Council. It is sad in some ways to see the work that isn't being done or isn't even being proposed. We are into three years of Gorbachev, and I must say that we are nowhere near the quality of research proposals we thought we would see in that area. In part, with the great opportunity we have been given with Gorbachev, we haven't reacted as a profession as well as I think we might have. We are making progress on some of the problems in the cadre area. One of the things we have done that I think is extraordinarily successful is to set up summer institutes for people who are working in various areas. We have had some people from the U.K. come to these. The first one was a summer institute in economics, in which young people – either PhD students or young post-doctoral individuals – are brought together for two weeks to meet on a daily basis to discuss their work. Some members of the profession come to spend a day with the group, but there is a permanent faculty of five or six people who work with them and essentially critique their research for them. That has been very successful. There is now a similar program in politics and one in Eastern Europe. That gives graduate students and young faculty spread out across the country (and indeed, across the world) a sense of community, a sense that there is a profession there. In this last year, for the economics workshop, we brought an esteemed Soviet academic to be one of the faculty members, something that would have been unthinkable a few years ago. So for two weeks, we had a Soviet there to critique students' work and to be critiqued in his work, and I think both sides enjoyed it immensely. There are now post-doctoral fellowships out of Title 8 money. There are also fellowships funding teaching posts in universities, in order to encourage universities to hire young people, particularly in economics but also in other areas. That, I must say, hasn't been as successful as we thought it would be, and I am not sure that that will continue. But it is one way that we struggled with to try to resolve this terrible problem in getting universities to do what we know they should do but won't do.

Further, a thought on the special opportunities for Gorbachev. I think it understates it to say we have many opportunities to meet Soviets – it is extraordinary now. I don't know about the rest of you, but at least in Washington, it's a sort of a Soviet a day now. Many of my colleagues hide when I call them and say: »Another Soviet is in town.« What is interesting is that the Soviets have reached out to the profession. I, Marshall Goldman, probably some of the rest of you have been published in the Soviet press now, were interviewed. We were asked by the Soviet to give our opinion on what they should do. We are involved in projects; I am involved in some projects with the Soviets looking at aspects of their economic policy. I never thought that this would happen. I have round tables now with the Soviets that I publish in my journal on Soviet economy, without any restrictions on what I publish. I never thought these things would happen. My impression is that the main limitation right now, today (I don't know about a month from now or a year from now) on working with the Soviets is in our heads. That is, there is almost anything we could propose, and at the very least, they will think about it; they will actually implement many of the suggestions. Bergson suggests cooperative effort in statistics; I think they are ready. I think they are flat-out ready to do that, and it is

401

really a matter of our pushing. It is we and not the Soviets who in many cases have been timid, in part because we have a lot of luggage we have carried with us. This is also because we obviously were somewhat careful, since we know it is a honeymoon period and one of these days the honeymoon will probably be over. But we might as well use it while we have it.

A final point I would like to make very briefly is about U.S. research versus that of Europe and another country we have not mentioned, namely Japan. I think in general Soviet studies in the United States is far better off than in Europe and long away from Japan. For those who have been there, Japan is an extraordinary place in terms of the quality of Soviet studies. I don't know how the national policy of a country that close to the Soviet Union could so suppress the field. But it is extraordinary, and it means that Japanese scholars in many cases have to cooperate with the U.S. to develop the most elementary parts of their profession. I agree with Jerry that there are parts of Europe that are better than we are, in part because of productivity (I have in mind per-capita productivity in both Germany and the U.K.). But in general as a profession, I think the U.S. Soviet-studies community is stronger; it is larger and that helps a lot.

It also helps that we have had strong support. I just end with the point that, of course, you are going to have to do something on a European basis – as Europeans. It is going to be much harder than it was in the U.S. In part, we had no qualms in using the fear of the Soviet Union to get funding at times. We had different purposes than our funders, and that was fine. Alas, you may have other problems with your funders. But you know creating an European institute for Soviet and East European studies is only the beginning. You have got to put serious money behind it: it has got to be long-term money, it has got to be somewhere in the neighborhood of $ 5-10 million per year, and the money has to be administered by scholars. If it becomes political, if the decisions become political, then it is useless – it is worse than useless, it is harmful. In the U.S., we have done some work on the Soviet Union through the Fund for Democracy, which was a congressional creation that came out of our effort to spread the good word about democracy to the rest of the world. Perfectly terrible work is done through the Fund for Democracy; perfectly terrible work is done with some money that goes directly from the Department of Defense to researchers. You need an independent board of scholars – independent from their funders and independent from retribution when they make decisions solely on the basis of quality. I am frankly skeptical of whether Europeans can do that as a group right now. I don't know. But that is what you need. You need serious money and that sort of setup. I wish you the best of luck.

Contributors

Leonid I. Abalkin: Academician; Director of the Institute of Economics; Member of the USSR Congress of People's Deputies, Moscow

Hannes Adomeit: Senior Researcher, Stiftung Wissenschaft und Politik, Ebenhausen

Vladimir G. Baranovsky: Professor; Head of the West European Studies Department, Institute of World Economy and International Relations, Moscow

Abram Bergson: Professor of Economics, Harvard University

Christoph Bertram: Foreign Editor, Die Zeit; former Director of the IISS, Hamburg

Anatoly V. Bolyatko: Major General; Deputy Head of Department, USSR Defense Ministry, Moscow

Alfred Cahen: General Secretary of the Western European Union, London

Armand Clesse: Special Counselor to the Government of Luxembourg; President of the Association Luxembourg-Harvard

Willem F. van Eekelen: former Minister of Defense, Netherlands; appointed General Secretary of the Western European Union

François Fejtö: Historian, Specialist on Eastern Europe, Paris

Luigi Vittorio Ferraris: Professor of International Relations at the University of Rome; Member of the Council of State

Renata Fritsch-Bournazel: Senior Lecturer, Institut d'Etudes Politiques, Paris

John Kenneth Galbraith: Professor of Economics, Harvard University

Marshall I. Goldman: Professor of Economics at Wellesley College; Associate Director of the Russian Research Center, Harvard University

Oleg A. Grinevsky: Ambassador at large, USSR Foreign Ministry; Head of Soviet Delegation at CFE talks in Vienna, Moscow

Ed A. Hewett: Senior Fellow, Brookings Institution, Washington

Jerry F. Hough: Professor of Political Science, Duke University; Staff Member at Brookings Institution, Washington

405

Andrei A. Kokoshin: Corresponding Member of the USSR Academy of Sciences; Deputy Director of the USA and Canada Institute, Moscow

Michail A. Krutogolov: Professor; Research Associate, Institute of State and Law, Moscow

Michael MccGwire: Senior Fellow, Brookings Institution, Washington

Albrecht A.C. von Müller: Director of the European Center for International Security (EUCIS), Starnberg

Alec Nove: Professor of Economics, University of Glasgow

Nikolai Y. Petrakov: Corresponding Member of the USSR Academy of Sciences; Deputy Director of the Central Institute of Econometrics; Member of the USSR Congress of People's Deputies, Moscow

Alex Pravda: Senior Researcher, Royal Institute of International Affairs, London

Lothar Rühl: former Secretary of State for Defense, Federal Republic of Germany

Thomas C. Schelling: Professor of Political Economy, John F. Kennedy School of Government, Harvard University

Dietmar Schössler: Professor of Political Science, University of Mannheim

Eberhard Schulz: Professor of Political Science, University of Bonn; Deputy Director of the Forschungsinstitut der Deutschen Gesellschaft für Auswärtige Politik, Bonn

Gerhard Simon: Senior Researcher, Bundesinstitut für ostwissenschaftliche und internationale Studien, Köln

Georges Sokoloff: Professor at the National Institute of Eastern Languages and Civilisation, Paris

Michel Tatu: Editorial Writer, Le Monde, Paris

Heinrich Vogel: Director of the Bundesinstitut für ostwissenschaftliche und internationale Studien, Köln

Gerhard Wettig: Senior Researcher, Bundesinstitut für ostwissenschaftliche und internationale Studien, Köln

Philip Windsor: Professor of International Relations, London School of Economics

Vadim V. Zagladin: Foreign Policy Advisor to the Chairman of the Presidium of the USSR Supreme Soviet; Member of the CPSU Central Committee, Moscow

Vitaly V. Zhurkin: Corresponding Member of the USSR Academy of Sciences; Director of the Europe Institute, Moscow

Selected Bibliography

Hannes Adomeit: Die Sowjetmacht in internationalen Krisen und Konflikten – Verhaltensmuster, Handlungsprinzipien, Bestimmungsfaktoren, Nomos, Baden-Baden 1983

Abel Aganbegyan: The Economic Challenge of Perestroika, Indiana University Press, Bloomington 1988.

Graham T. Allison: Testing Gorbachev, Foreign Affairs, Fall 1988, pp. 18-32.

Abram Bergson: Planning and Performance in Socialist Economies. The USSR and Eastern Europe, Unwin Hyman, Boston 1988.

Seweryn Bialer: The Soviet Paradox. External Expansion. Internal Decline, Alfred A. Knopf, New York 1986.

Seweryn Bialer and Michael Mandelbaum (eds.): Gorbachev's Russia and American Foreign Policy, Westview Press, London 1988.

Ellen Dahrendorf (ed.): Russian Studies. Leonard Schapiro, Penguin Books, New York 1988.

Jonathan Dean: Watershed in Europe. Dismantling the East-West Military Confrontation, Lexington Books, Lexington 1987.

François Fejtö: Histoire des démocraties populaires, 2 volumes, Edition du Seuil, Paris 1972.

Renata Fritsch-Bournazel: L'Allemagne: un enjeu pour l'Europe, Editions Complexe 1987.

John Kenneth Galbraith and Stanislav Menshikov: Capitalism, Communism and Coexistence. From the Bitter Past to a Better Prospect, Houghton Mifflin Company, Boston 1988.

Marshall I. Goldman: Gorbachev's Challenge. Economic Reform in the Age of High Technology, W.W. Norton & Company, New York 1987.

Mikhail Gorbachev: Perestroika: New Thinking for Our Country and the World, Harper & Row, New York 1987.

Mikhail Gorbachev: At the Summit. Speeches and Interviews, February 1987 – July 1988, Richardson, Steirman & Black, New York 1988.

The Gorbachev Challenge and European Security. A Report from the European Strategy Group, Nomos, Baden-Baden 1988.

Ed A. Hewett: Energy Economics and Foreign Policy in the Soviet Union, The Brookings Institution, Washington 1984.

Ed A. Hewett: Reforming the Soviet Economy. Equality versus Efficiency, The Brookings Institution, Washington 1988.

David Holloway: Gorbachev's New Thinking, Foreign Affairs, America and the World 1988/89, Vol. 68, No. 1.

Jerry F. Hough: Russia and the West. Gorbachev and the Politics of Reform, Simon and Schuster, New York 1988.

Jerry F. Hough: Opening up the Soviet Economy, The Brookings Institution, Washington 1988.

How Should America Respond to Gorbachev's Challenge? A Report of the Task Force on Soviet New Thinking, Institute for East-West Security Studies, New York 1988.

Robert G. Kaiser: The U.S.S.R. in Decline, Foreign Affairs, Winter 1988/89, pp. 97-113.

Robert Legvold: Soviet Foreign Policy, Foreign Affairs, America and the World 1988/89, Vol. 68, No. 1.

Michael MccGwire: Military Objectives in Soviet Foreign Policy, The Brooking Institution, Washington 1987.

Stephen M. Meyer: The Sources and Prospects of Gorbachev's New Political Thinking on Security, International Security, Fall 1988.

Uwe Nerlich / James A. Thomson (eds.): Das Verhältnis zur Sowjetunion: Zur Politischen Strategie der Vereinigten Staaten und der Bundesrepublik Deutschland, Nomos, Baden-Baden 1986.

Alec Nove: The Soviet Economic System. Third Edition, Allen & Unwin, London 1986.

Perestroika 1989, Charles Scribner's Son, New York 1988.

Lothar Rühl: Mittelstreckenwaffen in Europa: Ihre Bedeutung in Strategie, Rüstungskontrolle und Bündnispolitik, Nomos, Baden-Baden 1987.

Harriet Fast Scott and William F. Scott: Soviet Military Doctrine. Continuity, Formulation, and Dissemination, Westview Press, Boulder 1988.

Michel Tatu: Gorbatchev: L'U.R.S.S. va-t-elle changer?, Le Centurion, Paris 1987.